AMENHOTEP III: EGYPT'S RADIANT PHARAOH

This book follows the life story of Amenhotep III, one of the most important rulers of ancient Egypt, from his birth and into the afterlife. Amenhotep III ruled for about 38 years, from circa 1391 to 1353 B.C., during the apex of Egypt's international and artistic power. Arielle P. Kozloff situates Amenhotep III in his time, chronicling the key political and military events that occurred during his lifetime and reign as well as the evolution of religious rituals and the cult of the pharaoh. She further examines the art and culture of the court, including its palaces, villas, furnishings, and fashions as well as his extended family, officials, and international relationships. Through the exploration of abundant evidence from the period, in the form of both textual and material culture, Kozloff richly re-creates all aspects of Egyptian civilization at the height of the Mediterranean Late Bronze Age.

Arielle P. Kozloff, former curator of ancient art at the Cleveland Museum of Art, is a private consultant and lecturer for museums and private collectors in the United States and abroad. She is the coauthor of *Egypt's Dazzling Sun* and *The Gods Delight*. She has contributed chapters to volumes including *Egyptology Today*, *Amenhotep III: Perspectives on His Reign*, and *Millions of Jubilees* as well as articles to numerous journals, including *Journal of Egyptian Archaeology* and *American Journal of Archaeology*.

AMENHOTEP III: EGYPT'S RADIANT PHARAOH

ARIELLE P. KOZLOFF

CAMBRIDGE
UNIVERSITY PRESS

CAMBRIDGE UNIVERSITY PRESS
Cambridge, New York, Melbourne, Madrid, Cape Town,
Singapore, São Paulo, Delhi, Tokyo, Mexico City

Cambridge University Press
32 Avenue of the Americas, New York, NY 10013-2473, USA

www.cambridge.org
Information on this title: www.cambridge.org/9781107638549

First published 2012

Printed in the United States of America

A catalog record for this publication is available from the British Library.

Library of Congress Cataloging in Publication data
Kozloff, Arielle P.
Amenhotep III : Egypt's radiant pharaoh / Arielle P. Kozloff.
p.   cm.
Includes bibliographical references and index.
ISBN 978-1-107-01196-0 (hardback) – ISBN 978-1-107-63854-9 (paperback)
1. Amenhotep III, King of Egypt.   2. Egypt – History – Eighteenth dynasty,
ca. 1570–1320 B.C.   3. Pharaohs – Biography.   I. Title.
DT87.38.K69   2011
932'.014092–dc23   2011020072

ISBN 978-1-107-01196-0 Hardback
ISBN 978-1-107-63854-9 Paperback

To the archaeologists, inspectors, collectors, conservators, and curators who discover, guard, treasure, and care for Egypt's antiquities; to the scholars who study them; and to the amateur Egyptologists who always want to know more.

CONTENTS

ACKNOWLEDGMENTS

My mother, Marion Kozloff, introduced me to Egyptian art on visits to the University of Pennsylvania Museum. Elizabeth Finkenstaedt introduced me to Amenhotep III at Mount Holyoke College. John D. Cooney encouraged me first to look more closely at the monuments of Amenhotep III and then to step back and view the oeuvre as a whole. This has been a long journey, and these three, all "true of voice" and "repeating life," are just the first of countless individuals to be thanked, only a few of whom can be mentioned here.

In 1992, Betsy Bryan and I, after twenty years of dreaming and ten years of planning, were joined by Larry Berman and Élisabeth Delange and produced the exhibition *Egypt's Dazzling Sun/ Le Pharaon Soleil*, which was devoted to a better understanding of Amenhotep III's monuments. The book presented here is aimed more at the man himself, his life, and the issues confronting his reign, but I owe these three colleagues a great debt of gratitude.

Edmund S. Meltzer patiently read many drafts of this work and contributed innumerable bits of information and advice. His generous collegiality, wisdom, and erudition are remarkable, and his encouragement was a constant touchstone. Susan Giuffre read an early draft and Richard Wilkinson a later one, the latter sending me to Beatrice Rehl of Cambridge University Press, who was welcoming and patient. Virginia Krumholz read the penultimate draft and suggested areas needing expansion. Lisa Haney checked the bibliography, as did Dr. Meltzer. Ken Karpinski, Eleanor Umali, and James Dunn oversaw production.

Before any writing could occur, years of haunting libraries, museums, and, of course, Egypt, were necessary. On visits to Egypt, Head of the Supreme Council, then Minister of Antiquities, Dr. Zahi Hawass, and his assistant, Janice Kamrin, smoothed my way, gave me tremendous encouragement, and provided photographs or photographic permission. Former Chief Inspector Sayed Hegazy aided my travels in many practical ways, in addition to offering insights unknown to most foreigners. Egyptian Museum registrar Yasmin El Shazly and Supreme Council assistant Beth Asbury were also extremely helpful.

The staff members of the British Museum's Department of Ancient Egypt and Sudan were endlessly hospitable and generous with their time, space, resources, and thoughts, especially W. Vivian Davies, the head of the department; Susanne Woodhouse, librarian; and Richard Parkinson, John Taylor, Derek Welsby, Marcel Marée, and the rest of the curatorial and administrative staff. Over the years, the staffs of the Cleveland Public Library's Special Collections, especially the White Collection, and of the library of the Cleveland Museum of Art have also been extremely helpful and kind.

The American Research Center in Egypt has provided a platform for me to forward almost all the new ideas presented here, and I have benefited tremendously from the discussions generated. Undoubtedly, some colleagues will be disappointed that they did not change my mind, whereas others will be happy that they did.

In addition to those named earlier, I am endlessly grateful to the scholars and scientists who have discussed at length various points with me or have guided me through their excavations or museum collections, for example, Hourig Sourouzian, Peter Lacovara, Salima Ikram, Charles Van Siclen, Rita Freed, Angus Graham, Tom Hardwick, James Harrell, Martina Ullmann, David O'Connor, Helen Jacquet, Dorothea Arnold, Earl Ertman, Marianne Eaton-Krauss, Ray Johnson, Andrew Gordon, May Trad, Renée Dreyfus, Melinda Hartwig, William Peck, Gay Robins, Karola Zibelius-Chen, Regine Schulz, Christine Green, and Richard Fazzini. In addition, Ian Shaw, Maarten Raven, Lawrence Berman, Jiro Kondo, Louise Chu, Luc Limme, and Richard Wilkinson generously contributed photographs. Eric Gubel, Klaus Finneiser, Catharine Roehrig, Guillemette Andreu, Gabriele Pieke, and Claire Derriks also assisted (in addition to those cited in the captions) in obtaining photos and/or permissions.

Many outside of Egyptology answered questions or gave advice, for example, on the subjects of bubonic plague in Egyptian antiquity and ancient diseases in general, Drs. Joe Hinnebusch and Kent L. Gage (National Institutes of Health, Rocky Mountain Labs), Dr. Tom Schwan (Centers for Disease Control), and Dr. Eva Panagiotokopulu (University of Sheffield); and on the subjects of horse training and chariotry, Dariush Elghanayan and Rich Petersen. Medievalist Sara Jane Pearman and classical archaeologists Mary Ellen Soles and Sandra Knudsen gave excellent counsel.

My brother and sister-in-law Philip and Judith and their daughter Alexandra provided warm hospitality in New York and London on my semiannual research trips. They and brother David, along with his wife, Jeri, and their family, Jason and Daniel Brodkey, and theirs, Charlotte and Gordon Moore, and theirs, Brenda and Evan Turner, Barbara S. Robinson, and Betty W. Ratner (true of voice), offered endless encouragement over the years.

In keeping with the spirit of the salutations in the Amarna letters, I thank Daisy, Harry, Night Watch, and Sunny for insights into the intricacies of Kikkuli's horsemanship text while diverting me from my work. A series of incarnations of Bastet – Jezebel, Salomé, Rumpelteazer, Desi, and Lucy – supervised my work at home.

Most important of all, my husband, Jerald S. Brodkey, did everything to make writing this book possible. He has been an IT master of great patience in the face of my hopeless ineptitude and a tireless photographer both in Egypt and the United States. He has suffered my long absences (left to the devices of the preceding Bastets), found obscure bibliographical references, ordered books, organized photos, and otherwise tolerated my obsession with Amenhotep III with good humor.

Of course, none of these fine friends, colleagues, and family members is responsible for the inevitable flaws of this study, but I hope they will enjoy reading it and, perhaps, find some new and interesting ideas.

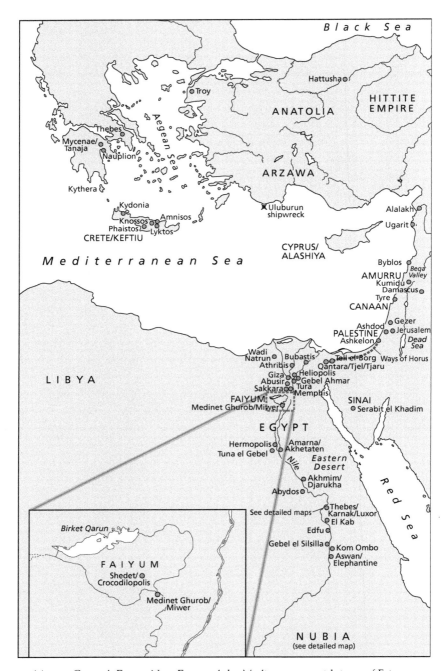

Map 1. General: Egypt, Near East, and the Mediterranean with inset of Faiyum.

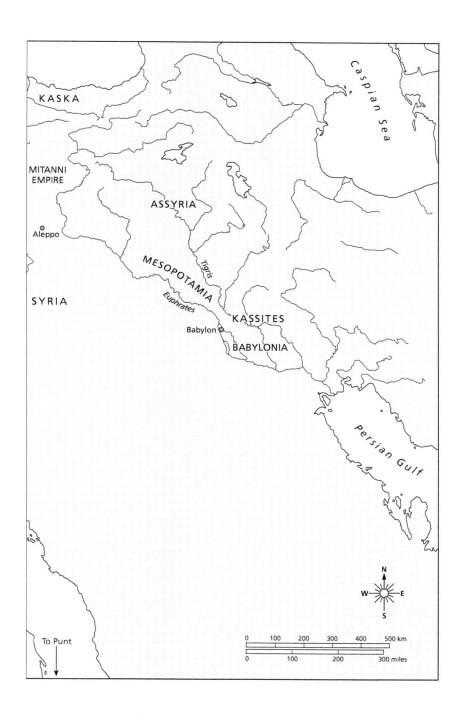

KASKA

MITANNI
EMPIRE

ASSYRIA

Aleppo

MESOPOTAMIA

Tigris

SYRIA

Euphrates

KASSITES

Babylon

BABYLONIA

Caspian
Sea

Persian Gulf

To Punt

N
W   E
S

0   100   200   300   400   500 km

0   100   200   300 miles

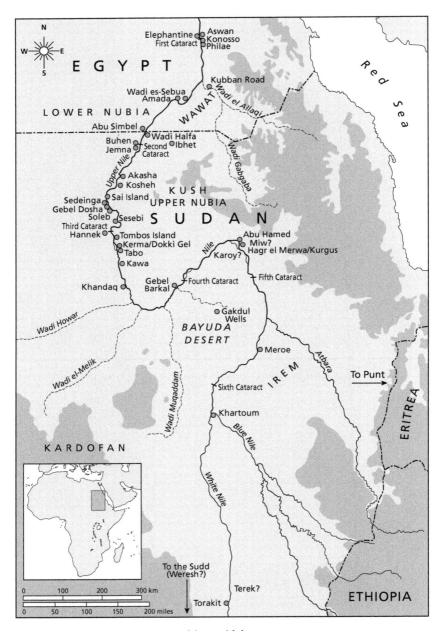

Map 2. Nubia.

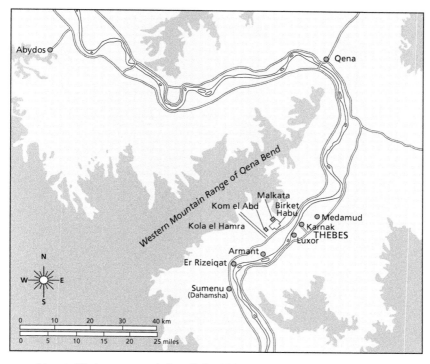

Map 3. Theban area, including Kola el Hamra's alignment toward Abydos.

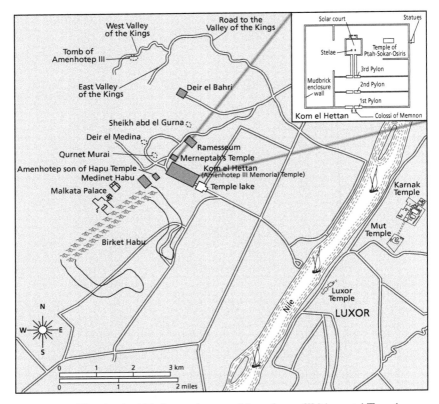

Map 4. West bank of Thebes with inset of Amenhotep III Memorial Temple.

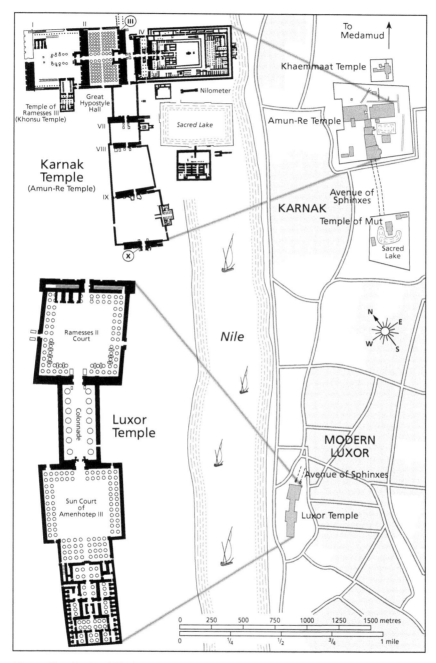

Map 5. East bank of Thebes with Karnak, Mut, and Luxor temples; including insets of Karnak and Luxor temples enlarged.

INTRODUCTION

AMENHOTEP III AS HE IS VIEWED TODAY

Beginning in 1391 B.C., Amenhotep III was for 38 years the richest man on earth and commander in chief of the largest, best equipped army of its day. A successful though infrequent warrior, he was also a thoroughly cultivated man – religious, literate, and an art lover – at the height of Egypt's Eighteenth Dynasty, what is often called her "Golden Age." His foreign vassals addressed him as "the Sun," and he justifiably called himself "dazzling," here termed "radiant" for his effect on the then-known world. One could search for his equal through all the rulers of ancient Rome, the emperors of China, the kings and queens of England and France, and the czars of Russia and generally come up wanting.

Yet, today, 34 centuries later, his heirs are the world-famous ones. Two of these were far weaker and less productive men. His son Akhenaten is regarded as a champion of monotheism (the so-called Amarna Revolution) in an age of nearly universal polytheism, when, it will be argued here, his new devotion was a reaction to the traditional gods having failed their country in a time of crisis. Tutankhamen, Amenhotep III's short-lived grandson, accomplished little in his lifetime but rose to superstardom when his tiny tomb crammed with golden treasures was found nearly intact in 1922, the finds subsequently paraded around the world in a series of traveling exhibitions. In the following dynasty, Ramesses the Great reigned for 67 years, usurping Amenhotep's statues and temples in his own name and leaving the false impression of a large artistic and architectural footprint. Living to 90 years of age, Ramesses was a successful sire, producing around 200 children; a lucky soldier; and finally, a Middle Eastern peacemaker in a land of eternal turmoil.

Among Egyptologists, however, Amenhotep III is a favorite. His reign produced prodigious amounts of sculpture and decorative arts in every medium, material, and size. Each is marked by a deliciously ornate

1

aesthetic and a quality of workmanship rarely equaled in world history. Even when successors usurped his statuary, enough traces of his original artists' incomparable technique and style can be found beneath the later, cruder chisel marks. He built extensively throughout the Nile Valley, not only in Egypt, but far south in the Sudan as well. His temples are elegantly designed and enormous in size, providing generations of excavators with infinite fields for study.

For epigraphers, linguists, and literary experts, Amenhotep III left plentiful records and texts to decipher, ponder, and discuss. For theologians, he revived and revered ancient traditions while gathering new influences from Nubia and the Near East. His most profound effect on religion, at the climax of his reign, was his own deification, perhaps creating a foundation for his son Akhenaten's retreat from many gods to one.

As a result of his artistic production and his apparent avoidance of major wars, the reign of Amenhotep III has traditionally been viewed as peaceful, idyllic, full of luxury, and devoid of problems. Women became especially prominent during his reign. More statues, carvings, and paintings of sensuously attired, exquisitely beautiful, and curvaceous women exist from his reign than from any other. As a result, and because of the number of foreign princesses Amenhotep III acquired for his harem, he has generally been viewed until very recently as a rather effete, though lovable, womanizing oriental potentate.

This general belief likely started with Jean-François Champollion's studies of Amenhotep III's cartouches on the thrones of the Colossi of Memnon along with the inscriptions on the Rosetta Stone, which led to his remarkable decoding of hieroglyphs in 1822. Once our king's name became widely recognizable during the nineteenth century, the elements of his persona most likely to titillate the Victorian mind-set began to emerge from monuments large and small such as the Colossi, where Amenhotep's regal form is surrounded by those of shapely women; two voluptuous statues of the goddesses Isis and lion-headed Sekhmet previously shipped by the eighteenth-century Italian traveler Donati to Turin; and numerous chance finds of exquisite cosmetic vessels and jewelry inscribed for Amenhotep and easily found on or near the surface at his unique city on the west bank of Luxor, Malkata.

One hundred seventy years later, the exhibition and catalogue *Egypt's Dazzling Sun, Amenhotep III and His World*, by Betsy Bryan (who, in 1991, had published her exhaustive study of Amenhotep III's father Thutmose IV), Lawrence Berman, Élisabeth Delange, and me, began to probe more deeply into our pharaoh's intellect and spirituality, seeking and finding greater meaning behind the earlier vapid impression. In 1998, David O'Connor and Eric Cline organized *Amenhotep III: Perspectives on His Reign*, a collection of essays concerning this king's family, administration, foreign relations, and artistic output, further adding to a sense of the intricacy and depth of this ruler's mind and the breadth of his scope. In 2000, Agnès Cabrol produced a book titled *Amenhotep III Le Magnifique*, organized as a series of topics about his life and reign, with some interesting new ideas and observations. The same year, Joann Fletcher wrote *A Chronicle of a Pharaoh: The Intimate Life of Amenhotep III*, an entertaining weave of a number of interesting facts and personalities, colorful tales, and fanciful details.

These works, organized thematically (the king's family, administration, statuary, etc.), form the foundation stones for the biography presented here, but this book takes a different approach. Studying a period by themes is a perfect way to begin organizing huge amounts of information, but it separates facts and events from the historical order in which they occurred. This book is the second step. It reorganizes the documentation into chronological order, forcing us to deal with the real-time framework in which events occurred and people lived. As a result, we arrive at new insights, some very much at odds with the assumptions of the past.

A true biography, in the sense of a chronological history of a person's life, is not possible for most of Egypt's kings, who rarely left enough records to provide a continuous and complete timeline. In the case of Amenhotep III, however, records exist in mind-boggling numbers. We know more about him than most of us know about our own great-grandparents. There are portraits of him as a young prince and youthful graffiti in his name. Large commemorative scarabs record two marriages, bull hunts, lion hunts, and the construction of a great lake. We know the names of several sets of his in-laws, both royal and common, and we have the mummies and burial treasure of his great queen Tiy's parents. We know the names of his nonroyal grandmother and mother, royal stepmothers, sisters, brothers, children, grandchildren, and even his first son's pet cat. We know the king's favorite colors, and Tiy's as well.

There are records of openings of quarries providing stone for the construction of certain temples and testimonials to his two brief military campaigns in Nubia. There are literally tens of thousands of statues, funerary objects, and other belongings of the king, his family, and his courtiers in museums and collections around the world, including, of course, in Egypt. This ancient land (including the Sudan) is virtually an open-air museum, with many of the structures built by Amenhotep III still above ground and visible, while many more have been excavated, retraced, and recorded.

The king's three jubilee festivals in Years 30, 34, and 37 of his reign are documented in temples and tombs, but even more remarkably by more than 1,000 potsherds, gift labels from jars holding donations of food to Amenhotep III and his family at his Malkata palace. These handwritten notations usually name the recipients and/or the donors, the latter coming from a cross section of Egyptian society. They often document the precise type of wine, ale, meat, honey, vegetable, and oil held in the jars and the year-dates the gifts were sent. Published by William Hayes of the Metropolitan Museum, these pithy records are rich nuggets of information about the players and their practices in the last years of Amenhotep III's reign.

In addition to the royal records, even more documentation comes from inscriptions left by private individuals in and on their own monuments. Courtiers amassed unprecedented wealth and power during Amenhotep III's reign and, as a result, were able to commission or have the king endow them with large tombs and impressive statuary of their own, some with autobiographical texts including important information related to their sovereign's activities.

Most of what we know about Egypt's international relations in the last years of this reign and the next two or so decades is revealed in correspondence found in an archive at Tell el Amarna, the capital founded by Akhenaten. This historical treasure holds more than 300 personally dictated letters between late Dynasty 18 royalty and Cypriote, Hittite, Mitanni (upper Tigris-Euphrates Valley), and Babylonian kings as well as Canaanite mayors and governors. One letter is dated as received by Amenhotep III at Malkata in the third to last year of his reign. When Akhenaten abandoned Thebes, he moved his father's palace correspondence file from Malkata to Amarna, and the exchange of letters continued.

Almost all the Amarna letters were written in Middle Babylonian Akkadian, the English of its day, which was a foreign language to all but Babylon and Assyria. Mitanni king Tushratta sent one long missive in his native tongue of Hurrian, and provincial Arzawa sent two in Hittite. Some of the Syrian and Palestinian mayors, vassals of Egypt, managed to slip terms from their own West Semitic dialects into the texts as well. All the scribes formed the words by punching cuneiform (wedge-shaped) signs onto large, damp clay tablets, which were fired to make them durable enough for long journeys. Just as the modern Latin-based alphabet is used by most Western languages today, cuneiform served many Near Eastern tongues and dialects in antiquity.

In 1887, the hoard was discovered accidentally in the remains of palace storeroom at Amarna by scavengers looking to take and reuse bricks from the ancient walls. The Assyriologist turned Egyptologist Reverend A. H. Sayce described the find:

> At the risk of repeating a well-worn tale, I will describe briefly the nature of the discovery in the ruins of a city and palace, which like the palace of Aladdin, rose out of the desert sands into gorgeous magnificence for a short thirty years and then perished utterly, some 300 clay tablets were found, inscribed, not with the hieroglyphs of Egypt, but with the cuneiform characters of Babylonia. They were, in fact, the contents of the Foreign office of Amon-hotep IV, the 'Heretic King' of Egyptian history.

Now these tablets are scattered among museums and collections in Cairo and abroad. They form the basis of important studies regarding the military, trade, economy, international marriage, social conditions, and chronology of this era.

Given all these documents, statues, tombs, and monuments – a virtual worldwide web of information – the reign of Amenhotep III *can* be studied chronologically, but some of the dearly held beliefs about this reign are upended in the process. For example, Cyril Aldred, one of the most dedicated and inspiring twentieth-century scholars of Amenhotep III's life and art, assumed that royal children were born only during kings' reigns. Of course, there is no biological or historical reason for this, yet Egyptologists, including me, continued to follow this line of thinking for decades. That meant refusing to entertain the possibility that our Amenhotep was born while his father was still prince, which in turn forced us to discount as fantasy our king's stelae inscribed with detailed accounts of the military campaign he led in Nubia in Year 5, whereas similar stelae recording similar events for other pharaohs were taken as fact.

The biography presented here takes the point of view that our Amen-hotep was born before his father became pharaoh. Doing the math of the ages of his recent ancestors and their length of reign seems to bear this out. Furthermore, it is suggested here that Amenhotep likely held an administrative position of great importance during his father's reign, that he was an adult when crowned king, and that he did lead the Year 5 campaign to Nubia, as he claimed. Most of the evidence is circumstantial, but a great deal of it comes from giving Amenhotep's writings the same respectful validity ascribed to those of other pharaohs. These inscriptions may be boastful, exaggerated, and arrogant, but they generally have their dates right and are a fair indication of the nature of the events, even when the win-loss column favors the texts' authors.

One of the most interesting features of Amenhotep's reign crystallizes in a period when there was not an abundance of records but a total lack thereof. In a reign otherwise flooded with documents, there is a long drought from Years 12 to 19, when there are none, zero. This phenomenon is often excused by pointing out that other periods in Egypt's history have similar gaps, but no other reign has the quantity, detail, and character of records that we find during Amenhotep III's good years. The eight-year silence in his chatty reign is remarkable, as is the subsequent radical change in Amenhotep III's life – and world – views in the second half of his reign.

The reason for both the historical gap and Amenhotep III's new approach is unknown, but it occurred at a time of voluminous production of statues of the goddess of war and pestilence, Sekhmet. More statues exist for her than for the king and all the other gods combined. Dozens more have been found in recent excavations at Kom el Hettan, the site of Amenhotep III's gigantic memorial temple. The general lack of major warfare during this period begs the historian to ask if this was a period of pestilence. This theory is hard to prove, but evidence gathered by infectious disease experts and Egyptologists is mounting. Gradually, the likelihood that Amenhotep's reign was victimized by a series of crippling plagues becomes more and more apparent according to some, and not ruled out by others.

There may also have been other problems caused by Mother Nature. Egypt is prone to earthquakes today, and it was in antiquity as well. Whether any might have occurred and done great damage during the reign of Amenhotep III is not yet known. Added to that is the recently gathered evidence that during these years, Egypt's lifeline and main highway, the Nile River, was changing its shape. This is normal for a river left to its own free will. What it meant for Karnak was that the temple's front gate needed to be moved gradually westward to keep up with the Nile's receding edge. At Kom el Hettan, across the river from Karnak, front gates were moved eastward toward Karnak. This seems to suggest that the Nile at Thebes, at least, was shrinking in width, which would have had devastating agricultural consequences.

In sum, there are many signs that Amenhotep III's 38 years on the throne were not the blissful and carefree period we have come to imagine on the basis of his stellar art production. In fact, his voluminous oeuvre, especially his colossal temple construction, may have been devised to win the gods' intervention against Egypt's decline. His plan and his efforts had no effect, however, and his family dynasty spiraled downward into oblivion in the decades following his death.

A bright spot is Amenhotep III's tremendous personal devotion to and esteem for his great queen Tiy, which is revealed not only in the sheer number and complexity of monuments he commissioned in her honor but also by the king of Mitanni, who wrote to her after Amenhotep III's death, making it clear that he regarded her as an impressive power and intellect behind the throne. The couple's relationship has no more touching evidence of their mutual love than a memorial left by the widow at her husband's birthplace. Such testimony to the depth and breadth of a royal marital relationship is extremely rare in Egyptian history.

One of the thorniest issues relating to Amenhotep III is the possibility of a coregency between him and his son Amenhotep IV/Akhenaten lasting anywhere from a few months to 12 years. The point of view of this book is that current evidence does not clearly support a coregency. The Amarna letters written to Akhenaten suggest that he was his father's successor, and they indicate that he needed tutelage in international affairs from the dowager queen Tiy. Obviously, he knew nothing about this arena firsthand as a coregent. Donald Redford's 1967 examination of the coregency was so thorough and logical that it should have put the question to rest. It continues, however, because the obscure details of the controversy are fascinating and the passionate arguments too much fun to resist. The decades-long academic debate has been full of provocative personalities, factions, and politics, and it deserves its own separate study.

This book does not pretend to have all the answers to all the questions about the life of Amenhotep III. The reader will not be surprised to see the words *perhaps*, *maybe*, *probably*, and other forms of hedging one's historical bets frequently throughout the text. The reasons for these best guesses are given, and the reader is directed to multiple sources in the notes.

Every year, new information appears in one way or another, either through excavations in Egypt, through discoveries in museums throughout the world, or in the process of scholars examining the period from new angles or with more updated methodologies and by sharing information with each other. Some of this will, as time goes by, undoubtedly alter some of the points made in this book.

GEOGRAPHIC, CULTURAL, AND HISTORICAL BACKGROUND

The Serpentine Nile

Egypt has an odd shape totally dependent on the world's greatest river, the Nile – a long, winding serpentine of swiftly flowing water, a few hundred yards wide and half a continent long. Patches of green crops emerge from the black soil sheathing each bank, adding to the snakelike image. North of Memphis, the Nile fans out into a delta of branches and streamlets before it empties into the Mediterranean Sea. From the air, this broad, green swath forms the Nile's cobralike cape and head. Before modern dams were built, the Nile annually swelled with the melted snows and silt of Ethiopia and central Africa. It flooded its banks in northern Sudan and Egypt and sloughed off the fertile, black mud it had transported – like a reptile shedding its skin – renewing itself and the valley for another year. This inspired Greek historian Herodotus to memorialize Egypt as the "gift" of the Nile, as if the river were benign and inexhaustible, when it could be, in some years, devastatingly stingy and in others over-generous to a fault. Even in good years, which, thankfully, outnumbered the bad, the gift, as is often true, required a tremendous amount of management and capital expenditure in order to provide a dependable agrarian economy.

Egypt's ancient name, *Kemet* (the Black Land), refers to the Nile's sable banks and contrasts with *Deshret* (the Red Land), the broad deserts lying east and west. On a map, this sinuous empire, 1,000 miles long, including Nubia in the northern Sudan, and sometimes only a very few miles wide, looks impossible by every standard – impossible to control, impossible to defend, and impossible to unify under a single religion, culture, or language. Yet the reason for its peculiar shape, the Nile, also made the impossible possible for it provided about 675 land-miles of nearly uninterrupted, easily navigable waters from the First Cataract, just south of Aswan, to the Mediterranean Sea. It was, for all practical purposes, a super-highway making both travel and communications quick and easy.

The Nile was so basic to Egyptian thought that it had no name but *iteru*, "The River." Its modern name may descend from a form of that – *nai-iteru* – changed in Greek to Neilos. It was so crucial to Egyptian travel that the wheel was not adopted as a means of transportation until long after the Pyramid Age, many centuries into Egypt's known history. The words meaning "to travel north" and "to travel south" were written with hieroglyphs in the form of sailboats, the one, with sails furled, taking advantage of the river's northward flow, and the other, in full sail, carried by the prevailing north to south wind.

Egypt's strung-out geography meant that early cult centers along the ancient Nile had developed their own creation myths somewhat similar to each other in theory but with different names and duties given to the paternal gods, mother goddesses, and pantheons. The various divinities married each other, had children, and carried out heavenly tasks and duties. This meant that they interacted and communicated with and related to each other in ways that made them understandable to humans.

Each deity had its visible symbol or avatar, sometimes more than one, and sometimes one served several deities. The god of wisdom and writing, Thoth, could be represented by an ibis or a baboon. The sycamore tree could be home to the goddess Nut, Hathor, or Isis. Yet Hathor could also appear as a cow, and Nut could also personify the Milky Way as a golden-bodied, nude young woman, arching her body across the nighttime sky. Their devotees had personal amulets or drew personal images of their special deity's avatar to use as focal points for their devotions. Any official petition to a god or goddess, however, could only be made by or with the assent of the king, who represented all deities on earth and who commissioned statues of them and built temples to them.

The easy coexistence, overlap, and occasional mergers of these many cult systems are a tribute to the success of the unification and the religious tolerance of the ancient Egyptian people. There was never a sense, except during the benighted Amarna period, that only one set of belief systems was correct and that all others were either anathema or substantially inferior. Furthermore, the ancient Egyptians welcomed foreign deities into their spiritual fold. It is interesting that this open-minded and intellectual approach of ancient Egyptian spirituality did not extend to human encounters. For the Egyptians considered themselves culturally superior to all others – Nubians, Syrians, Cretans, and dozens of other ethnic groups. Foreigners were traditionally depicted as bound prisoners writhing beneath the pharaoh's delicately sandaled feet. '

Egypt's Early History: From the Unification to the First Intermediate Period
(ca. 3000–2040 B.C.)

No kingdom on earth has a longer continuous history than ancient Egypt. It began sometime around or before 3000 B.C., when the towns dotting the banks of the long Upper (southern) Nile were joined politically with the settlements of the Lower (northern) Nile and the Delta (Map 1). The unification, traditionally ascribed to a king named Menes, set the cornerstone for the first three dynasties that comprise Egypt's Early Dynastic Period (ca. 2920–2575 B.C.).

From that time forward, every pharaoh held the title King of Upper and Lower Egypt, wore the two lands' combined crowns, and used their combined insignia. Menes placed his capital, "White Walls," at the juncture of Upper and Lower Egypt, at what is now Memphis, south and west of modern-day Cairo. Memphis was the cult center of a most ancient god, Ptah. The town's ancient name was "Hikuptah" (Mansion of the Spirit of Ptah), from which "Egypt" is derived. According to the theology of Memphis, Ptah was the creator god depicted as a mummiform man. He was thought to have sculpted the earth itself, and he created individual beings from clay on a potter's wheel. Not surprisingly, Ptah was the god of craftsmen and of the arts.

Heliopolis (ancient "Iunu"), now beginning to come to light under the modern El Matariya area of eastern Cairo, was the other northern city of great prominence. This was the cult center of Re, who was both the creator of life on earth (according to the Heliopolitan creation myth) and the physical embodiment of the sun. The Egyptian king was thought to be the son of this sun god. When he died, the king joined the sun god in his travels through the sky, while *his* son replaced him as the earthly son of the sun god. With few exceptions, every pharaoh from Dynasty 5 (beginning ca. 2490 B.C.) until the Roman invasion (30 B.C.) used some form of "Re" in his throne name.

After the Early Dynastic Period, the succeeding five dynasties of the Old Kingdom (2575–2134 B.C.), the Pyramid Age, lasted over 400 years. Memphis blossomed during this period. On the desert escarpment just to the west, huge pyramids were built as royal tombs for Djoser, Khufu, Khaefra, Menkaura, and others. Pepy I's pyramid was named

Men-nefer, which survives today in a Hellenized form of Memphis's name. These great tombs, the temples associated with them, and the Great Sphinx associated with Khaefra's pyramid cast a grandeur over Memphis unequaled by any ancient city in the then-known world. Avenues of lavish courtiers' tombs with delicately carved and gaily painted scenes of fruitful harvests, elegant furniture, and ornate jewelry suggest that life in Memphis was sweet, at least for the elite.

Amenhotep III was born and lived his early years not far from Memphis and Heliopolis. The centuries-old cults, monuments, and traditions of this area clearly wielded influence on his reign. The Memphite Ptah was prominent in our king's reign, and Ptah was given sacred land south in Thebes. Re had already found a home at Karnak before Amenhotep III, but solar imagery and solar deities usually more associated with Heliopolis came to dominate Amenhotep III's reign, especially toward the end. The temples at Heliopolis and Memphis, both of which must have been large and complex by this time, and the pyramids and memorial temples at Giza and Sakkara, obviously still impressive today, must have posed both a challenge and an inspiration to a creative and ambitious young prince growing up nearby.

At the end of the Sixth Dynasty, Egypt's power became decentralized, and her wealth shrank with her diminished tax base. Egypt dissolved by the end of the Eighth Dynasty into a period of anarchy known as the First Intermediate Period (2134–2040 B.C.). Some scholars place this as the time of the biblical patriarch Abraham, who apparently wandered into Egypt to escape even worse climatic conditions in the Levant.

The Middle Kingdom, the Rise of Amun, and the Second Intermediate Period (ca. 2040–1550 B.C.)

After about 100 years, Mentuhotep II of Thebes (ancient "Waset" ("Scepter")), in southern Egypt, rallied to reunite the land, founding the Eleventh Dynasty. This started a new era, now called the Middle Kingdom, Dynasties 11–14 (2040–1640 B.C.), Egypt's "classic" period of literature and language, when some of ancient Egypt's greatest stories and poetry were written. The visual arts also reached a high point with the quality of hard stone sculpture and intricate jewelry being exceptionally fine.

The sudden rise to power of an Upper Egyptian family brought the southern god, Amun, to the forefront of Egyptian theology. Amun, "the Hidden One," now became the national god of Egypt, with a cult temple at Karnak at the northern end of Thebes. Amun was increasingly joined with Re, creating Amun-Re. The two were a yinyang of deities, the sun god Re being radiantly omnipresent during the daytime and Amun being permanently hidden away and invisible.

Despite the importance of the Theban region as their birthplace, the pharaohs of the Middle Kingdom eventually moved their capital northward to the entrance of the huge Faiyum oasis just west and upriver from Memphis. Here Amenemhet III, the last great king of Dynasty 12, undertook vast irrigation projects and built a tall pyramid, now reduced to rubble, with colossal sculpture known today only from inscriptions. The grand, labyrinthine memorial temple associated with his pyramid was still a wonder in the days of Herodotus, who said that while the pyramids "beggar description," the labyrinth "outstrips even the pyramids." Our Amenhotep was born in the shadow of these monuments, and memory of them is indelibly stamped on his own work.

Toward the end of Dynasty 13, the Hyksos ("foreign princes") from western Asia stormed through the Delta and overtook Lower Egypt. Their success rode on the wheels of a powerful new war machine: the horse-drawn chariot, both the vehicle and the horse being completely new to the Nile Valley. A thousand miles south, a consortium of Kushite (Nubian) tribes inundated the valley from the Sudan. The glorious history and culture of ancient Egypt were perilously close to being extinguished between these two human tsunamis. The stronger of the two groups, the Hyksos, reigned over Egypt during what is now called the Second Intermediate Period (1640–1550 B.C.). The biblical story of Joseph, sold by his brothers into slavery and taken to Egypt, where he rose to become a court favorite, is often said to relate to these years.

The Early New Kingdom: Dynasty 18, Amenhotep III's Ancestral Line, and the Rise of Thebes (ca. 1550–1411 B.C.)

The tides turned with the arrival of Kamose, who sat "together with an Asiatic and an African, each man holding his slice of Egypt," as he memorialized his reign on a stela. Considered the last Egyptian king of Dynasty 17, Kamose made some strides against the Hyksos as far as the Delta and also invaded Nubia, sending the insurgents back beyond the Second Cataract. He was followed by Ahmose I (1550–1525 B.C.), the first king of Dynasty 18, who beat the Hyksos back to Canaan and reaffirmed Kamose's efforts in Nubia. On the foundations these two leaders laid for Dynasty 18 and the New Kingdom, Egypt dominated North Africa and the Near East for the next four centuries. This is the family line into which Amenhotep III was born.

A series of military campaigns maintained Egypt's supremacy. Thutmose I (1504–1492 B.C.) penetrated western Asia as far as the Tigris-Euphrates Valley. Thutmose III (1479–1425 B.C.) led wave after wave of attacks along the eastern Mediterranean coast into what is now Syria and penetrated deep into Nubia. By the end of his reign, Egypt's military was ensconced in fortresses as far south as Gebel Barkal, near the Nile's Fourth Cataract in the Sudan, and was regularly extracting tribute in the form of ivory, ebony, exotic animals, slaves, and gold. At the same time, local rulers along the Levantine coast became Egypt's vassals.

Amun-Re's burgeoning temple at Karnak was a primary beneficiary of the riches coming in from Thutmose III's adventures abroad. New walls recorded all variety of donations and feasts resulting from the victories in Asia. Delicate relief carvings on the wall of one chapel recorded the strange flora and fauna discovered abroad. The result was a botanical and zoological study of great sophistication. This combination of military aggression and scientific inquiry gave Thutmose III the modern sobriquet "Napoleon of ancient Egypt," since Bonaparte's military expedition to Egypt in 1798 included academics and scientists of all kinds, who recorded everything from wildlife to monuments and laid the foundations for the study of Egyptology as it is known today.

Thutmose III had become king at the age of two, when his father died. His father's widow and sister, Hatshepsut, stepmother and aunt to toddler Thutmose III, became his regent. Eventually outliving her, Thutmose III became sole ruler when he was about 16, after which he ruled for another 38 years. He must have been in his middle to late teens when his eldest son was born. This child became Amenhotep II and must have been in his late thirties when he finally ascended the throne around 1427 B.C., perhaps sharing rule for two years with his father. Amenhotep II must have had a number of children by the time of his coronation. Several sons are known.

Prince Thutmose was one of the younger ones, likely born early in his father's reign, since he was big and strong enough to race a chariot with its pair of stallions while he was still a prince, according to the "Dream Stela" he set up at Giza, but apparently not yet mature enough to have moved on to more dignified occupations. By this time, the future Thutmose IV was old enough to produce his own first son, who would become our Amenhotep III. In other words, at the time of our king's birth, his father was a junior prince around ten years away from succeeding to the throne.

Meanwhile, during Dynasty 18, Thebes had grown into a major metropolis. During the Middle Kingdom and early Dynasty 18, one or more branches of the river curled eastward of the main flow, creating islands of the sites where Karnak, Mut, and Luxor temples now stand. These branches eventually withered, leaving the sacred lakes at the Amun-Re and Mut temples, but a large area of swamp suitable for fishing and fowling still existed in early to mid-Dynasty 18.

As the marsh gradually filled in, becoming firm enough for farming and settlement, Karnak island joined up with the east bank, and the small shrine began to spread out, eventually, over many centuries, transforming itself into the great religious complex known today. This evolution is evoked in an ancient anthem to the city of Thebes: "Thebes is the pattern for every city. Both waters and land came from her in the Beginning. [Then came the sands and] her foundations on the heights become land. Then mankind appeared within her." The temple's papyrus-shaped columns relate not to myth but to reality.

In Dynasty 18, Thebes effectively became Egypt's administrative capital. By the time of our king's birth, the main city of Thebes, according to New York University professor David O'Connor, covered about 1,500 acres and had 90,000 inhabitants, about the same as the city of Albany, New York, or Bath, England. Its west bank was the new location for the royal cemetery, a series of closely connected and well-hidden western desert ravines now called the Valley of the Kings. Royal memorial temples were set out in the open along the western edge of the agricultural land separated from secluded Kings' Valley by a row of desert hills. Many courtiers of high rank, especially from mid-Dynasty 18 onward, even if they had been born elsewhere, made their own burials, or at least cenotaphs, in the easily accessible hills above the royal temples (Map 4).

Memphis, by virtue of its location, remained a great economic center and focus of both domestic and international trade. Most foreign goods from the north and east entered Egypt through its eastern Mediterranean seaports or via the land routes across the Sinai, and almost all of these must have passed through Memphite docks for sale or distribution along the river farther south and west to the oases. Grain, wine, and other foods grown in the great Delta breadbasket also passed through Memphis on their way to storehouses and markets upriver. Therefore, even as Thebes became a more active administrative center, kings maintained palaces at

Memphis, and the older city held the hearts and affections of its native sons, including those called south by duty.

A NOTE ON THE SPELLINGS OF ANCIENT EGYPTIAN NAMES

There are very clear philological rules regarding the transliteration of Egyptian hieroglyphs into the Latin alphabet. These do not include vowels because the Egyptians generally did not write them, leaving us mostly to guess at how to fill them in. Furthermore, not all the consonants transliterate easily, so Egyptologists use diacritical marks – apostrophes, dots under letters, and so on – to signal to each other which consonant or vowel is meant. The name "Amenhotep," for example, is strictly transliterated as *imn ḥtp*, and the *ḥ* should have a dot under it. Over the centuries, this name has been presented to readers in a surprising number of ways, from the Hellenized "Amenophis," which is now considered old-fashioned, to the philological favorite "Amenhotpe," which results in a difficult, even distasteful, pronunciation. The name "Amen," alone, is often spelled "Amun" or "Amon."

Most authors these days spell our king's name Amenhotep, and so do I. On the other hand, I have decided to spell the deity's name with a *u*, as in "Amun." I have followed this pattern throughout the book, spelling names when they are applied to divinities one way and when they are applied to human beings (even royalty) another way. I hope that this will help new readers to discern more easily the gods from the historical figures. The gods are, for example, Amun, Re, Sobek, and Montu. The human beings are Amenhotep and Sitamen, Khaefra and Ramose, Sebek-hotep and Sebek-mose, and Mentuhotep. There are exceptions, of course. Atum, for example, is spelled the same way as a god and in private names.

Occasionally, I have stuck in a hyphen where I thought it would help, and sometimes I have simply taken free license to double a consonant to help pronunciation – not that we know how these words actually sounded in antiquity.

PROLOGUE

THE BIRTHPLACE OF
AMENHOTEP III

THE FAIYUM OASIS

The Faiyum oasis, the once-idyllic birthplace of Amenhotep III, lies southwest of ancient Memphis in the Libyan desert (Map 1). At 40 miles wide, it is Egypt's second broadest stretch of arable land after the Nile Delta. On its northern edge, 150 feet below sea level, is its largest feature – the shrunken, brackish inland sea called Lake Qarun (Horn). In the past, connecting streams and canals made Qarun a catch basin for the Nile's annual floodwaters when they were especially high. Herodotus wrote that the lake (called "Moeris" in his day) was actually man-made, which, considering what we shall see of Amenhotep III's projects, is not entirely impossible, and that water flowed into it from the Nile six months of the year but reversed itself the other six months.

Waterfowl, fish, and other aquatic life were abundant there – so much so, according to the Greek historian, that taxes were paid to the royal treasury on their account. The perch was worshiped as a local god, as was its nemesis, the crocodile, Sobek, the principal god of the Faiyum's administrative seat, Shedet (Greek Crocodilopolis). The surrounding land was rich, producing wheat, barley, flax, hemp, figs, pomegranates, and grapes. Uncultivated wild heath was home to game animals such as gazelles, feral cattle, and hare as well as their predators, foxes and jackals.

The Faiyum, as noted in the Introduction, became a favorite royal spot in the Middle Kingdom. Monuments like Amenemhet III's 90,000-square-yard labyrinth on the lake's shore were legendary throughout antiquity. Even more amazing, if we swallow Herodotus's description, were the "two pyramids which rise out of the water to a height of fifty fathoms, with the same amount built underwater; each of them crowned by a stone figure seated on a throne."

16

1. View of Medinet Ghurob from the northeast corner of the enclosure wall toward the canal. Photo courtesy Ian Shaw, University of Liverpool Excavations at Medinet Ghurob.

In Dynasty 18, the Faiyum became a country getaway for the kings and their court. Amenhotep III's great-grandfather, Thutmose III, founded a fortress and walled town about 660 yards in circumference at the oasis's eastern edge, toward Memphis. The town was called in antiquity "Mi-wer," translatable either as "Great Lake" or "Grand Canal," but its modern name, Medinet Ghurob (Crow City), is more evocative of the desiccated wasteland it has become in modern times (Figure 1).

Unfortunately, our knowledge of this site is very sketchy because it was only tentatively and sporadically excavated, mostly in the nineteenth century, and was looted for its treasure and quarried for its building materials for decades before and after that. Since 2006, archaeologists from University of Liverpool, under the direction of Ian Shaw, have begun to reevaluate the site.

THE FAIYUM'S HAREM AND ITS CULTURE

One of the most significant features of Mi-wer was its harem — a sort of luxury work-villa for royal women, including queens, consorts, princesses, and female chattel acquired through conquest and other means. Some of the women in royal harems were from noble Egyptian households – daughters of courtiers depicted in their fathers' tombs wearing ornate royal jewelry and bearing the titles "Royal Ornament" and "King's Favorite." By tending to the king and his court, these young girls were educated in proper manners and customs, making them attractive marriage candidates for favorite courtiers if not retained by the king himself. The enormous quantities of beads and other jewelry items still remaining on or near the surface of the site today are indirect testimony to the favor these women held at court.

The Turkish word *harem* comes from the Arabic meaning "forbidden," and in Turkey, such premises were in the most remote rear corner of a sultan's palace precinct, where they were closely guarded by eunuchs. Dynasty 18 Egyptian harems were found both within the king's main palace grounds and as separate institutions. While they undoubtedly had carefully chosen staffs and attendants, there is no evidence that they were attended by eunuchs.

Nevertheless, one ancient Egyptian word for "harem" was *kheneret*, and it is related to the words for "restrain," "confine," and "prison." Inmates of both harems and jails were called *khenerut*.

The more common word for "harem" was pronounced something like "ippet." *Ippet* is similar to the word for "counting house." This makes particular sense at Mi-wer, where all aspects of the town – its women, its children, and its output of finely woven linen – were royal property and required careful accounting. *Ippet* is also related to the word "rhythm." The ancient Egyptians enjoyed symbolic plays on words. Perhaps this was a pun referring to a woman's biological cycles.

Young harem girls were called *neferut* (beauties). According to an ancient papyrus, this term was applied to women "beautiful of their bodies, being buxom with braided hair, who have not yet opened in childbirth." Musically talented ones acted as royal entertainers and concubines. Colorful paintings in the tombs of the richest courtiers at Thebes depict attractive women – some richly clad, some nude – playing flutes and percussion instruments, usually accompanied by a blind male harpist, while athletic girls dance and perform gymnastics wearing nothing but jewelry – beads, hair ornaments, earrings, and hip – bands. Ancient stories describe pharaohs listening to stories – something like the 1001 Arabian nights – or delighting in boat rides powered by beautiful, naked young women.

Although women of the harem had little control over their own destinies, it was arguably the best life females could have in ancient Egypt. They had the finest of everything: linens, jewelry, ointments, glass vessels, perfumes, food, wine, furnishings, and even opium imported from Asia.

However, these enclaves were not places for the timid or the politically inept. Stories of plotting by queens and other harem women crop up intermittently in history. For example, trial records of a harem-sponsored royal assassination attempt in Ramesside times suggest that some of the guilty were sent home to commit suicide by drinking poison potions. Others may have been burned alive on braziers at the temple gates.

THE HAREM'S PLACE IN THE ROYAL EXCHEQUER

Mi-wer's two major industries were the manufacture of linen and the production of children. As far as the first was concerned, weaving was one of the few occupations allowed, even encouraged, among royal and noble women throughout antiquity, and it was a hallmark industry at Mi-wer. It seems that the first influxes of weavers at Mi-wer were skilled captives fetched by Thutmose III and his successors from Asia during decades of war. These included women from Canaan, the Tigris-Euphrates Valley, and elsewhere in the Near East who were adept at recently invented Eastern-style embroidery and intricate weaving techniques. Men, probably also from the Near East, operated the most recent mechanical invention: large, vertical looms.

The Amarna letters often list royal linen among the gifts sent from pharaoh to foreign kings, while wool garments came back in exchange. The palace even paid staff salaries and bonuses in cloth. Since linen's shelf life was longer than that of grain or flour, it could be stored or banked away long term as a sort of a trust fund or rainy-day account. Linen was graded according to quality, "royal" and "fine" being the sheerest and most delicate, suitable for the king and divine cult statues. The value of a fine-grade garment has been reckoned as equal to an ox, perhaps equivalent to a small automobile today. The lowest or coarsest grades served as toweling, bed coverings, wrapping paper, personal tissues, bandages, horse blankets, ships' sails, and lamp wicks. The quality of mummy bindings depended on a family's means, and sometimes these wrappings were scavenged from worn-out clothing.

THE HAREM AS ROYAL INCUBATOR

During the reign of Amenhotep III's father, Thutmose IV, the population was likely something of a mix of highborn and royal women and skilled immigrants. The production of children, especially royal children, was a natural outcome. Mi-wer's subsequent function as an incubator for palace children was inevitable. Children's toys, clothing, and even burials of tiny bodies have been found there, as have amulets associated with childbirth, such as small images of its chief goddess, Taweret, an appropriately shaped, upright-walking hippopotamus, and Bes, the lion-faced, dwarflike god of the hearth and protector of children.

Current excavations there may eventually turn up a birthing house, which Gay Robins calls the "specially built structure erected perhaps in the garden or on the roof" to keep the mother, the process, and the eventual newborn isolated from the community. The hieroglyph for childbirth is in the form of a kneeling woman with a child diving out from beneath her. More detailed artists' sketches and literary references depict the mother, her long hair loosely tied up, squatting on two bricks while tended by young girls, all of them nude, except for jewelry and amulets. The postpartum woman is depicted dressed in fine linens sitting on a bed, babe in arms.

It appears that here, between two bricks in a hut within a royal harem in a garden oasis in Egypt's western desert, is where one of ancient history's richest and most powerful rulers came to light. This is where the biography of Amenhotep III begins.

1

AN HEIR UNAPPARENT

(Reign of Amenhotep II, Years 15–25, ca. 1411–1401 B.C.)

PARENTS OF THE FUTURE KING

The infant Amenhotep was born at Mi-wer to Prince Thutmose, a son of Pharaoh Amenhotep II, who was in the fifteenth year of his reign, about 1412–1411 B.C. by modern reckoning. The little boy was not perfect: he had a clubfoot, but that was a relatively common feature of this family, judging by the mummies thought to be theirs. This malformation would never appear in any of his portraits, nor was there a hint of it in his inscriptions.

The new father, Prince Thutmose, was, at least in his own eyes, as handsome as a god. A pillar from the hall built during his reign at Karnak shows this quite literally as now King Thutmose IV faces a mirror image of himself in the form of the god Amun, the two of them distinguished from each other only by their crowns (Figure 2).

The portrait statues Thutmose IV eventually commissioned depict a symmetrical face with slightly slanted eyes and a strong nose, broad shoulders, a thin waist, and legs like tree trunks. Although the royal sculptors rarely produced any but the most idealized physiques, in reality, the young prince's body must have been honed and hardened and his skin tanned by his favorite pastime of racing his father's chariots in the desert west of Memphis. His best-known, smaller-than-life-size portrait shows him seated side by side not with a wife, as many kings and nobles were depicted, but with his mother, Tiaa, a minor harem lady who would have been invisible to history had her son not become pharaoh. She acquired the title of queen, or Great Royal Wife, only after the death of her husband, Amenhotep II, and the succession of her son, Thutmose IV.

Newborn Prince Amenhotep's mother was a woman named Mutemwia. Her origins are shadowy, and exactly how she fit in among

2. Pillar from Thutmose IV's Karnak hall before reconstruction showing the king with Amun and a jubilee inscription. Photo: APK/JSB.

the royal women is not known. Traditionally, pharaohs endowed their sons with harems when they came of age, so perhaps Amenhotep II had given her to young Prince Thutmose when he reached adulthood in his mid-teens. As was the case with Tiaa, Mutemwia would have been lost to oblivion had her son not eventually become King Amenhotep III.

Mutemwia's name, meaning "Mut is in her (sacred) boat," was uncommon in Dynasty 18. The word *mut* was Egyptian for "mother," which took the written form of a hieroglyph in the form of a vulture. It was also the name of an Upper Egyptian lion-headed goddess, who first became prominent in Dynasty 18. Mut was celebrated as Amun's consort at

3. Mutemwia's sacred bark sculpture from Karnak, granodiorite, L. 90 inches, EA 43. Courtesy the British Museum.

Thebes, where she had a temple, the site of an important school for princes and well-born young men (see Chapter 2).

Mutemwia's name would eventually be memorialized by Amenhotep III in a unique rebus: a seven and one-half foot long sculpture carved in hard, black granodiorite depicting the lady in completely human form enthroned on the deck of the sacred bark (*wia*) she rode in festival processions. A larger-than-life vulture (*mut*) stands behind her, its great wings hunched around her like a mother bird protecting its nestling. Some scholars see Mutemwia as Asiatic, but the portrait head now separated from the rest of the sculpture reveals negroid features, including a short, broad nose. Originally placed in Karnak temple, the statue is currently a central exhibit in the British Museum (Figure 3).

This rebus portrait is just one of the many monuments Amenhotep III would commission for his mother. Most of them come from the Faiyum oasis, making it clear that this place had some meaning for Mutemwia, and she must have spent a great deal of time there. What originally brought her to Mi-wer is not known, whether it was her skill as a weaver, her musical talent, political exchange, or a family connection. Whatever the reason, she must have been beautiful. Her son remembered her on her monuments as "sweet of love, great of grace, who fills the Hall with the fragrance of her dew."

Amenhotep III would describe his parents' union in imagery and verse years later on the walls of Luxor Temple, which he built in celebration of his own divine birth. He made his father a god and his mother a queen, and described their evening together with great passion and spirituality. He recounted how his father found Mutemwia

> as she was resting in the beauty of her palace. She awoke on account of the aroma of the god and cried out in front of his majesty. He went to her straightaway . . . and he caused her to see him in his form of a god . . . She rejoiced at the sight of his beauty, and love of him coursed through her limbs. . . . And then the majesty of this god did all that he desired with her.

Once the child was conceived, the god of wisdom and writing, Thoth, counted the days until his birth, and the potter god Khnum formed the infant prince from clay on his potter's wheel along with a twin, the boy's *ka*, or "spirit." Finally, the god spoke to Mutemwia:

> Amenhotep, ruler of Thebes, is the name of this child I have placed in your body. . . . He shall exercise the beneficent kingship in this whole land. . . . He shall rule lands like Re forever.

Reality was quite the contrary. At birth little Amenhotep was a fairly insignificant soul. His father was somewhere around fifth in line to the throne. Because Thutmose's older brothers must have had sons of their own, the newborn Amenhotep's place on a theoretical proximity-to-the-throne list must have been near the end of the papyrus scroll. This relatively low status may have worked in the child's favor, making him less of a target for palace intrigue during his vulnerable early childhood. It enabled the future king to spend his earliest years – during his grand-father's last ones – in relative anonymity inside the protected nest of Mi-wer, under the wings of his mother and paternal grandmother. Life at Mi-wer must have taught its own lessons just by the nature of the place. Some of the characteristics of Amenhotep's reign – his appreciation for women, his adroitness at international relations, and his love of expert craftsmanship and fine design – were almost certainly imprinted on him as a young child.

The child's name, meaning "the god Amun is at peace" (or "Amun is gracious"), was probably chosen to honor his grandfather, but it is also important for its southern bias as Thebes, the center of Amun-Re's cult, became more and more the center of the empire during these years. The spiritual importance of ancient Egyptian names cannot be overstated.

Expunging an individual's name from his or her tomb wall was a way of condemning the person's memory and soul, whereas speaking the name of the deceased kept him or her alive. How much Amenhotep III's eventual and rather complete architectural transformation of Thebes drew inspiration from his own name can only be imagined.

AMENHOTEP'S EARLY CHILDHOOD AT MI-WER

Amenhotep was surrounded by siblings and half-sibs at Mi-wer. The names of about 17 are known or suspected. There was an older sister Tiaa, named after her grandmother. She may have been the daughter of Nefertiry, Thutmose's first official wife or queen other than his mother after he became king. Tiaa and another sister, Py-ihi, would survive well into their brother's reign, their names being found together in a tomb with those of other royal women. Brother Aakheperura bore the throne name of their grandfather and was a close companion of Prince Amenhotep. A baby brother named Temy was born during Amenhotep's childhood and given to the royal steward Tjanuna to mentor. A tiny blue glazed figurine in the British Museum shows Tjanuna squatting with the little boy between his knees, the two of them enveloped in a heavy cloak. Brother Amenemhet (given the title King's Son of His Body) was named after great kings of the Middle Kingdom who had left so many grand monuments nearby in the Faiyum.

Other recorded or suggested names of Amenhotep's siblings are Amenemopet, Penttepihu, Tawy, Merymose, Meryt-ptah, Sathor, Neferamen, Wiay, Hentiunu, and Khatnesu. Another possible brother, Ahmose, was named after the first great king of Dynasty 18 and became High Priest of Re at Heliopolis.

Of course, many children never reached adulthood. This is not surprising considering that the best medical treatments of the day were magic spells or little amulets worn to ward off evil. One ancient medical prescription called for a sick child to eat a cooked mouse then tie up its bones in a collar of "fine linen" knotted seven times around the neck. Prince Amenemhet, named earlier, and a sister called Tentamen succumbed in infancy or early childhood, and their canopic jars were placed in their father's tomb. Infant burials are also numerous at Mi-wer.

What may be our Amenhotep's first baby portrait, with three of his siblings, was found fairly recently (Figure 4). A princess and her two sisters and one brother are sculpted on the lap of a statue of a

moon-faced nurse found in the eastern Delta at Zagazig, the modern
name of the area that includes the temple of the feline mother goddess
Bastet at Bubastis. The statue is now in the Cairo museum. Carved
in limestone about half life-size, her eyes inlaid in contrasting stone,
the unnamed woman sits on an elegant, high-backed chair with pet
monkeys, an expensive bronze mirror, and a kohl (eye paint) jar carved
in the spaces between the chair's legs. She wears a voluminous wig and
fine jewelry. Her capacious lap holds four children: an elegantly attired
teenage girl sitting sideways and, behind her, a small boy and two girls –
all nude – leaning against the woman's chest. The boy, his hair braided
into a side lock, and the girl to his right each wear a heart amulet on a
cord inlaid in red jasper, suggesting that they are royal. Therefore, the
lady was likely a royal wet nurse or governess and the children on her
lap a prince and princesses she fed in their infancy.

The statue has been dated to the reign of Amenhotep II, the period
of our little prince's early childhood, but the style of chair on which
the nurse sits and the necklace she wears were in fashion as late as
Thutmose IV's reign. The heavily braided wig is the forerunner of a
style that became popular early in the reign of Amenhotep III. The age
relationship between the older, big sister sitting cross-wise and the little
boy behind her is very reminiscent of Thutmose's daughter Tiaa and
Prince Amenhotep. The lack of inscription fits the scenario that the
eventual disposition of these children was not yet clear.

Children of the Kap

Amenhotep's and his brothers' earliest education would have begun in
Mi-wer's *kap*, a murky word usually translated as "nursery." The *kap* is
thought to have been a secluded and protected area within the harem.
Whether it was a room or a discrete structure is not known, but, apparently, it was a gathering point where a select group of very young boys
received their most basic education. Some of these children were blue-
blooded, but others – judging by their eventual careers – were likely the
offspring of valued employees or were even unacknowledged children
of royals. In this light, the *kap* appears to have been an unusually demo-
cratic institution, allowing an egalitarian learning environment for boys
of ultimately disparate social strata. Its members felt an *esprit de corps*,
and alumni of this royal nest carried the title *khered en kap* (Child of the
Nursery) proudly to their graves.

4. Statue of royal nurse from Zagazig (Bubastis), limestone with colored stone inlays, H. 32–1/2 inches. Egyptian Museum, Cairo. Photo by Kenneth Garrett. Courtesy Dr. Zahi Hawass and Egyptian Museum, Cairo.

Two children of Amenhotep's nursery are known. One of these was Amenemopet, who grew up to be an administrator of a hammock workshop, with the title Chief of Rope, thus, overseer of an important craft at Mi-wer. The other was Inena, who became "Chief Craftsman of the Shipwrights of the Boats of All the Gods of Upper and Lower Egypt." Inena was the son of Hamesh, a name with a Semitic ring, who was

Chief Craftsman of the King. Inena's grave stela, now in the British Museum, lists his major projects, including a divine processional bark that he made for Sobek of Shedet, the Faiyum's capital, in addition to a barge for Amun, probably the one described eloquently by the king himself years later on a stela at Thebes.

A young man named Meryra, according to a much later inscription in his tomb at Sakkara, was a supervisor of Amenhotep III when he had been a small prince, an *inpu*, a word that is written with a hieroglyph in the form of a lap child with his index finger raised to his mouth. This word is thought to mean something like "puppy" – probably not unlike the way an American teacher might say she knew the president of the United States when he was a "young pup" – but its use in Egyptian inscriptions gives it a richer meaning. Our prince's father was just about to use this term on his most important stela (see Chapter 2), saying about himself, "When His Majesty was an *inpu* like Horus in Chemmis," in other words, like the child-god Horus when he was still a nursling.

Because of the reference to Horus, some authors take *inpu* to mean "crown prince," but this interpretation is reflexive. According to Meryra's view of history, he was indeed the supervisor of an *inpu* like Horus in Chemmis, but only in hindsight, retrospectively, as Bryan thoughtfully decided about Thutmose IV's use of the word in his own inscription. Subsequently, Meryra became a lifelong personal friend of the future king, eventually attaining high office as chancellor or Keeper of the Privy Seal, and he was entrusted as a tutor for one of Amenhotep's sons, Si-Atum, who probably grew up in the area of Memphis since Meryra's tomb is nearby.

Young students, perhaps as early as their days in the *kap*, learned to sit cross-legged on the floor – like grown-up scribes – pulling their kilts tightly across their thighs to form writing desks, and to begin learning basic words and texts in hieratic, the cursive form of the language, which was used in business documents and on many papyri but not on temple walls and major monuments. This script would have been a useful tool for everyone, including future kings, officials, shipwrights, and workshop foremen, and training in hieratic may have started quite early. Their tablets were exactly that: small sheets of limestone or plastered wood planks, either of which could be wiped clean and reused, papyrus being far too expensive. Thoth, the god of writing, is often depicted scribbling on palm leaves, and these likely served students as well.

Not all students went on to study their language's word forms and grammar as written in hieroglyphs, which consisted of hundreds of signs – some of them representing sounds and some representing ideas. Egyptologists Rosalind and Jac Janssen have written that pupils memorized polite, formulaic phrases to be used in correspondence and standard clichés for official documents, and they chanted their grammar, much like first-year Latin students reciting "amo, amas, amat. . . ."

After the boys had learned to read and write, and perhaps not until they went on to higher education, they tackled the classic texts of the Middle Kingdom; each of these stories had morals and instructions to be learned by the students. One was the *Tale of Sinuhe*, an official of Amenemhet I who fled in a panic from Egypt when his king was murdered. He settled in Palestine, where he did very well for himself. In his later years, however, he became homesick and returned to Egypt to be pardoned by Amenemhet's son and successor, Senwosret I. Another story, the *Tale of the Eloquent Peasant*, was about a man from the oasis who was robbed of his donkeys. His complaints to the king's high steward were so beautifully phrased and spoken that the king righted the wrong done to him. There were also histories, perhaps more correctly called "legends," of ancient kings, one of them recounting the magical conception and birth of triplets: the first three kings of Dynasty 5.

Arithmetic was naturally an important subject for boys who would become treasurers, granary supervisors, and even shipwrights. In school, these youngsters learned to calculate silently and quickly. Numbers were written in the form of hieroglyphs: a stroke for the number 1, a tadpole for 100,000. The number 400,000 was written in cursive hieratic as a tadpole with four strokes under it. Fractions in weight and linear measurements were various parts of the sacred eye of the god Horus, the iris being 1/4 and the eyebrow being 1/8, for example. Exactly how an Egyptian visualized complex calculations in his mind's eye is hard to imagine.

Music was also part of the core curriculum, and schoolboys learned "to sing to the reed-pipe, to chant to the flute, to recite to the lyre," according to the Janssens. Evidence in the form of students' sketches found in a school inside a royal memorial temple on the west bank of Thebes suggests that art, too, figured prominently in lessons.

Prince Amenhotep must have taken these studies seriously, for they bore fruit in every aspect of his reign. As pharaoh, he would become one of the greatest patrons of the arts in world history, commissioning incalculable square feet of temples, all decorated with painted relief carvings of exceptional quality. He demanded the best materials and attention to the tiniest details of fine workmanship. His most highly skilled artists drew the human figure with a sensually curving line that made two-dimensional figures seem to emerge from the wall. This line became a signature of his style.

During his reign, he would create an enormous number of written records on large commemorative scarabs, temple walls, monolithic ste-lae, clay tablets, statuary, and so on. Many seem to have been dictated personally by him, and they have a certain meter and elegance approaching poetry. Music and dance increased in frequency and prominence as subjects in courtiers' tomb decorations and on smaller works of art as well. It seems that patronage and appreciation of the performance arts stepped up considerably during his reign. His own grasp of arithmetic is impossible to calculate, except for the suspicion that every time his architects drew up plans, he came back to them with the command to double or triple the size of the planned buildings.

At a certain age, Amenhotep and the most promising of the other boys were sent away to school. The Eton or Harrow of ancient Egypt was the palace school at Memphis, and its principal product was an elite class of scribes and officials. These were the tiny percentage of Egyptian boys who would fill the pharaoh's administrative posts, from the highest vizier to the lowest military scribe or entry-level priest. Classes were made up of royal children, of course, but also of sons of favorite courtiers being groomed for important careers. In addition, highborn foreign boys were imported and brought up within the palace nursery and schools and then returned to their native lands to rule as vassals.

The palace school also provided an internship in politics and courtly behavior. By serving as pages and lackeys to the court when not in class, the young prince and his fellow students learned how the pharaoh and officials acted and communicated with each other. An ancient text, *Satire of the Trades*, probably first written half a millennium earlier and copied and recopied by generations of school boys before Amenhotep's day, instructs as follows: "If you walk to the rear of officials, approach from a distance behind the last. . . . When an official sends you as a messenger, then say what he said. Neither take away nor add to it."

Sports were also a crucial aspect of a prince's training, in particular archery and chariotry, which were central activities in Late Bronze Age warfare. Grandfather Amenhotep II appears as a preadolescent archery student in two tomb scenes of his mentor Min, the mayor of Thinis and father of Sebek-mose, one of Amenhotep III's important officials (see Chapter 10). The boy's shooting practice is said to take place in the court of the palace at Thinis. The exact location of the city of Thinis itself is not now known, but it is thought to be associated with Girga, about 70 miles northwest of Thebes. Did a specialized royal military school or sports training center exist there?

According to Amenhotep III himself, he excelled at all of his childhood tasks and tests. Never one to be needlessly modest, once he became king he had a temple wall inscribed that he was the "foremost of . . . children," and that it was ordained when he was a "weaned child," in other words, after he had graduated from the *kap*, that he would rule Egypt. The latter statement has only a slightly more realistic ring than his birth story on Luxor Temple's walls, especially since his father had not yet engineered his own succession to the throne.

2

THE MAKING OF AN HEIR
APPARENT

(Reign of Thutmose IV, Years 1–5, ca. 1400–1396 B.C.)

THE PROMISE OF THE GREAT SPHINX

Around 1400 B.C., Prince Amenhotep's father became King Thutmose IV. How the four princes standing between him and the throne disappeared is not clear, but many Egyptologists suspect the worst: murder by Thutmose's own hand. The evidence is circumstantial but compelling. Stelae set up by the elder brothers at the temple of Giza's Great Sphinx in the days when they had royal aspirations of their own were found hammered into pieces in a context suggesting Thutmose's handiwork. The violence and simultaneity imply brutal premeditation.

The new king had the perfect alibi, however: the Sphinx itself. This was the huge, pharaoh-headed lion carved from a knoll of Giza's living rock. It guarded the desert edge leading up to the grand pyramid of Dynasty 4's Khaefra. The Sphinx was an avatar of Pharaoh, and by Dynasty 18, it was considered a god in its own right: *Hor-em-akhet*, "Horus on His Horizon," or Harmakhis, as he was eventually known to the Greeks. Thutmose IV recorded his version of events in hieroglyphs on a large stone plinth – today called the Dream Stela – dated it Year 1, month 3 of Inundation, day 19 (around mid-September); and installed it between the lion's paws.

In this his most important and famous text, Thutmose started by describing himself in days past: "When His Majesty was an *inpu*, like the young Horus in Chemmis . . . he was seen like a god himself." He then brought his brief vita up to present time by saying that "now" he passed time on the Giza plateau at archery practice, hunting, and chariotry. One day, Thutmose continued, he stopped to rest in the shade of the Sphinx and fell asleep. As the prince dreamed, the god spoke, promising him the kingship, and then the Sphinx fell into moaning about his ruined limbs and the encroaching sand that weighed them down.

This speech has traditionally been taken as a bargain between god and prince: if the prince clears away the sand, the Sphinx will give him the throne. On the other hand, the divine beast's piteous self-description is the perfect metaphor for the elderly Amenhotep II's own physical condition at the end of his life. Judging by the mummy considered to be his and preserved in the Cairo museum, he suffered from arthritis, and his entire body was covered with strange subcutaneous nodes still visible today but undiagnosed. Considering Amenhotep II's age and ill health, the Dream Stela may actually recount a last moment between father and son, when the dying king chose his youngest, most viable offspring as successor.

It sounds like a thoughtful move by a wise old man who knew from experience that a pharaoh needed youthful bravado and energy. Because Thutmose III lived to his late 50s, his eldest son, Amenhotep II, must have come onto the throne as a fully mature man. If Amenhotep II was nearing 40 when he was crowned, then he lived to 60 or more by the end of his reign, making him among the longer lived of Egypt's pharaohs. At his death, his elder sons would have been about the same age as he had been at his own accession and well past their primes as far as ancient life spans were concerned. Could he have decided from his own experience that their athletic junior brother was indeed the strongest candidate for pharaoh?

Whether by decree, foul play, or accident, Thutmose became the eighth king of the Eighteenth Dynasty, the fourth Thutmose to rule Egypt. In gratitude to the Great Sphinx, he cleared away the sand that had drifted over it, surrounded it with protective retaining walls stamped with his throne name, *Menkheperura*, and erected the Dream Stela.

ROYAL PROPAGANDA

Thutmose IV's work at Giza was just the beginning of a propaganda campaign to clarify and justify his right to the throne. Next he tackled the status of his mother, Tiaa, by promoting her from faceless concubine to queen. Two statuary fragments of Tiaa from Giza invoke the blessing of the Great Sphinx. The inscription includes archaic titles meant to revive the past and legitimize the present by their use. Though this may seem quite cynical and self-righteous to the modern mind, the pharaonic view was likely a fervent sense of divine right and a quest to create and preserve the correct order of things – what the ancient Egyptians called *ma'at*. Just as American presidents repeatedly recall, reuse, and stand on the words and ideas of the Founding Fathers and Abraham Lincoln, Thutmose IV apparently researched and invoked lapsed principles that had served the empire well in more ancient times.

The Karnak statue of Thutmose IV as pharaoh seated next to and embracing his mother, Tiaa, as regnant queen was one of his most flagrant revisionist monuments. No other pharaoh is known to have done this before; perhaps none needed to. Hieroglyphs carved on the throne call her Great Royal Wife, the Egyptian term for "chief queen." This title had been withheld from her by her husband but was now ordained by her son. On a statue found in the Faiyum, she is "King's Mother, Great Royal Wife, Tiaa" and "beloved of (the crocodile god) Sobek of Shedet." The new king even went so far as to add Tiaa to his father's monuments at Karnak, as if she had been queen all the time.

Finally, Thutmose turned his attention to his heir. By now, it must have been apparent that Prince Amenhotep looked nothing like his father, judging by the pair statue with Tiaa. In that image, Thutmose bore the thin lips and aquiline features of the dynastic line. Little Amenhotep had distinctly different and remarkably southern features – a short, broad nose and thick lips, the upper one being considerably thicker than the lower one. He would imprint these features on the royal family through the end of the dynasty, including on the famous face of Tutankhamen. The lack of resemblance between father and son may have been glossed over during the boy's first years when he was so far from succession to the throne. Once his father became king, however, it surely mattered.

To set matters straight, Thutmose commissioned a granite statue where the long-legged boy, at least ten years old, perches on the lap of his tutor, Royal Treasurer Sebek-hotep both individuals now headless (Figure 5). The older man sits in the traditional scribe's pose, cross-legged on a thick cushion, his hands crossed protectively over the boy's chest. The prince wears the royal calf-length kilt. The remains of one long lock of hair braided to the side in the traditional child's coif – the same as that worn by the boy on the nurse portrait from Bubastis – touches his shoulder.

Sebek-hotep's statue, now in Brussels, is inscribed as a gift of the king to the two principal deities of the Faiyum and was probably originally placed at the temple of the crocodile god Sobek at Shedet in the Faiyum, where Sebek-hotep had once served as mayor, a position gained by marriage. His wife, Meryt, was the daughter of the former mayor of

5. Prince Amenhotep on lap of treasurer Sebek-hotep, granodiorite. Height 21 inches, E6856. Copyright Royal Museums of Art and History, Brussels.

Shedet and, as a woman, could not inherit the family office. Apparently, she had no eligible brothers, so Sebek-hotep landed his first major job by succeeding his father-in-law as mayor and then eventually rose from there to treasurer.

The royal treasurer was in charge of all royal workshops, their income, and their assets, so Sebek-hotep controlled all aspects of nearby Mi-wer, from its manufacture of royal linen to its production of royal children. The sex lives of the royal women, in particular, required meticulous supervision. The days between royal conjugal visits and children's births apparently were carefully counted to be sure that no interlopers could have breached harem security. This practice is recorded for later harem cultures, for example, in Turkey, but is only implied in ancient Egypt. The ibis-headed god of wisdom and writing, Thoth, appears in birth room scenes such as Amenhotep's Luxor Temple description of his parents' union, in which the deity writes the number of days from conception to birth on a palm leaf. Sebek-hotep and his scribes likely kept similar accounts on Mutemwia and other royal consorts. This would have made Sebek-hotep the guarantor of every royal child's legitimacy, giving him a special place in their lives.

The statue's inscriptions name the boy "King's Son of His Body, Amenhotep, Who Loves Strength." The phrase "of His Body," was never used in an honorific sense, as "King's Son" sometimes was for special courtiers, but could only be used for legitimate children of the reigning king. Therefore these words carved onto the image of this most trusted and highly placed courtier, who counted the days from conception to birth, virtually guaranteed Prince Amenhotep's legitimacy. It proclaimed that Thutmose had produced an heir to the throne and that the succession was safe. Reflexively, the existence of an heir reconfirmed the king's own legitimacy as ruler.

No matter how Thutmose IV had climbed onto the throne, he had now secured his rights by both divine and natural law. First, the Dream Stela proclaimed the kingship by divine decree. Second, mother Tiaa was a queen. And third, the king had produced a healthy and strong heir. Thus Thutmose IV's credibility as ruler of Egypt was indisputable and sealed from all sides. He had guaranteed *ma'at*, the right order of things.

PRINCE AMENHOTEP'S HIGHER EDUCATION AT THEBES

Sebek-hotep's statue is inscribed with the words *ma'a kheru*, after his name meaning "true of voice" or "justified," a phrase used for individuals whose souls had successfully passed the tests of the last judgment, been found pure, and been allowed to enter heaven. Therefore, at the time the statue was made, Sebek-hotep was probably dead, and Prince Amenhotep was no longer under his aegis. By this time, the boy may have left for school upriver at the temple of the goddess Mut on the east bank of the Nile at Thebes.

Although Thebes had begun to come to prominence about 600 years earlier, it was not until Dynasty 18 that the city blossomed on both sides of the Nile (Maps 3–5). The western bank was a broad, flat, low-lying plain that flooded every summer. When the river subsided, leaving new layers of fertile silt, the farmers tilled, sowed, and harvested their crops. At the edge of this farmland, desert ridges rose hundreds of feet, offering from their summits a panoramic view of the entire Theban valley to the eastern mountains 20 miles away. The faces of the western hills, warmed daily by the rising sun, became the catacombs for

Egypt's nobility. A network of valleys farther west, crowned by a natural rock pyramid, served as the Valley of the Kings, the legendary royal burial place of Dynasties 18, 19, and 20. The belt of land joining desert to farmland was gradually studded during the New Kingdom with temples built by each pharaoh in his own honor. Called mortuary or memorial temples, these grand edifices probably did serve a purpose related to the kings' funerals and afterlives, but they were also used during the kings' lifetimes as venues for festivals.

The east bank stood higher after centuries of occupation. It was the land of the living: the main city with the royal administrative palaces; temples to the local gods, especially Amun-Re; courtiers' villas; city dwellings; markets; harbors; and so on. The ancient New Kingdom city is now mostly underneath the modern city of Luxor, making it nearly impossible to excavate. According to O'Connor's previously cited estimate of the size of New Kingdom Thebes, the town was substantial, covering about 1,500 acres (one-tenth the area of New York's Manhattan Island) and containing about 90,000 inhabitants (about 6% of Manhattan's actual residents).

Judging from other ancient towns of the same date, the center must have been a dense warren of narrow paths and alleyways crowded by slim, single- and multiple-storey adobe houses with tiny, dark rooms and hearths in interior courtyards. Some had room for the family donkey, cow, and other animals. The wealthy officials' large villas, with their attendant workshops, gardens, arbors, and pools, likely claimed prime real estate along the river's edge, just as in modern times. The city's current name, "Luxor," comes from the Arabic meaning "palaces," referring to the grandeur and prominence of the temples bracketing the eastern shore and studding the edge of the western desert.

Prince Amenhotep's final years of schooling took place on the east bank in Mut Temple on the southern side of the great Amun-Re temple at Karnak in northern Thebes, the opposite end of the city from Luxor Temple. Exactly why Mut Temple was chosen to house a major school is not clear, unless it had to do with the goddess's aspect as a consort to the national god and the mother of his son, Khonsu – in other words, as nurturer of divine and royal heirs. She was also virulently protective of her Egyptian kings, burning their enemies alive in her brazier.

Images carved on Mut Temple's interior walls suggest that this was also the location of a rite of passage that marked the end of boyhood and the entry into manhood: circumcision. The mummies of both Thutmose

IV and his father, Amenhotep II, show signs of having undergone this ritual. The mummy of our king, Amenhotep III, is not in good enough condition to tell for sure. Circumcision as a sign of having reached maturity and joined the ranks of his elders was a turning point in a young man's life. Whereas birthdays were apparently not tracked or used as age measurements, the years since a man's circumcision were occasionally a matter of record. For example, Amenhotep III's great-grandfather, Thutmose III, is reported as having asked his vizier, User-amen, not the man's age but, "How many years ago were you circumcised?"

THE SCHOOLMASTERS HEKARESHU
AND HEKARNEHEH

Royal Tutor Hekareshu and his son Hekarneheh ran the school at Mut Temple. They likely came from Nubia, where, among the more Egyptianized populace, names beginning with the word *heka*, meaning "prince" or "ruler," were their way of showing loyalty to the king. Mut Temple was Thutmose IV's alma mater, and Hekareshu was his teacher. Hekareshu's son, Hekarneheh, was a child of the *kap* (probably a contemporary of Thutmose). As a youth, he acted as a "page in the inner palace." When he grew old enough, he joined the military, rising to Commander of Cavalry. Later he returned to Thebes and, following in his father's footsteps, took up the quieter life of educating the royal children and their cohort. One might fantasize – on no grounds other than her presumed Nubian appearance and her name – that a third member of this family was Mutemwia. If so, then Thutmose met her when he was just an adolescent.

The elder teacher, Hekareshu, seems to have had a special affinity for Egypt's most ancient history, according to the exceptionally fine objects he left at Abydos, the legendary burial site of the god of the dead, Osiris. Abydos was also the location of tombs for Egypt's first kings. As early as the Middle Kingdom, individuals left small mummiform statuettes, called *shawabtis*, at Abydos. In general, *shawabtis* were meant to substitute for their owners as agricultural workers in the afterlife, and everyone who could afford to was buried with a full complement of 401. Their name comes from the promise inscribed on them. If the god calls on the deceased person for field labor, it is written "I will answer (for him or her)," and the little figures were usually depicted holding agricultural implements in their hands. The special, individual *shawabtis* donated at Abydos offered the added benefit of assuring their owners' proximity to Osiris in death.

6. Thutmose IV on lap of teacher Hekareshu with Prince Amenhotep on dais before Hekarneheh. From Theban tomb 64. After Lepsius.

Hekareshu left the finest group of *shawabtis* discovered at Abydos so far – one in alabaster, another in blue glass covered in gold foil, and a third in ebony – such a remarkable group that the find spot was named "Hekareshu Hill" by the excavators. Aside from demonstrating the output of the best imperial workshops, these three objects testify to the deep interest and respect Hekareshu had for Egypt's most ancient traditions, which he must have instilled in his students.

Most of what we know about the Hekas comes from Hekarneheh's tomb in the Valley of the Nobles on the honeycombed desert hills of the west bank of the Nile opposite Karnak. Like all the best nobles' tombs, it had a large open room decorated with brilliantly painted scenes representing aspects of or events in their lives. Such rooms, unlike burial shafts and chambers, were accessible to family, friends, and other visitors, before and after the owners' deaths, and served as gathering places at holidays.

Painted on the tomb walls are figures of the two teachers and a bevy of royal youngsters – a hall of fame of the school's most important pupils – in particular, Thutmose and Amenhotep (Figure 6). The former, dressed as a prince, sits on old Hekareshu's lap, but his throne name is written above, indicating that the scene was painted after he had been crowned king. A diminutive Prince Amenhotep, wearing the braided side lock of youth, stands in a position of honor on the dais at Hekareshu's knees. The younger teacher, Hekarneheh, handsome and fit, stands behind the boy. Other princes, most of whose names are lost or were never filled in to begin with, march in cookie-cutter rows behind Hekarneheh. Elsewhere in the tomb, Amenhotep performs rituals together with Hekarneheh, the teacher guiding his student through the arcane steps of each rite. In these scenes, Hekarneheh is called Amenhotep's "nurse." The Egyptian spelling includes a hieroglyph in the form of a pendant breast, suggesting the protective and nurturing aspect of the teacher's role.

THE TOMB OF SEBEK-HOTEP AND MERYT

The Theban tomb of Prince Amenhotep's beloved childhood mentor and protector, the treasurer Sebek-hotep, is right next door. A devoted northerner, he was probably never meant to be buried there, but as one of the court's highest officials, a monument near the Valley of the Kings was due him. The most famous scene from the tomb highlights his wife, Meryt, who had been a Royal Ornament in the palace of Amenhotep II before being married to Sebek-hotep. In the tomb scene, Meryt holds Prince Amenhotep's older sister, Princess Tiaa, on her lap under the label "nurse of the King's daughter, Tiaa."

Royal Ornament Meryt was well practiced in the manners and customs of court ladies. As "great one of the musical troupe," she was choral and instrumental director of an ensemble most likely attached to the temple of crocodilian Sobek in her hometown of Shedet, near where Amenhotep and his sister Tiaa were born and reared. It would have been Meryt's job to oversee the training, rehearsal, and performance of musical aspects of the religious rites at the temple. She was, therefore, by heritage, history, intelligence, and rank, a woman of great esteem and honor in the community and the perfect woman to mentor Tiaa and to train her in the liturgy and rites of the cult. Likely she taught her to read and write as well, for to carry out all her duties, she must have been literate herself.

Just inside the doorway of Sebek-hotep's otherwise fully decorated tomb is a large, blank space. By all rights, it should hold a scene of Sebek-hotep with Prince Amenhotep equally as important as the one in Hekarneheh's tomb. One can only imagine the possible scenarios that might have prevented this, not the least of which is jealousy.

As Theban residents, the Hekas had much more control over what was being accomplished across the river than did someone living hundreds of miles north, and they could make sure that their own scene with Thutmose IV and his heir was executed in full color, whereas Sebek-hotep could not. On the other hand, many Theban tombs were never finished. Possibly Sebek-hotep died before commissioning his most important wall.

Prince Amenhotep probably spent only a few of his youthful years at Thebes, but they were crucial to his intellectual and spiritual development. It would have been here more than at any other site in all of Egypt that the seeds were sown for a new vision and new world order eventually expressed in extensive city planning and lavish architectural development throughout the empire.

3

THUTMOSE IV AND KING'S SON AMENHOTEP IN NUBIA

(Reign of Thutmose IV, Years 5–8, ca. 1396–1393 B.C.)

TROUBLE IN UPPER EGYPT AND NUBIA

In Year 5 of Thutmose IV's reign, according to an economically worded stela of poor and provincial style, Amenhotep III's father, Thutmose IV, gave a land grant to Medamud Temple, just a few miles north of Thebes (Map 3). Medamud, ancient *Madu*, was the cult city of war god Montu, the second most important god after Amun for the founders of the Middle Kingdom, several of whom were named "Mentuhotep." According to the stela, Montu had helped in a "restoration of order," the details of which are unknown.

Some of Thutmose IV's more important inscriptions from these years deal with troubles much farther south in Nubia, modern Sudan (Map 2). Nubia was the source of most of Egypt's gold during the New Kingdom, and many scholars derive the classical name "Nubia" from *noob*, the ancient Egyptian word for "gold." Additional luxury materials and chattel came from there, just as in more recent times. These included slaves, cattle, exotic pets (monkeys, giraffes, unusual types of antelope), ivory, and rare woods. Ebony came from deeper Africa via Nubia, and our word for this black wood probably stems from the ancient Egyptian *hbny*.

The northern part of Nubia, Wawat, lay just south and east of the First and Second cataracts. Wawat was the heart of Nubia's gold lands, supplying ten times as much gold to Egypt as the rest of the southern mines put together. Thanks to the foundations laid earlier in the dynasty, particularly during the reign of Thutmose III, settlements in Wawat and south as far as the Third Cataract were well acculturated into Egyptian customs, language, and religion, and many Egyptian foreign service officials, merchants, and military men resided there. These included native-born Egyptians as well as Nubians educated in Egypt and mercenaries often called on by Pharaoh to fill out the military. Despite the strong Egyptian presence, fortifications at gold-working sites in Wawat and along the nearby Nile testify to the reality of frequent threats from miscreants, even during the height of pharaonic control.

The ancient Egyptian name for all of Nubia, "Kush," also had a specific geographical meaning for the area south of Wawat, between the Second and Fourth cataracts and east to the Abu Hamed bend of the Nile stretching across the Nile's horizontal, S-shaped curves between the twentieth and eighteenth parallels. The Third Cataract, in particular, was something of a demarcation line. Throughout the New Kingdom, settlements north of the Third Cataract pretended to be as Egyptian as possible, whereas settlements to the south, with few exceptions, remained Kushite to the core, with different ceramic styles, burial customs, and so on, and were to the ancient Egyptians something like the Wild West as viewed by nineteenth-century Philadelphians. Today, places called "Akasha" and "Kosheh" echo the ancient name. In ancient Egyptian, the name "Kush" was almost always accompanied by an adjective meaning "wretched" or "vile," commemorating that it had been a repeated threat to Egypt's security, despite being a source of great riches and delights.

South of Kush was Karoy, another important source of gold for pharaohs from Thutmose III to Amenhotep IV. Likely situated on the left bank of the Nile between the Fourth Cataract and the Abu Hamed bend, Karoy was often named in texts as the southern limit of the Egyptian empire.

INSCRIPTIONS OF THUTMOSE IV AND HIS FAMILY AT ASWAN

Attempting to maintain stability and boost loyalty in this area, Thutmose IV commissioned shrines and temples throughout Nubia. However, monuments with actual dates on them have not yet been found farther south than the First Cataract at Aswan, leaving open the question of how far south he traveled personally. Apparently he visited Aswan twice, leaving some of the last inscriptions of his reign there. A scene dated Year 7 at Konosso Island shows Thutmose IV smiting foreigners under the benign gazes of the gods and Queen Iaret, who holds a mace, as if ready to tag-team. The presence of Iaret, who had apparently been promoted after the deaths of Nefertiry and the dowager Tiaa, suggests that this imagery is honorific rather than historical record.

Konosso Island, with its huge, river-polished, black granodiorite boulders, was a favorite spot for formally and informally carved inscriptions of Thutmose IV, his family, and his court (Figure 7). Prince Amenhotep left his mark there twice. The first was a dedication to the elder teacher, Hekareshu: "Favored of Amun-Re, God's Father, Hekareshu, *ma'a kheru* (justified)." Our prince signed it with his brother, Prince Aakheperura. The title God's Father was an honorary one given to a king's favorite elders, in this case, by Thutmose IV to his beloved teacher. As on Sebek-hotep's statue, the word "justified" probably indicates that Hekareshu had died, and this may be a memorial inscription for the old man in his homeland, if his name is an indication of southern origin. If scholars are right about Thutmose's Year 7 voyage being a state visit, this inscription probably dates to that trip. By now, Prince Amenhotep was at least 17 years old.

The second inscription, apparently carved at a later date, gives the names of four individuals, three of which are followed by the phrases "justified" or "repeating life (in the next world)," suggesting that they had died in the meantime. The first two are the younger teacher, Hekarneheh, and Prince Aakheperura, and the third is Royal Herald Re'a, whose best-known monument is his tomb at Thebes. The royal herald served as a mediator and a local representative of the central administration, functioning as both sheriff and town clerk. The fourth name, King's Son Amenhotep, is the only one not followed by a memorial epithet.

This second rock-cut graffito at Aswan may be contemporary with a police action Thutmose IV undertook in the area and recorded on a rock at Konosso and dated the second day of the third month of winter on the cusp of Years 7 and 8 of his reign. According to Thutmose IV, the adventure started at his palace at Karnak. There he received the news that Nubian troublemakers were advancing downriver toward Egypt's southern border.

The king wrote as follows (paraphrased from Bryan's translation):

> Now his Majesty was in the Southern city at the quay of Karnak... He prayed to his [divine] father Amun, who had given him eternity as king forever...

> ... [A messenger arrived to report] to his Majesty: The Nehesy (a tribe living between the Second and Fourth cataracts of the Nile) have descended from the vicinity of Wawat (have traveled northward from the hills of the eastern Nubian desert), and have

7. Inscribed boulders at Konosso. After De Morgan.

planned rebellion against Egypt, collecting for himself all the foreigners and rebels of the other country.

[At dawn] The king [proceeded] to the temple in order to give offerings . . . and [placed] himself in the presence of the ruler of the gods, asking his advice. . . .

Then the god informed him what would happen; showing him the correct way to do what his ka (his spirit) desires, like the words of a father to his son. . . . The king went forth . . . his heart being joyful.

And he commanded that his army be collected immediately. He sent it off in valiance and strength.

. . . he being brave in his golden ship like the [sun-]god Re . . . his sails were filled with bright red and green linen, and spans of horses and troops accompanied him. His army was with him, the champions in two rows, with the elite troops at his sides, and the [smaller boats] equipped with his retainers.

The king fared south like Orion, making Upper Egypt gleam with his beauty: the men shouted their admiration for him, and the women ululated (a shrieking sound still used today at times of great joy or sadness) at the news . . . every god of the Southern region bore a bouquet for his nose.

The king alighted at Edfu to attend a festival. Then the Good God [King Thutmose] went forth like Montu (the god of war) in all his forms [and like Seth, and with Re behind him]. . . .

. . . and then he went forth with one sole companion from his retinue . . .

Without waiting for his army . . . he made a great carnage with his powerful scimitar. His terror entered into every belly . . . He opened the road like the Southern jackal, seeking the source of the attack . . . He found all the enemies . . . in a hidden valley . . . concealed from even the mountain dwellers . . . in a little-traveled land . . .

. . . . Then he removed the leaders together with their relatives, their cattle, all their possessions with them . . . "

Like many royal inscriptions, Thutmose's record of his Nubian campaign is full of bombast but light on geographic details. Where the battle took place can only be guessed. The Nehesy were traveling north, according to the word "descended," which meant they were heading from the south to the north toward Egypt's border, probably into the wadis (dry valleys or arroyos) running through the desert toward the Nile. Placement of his Victory Stela at Konosso adjacent to Aswan suggests that the battle was waged south of there, and his monument would serve as a warning to others with mischievous ideas.

"The road" Thutmose IV opened "like the Southern jackal" was probably the Kubban Road, which, during the New Kingdom, was the principal route from the First Cataract to the gold mines and quarries of the Wadi Gabgaba and the Wadi el Allaqi in Wawat (Map 2). This remote track could easily have been interrupted for a time by surprise attacks by even a small number of thugs, and the flow of gold into Pharaoh's coffers would have been halted. But the Nehesy were likely armed with nothing more than stealth, sticks, and stones. They would have been no match for the Egyptian king's superior might, with his horse-drawn chariots and bronze weaponry.

Who was the "one sole companion from his retinue"? Most kings did not name individual officials on such monuments, and Thutmose need not have mentioned a companion at all. He was the king, after all, and could have taken sole credit for the victory. Was it Prince Amenhotep? Or was it Thutmose's viceroy of Nubia, also named "Amenhotep," an increasingly common name at the time?

VICEROY OF NUBIA AMENHOTEP

The vice-regency of Nubia was a relatively new administrative post established by Dynasty 17's Kamose to maintain pharaonic authority in the south. There was no other office like it in the government, and it made Kush a special province of Egypt. This official's two most important duties, other than peacekeeping, were shipping gold, goods, rare animals, and slaves safely to Egypt and overseeing the king's building projects.

The late Eighteenth Dynasty title of the viceroy translates literally as King's Son of Kush, often abbreviated simply to King's Son. Some of these viceroys were not true royal blood but had been promoted from the ranks of *toparchs*, local headmen, and were given the honorific title of King's Son even though they were not. Other highly regarded Nubian locals also occasionally bore the title King's Son. For example, a King's Son existed at ancient Miam (modern Aniba in northern Sudan), adding more confusion to the viceroy's title.

Viceroy Amenhotep was the fifth to hold this post. A stela in his honor from the ancient fortress of Buhen bears a cartouche of Thutmose IV, securing him to that reign. He is also known from graffiti at Aswan's Sehel Island near inscriptions of Thutmose IV and Prince Amenhotep. At Sehel, Viceroy Amenhotep calls himself "Overseer of the Cattle of Amun, Director of Works in the South and in the North, Head of the Stable of his Majesty, King's Son of Kush, Overseer of the Southern Lands, mighty one of the king, praised one of the Good God, King's Scribe."

His titles and epithets reflect a new sense of royalty. Viceroy Amenhotep was the first to be called King's Son of Kush, as if to distinguish him from all the other Nubian so-called princes. He was the first to come to the post as Overseer of the Cattle of Amun, a common title of true kings' sons. He was the first to use the title Master of the King's Horses, a traditional office among true royal princes, although not restricted to them. He was also the first on his Buhen stela to be called Fanbearer on the Right of the King, a title that obviously implied close personal contact with his liege. And, he was the first to be depicted carrying a special royal accouterment, an ostrich-plumed *sekhem* scepter.

Viceroy Amenhotep's parentage and origins were never mentioned anywhere, perhaps because both were obvious. He disappeared without a trace after Amenhotep III was crowned. There are no burial objects — canopic jars, *shawabtis* — and no tomb known for him. Burial objects and/or tombs are known for his two predecessors in the post of viceroy and for two of his immediate successors. If he had died bearing the title, there should be some trace of him. On the other hand, if Viceroy Amenhotep was our Prince Amenhotep and became Amenhotep III, on ascending the throne, he gave up all princely titles as superfluous, and he was buried decades later in Kings' Valley with the accouterments not of a viceroy but of a pharaoh.

If the two Amenhoteps were one and the same, this is a rare glimpse into crown princes' careers. It would have been fitting to install the future Amenhotep III in Nubia as overseer of this important province to gain practical administrative experience – and perhaps to keep him out of the way of his father. This scenario recalls the centuries-old *Tale of Sinuhe*, studied by young Egyptian boys at school. Sinuhe explains that his king, Amenemhet I, "stayed within his palace and his son [Senwosret] reported to him that what he ordained was done." According to Sinuhe, Senwosret was leading the army in Libya when Amememhet died (apparently the victim of a harem plot), causing the prince to hurry back to the capital and assume the throne as Senwosret I (see also Chapters 4 and 5).

As far as Viceroy Amenhotep's assignments are concerned, most of what Thutmose IV ordained in Nubia was construction in his own name. Both the architecture of his temples and the southern reach of his work would find echoes in Amenhotep III's upcoming reign. On Elephantine Island, which stands in the middle of the river at Aswan, Thutmose IV expanded the temple of the ram-headed god Khnum with a pillared hall. The temple to Amun-Re and Re-Harakhte at Amada, about 110 miles south of Aswan, also grew a pillared hall, which was decorated with a reference to Thutmose's otherwise little-known *sed*, or jubilee festival, an event that normally occurred much later in a king's reign (see Figure 2 and Chapter 13). Amada stood on the east bank of the Nile in what the 1929 edition of Baedeker called "the most fertile portion of Nubia . . . [where the] belt of cultivable land along the river is comparatively broad." Likely it had not changed much from antiquity until Baedeker saw it, except for the gradual desiccation of the entire Nile Valley over the centuries. Nowadays, this farmland is submerged under Lake Nasser, formed by the High Dam at Aswan, and the temple was moved between 1964 and 1975 to higher ground.

Farther south, halfway between the Third Cataract and the great S-shaped bends in the Nile River, lies Kerma, the ancient capital of the Nubian kingdom. At a site half a mile north is Dokki Gel, known in antiquity as Pnubs, the "jujube tree." Here Thutmose IV built a sandstone temple to Amun on mud brick foundations of Amenhotep II. Though it is not a very large site, the architectural plan was rather complex. The temple is known to have comprised a tripartite sanctuary with a vestibule and a columned hall, but the iconography of the wall decorations was lost when Akhenaten demolished the building. The entrance of the temple was connected by a paved walkway to a building thought to be a ceremonial palace, and the sanctuary was surrounded by bakeries and storerooms for preparing and holding offerings. Meager remains suggest that Thutmose IV also built onto a temple started by his father, Amenhotep II, at Tabo on Argo Island, not far from Kerma.

Southernmost, about 25 miles downstream from the Fourth Cataract, is spectacular Gebel Barkal, a mountain (*gebel*) rising straight up out of the sand to a height of 302 feet like a southwest American mesa. A pinnacle formation facing the river suggested the shape of the sacred cobra or uraeus, the protector of kings and queens. The site was sacred to Amun-Re, whose primeval aspect was thought to reside within the giant rock. His temple at its base served as a sort of spiritual double for his cult center at Karnak. The original temple was started during Thutmose IV's reign, according to deposits found there, but later constructions during the height of Kushite power in the first millennium B.C. have erased all but traces of that structure.

A tenure as viceroy overseeing these projects would have allowed Prince Amenhotep to become familiar with Nubia, laying a firm foundation for events, projects, ideology, and worldview in the years to come. In his fifth year on the throne, he would wage a military campaign there, and he would send another army there in Year 26. Late in his reign, he would build temples deep in Nubian territory, as if this were a land he knew well. Aspects of Nubian religion would also become important during Amenhotep's reign. One of these was an emphasis on fertility, female fertility in particular, which meant a rise in the popularity of the dwarf god Bes, who protected women in childbirth and their children, as did the cat goddess Bastet and the upright-walking hippopotamus Taweret, nearly a caricature of the pregnant woman. Female deities would also become more prominent, especially daughters of Re, such as Ma'at and Mut/Hathor/Sekhmet, who spent part of every year in Nubia. The other deep African influence was an emphasis on ancestors and tradition that would become extremely important to Amenhotep III as he eventually began to prepare for his first jubilee in Year 30.

Prince Amenhotep must have been close to 20 years old at the end of his father's reign. He certainly had a harem of his own and very likely a number of children. The woman who would become known as his principal wife, Tiy, was surely with him, although she was neither acknowledged nor given her full status as queen until the end of his first decade as monarch. Her first born son and daughter, Thutmose and Sitamen (Daughter of Amun), were likely brought into the world while their grandfather, Thutmose IV, was still alive. Her son Amenhotep, who would eventually succeed his father as Amenhotep IV, later changing his name to Akhenaten, was likely born much later. A little prince named Aakheperura, probably named after our king's deceased brother may have been her son. He appears on the lap of an unnamed male nurse, the owner of Theban Tomb 226, who flourished early in Amenhotep III's reign (see Chapter 4). Another possible early son was Si-Atum, who lived long enough to produce a daughter, who matured in the third decade of the reign.

4

LE ROI EST MORT, VIVE LE ROI!

(Reign of Amenhotep III, Year 1, ca. 1391 B.C.)

THE BURIAL OF THUTMOSE IV

"The falcon has flown to heaven and Nebmaatra Amenhotep Ruler of Thebes is arisen in his place." Such was the announcement for every New Kingdom monarch. Prince Amenhotep succeeded to the throne at his father's death, sometime around 1391 B.C., the latter's reign having been rounded out by scholars to ten years. As mentioned previously, there is evidence that Thutmose IV had made some plans or an attempt at having a jubilee festival, and Melinda Hartwig has suggested that he deified himself, both of which seem at best premature in such a short reign. Had he become mortally ill, or was he fatally wounded in battle? In this case, a quickly planned fete or self-deification might have been hoped to revive him. Obviously, it was futile.

Like Senwosret in Sinuhe's tale, if our Amenhotep was viceroy of Nubia, he must have returned urgently to Memphis, or at least Thebes, to secure his transition to the throne. There is no evidence that he had rivals, but even Senwosret, despite having been named years earlier as his father's coregent, worked under Amenemhet's orders, suggesting a de facto secondary status. At word of the old man's death, Senwosret rushed back to the capital to officially claim the seat and crowns already due him.

It would take close to three months to lay Thutmose IV to rest. The first 70 days were devoted to the complex procedures associated with mummification, and it was an official period of mourning during which people fasted and men did not shave their beards. According to tradition, 70 days was the length of time the god Osiris lay dismembered before the conjurations and rituals performed by his wife, Isis, brought him back together and to life. It was also equated with the number of days the bright star Sirius disappeared from the nighttime sky every year.

During this period, the deceased Thutmose IV underwent a series of operations designed to prepare his body for the afterlife. First, his brain was removed, and then his internal organs were treated and potted separately in jars dedicated to specific deities. Next the body was packed with natron to desiccate it, then washed with Nile water, dried, anointed with sweet-smelling oils such as myrrh, and finally, completely wrapped in fine linen bandages, his finger tips and the tips of his toes sheathed in gold.

Most significant of the funerary rituals was the "opening of the mouth," during which special implements were touched to the mouth of the mummy, magically animating it and making it able to breathe, speak, and eat in the next world, just as Osiris was revived and able to do all of this, plus impregnate Isis with their son Horus. Magically alive once again, the dead king, as Osiris, joined the falcon-headed sun god Re-Harakhte's journey through the sky by day and through the underworld by night.

Thutmose IV's mummy was laid to rest inside a huge brown quartzite sarcophagus decorated with figures of deities and inscribed with column after column of funerary text. The deeply carved glyphs were filled in with orpiment (arsenic sulfide), a pigment imitating gold, as its name suggests. Buried with him were his son Amenemhet, daughter Tentamen, and a third, unnamed individual. All the things he needed for the afterlife must have accompanied him: chariots, furniture, throw sticks for bird hunts, mace heads, gloves, vessels, statues, a board for playing *senet* (which looks something like chess), and a fragment of linen delicately embroidered in several colors, perhaps at Mi-wer, perhaps by the hand of Tiaa, Iaret, or even Mutemwia. A full set of *shawabtis* (servant figurines) was certainly placed there so that the king would not have to undertake any work in the agricultural fields of the next world.

Thutmose's tomb, now numbered KV 43, is in the main part of the Valley of the Kings. It is a fairly large tomb with long corridors, pillared halls, and walls decorated with scenes of the king before various deities who promised him eternal peace. Contrary to his image on the pair statue with mother, Tiaa, and some of his other statuary, Thutmose IV's portraits painted on the walls of his tomb are endowed with more negroid features, like his son's.

Eternal peace was not the case for this king because his tomb was robbed, probably within a few decades of his death, during the Amarna period. It was repaired a few years later under orders of Horemheb, an army general who had become, lacking a better alternative, the last king of Dynasty 18. His overseer of the treasury, Maya, was in charge of the restoration, assisted by Djehutymose, steward of Thebes. The record of their work is written in hieratic in a beautiful calligraphic hand on the wall of the tomb's antechamber.

The tomb was rediscovered in modern times in 1903 by Howard Carter, who, 19 years later, would discover King Tut's tomb. He wrote about Thutmose IV's, "Our eyes became more accustomed to the dim light of our candles, and . . . we realized in the gloom that the upper part of the walls of this well were elaborately sculptured and painted. The scenes represented the Pharaoh . . . standing before various gods and goddesses of the Netherworld. Here was final proof that I had found the tomb of Tuthmosis IV."

ASCENSION AND CORONATION OF AMENHOTEP III

Judging by the funerary scenes in Tutankhamen's tomb, it was up to the king's successor to act as priest at the burial, just as nonroyal sons normally handled the rites at their own fathers' burials. In Tut's tomb, his successor, Ay, officiates, wearing a crown as if already named king, even before his predecessor's actual burial. It would have made sense for the sake of security, if nothing else, for the new king to ascend the throne and start forming his court immediately on his predecessor's death, delaying the actual coronation until after the burial. A modern example is that of Queen Elizabeth II, who, in February 1952, on being informed of her father's death, immediately returned to England from Africa and took the Royal Oath, sealing her accession. She scheduled her coronation 16 months hence to make plans and, in England's case, hope for better weather.

Reliefs at the temple Amenhotep III built at Sedeinga in Nubia hint that there were indeed two steps up to the throne in the case of our king as well – the Royal Ascent and the coronation. Whether Amenhotep was in Nubia or nearby, his installation was surely accomplished more quickly than his coronation, a long and lavish event in keeping with the ancient Egyptian penchant for ornate ritual and protracted festivities. Coronation ceremonies, which seem to have occurred primarily in Thebes during Dynasty 18, needed a great deal of planning and preparation, considering the number of priests and officials participating, the scores of items of new regalia, and the numbers of sacrificial offerings, not to speak of the necessity for planning according to favorable stars. The rituals were complex, and the gods certainly demanded that they be carried out with precision. This meant days, if not weeks and months, of rehearsal. Although no images of Amenhotep III's own event are known, records and images of the coronations of Queen Hatshepsut (his great-great-grand-aunt) and King Horemheb (the last king of his dynasty) suggest what must have occurred for him.

Whether in late spring or late summer, the two dates suggested by scholars for Amenhotep III's crowning, in Thebes, the sun would have been dazzlingly bright when the god Amun, in the form of his cult statue, emerged from his Holy of Holies in the darkest recesses of Karnak Temple, traveled across Luxor, and participated in – in fact, adjudicated at – the crowning of the new king. The statue, which no longer exists, was made of "fine-gold, lapis lazuli, turquoise, and every rare, costly stone," as later described by our king's grandson, Tutankhamen. The only equivalent Egyptian cult statue surviving from antiquity is a solid silver, gold-leafed, glass and semiprecious stone encrusted, seated falcon-headed god now in the Miho Museum outside Kyoto. Though only 16 1/2 inches tall, it weighs 36 pounds, truly worthy of a god!

Amun's cult statue had been bathed, fed, and dressed in the finest linens and rode shrouded inside a portable shrine on a sacred boat carried on four poles on the shoulders of files of priests. Priestly escorts burned incense to perfume the air for god and king and waved ostrich plume fans, dispersing heat and flies.

The royal candidate was led from the palace in a procession that wound through Karnak Temple. He was ritually purified with holy water from one of the sacred lakes, perhaps Karnak's, an act that some scholars identify as a predecessor of baptism. The procession then made its way through throngs of onlookers. Men cheered, and women ululated high-pitched notes of joy. The hieroglyph for "common folk" was a small ploverlike bird ("lapwing") endowed with both flapping wings and upraised human arms. The plover family is known for shrill voices and large flocks, making these birds the perfect symbol for swarms of screeching hoi polloi. Everyone tried to catch a glimpse of the new king and of the god's statue, reading omens in each movement caused by the priests' swaying shoulders as they passed Mut Temple and continued on to Luxor at the southern end of Thebes.

Amenhotep III's coronation probably took place inside a shrine or temple built by Hatshepsut or Thutmose III at what became during our king's reign the southern end of Luxor Temple. Upper Egypt's tall, conical white crown with its bulb-shaped point was presented by priests wearing masks representing the gods of the south. Lower Egypt's platform-shaped red crown with its spike at the back and curlicue in the front was presented by masked priests representing the Lower Nile cult centers. The two crowns merged perfectly to form a Double Crown, the white one inserting itself into the platform of the red, between curlicue and spike, representing the perfect fit of Upper and Lower Egypt into a unified realm. Perched above the center of the king's forehead was a gilded and bejeweled sacred cobra (uraeus), its tail curled tightly over the crown like a coil ready to spring the head forward to spit poison into the eyes of anyone daring to gaze directly at the king.

In return for Egypt's crowns, the king promised to build the army, maintain and enhance the temples, and assure the income necessary for the priests. All of this depended on the king's primary duty to guarantee the evenness of the Nile's annual flood throughout the valley and Delta, resulting in bountiful annual harvests. Too high a flood was destructive; too low a flood left drought. The annual waters were controlled partly by the gods and partly by the royal administration's ability to maintain its system of grand canals, irrigation ditches, and reservoirs.

Before Amenhotep emerged from Luxor's shrines, the Double Crown was exchanged for another, deep blue in color, the *khepresh*. This is the crown Ay wears as he officiates in Tut's tomb. Amenhotep may also have worn it from the time of his initial installation until the coronation, and he favored it throughout his reign. It was more aerodynamic than the others – tall and rounded in the front, arching to a slanted, cross-wise fin shape at the back and holding the obligatory uraeus in the front. It was the crown kings wore as they drove or rode in their chariots on festival days, on hunts, and to war. On his upper body, he wore a short-sleeved tunic of gossamer transparency, the fine form of his body showing through. Below he wore a long, transparent kilt around which was wrapped a pleated, red, sarong-shaped garment, and over that a metal apron inlaid with semiprecious stones and/or glass. A (mighty) bull's tail hung in the back when he walked but was pulled around his hips and draped over his lap when he was enthroned. A beaded waistband with his throne name in a cartouche held the kilt in place.

Around his neck, Amenhotep III wore a double row of disk-shaped gold beads – the Gold of Honor – perhaps awarded by his father at his jubilee. These choker-length necklaces rested on a broad *wesekh* collar of multiple rows of multicolored faience beads representing flower petals, persea fruits, and probably hieroglyphic amulets. In his hands, Amenhotep carried the three crucial insignia of his office: the shepherd's crook in gold and blue (lapis lazuli or blue glass), a hard stone mace head on a gilded and inlaid staff, and a flail, also made of precious metal and colored stone inlays. The king's sandals were made of the finest leather, and, if they were like his grandson Tutankhamen's, had images of conquered foreigners dyed and embossed into the soles beneath his feet.

AMENHOTEP III'S OFFICIAL NAMES

As he appeared before the crowds for the first time officially crowned, his five official "great names" were revealed and pronounced. Each was specially chosen to fit a certain facet of the whole titulary, and when taken together, the names evoked both the personality of the king and what he projected as the gestalt of his reign. The Horus name identified the king with the falcon god, who flew through the sky each day as the sun. The Two Ladies name placed the king under the protection of two primeval goddesses: Nekhbet, the chief goddess of Upper Egypt, whose cult center was at El Kab, in the eastern desert not far from Thebes, and Wadjet or Edjo, the cobra goddess of the North. The Golden Horus name's meaning is not known with certainty, although there are several theories.

Altogether our king's names were Horus, *Ka-nakht kha-em-maat* (Mighty–bull appearing–in–truth); Two Ladies, *Semen-hepu Segereh-tawy* (Who–establishes–laws, Who–pacifies–the–two–lands); Golden Horus, *Aa-khepesh hu-Setiu* (Great–of–strength, Smiter–of–Asiatics); King of Upper and Lower Egypt, *Nebmaatra* (Re-is-Lord-of-Truth); Son of Re, *Amenhotep*, Ruler of Thebes. The last two, the throne and birth names, were the only ones written inside cartouches, name rings signifying eternal rule. Images on Luxor Temple's walls show Amenhotep III crawling toward a seated deity and holding in his outstretched hand two cartouches. If accepted by the gods, the names would be written on the leaves of the sacred persea tree at the Re sun temple in Heliopolis, up north near Memphis, and this event was probably commemorated in a second rite there after the ceremonies at Luxor.

He was the third ruler named Amenhotep. The name "Amun-is-at peace" obviously honored the southern god. Neither the Amenhoteps nor any other pharaohs used numerals of any sort after their names. Our monarch's epithet "Ruler of Thebes" distinguished him from his grandfather, the second Amenhotep, whose epithet "Ruler of Heliopolis" separated him from the first Amenhotep.

Amenhotep III's throne name, Nebmaatra, was unique to him. It was the name he would go by in his own day. Even his beloved Tiy wrote that name first on the most tender of documents. He also used it in foreign correspondence and other rulers addressed him thus, although in Middle Babylonian Akkadian, the international court language, it came out something like Nimmuriya. Nebmaatra meant "the god Re is Lord of Truth," and it invoked both the god Re and his daughter Ma'at, the goddess of Truth and the Right Order of Things, the opposite of Chaos. Amenhotep's emphasis on establishing and maintaining the concept of *ma'at* would remain an important principle throughout his reign. The balance achieved by pairing names, one with a northern bias and the other southern, was part of establishing *ma'at*. When choosing his throne name, Amenhotep III may also have been recalling "Nemaatra," the throne name of Dynasty 12's Amenemhet III, whose colossal monuments surrounded his childhood in the Faiyum oasis.

As for his Two Ladies name relating to laws and peace, Amenhotep III's 38-year reign would stand out in the annals of Egyptian history as one of nearly unparalleled peace and political stability. His Golden Horus name, "Smiter of Asiatics," seemed to contradict the Two Ladies. It was more traditional in spirit than characteristic of Amenhotep III, and it probably sat well with some factions of his court and military.

THE NEW KING'S FIRST OFFICIAL RECEPTION

After the temple ceremonies, the new king returned to his palace, where he received courtiers, some of whom, like an army captain whose name is now lost and his first vizier, were holdovers from the reign of Thutmose IV. A few of these men had panoramas of their audience with the monarch painted on walls in their tombs across the river.

The most lavish of these scenes, now restored from fragments in the Luxor Museum, comes from the destroyed tomb (TT 226) of an overseer of royal tutors whose name is lost (Figure 8). The wall provides a detailed, colorful image of the newly crowned king ensconced in his palace. Dressed as described on his emergence from Luxor Temple and holding the symbols of office, Amenhotep sits enthroned on a high-backed ebony chair with intricately carved floral tracery. This throne rests on a dais bearing traditional representations of Egypt's foreign enemies kneeling with their arms raised up toward the king, who literally sits on them. The throne and dais are nested inside graduated baldachins with cornices of gilded cobras, feathers, and grape clusters resting on shafts in the shape of lily and papyrus stalks. The outside baldachin, if drawn to scale, was at least ten feet tall. The audience hall itself must have been huge.

Mutemwia stands behind the throne dressed in starched white linen with a red sash at her waist, a broad collar of fine beads, and a golden headdress in the form of a vulture. This was the crown of a goddess and of a queen, and her name was written above her in a royal cartouche, the word *mut* (mother) being written as a hieroglyph in the form of a standing vulture, the protectress of the king. The vulture was often shown hovering above the king with its wings spread around him. Here Mutemwia takes the place of the goddess, her arms embracing her grown son's broad shoulders. Mutemwia had never been queen during her husband's life, but now her son gave her the position and esteem that had previously been withheld. The title King's Mother is written before her cartouche.

Two ostrich plume fans are held up toward the king by attendants whose images were lost when the wall crumbled. Not only did these grand feathers bring pure, clean, cool air to the pharaoh's nostrils, but they also represented two deities – Ma'at, the goddess of Truth, and Shu, the god of air and sunlight. Ethereal in nature these two would become central figures in Egyptian religion as solar worship gradually increased over the next 40 years. Even in the early years of Amarna monotheism, Shu and Ma'at, representatives of purity and cleanliness, were not abandoned.

The scene adjacent to the enthroned king is lost, but Sinuhe, the Dynasty 12 official who had returned to court after an absence without leave, gave a glimpse of what a royal audience was like:

> When it was dawn, very early in the morning . . . ten men came . . . ushering me to the palace: I touched the ground between the statues of sphinxes, as the royal children who stood in the doorway came to meet me, and the friends who usher to the columned hall put me on the way to the inner palace. I found His Majesty on the great throne in the portal of electrum (a natural alloy of silver and gold). Then, I prostrated myself, not knowing myself in front of him, while this god addressed me amicably, but I was like a man seized in the dusk, my soul had gone, my limbs being weary, my heart was not in my body. Then His Majesty said to one of these friends, Raise him and let him speak to me!

8. Amenhotep III with mother Mutemwia in a kiosk. Scene from Theban tomb (TT) 226, facsimile painting (tempera on paper) by Nina de Garis Davies, height 89 inches. Courtesy Metropolitan Museum of Art, Rogers Fund (15.5.1). Image copyright the Metropolitan Museum of Art.

The images in Theban tomb 226 and literary passages from classic texts give impressions of the opulence and omnipotence of Egypt's throne but none of the drawbacks of being Pharaoh. It was a life of luxury and power, indeed, but not one of total freedom. Sicilian-Greek historian Diodorus Siculus described in the first century B.C. (the time of Cleopatra and the last Ptolemies) the restrictions of a pharaoh's life and the benefits resulting from them:

> There was a set time not only for his holding audiences or rendering judgements, but even for his taking a walk, bathing, and sleeping with his wife, and, in a word, for every act of his life. . . . the kings were not allowed to render any legal decision or transact any business at random or to punish anyone through malice or in anger or for any other unjust reason, but only with the established laws relative to each offense.

And he continued,

> Consequently . . . they maintained an orderly civil government and continued to enjoy a most felicitous life, so long as the system of laws described was in force; and, more than that, they conquered more nations, achieved greater wealth than any other people, and adorned their lands with monuments and buildings never to be surpassed, and their cities with costly dedications of every description.

The degree of truth of these statements certainly varied depending on individuals and circumstances, but Diodorus Siculus's perceptions fit what we know of coronations and other rituals of Dynasty 18, Amenhotep's titular insistence on law and justice – on *ma'at* – and finally, his unprecedented success in monument building.

At his coronation, the gods promised Nebmaatra Amenhotep Ruler of Thebes a reign of millions of years. In earthly terms, that number would eventually translate to a mere 38. Even so, four decades were almost as good as an eternity in those days. A child born on Amenhotep's coronation day, if he survived the perils of childhood, was very likely to die before his king. For most of Egypt's population between 1391 and 1353 B.C., Amenhotep was the only king they would ever know. Crowned around the age of 20, well fed, comfortably housed, and cared for, Amenhotep III would live to be a grandfather nearly 60 years old, outlasting several of his own children and at least one grandchild.

ESTABLISHING DIVINE MIGHT AND DIVINE RIGHT

(Reign of Amenhotep III, ca. 1391–1388 B.C.)

OPENING NORTHERN LIMESTONE QUARRIES AND FOUNDING A CEMETERY FOR BULLS

It was the eternal duty of a newly crowned pharaoh to refresh and refurbish the temples studding Egypt's landscape. Considering the hundreds of local village and town gods and goddesses as well as major deities in all their various guises and permutations, there must have been hundreds of shrines and temples requiring Amenhotep III's attention. During the next 38 years, not only would many receive major additions and/or be completely renovated but entirely new temples would rise from scratch. Amenhotep III was to become the most prolific builder in Egypt's history. There is hardly a king, emperor, or national leader in premodern world history who can match him. He truly earned his ancient sobriquet *menwy* (monument man).

Before he could build, however, he needed to supply his contractors with the necessary materials. He started right away in Year 1, on day 1 of the third month of summer, by opening new limestone quarry chambers at Deir el Bersha in Middle Egypt. His dated inscription mentions a monument to wise god Thoth at nearby Hermopolis (its classical name coming from Hermes, the Greek equivalent of Thoth). That monument must be the Thoth temple at neighboring El Ashmunein, where architectural remains from early in the reign have been found. Much later, in preparation for one of his jubilees, Amenhotep would add four colossal, brown, quartzite baboons (one of Thoth's avatars) standing with their paws raised as if shrieking toward the rising sun at dawn.

At Tura (ancient Ainu), near modern Cairo, in Years 1 and 2, Amenhotep reopened previously abandoned quarries, where stelae of

Middle Kingdom's Amenemhet III and our king's grandfather Amenhotep II stand. Amenhotep III's stela there, a piece of which is in the
Toledo Museum, states, "His Majesty commanded quarry chambers to
be opened anew to hew fine limestone of Ainu to build his mansions of
millions of years (temples), after His Majesty found the quarry chambers . . . falling into ruin greatly since the times that were before. It was
His Majesty that did it anew, that he might be given life, stability,
dominion, and health like Re forever." In a scene above the inscription,
Amenhotep burns incense in front of four deities, the first three being
rubbed out by ancient vandals and the last being Sekhmet, the goddess
of pestilence and war, who would become a major force in his reign (see
Figure 24).

Sekhmet's presence there may be due merely to her status as consort
to Ptah, the god of Memphis, where Amenhotep III built a "mansion
of millions of years." One cannot help but wonder, however, about
her pestilence aspect and the tale told by third-century B.C. historian
Manetho about the diseased persons cast by a king named Amenophis
into the stone quarries east of the Nile to work separately from everyone
else (see Chapter 9).

Limestone was the building stone of choice for northern temples, and
Tura limestone was the best in Egypt. It had the same cachet as Italy's
Carrara marble in the Renaissance. In fact, the name "Tura" became the
term for the finest grade of limestone and was applied to blocks from
other quarries that measured up to the same high standard. Though
ordinary limestone was good enough for basic temple construction, Tura
was reserved for fine-quality wall reliefs and for sculpture and funerary
furnishings made by the best palace and temple workshops. The small,
tight grains of Tura allowed talented carvers to execute exquisite detail
in their work. For example, a two-inch-high hieroglyph of the owl-
shaped letter *m* could be represented down to the shafts and vanes of
individual feathers. Tura also held paint well, and its finished surfaces
were painted in rich earth tones, golden yellows, lively reds, brilliant
blues, and bright greens nearly vibrating against Tura's dazzling white
background.

Amenhotep III may have used stone from one of these quarries for
a cemetery he founded at Sakkara in honor of the bulls of Memphis's
ancient, perhaps prehistoric, Apis cult. Its mythology was complex,
having morphed over the millennia, and it is imperfectly understood
today, yet some principles and ideas can be outlined. It was Apis's job to
protect the city of Memphis, an appropriate task since bulls are fiercely

territorial, especially when females are nearby. The custom of running the bulls around the city walls at the time of the king's jubilee is known from early times. The element of fertility associated with the bull speaks for itself, and, as previously noted, pharaohs affected the bull tail as part of their costume.

Each Apis bull was chosen for specific details of conformation and markings, which were described centuries later by a confused Herodotus as either totally devoid of black hairs (in Book 2) or "black except for a white diamond on its forehead and the image of an eagle on its back, its tail hairs are double, and it has a beetle-shape under its tongue" (in Book 3). Its mother was said to be a cow on whom "a beam of light descends," and she cannot conceive offspring after this calf's birth. The Apis bull was meticulously managed throughout its life, its every movement watched for omens.

Considering the bulls' fine care, they must have been long-lived, achieving perhaps 10 or 15 years, or more, each. Since Amenhotep III is known to have buried two of them, he likely founded the original cemetery early in his reign. Giving the Apis bull a proper burial allowed it to join Osiris and, through him, find renewal and resurrection. Therefore it was carefully embalmed, its mummy placed inside a huge stone sarcophagus and its internal organs potted in appropriately enormous limestone canopic jars, each weighing several hundred pounds. The jar lids abided by the customs of the time and were carved with human faces, these particular ones in the image of Amenhotep III himself.

In the mid-nineteenth century, the French archaeologist Auguste Mariette described the early Apis tombs, which have since become resubmerged beneath the sand. Each bull had a relief-decorated funerary chapel; one depicted Amenhotep III with his eldest son, Prince Thutmose, offering incense to the sacred bull. A ramp led from there underground to Apis's final resting place. Alabaster jars inscribed for Prince Thutmose were found in a burial chamber, as were a bull's canopics, which are now in the Louvre. The cavernous, multichambered burial known today as the Serapeum, which still contains many of its original taurine sarcophagi, is a later construct.

It is rare in Egyptian art for a prince to be shown with his father. Other than the surprising news of his existence and his context, this scene offers us little information about the boy. Likely, as previously mentioned, he was born before Amenhotep III became king, and he was probably old enough and learned enough to begin participating in temple rituals when he was a young adolescent. Therefore this relief was probably not carved until somewhere around the end of our king's first decade. Prince Thutmose is discussed further in Chapter 9.

BULL AND LION HUNTS

The most colorful and dramatic events of Amenhotep III's early years are inscribed on the undersides of commemorative scarabs (Figure 9). These amulets are effigies of the sacred scarab beetle, which, according to ancient Egyptian belief, pushed the sun across the sky every day just as a real beetle pushes a ball of dung (the eventual petri dish for its eggs) backward with its hind legs to its destination.

Most of Amenhotep III's cover the palm of a hand and are beautifully carved, with every anatomical detail of the insect in place. The undersides are planed flat and incised with rows of carefully formed hieroglyphs. Almost all were glazed to a bright blue-green sheen that made them sparkle, nearly gemlike. There was nothing more recognizable as Egyptian, and their color and size made them quintessentially royal. They were sent as propaganda around the kingdom and abroad, turning up as far away as Syria and Nubia. Their texts were meant to be recited aloud by the few who could read to the many who could not.

The first series, of which only five are known, is dated to his second year on the throne. It bears the story of a brutal wild bull hunt in the region of Shetep, probably the Wadi Natrun (Natron Valley), a small oasis halfway between Memphis and the Mediterranean Sea. The site's modern name comes from a rich supply of the principal material used in mummification. The king wrote that he had received word of wild bulls ravaging the area, and like a lion sensing his prey, he moved quickly within range. "His Majesty sailed downstream (north from Memphis) in the royal barge Kha-em-maat ("Appearing in Truth") at the time of evening, making good time, arriving in peace at . . . Shetep [in the] . . . morning. [He] instructed the officers and private soldiers . . . and the children of the nursery to keep a watch on these wild bulls."

"His Majesty commanded. . . . that one surround these wild bulls with an enclosure with a ditch, and His Majesty proceeded against all these wild bulls," first by driving them into the ditch, and then finishing them off with his bow the way native Americans killed bison. The total number of live bulls counted was 170, and the king claims to have slaughtered one-third of them that day. Though the reader might swallow 57 bulls being murdered by one man in one day, the suggestion that an entire wild herd was made up only of stray bulls with no cows and

9. Commemorative scarab recording the "marriage" of Amenhotep III and Tiy. Faience. Dimensions 2 × 3 inches, 37.475E. Courtesy the Brooklyn Museum (http://www.brooklynmuseum.org/opencollections).

calves seems unnatural and highly unlikely. Yet the text is clear; it says "bulls."

The second dated series, of which about 123 are known today, encompasses Amenhotep's first ten years on the throne. Here the victims are lions, and Amenhotep brutally slew 102 (or 110, depending on the scarab) over the decade "with his own arrows." Because lions roamed not just sub-Saharan Africa but as far north as Syria in the fourteenth century B.C., these lion hunts could have occurred almost anywhere in the region.

There is something about these two series of "hunt scarabs" that begs them to be understood metaphorically rather than literally, and this is where Amenhotep III's most important and most trusted official enters the picture.

THE PRIEST AMENHOTEP SON OF HAPU AND THE SYMBOLISM OF THE HUNTS

Both the bull massacre and the sporadic lion culls recall stories told by Amenhotep son of Hapu, a priest of Horus Khenty-Khety, the local god of Athribis, a small town in the Delta, during the reign of Thutmose IV, and probably even before that during Amenhotep II's reign. In his auto-biography, Hapu's son claims to have been plucked from obscurity and made a "royal scribe" by Nebmaatra, the eldest son of Harakhte, the sun god. Since the deceased king becomes united with the sun god at his death, Thutmose IV must have just recently died, and Amenhotep son of Hapu joined the new king's court in its formative days or months.

One of his important memorial statues commissioned at the end of our king's reign and eventually placed at Karnak Temple is inscribed on all sides with the priest's autobiography. Early in the text, and therefore early in the reign, he describes two otherwise unknown fracases with familiar settings and plotlines, except that he is the hero. In regard to the first, Hapu's son claims to have repulsed pirates at the mouths of the Nile in the Delta, "quite apart from the crews of the royal sailors." Were these the same royal sailors and was this the same event as the Year 2 bull hunt, when the king hastened to the Delta on his royal barge?

Son of Hapu's second incident involved putting "troops at the head of the Road in order to repulse the foreigners from their places which surround (Egypt) by keeping an eye on the traveling of the Sandfarers." "The Road," like "the River," seems to have been a generic name given to a specific geographic feature, in this case most likely the coastal road (aka "Ways of Horus") leading through the eastern Delta across what are now the straits of Suez and over the northern Sinai to Canaan. Likewise, "Sandfarers" probably applies to groups of nomads or Asiatics using this route. It sounds like a chronic and recurring problem with interlopers in the eastern Delta over a period of time, in the same way that the lion hunts stretched out over a number of years. Were the bulls and lions in the scarab texts metaphors for the various human miscreants whom Amenhotep son of Hapu had helped his king to squelch?

Using bulls and lions as symbols for enemies explains why a herd was composed entirely of bulls, and simultaneously, it dehumanizes the enemies, reducing them to beasts, sending a message that they were mere game for the pharaoh's bow and arrows. The audience for this message was widespread. One scarab was found in northern Syria at Ras Shamra, its contents likely read aloud and translated for the local audience, who surely saw through its symbolism.

At home, these veiled stories prevented alarm that the homeland had been under attack, which must have been a sensitive issue considering Egypt's history with the Hyksos. It may be no coincidence that the last "lion" was hunted just before Amenhotep III signed an agreement with the king of Mitanni, north of Syria, marrying his daughter and forever binding the two as family, attempting to guarantee some stability not only for themselves but also for the lands lying between these two imposing empires.

It is perhaps ironic that Egyptian kings from the beginning of history used the same symbolism for themselves as for their prey, but pharaohs were "Mighty Bulls," whereas foreign kings who used similar metaphors for themselves were, in Egyptian eyes, lesser examples of the species.

Hapu's son must have been a vigorous 50-something at the time of these Delta and desert skirmishes because he boasted of being 80 years old at the first jubilee in Year 30. His second title, Scribe of Recruits, which became one of his favorites, reflects his success at mustering and leading troops, probably from his priestly parish in his early days. Likely the same groups of men, at least at the lowest levels, were involved in all basic physical endeavors, whether military or construction. Therefore his skills as a military commander would have served Hapu's son well managing gangs of workmen in the quarries and on the building sites that formed part of his portfolio decades later as the king prepared for his jubilee.

THE YOUNG KING IN THE SOUTH AT EL KAB AND THEBES

One of our king's earliest constructions in the south was at El Kab, upriver from Thebes, where he continued work begun by his father. About the size of a one-car garage, the chapel at El Kab sits out in the desert at the entrance to the Wadi Hellal, which led to semiprecious stone quarries and gold and copper mines and to the overland route to Nubia. El Kab's chapel honors the vulture goddess Nekhbet, whose center, the prehistoric town (ancient Nekheb), lies a bit more than one mile away. Nekhbet was a special protectress of every pharaoh and was often shown flying above his head in carved and painted scenes. The chapel is built of sandstone, the material of choice and convenience in the south, and the quarries at Gebel el Silsilla, across the river and to the south of Luxor, provided some of the best.

El Kab chapel's simple, hollow-cubic design, with its single doorway, looks like a mere wayside hut – which, in a sense, it was, because it served as a processional station for the sacred boat of the goddess as it was carried out from her temple on festival days. Images of the bark are carved in low relief inside the chapel. Unlike many larger structures its age, the chapel still retains its roof, held up by four 16-sided columns with heads of the goddess Hathor as capitals. Betsy Bryan confirmed the early date of El Kab's wall decoration by the slim proportions of the royal figures, which match those of Amenhotep III on the dated stela from Tura, in other words, very early in his reign.

But was it his reign alone, or did he briefly share the throne with his father? El Kab's interior walls include images of Amenhotep III and Thutmose IV enthroned side by side as though they ruled simultaneously (Figure 10). A contemporary Theban tomb of an unnamed troop commander has images of Thutmose IV receiving revenues from northern lands, while adjacent images of Amenhotep III receive from the south. Adding together El Kab, the tomb scenes, and the strong possibility that our king was the viceroy of Nubia, one might imagine a period of coregency between father and son, but such propositions are fraught with uncertainty without the linchpin proof of inscriptions. It is worth remembering, in the case of Sinuhe's two kings, that in Year 20 of his reign, Amenemhet I actually appointed his son Senwosret as his coregent. Nothing of the sort is yet known for Thutmose IV and Amenhotep III.

At Thebes, Thutmose IV had undertaken or at least begun work on several structures at Karnak, and young Amenhotep III proceeded to carry out some of his father's efforts. For example, he completed construction or at least finished the decoration of an alabaster shrine for Amun's sacred boat. The shrine had been enlarged to accommodate a new and grander sacred bark, one with five carrying poles. Later he tore down the shrine and tossed it into the foundations of a much larger structure of his own. At the southern end of Thebes, he began a complete reorganization of Luxor Temple, where a number of small-to medium-sized shrines remained from previous Dynasty 18 pharaohs, including Hatshepsut and Thutmoses III and IV. These were eventually jostled about like used furniture and combined into parts of later structures at Luxor Temple.

Amenhotep started new construction at what is now Luxor's southern end, where he built a multichambered structure, including the so-called Birth Room, whose walls describe the divine events leading up to his appearance on earth. His path to the throne had been carefully paved by his father, and there is no clear sign of controversy. Yet scenes of this type were not common. Those in the funerary temple of Hatshepsut, whose claim to her own throne had, indeed, needed some bolstering, seem to have provided the inspiration for Amenhotep III's scenes, and so one cannot help but wonder if he felt himself in a similar predicament. The exact date of execution of Luxor's Birth Room

10. Interior scene of Amenhotep III and Thutmose IV enthroned side by side at El Kab. After Tylor et al.

scenes is not clear, but one could argue that they were among the first things on his agenda as a very important piece of propaganda establishing his divine right, just as the hunt scarabs had established his divine might.

Amenhotep's mimicry of Hatshepsut's birth scenes is interesting for another reason. His throne name, "Nebmaatra," looks in its cartouche form very similar to Hatshepsut's "Maatkara." In both instances, the seated figure of Ma'at is the central glyph, accompanied by the sun disk for Re. Repeatedly throughout his reign, Amenhotep undertook projects started by Hatshepsut or reflecting her ideas. In the years to come, other features of Amenhotep's reign will recall Hatshepsut's not only in individual details but in the overall style of rule as well.

"THE FIRST CAMPAIGN OF VICTORY": AMENHOTEP III'S RIVER WAR

(Reign of Amenhotep III, Year 5, ca. 1387 B.C.)

WORD OF A REBELLION

In Year 5, word of a Nubian rebellion reached Amenhotep III in Memphis. Our conjectured absence of a viceroy would have created a power vacuum – the perfect opportunity for a local chieftain, "Ikheny the braggart," as he was called in the report, to cause trouble. The exact date of the bulletin is not known, but the most effective time to plan a rebellion in Nubia was flood season, which started around the end of June or beginning of July, when fields were under water and farmers out of work. Amenhotep's response to this threat became one of the most celebrated, well-recorded, and lucrative events of his reign, and it guaranteed a steady flow of Nubian gold into Egypt's coffers for years to come. His account of the adventure is carved onto a stela near Aswan and Konosso, where he had previously left memorials as a prince.

After receiving the bulletin, Amenhotep gathered his officials, several of whom also left graffiti on the boulders at Aswan. Primary among these men was Amenhotep son of Hapu, who, in his autobiographical inscription, claimed to have organized combat troops to "smite the Nubians and the Asiatics." In his words, he "levied the troops of my Lord" and "separated the *gangs* from their homes," the word *gang* being the term commonly used for a team of workers.

Barely secondary was Neferhabef, nicknamed "Heby" (sometimes "Neby"), mayor of Memphis. There was no one in a better position to muster a large number of troops from the sprawling fields around Memphis. Heby knew his men, their qualities and weaknesses, and

70

their families. Because the soldiers were organized into "companies of troops . . . commanded by commanders, every man [assigned] according to his village," Heby could identify both the courageous soldiers and the weak ones and no doubt see that rewards and punishments were correctly meted out. It must have been added incentive to the troops that word of both heroism and cowardice could reach friends and family back home through this civic leader.

Heby is better known to history through his sons from two different wives, half brothers Amenhotep and Ramose, who developed into two of the most powerful men in the later years of Amenhotep III's reign (see Chapters 12 and 15). The elder boy, Amenhotep (nicknamed "Huy"), who became high steward at Memphis, may have been old enough to join in on this campaign, but Ramose, who became governor of Thebes and southern vizier, was probably too young.

Only a few of Amenhotep III's other military men are known, and they seem to be from the south. One is a captain of the troops and overseer of horses whose name is lost but who left an important tomb at Thebes (TT 91). Nebamun (TT 90), was a police captain and standard-bearer for Amun's sacred bark whose tomb scenes show him actively engaged with large numbers of soldiers. Both men were holdovers from the previous reign, and their tombs are located close to those of Thutmose III's First Priest of Amun Menkheperra-seneb (TT 86) and of Paser (TT 367), the chief of archers (and child of the *kap*) of Amenhotep II, as though these plots were assigned to individuals who belonged together through career and/or family. Nebamun's daughter Segerttaui was a member of the royal harem and is pictured prominently in her father's tomb both at the entrance and inside receiving offerings from her parents and a sister.

Overseer of All Royal Scribes of the Army, Horemheb (TT 78), was also exceptionally close to the king and had on one tomb wall an image of Princess Amenemopet (Amenhotep III's sister) sitting on his lap. He started his career, however, in the reign of Thutmose III and was by this time certainly decommissioned. The touching vignette of him tending sweetly to a princess foreshadows Amenhotep son of Hapu's last post, as steward to the eldest daughter of Amenhotep III (see Chapter 15).

THE ROYAL ARMY AND ITS DIVINE ARSENAL

The Egyptian army was large and well organized and had certain specialties developed over the centuries. The largest permanent contingent consisted of standing infantry soldiers, who waged battle, guarded the borders, and, during peacetime, worked on pharaonic building projects. They were augmented every summer during Inundation by farmers whose fields were temporarily submerged but also aided those farmers at harvest time. Some were conscripts — even from the priestly ranks — but others were volunteers, for this was by far the primary means by which individuals of low birth could advance to a better life.

Children were drafted as aides for the "made" infantrymen. If they served well, they were promoted to infantrymen as adults. Desert mercenaries were hired from Nubia, particularly from Wawat in the north and from the Medjay tribe. These were skilled and hardy fighters and were specifically requested by foreign rulers in the Amarna letters as *Meluḥḥa* — "dark-skinned" warriors — when in need of backup from Pharaoh. Within Egypt, particularly Upper Egypt, they served as something of a desert police force.

The finest soldiers were called in ancient Egyptian *neferu*, literally meaning the "beautiful ones" or "good ones." The most effective of the *neferu* were archers with devastatingly powerful composite bows, a sophisticated device first used in Egypt by the Hyksos. They are said to have been accurate at 60 yards, effective at 200, and useful even up to 500 yards. Naturally, they, too, were sought by Canaanite allies in times of trouble.

Chariot teams — the awesome war engines of antiquity — were a special division of the army. It is astonishing to think that horses and their obvious pendant, the chariot, were completely unknown in Egypt for the first 1,500 years or so of its written history, until the Hyksos invasion. Dynasty 18 pharaohs, however, quickly came up to speed in horsemanship, including breeding, husbandry, training, and driving. By Amenhotep III's time, Egypt regularly imported fine horses from the Near East and had also developed breeding programs of its own, which, by then were somewhere around their thirtieth or fortieth generation of steeds.

Munitions factories and armories were strategically housed in the great temples at Memphis and Karnak. Major infantry training areas were nearby. Memphis was obviously better located for arming soldiers in the Delta and beyond to the Near East, whereas Karnak was more convenient for platoons heading south to Nubia. A large scene painted in High Priest Menkheperra-seneb's tomb shows him inspecting the workshops in his great temple at Karnak (Figure 11). Three of the registers, one after another, roll out views of three different workshops — one for chariots and tack, one for archery gear, and one for sacred vessels — as

11. Workshops at Karnak Temple: chariotry, munitions, weighing precious materials, ritual vessels. Tomb of Menkheperra-seneb (reign of Thutmose III), TT 86. Photo: APK/JSB.

if these three stood side-by-side on equal footing within the temple precincts, where the costly materials used in production were also stored.

The list of arms, both offensive and defensive, manufactured in Dynasty 18 is long. Aside from those mentioned earlier, there were carefully shaped throw sticks, javelins, bronze daggers, swords, stone mace heads on cubit-long dowels, and a variety of axetypes, along with quivers and other carry cases and shields made of wood and covered with cowhide, the spotted ones being especially beautiful. King of swords was the *khepesh*, a masterpiece of Late Bronze Age ergonomics. The cutting edge was on the outside rim of an arc dipping down from the line of the handle. This meant that the weapon could be made very light, enhancing its user's clout by design rather than weight. This is the scimitar often shown in the hands of pharaohs and gods in paintings and reliefs (Figure 12).

Menkheperra-seneb's tomb also shows foreigners bringing offerings of plumed helmets, and other representations of helmets exist from Dynasty 18, but they seem not to have been employed broadly until later in the New Kingdom. Gloves like those found in Tut's tomb were supplied at least to the king and the top brass. Charioteers would have found them desirable, if not necessary, for driving, even though they are rarely shown in use in tomb and temple scenes.

The king, however, did wear body armor, and so did the (male) gods. There was more than one type, judging from what has been found in King Tut's tomb and in scraps found in excavations. One, perhaps ceremonial, was made up of cloisonné elements – metal cells inlaid with stone and/or glass – linked together to form, in the case of Tut's, an overlapping feather pattern, which was then designed as a corselet with shoulder straps. The solid part covered the tender midsection of the body, while allowing body heat to escape and a full range of movement in the shoulders. Another type was a more pliant T-shirt or tunic made of tinted leather, also cut into tongue shapes and overlapped in a feather pattern. Sometimes these leather tabs were ribbed and dyed to imitate feathers.

In a damaged throne scene in the tomb of Amenmose, the steward of Thebes (TT 89), Amenhotep III appears to have donned the T-shirt variety of overlapping leather feathers, each one tinted red, white, and blue, and it is one of the very few times he is so attired. Possibly this body armor was more often substituted in art symbolically by the enveloping wings of a protective goddess. Male deities, on the other hand, often wear one of these items of body armor in tomb and temple wall scenes from the New Kingdom onward.

The fastest way for all of the king's men, munitions, and even horses to arrive in Nubia was by boat. During Inundation, stretches of river considered impassable most of the year, including some cataracts, disappeared beneath the swollen waters or were at least mitigated by providing broader passages of swift but navigable waters. The prevailing north wind eased the strain of rowing upstream against the current, giving a boost to the sails and slight relief from the searing summer heat. With a full complement of strong rowers on each side and a decent breeze, even a fully loaded ship could have made the journey in a few days, including occasional necessary portages.

MONUMENTS RECORDING THE CAMPAIGN AND THE KING'S ITINERARY

Monuments related to the "First Campaign of Victory" were set up from Thebes to the Third Cataract in the Sudan. Some have been found with dates, place-names, or tribal names, allowing speculation on the king's

12. Amenhotep III braining a Nubian, detail of Amenhotep III's victory stela. After De Morgan.

itinerary. One of the most important and informational is the Victory Stela dated Year 5, month 3 of Inundation, day 2 (around the end of August), along a road between Aswan and Philae Island (now mostly submerged under Lake Nasser). This is the one recording the initial bulletin about the uprising.

In the arched space at the top of the stela is a figure of the king, surrounded by deities, trampling on one Kushite while holding two others by their topknots, his arm raised to behead them (Figure 12). The text below the scene reads as though dictated by the king himself, beginning with the date, followed by a list of his own titles, epithets, self-laudatory adjectives and metaphors, and then a description of the event, including the initial report. "Ikheny the braggart within his army, he was not aware of the lion that was in front of him, for Nebmaatra is the savage lion who grasped [with] his claws vile Kush." As self-aggrandizing as this statement is for the king, it is, at the same time, somewhat naive because it memorializes the enemy's name and promotes Ikheny from anonymous troublemaker to royal opponent, raising him from obscurity to indelible history. It also suggests that this Ikheny was someone Amenhotep knew, perhaps from his stint as viceroy.

What it does not tell us is where Ikheny operated, but circumstantial evidence suggests that he was well south of the Second Cataract, a 50-mile-long trough of rapids (in Arabic, Batn el Hagar, "Belly of Rocks") now submerged under Lake Nasser, and likely he was south of the Third Cataract as well (Map 2). A stela found at Buhen (the Second Cataract fortress where Viceroy Amenhotep had previously left a stela with Thutmose IV's cartouche) is dated to Year 5, the first month of Inundation (mid-July). This is the earliest date of all the monuments from this campaign and probably marks the king's arrival in the area. It does not mention the battle, presumably because it had not yet occurred. It calls Amenhotep III "beloved of the gods of Wawat." Clearly he was still in friendly territory.

The only other dated inscription is a wall text marked Year 5, month 2 of Inundation, day 24 (?) at the southern end of the Second Cataract at Sai Island (ancient Sha't), a Dynasty 18 colony of great strategic importance. Soft, fertile, peaceful, and broad, Sai Island was a true gift of the Nile. It was the perfect spot for a trading post, local agriculture being particularly rich. Southbound sailors could rest here after their ordeal with the Belly of Rocks, while northbound ones could catch their breath before heading off. Travelers in either direction were at the mercy of Sai's local ruler.

The New Kingdom settlement and its half-mile-wide necropolis are at the northeastern end of this pinwheel-shaped island, within view of its pivot point, a 100-foot-tall butte today called Gebel Adou. A small temple was constructed in the reign of Thutmose III, but Amenhotep III, one of the major builders there, added to it, most likely at the time of this campaign, as he would again 20 years later. The dated inscription here is very fragmentary but has the look of a victory stela carved on the way home from a battle still farther south.

Just eight and fifteen miles south of Sai are Sedeinga and Soleb, where Amenhotep would eventually build the two most beautiful temples in Nubia (see Chapter 12). Thutmose III had already established a settlement at Soleb with a small rock-cut sanctuary (doubling as a lookout post?) just a few miles north at Gebel Dosha, in a cliff side at the very edge of the Nile. This part of Kush north of the Third Cataract was probably too well acculturated and Egyptianized for a major rebellion. Such unrest was more common south of the Third Cataract near Tombos, where the river divides into several large and small branches, forming a clot of islands.

Tombos, the site of a decisive victory of Thutmose I over the king of Kush, ending in the latter's dead body hanging from the bow of the victor's ship for the homeward journey, suddenly rose once again to importance during Amenhotep's reign. The cemetery contains a great many scarabs with our king's name, and its unique granite gneiss quarries came to be used later in the reign for colossal ram figures set up at Soleb Temple. On the west bank of the river near Tombos are numerous small sites from fortified Hannek in the north to Sahaba and Khandaq in the south. These sites show evidence of an earlier type of local culture surviving through the New Kingdom, despite evidence of Egyptian settlements in the region. Ikheny, his name perhaps echoing in the modern names of "Hannek" and "Khandaq," may have been a local chieftain who briefly stepped out of line.

Wherever the battle occurred, Amenhotep III led from his royal chariot, with a driver handling the flinty-hooved engines and a shield bearer managing a stash of arms within the car, leaving His Majesty free to fire from his bow. It must have been quite a terrifying sight: Amenhotep in his tall, domed, blue war helmet, sparkling white linen, and body armor in a dazzling chariot drawn by swift, expertly trained horses, surrounded by more of the same, with companies of elite archers and platoon after platoon of well-equipped infantrymen led by braying trumpeters, pounding drums, and flashy standard-bearers, with weaponry constantly resupplied from horse-drawn materiel carts.

On his Philae monument, Amenhotep described himself as "stouthearted while killing, and cutting off hands (of the dead as trophies)," "30,000 men as [living] captives – he let them go as [much as he] liked, so that the offspring of Kush is not [totally] cut off." The lucky Kushites who were allowed to remain and reproduce may have provided manpower for his future quarry work and temple construction in both Nubia and Egypt proper. Egyptian soldiers picked up as many severed hands as they could, attached them to their belts, and received compensation for them in the form of land and slaves when they returned home (Figure 13).

According to his monuments, the king did not return straight home after his victory. A stela set up at Thebes, but now in the Cairo museum, tells us that he traveled to Miw, a spot so remote it is rarely mentioned in pharaonic inscriptions. Miw's location had been a mystery parsed and argued by scholars for decades until finally, in the early years of the current century, a team of archaeologists from the British Museum, led by W. Vivian Davies, identified Hagr el Merwa, in which the name reverberates, as part of Miw. Hagr el Merwa is a rock outcrop near Kurgus, north of modern Khartoum, where Thutmose I and Thutmose III had established the southernmost extent of the Egyptian empire. Miw may have included areas on either side of the river. Until now, no inscriptions definitely ascribed to Amenhotep III have been found at Kurgus. His statement on the Theban stela is the only evidence that he entered Miw.

Another inscription (at Konosso) tells us that King Amenhotep traveled as far south as a site even more remote and perhaps only legendary, the Kebhu-Hor, "Pool(s) (or Fountains) of Horus," where he set up a victory stela. Stating that he left a monument there makes Kebhu-Hor sound like a real location. This sentence, however, follows one declaring that the king had expanded his realm to the Four Pillars of Heaven, a traditional symbolic term. Sometimes the name "Kebhu Hor" was also metaphorical, referring to the peripheral areas at the edge of the world to and from which migratory birds fly.

But if the Pools of Horus were a real geographical feature, where were they? Derek Welsby suggested privately that one landmark fitting this scenario lies in the center of the Bayuda desert and is called today the Gakdul Wells. According to a nineteenth-century British traveler, the Gakdul Wells were "as wild and romantic as you can imagine, the wells being hidden away in deep caverns with precipitous sides, in the midst of frowning rugged rocks. The sailors, with their contempt of heights, and entire freedom from giddiness, swung themselves down into the most horrible abysses, if only they had a rope made fast at top."

Gakdul is at the midpoint of the route that cuts across the Bayuda desert, presumably part of Miw, and is considered a preferable and faster alternative to sailing the treacherous bend in the river north of Khartoum. In 1896, Winston Churchill wrote in *The River War* that it took Lord Kitchener's British troops three days to travel from the Fourth Cataract to Gakdul by camel. Of course, the ancient Egyptians did not have camels, and it may have taken them a bit longer as they rested by intermediate wells or small desert reservoirs along the way.

If Amenhotep III did set up a victory stela at the Gakdul Wells or elsewhere in Miw, it would have served as a warning to individuals, groups, or lands existing farther south, such as Irem, Terek, and Weresh, additional victims of this First Nubian Campaign, according to

13. Displaying severed hands taken from war victims. Temple of Ramesses III, Medinet Habu. Photo: APK.

Amenhotep III's monuments. Irem has been most recently placed by scholars between the Atbara River and the Blue Nile on the island of Meroe, the modern name almost a mirror of the ancient one.

The last two victims listed by Amenhotep III, Terek and Weresh, must be still more remote because their names occur very infrequently in Egyptian texts. "Weresh" is an unusual name. When divided into two ancient Egyptian words, *wer* meaning "great" and *esh* meaning "swamp," it recalls the Sudd, the nearly impenetrable, huge marshes in the Upper White Nile south of Kordofan. Though Amenhotep may never have traveled there, he must have known of their existence. The "tall Terek" people of antiquity raised long-horned cattle like the tall, slim Nuer people of the Sudd today. Place-names like Torakit, and others ending in the sequence -*ok*, exist here. Amenhotep III may have encountered representatives of Terek or Weresh either in trade or in combat at his southernmost stop, wherever it was.

One more spot, Karoy, a well-known and rich gold-producing region, is mentioned on monuments as part of Amenhotep's Nubian itinerary. Karoy's location, on the left bank of the river between the Fourth Cataract and the Nile bend downriver from (north of) Khartoum, would have been a convenient spot for Amenhotep III to stop on his home-ward journey from Miw. He eventually claimed to use the gold he won from Karoy on this campaign as the financial foundation for his major construction at Karnak Temple.

How the ancient Egyptians traveled between the Fourth and Third cataracts, which lay on either side of a huge, south-pointing peninsula, is a puzzle because no supportive Egyptian settlements dating to this period or earlier are yet known along this stretch of the Nile. Perhaps they traveled overland following the method traditionally used (even in the twentieth century) by desert nomads as they crossed long, parched expanses: refilling large water pots submerged at intervals in the sand as they headed into the middle of the desert, relying on others to have done the same from the other direction. Feces piled on top of the jar sites marked them and warded off predators.

As Amenhotep III traveled toward home, he set up his victory stelae. The first one, on Sai Island, was dated the twenty-fourth day of the second month of Inundation. A statue from Sai of the king enthroned beside a goddess may be contemporary because the style is extremely conservative and must belong to the early years of the king's reign. It bears several inscriptions, the main one stating that he "has made his name famous among . . . of the vile Kush."

Continuing northward, he may have stopped at Wadi es-Sebua (Valley of the Lions), 93 miles south of Aswan, just north of the Second Cataract. This site was strategically important, probably serving as a way station and travelers' respite, for there was little or no local populace to serve. Here Amenhotep decorated a tiny (70-square-foot) rock-cut sanctuary with painted plaster walls. It is now submerged under Lake Nasser, but the paintings were removed from the walls and deposited in the Cairo museum in 1964. The scenes underwent three phases of decoration during our king's reign, according to Yale University's Martina Ullmann. The earliest one highlighted Amun as Lord of the Ways, and it likely dates to these early years. The other, later phases reflect new developments in religion and in Amenhotep III's self-image as the reign progressed (see Chapter 12).

Finally, near Philae, Egypt's threshold, Amenhotep III set up a second victory stela relating to this Nubian war, and he dated it day 2 of the third month of Inundation, marking the end of the campaign.

The entire adventure must have covered just a few weeks, starting with Amenhotep receiving the report in Memphis at the onset of Inundation, traveling to Buhen at the Second Cataract, waging war upriver from the Third Cataract in the middle to the end of that month, traveling to Miw in the first half of the second month of Inundation, returning through Karoy in the second half of that month, setting up a stela at Sai on the twenty-fourth day, and finishing back in Egypt near Aswan at the beginning of the third month of Inundation, undoubtedly with great celebration. The success of this campaign and the riches gained provided the foundations for the rest of Amenhotep III's reign.

7

THE SPOILS OF WAR

(Reign of Amenhotep III, Years 6–9, ca. 1386–1383 B.C.)

HUNDRED-GATED THEBES: "THE LIKE HAD NEVER BEEN MADE"

Thanks to the countless captives and heaps of gold Amenhotep III hauled back from his Nubian campaign, Karnak Temple received a grand new gateway facing the Nile (Figures 14 and 15). Part of the text carved on a stela from his mortuary temple acknowledges the source of the structure's construction funds: "His Majesty brought the gold for it out of the country of Karoy on the first campaign of victory of massacring the wretched Kush." This new gateway, called a "pylon" in Egyptian architecture, has two wide wings with broad bases and walls slanting inward to narrower tops. Between them, an enormous bivalve, richly decorated cedar door once swung on bronze hinges pinned into granite sockets.

Amenhotep himself described the pylon on a stela in his memorial temple and now in the Cairo museum:

> The king made a monument for Amun, making for him a very great gateway before Amun-Re lord of the thrones of the two lands, sheathed entirely in gold, a divine image according to respect, filled with turquoise [one-half ton], sheathed in gold and numerous precious stones [two-thirds ton of jasper]. The like had never been made. . . . Its pavement was made with pure silver, its front portal inset with stelae of lapis lazuli, one on each side. Its twin towers approach heaven, like the four supports of the sky. Its flagpoles shine skyward sheathed in electrum.

Drill holes for securing the silver flooring sheets are still visible on the passageway. Its original finished height is unknown since its top has obviously broken away, but it must have been huge because it was said to have had eight flagpoles, each 130 feet tall, their pennants waving only slightly above the walls, according to near-contemporary representations.

The new pylon arose just in front of the previous front gate on soil deposited relatively recently by the river as its eastern bank extended itself westward. Amenhotep's is now numbered and universally known as the Third Pylon behind two others built over the next 1,000 years in ongoing pursuit of the river's edge (Map 5). The Second Pylon was put up at the end of Dynasty 18 by Horemheb, a commoner who rose through the military to the throne for lack of blue-blooded heirs. The First Pylon was built ten centuries later by Nectanebo I, whose 18-year renaissance briefly interrupted the millennium-long decline of Egypt's world supremacy. The First Pylon, Karnak Temple's current front entrance, now stands 550 yards away from the quays where tourist boats dock.

In all, there are ten numbered pylons in Amun-Re's temple, not counting the ones at smaller, subsidiary temples within the precinct and the dozens at other temples in the Theban valley. In the *Iliad*, Greek balladeer Homer only slightly exaggerated the wealth and monuments of ancient Thebes as the city "with the hundred gates," a place "where the houses overflow with the greatest troves of treasure."

Ironically, construction of the Third Pylon required Amenhotep III to dismantle his father's most important structure at Karnak – a portico inserted into the festival court of Thutmose II in front of the Fourth Pylon – as well as two obelisks and several other monuments. The portico had only recently been completed by Amenhotep III himself. Inside the Third Pylon's foundations, excavated by the French archaeological mission at Karnak, were blocks from previous Karnak structures including a block from a jubilee structure, but whose?

Adding to the list of questions about this monument is the evidence that the main scene of processional boats on the interior face of the better-preserved north wing of the Third Pylon (Figure 14) was revised after a period of time, leaving ghosts of the figures removed (Figure 15). Some scholars think the scene was recarved during a coregency between Amenhotep III and his son, and others see Tutankhamen's handiwork.

The point of view taken here is that Amenhotep III himself commissioned the scene early in his career, shortly after Year 5, and revised it close to his jubilee (see further discussion in Chapter 10).

14. Karnak, Third Pylon, Sacred Bark of Amun. Photo: APK.

THE GOD'S BARGE AND THE OPET FESTIVAL

The subject matter of the main scene is fairly well understood. It shows two ships that were probably moored at a quay on the other side of the pylon when not in use. On the viewer's left (the stern partially visible in Figure 14) is a vast 60-oared boat with a large shuttered cabin amidships, its crew assisting the sails (now lost with the top of the wall) by pulling hard against the current to propel the boat upstream toward Luxor. It tows the second (Figure 14), the *Amen-em-Userhet,* a brand-new sacred bark of Amun.

Amenhotep III's lavish description of the god's barge rivals Plutarch's rapturous narrative 1,300 years later of Cleopatra and Marc Antony's floating love nest. Our king wrote that his own was made "of new cedar which his Majesty cut down in foreign countries of the land of God." It was dragged from Lebanon over the mountains by "princes of all countries. It was . . . very wide and large . . . adorned with silver, wrought with gold throughout, the great shrine [is] of electrum so that it fills the land with its brightness." Completing the description from the visual evidence of the pylon's scene, it was virtually a floating

15. Detail of erased figure on Third Pylon. Photo: APK.

temple complete with obelisks, offering tables, statues, and of course, a sanctuary. Decorating its hull were one register of Nile gods bringing offerings and another of Amenhotep III in the company of gods such as Re-Harakhte, Amun, and Min.

The gold, silver, and electrum fittings and overlays that filled the land with brightness doubled their effect by reflecting on the shimmering Nile. The *Amen-em-Userhet* appeared to float on the water like the sun in the sky, simultaneously harkening back to Egypt's ancient imagery of the sun god sailing above the earth in a magical boat and animating the king's "dazzling sun disk" epithet.

The good ship *Amen-em-Userhet* was probably built in the main royal dockyards at Memphis by Amenhotep's *kap-mate*, Inena, who noted on his grave stela that one of his major accomplishments was fabricating a boat for Amun. British Egyptologist Glanville wrote, "Inena was no mere foreman in the shops, but the official actually controlling the construction of the boats in question." The attention to detail and dedication to fine workmanship demanded by this important commission were undoubtedly traits instilled in Inena in the royal nursery of Mi-wer.

Amenhotep wrote that he had commissioned the *Amen-em-Userhet* specifically for the annual Opet Festival. This uniquely Theban event coincided with the Nile's annual flood, during which the king's *ka*, his divine spirit, was celebrated and renewed and his right to rule was reconfirmed. Lanny Bell, former director of the University of Chicago's Chicago House (at Luxor), which has undertaken a decades-long study of Luxor Temple and its relief carvings, has written that this was an occasion of cosmic significance.

> Gods became weary by the end of each year, when the agricultural cycle had run its course. They and their creation needed a recharge, a fresh input of energy. The dying gods needed to step outside the created world to tap the pure, uncontrolled power of the boundless chaos surrounding the cosmos . . . Opening the door to the uncreated was no simple operation and was fraught with danger. Improperly done, it could unleash the full destructive potential of disorder. But properly done, through the prescribed rituals of the Opet-festival presided over by the divine king, the opening could produce rebirth and re-creation.

According to scenes carved on walls at Luxor Temple, Amenhotep III initiated the festival from his residence at Karnak, a palace named after himself, *Nebmaatra-tjehen-Aten*, "Nebmaatra Is the Dazzling Sun Disk." From there he proceeded on foot the short distance to the Amun-Re temple, forming a procession with priests carrying the portable bark housing the king's *ka* statue. As they progressed through the sanctuaries of Amun-Re, his consort Mut, and their son Khonsu, the king made offerings, and their barks and retinues joined the procession, boarded the great ships, and sailed south to Luxor.

Bell describes the scenes as follows:

> Nearby, large crowds mass to view the flotilla. Loud roars must have erupted as the king, queen, and gods sailed past. On land, paralleling and keeping pace with the flotilla, Egyptian and foreign detachments of the army – some with [feathers in their hair indicating high rank], all in full battle array – march behind standards adorned with colorful plumes and streamers. Horses and chariots appear, similarly decorated. People chant and clap; musicians pluck lutes and shake sistrums (ornate metal rattles) and beat drums. Acrobatic dancers perform . . . trumpeters signal the various movements of the drama. Finally, the water procession arrives [and] is met by the lines of princes, princesses, and high officials who are now at the head of the overland group, carrying bouquets and other offerings and leading fattened, festooned cattle . . . destined for sacrifice.

The barks are off-loaded and transferred into Luxor Temple, where the rites occur.

By now, Amenhotep III had renovated the southern end of Luxor Temple into a series of small, dark chambers with narrow doorways offset from each other so that the path through the chambers to the sanctuary was a maze. Amun's bark shrine was along the temple's central access at the rear of the edifice, with the sanctuary hidden behind it. Once inside the dark temple, the king accompanied Amun-Re's bark to its resting place and then entered the Opet sanctuary, where he performed a ceremony setting in motion a new cycle, creating a new life force by which to reenergize Amun-Re, who then recrowned the king. The small cadre of participants then reemerged into the sunlight to be greeted by the closest officials and eventually by flocks of shrieking, waving commoners. Finally, instead of returning on foot to Karnak, as had his predecessors, Amenhotep III sailed back to Karnak, while officials and retainers marched back through town. We can only wonder if or how much his clubfoot may have weighed into this change in the traditional itinerary.

Every festival included days of feasting around the temples, if we judge from the offerings of bread, beer, cakes, vegetables, cattle, and fowl amassed for each day of the event. For just one day of one late New Kingdom festival, less important than Opet, five cattle, 200 birds, and 3,600 loaves of bread were listed. Presumably these gifts did not rot on the offering tables but were prepared and apportioned out to the priesthood and involved laity, with leftover scraps eventually going to the pilgrims (the screeching plovers) who had come from near and far.

MORE CONSTRUCTION AT LUXOR AND KARNAK

Amenhotep III's early architecture at Karnak included a gemlike shrine seen and recorded there by the mid-nineteenth-century French amateur archaeologist Émile Prisse d'Avennes but which has disappeared since then. His tantalizing renderings of the building, with its square pillars, cavetto cornices, and images of the king before various deities, are all that remain of this structure so pristine it still retained its original color.

The most complete and well preserved of his early works at Karnak is the tiny Kha-em-maat temple a few hundred yards away from the Third Pylon in north Karnak. The king wrote that it was "a splendor of fine gold, a resting-place for my father [the cult image of Amun-Re] in all his feasts. It is built of fine sandstone, worked with gold throughout. Its pavements are adorned with silver, all its portals with gold. It is equipped with two tall obelisks, one on each side, so that my father rises between them while I am in his retinue. I have assigned to him thousands of oxen, so as to present their choice cuts." Building on foundations of Thutmose IV, our king named the temple after himself, using his Horus name, "Kha-em-maat" (Appearing in Truth), the same name as the boat he sailed to the Delta to confront wild bulls, and the same name he would eventually give to his temple at Soleb in Nubia.

Kha-em-maat temple must have been utterly rococo, with its icing of glittering foil and gleaming, colorful inlays. One inventory lists it as being decorated with 31,485 *deben* (about 3 tons) of electrum; 25,182 *deben* (more than 2.5 tons) of gold; 4,620 *deben* (less than ½ ton) of copper; 14,342 *deben* (about 1.4 tons) of bronze; 6,406 *deben* (about 2/3 ton) of lapis lazuli; 1,731 *deben* (about 350 pounds) of cornelian; and 1,075 *deben* (about 200 pounds) of turquoise. Multiplying the amounts of costly materials used on this relatively modest structure by the exponentially larger and more central structures elsewhere at Thebes – not to speak of projects in the rest of Egypt and the Sudan – results in a mind-boggling amount of resources, both human and mineral, and it suggests that when Amenhotep III was finished, the entire metroplex of Karnak–Luxor must have dazzled the eye.

Medamud, Montu's town, may have been drawn into events at Karnak, requiring processional avenues and waterways to link the two sites (Maps 3 and 4). Now landlocked, in its day, Medamud must have been within easy range of Karnak by boat. The temple has a quay dating to the Old Kingdom, and there may be later docks and canals as yet undiscovered beneath the agricultural fields, villages, roads, and other impediments separating Medamud from the Nile and from Karnak today. A corresponding quay and traces of a silted-in canal lie at the base of Kha-em-maat's now landlocked processional way, perfectly positioned to send and receive waterborne processions to and from Medamud. A ceremonial connection between Medamud and Karnak would explain why the Kha-em-maat temple was built as a resting place for Amun's cult image as it traveled "in all his feasts." Where else would it have gone to or come from if not Medamud?

There are good religious and ritual reasons for the two temples to be aligned. Montu – a manifestation of the sun god Re and represented, like him, as a falcon-headed deity – was the patron deity of the nome or territory of Thebes even before it became a capital city in the Middle Kingdom. Other sites sacred to Montu were Tod and Armant (the latter retaining the god's name), a few miles south of Thebes, the former on the east bank and the latter on the west. Therefore Karnak lay between Medamud and Tod–Armant. Karnak's Kha-em-maat temple became known later in its life as a Montu temple, and its position midway among the other sacred Montu sites may have created some association during Amenhotep III's reign as well.

Medamud was also the ancient "mound" of the earth god Geb, husband of the sky goddess Nut, one of the mother goddesses especially cherished during the New Kingdom. She swallowed the sun at dusk on the western horizon, it passed through her body at night, and it was magically reborn from her the next morning on the eastern horizon. Her image appeared on the ceilings of royal tombs and on the lids of coffins and sarcophagi as a guarantee of resurrection.

Kha-em-maat's "two, tall obelisks," between which the sun rose, stood on what is today usually considered the north side of the temple. At Thebes, however, river-north was not true north because at Thebes, the Nile River's northward flow is north-northeasterly.

In February at Thebes, the sun seems to rise from Medamud precisely in a line with the front gate of the Kha-em-maat temple, and it appears to set at Armant, a few miles upstream from Karnak on the west bank of the river, following a northeast to southwest route. Theban natives today easily speak of winter sunrise and sunset in these terms: "rising in Medamud and setting at Armant." In antiquity, the annual timing would have been different due to precession and recession of the earth's axis, but the phenomenon was likely the same. Thus the sun appeared to rise or "Appear in Truth" between Kha-em-maat's two obelisks, bringing the temple's name to life. From the obelisks and gate, a processional way lined with recumbent rams points toward Medamud only three miles away, where Thutmose IV had thanked the god Montu for help at a time of crisis.

This line bisects Karnak Temple perpendicularly to its original axis and may have been the basis for a new north-south axis left incomplete by Queen Hatshepsut at her death. Our king would eventually revive this visionary plan. Clearing and widening the pathway between his pylon and the Fourth Pylon was likely the beginning of this effort.

PHARAOH'S TEMPLE

Amenhotep III's greatest architectural project, which he began early in his reign, was his memorial temple, or "mansion of millions of years," on the west bank of Thebes at a site now called Kom el Hettan

(Whale Hill), perhaps after skeletons once found there (Figure 16 and Map 4). It was larger by far than his predecessors' memorial temples fringing the desert's edge. Northernmost and backed up into the cliffs is the grand, tiered temple of Hatshepsut at Deir el Bahri, lying on nearly the same axis as Karnak Temple. Temples of Thutmose III, Amenhotep II, and Thutmose IV, now destroyed, stood to the south of Hatshepsut's, and our king's enormous structure reached northward to meet them. The main part of our king's temple stretched east-west from the edge of the desert toward the bank of the Nile, the line of its axis intersecting perpendicularly with that of Luxor Temple across the river.

The king himself described his edifice on a stela as

> a noble temple on the west side of Thebes – a fortress forever and ever, made out of fine white sandstone, wrought entirely with gold, its floors decorated with silver, and all of its doors electrum . . . well-endowed with statues . . . made out of granite of Elephantine, quartzite, and every noble and costly stone. . . . Flagstaffs were set up in front of it, wrought with electrum, and representing the horizon of Heaven with Re shining in it. Its lake was filled by the high Nile – possessor of fish and ducks, and brightened with baskets of flowers. Its workshops were filled with male and female servants and with the children of the chiefs of every foreign country of His Majesty's captures. . . . Its cattle were like the sand of the sea-shore, amounting to millions.

Sadly, in the past 3,330 years, Amenhotep III's "mansion of millions of years," probably the largest and most extravagantly furnished temple in human history, has almost entirely disappeared. It apparently did not even last until classical times. It is absent from Greek lists of the Seven Wonders, and historians like Diodorus Siculus did not mention it, presumably because it had vanished from sight in the intervening centuries due to both natural and human destruction.

Some of Dynasty 19's kings, including Merneptah and Ramesses II, built their temples on top of Amenhotep III's northern wing, obliterating it and usurping its statuary and architectural elements. The stela with its evocative description, now in the Cairo museum, was defaced during the Amarna period, restored by Sety I, and reused by Merneptah in his own temple. At Ramesses II's temple, the Ramesseum, a gigantic black granodiorite statue, its head now lying on the sandy floor, was almost certainly recut from one of Amenhotep III taken from Kom el Hettan. It was made famous in classical times by Diodorus Siculus and then more

16. Year 2008 view of excavations at Amenhotep III's memorial temple. Photo: APK.

recently by Percy Shelley as Ozymandias. Over the centuries, collectors purloined surface pieces from Amenhotep's temple, while agriculture, roads, and modern buildings buried the rest.

Nature also took its toll. Nineteenth- and early-twentieth-century photographers recorded images of annual floods washing across the entire area before Aswan's high dam brought this event to a halt. The temple's walls were constructed not entirely of sandstone as the inscription implies, but mostly of cheap mud brick sheathed in sandstone reliefs, which obviously could not withstand floods or the valley's occasional earthquakes as well as solidly stone-built Karnak and Luxor have.

By the twentieth century A.D., most Egyptologists who visited the site assumed that there was nothing left to find, and attempts at surveys were discouraging. It seemed that little more remained than the two lonely 59-foot tall "Colossi of Memnon," enthroned images of Amenhotep III made later in the reign (see Chapter 10 and Figures 23 and 24). They rest in front of the temple's long-gone first pylon like guardians who fell asleep on the job, allowing the entire monument behind them to be stripped bare and silted over.

Finally, in the early years of this century, the Amenhotep III Temple Conservation Project, directed by Hourig Sourouzian, began to make astounding discoveries, unmasking an apparent wasteland as a virtual treasure trove. In just a few seasons of work, she and her team added immeasurably to our understanding of the original scope and appearance of what must have been in its day one of the greatest architectural marvels of all time. Over the coming years, this international team will certainly change the scene entirely as they uncover and, it is hoped, rebuild the pylons and courts, repositioning the innumerable statues of king, queen, and deities in this grand edifice.

Amenhotep's earliest structure at this site was not particularly imposing – a sanctuary at the edge of the desert honoring Ptah-Sokar-Osiris, a form of the Memphite creator god Ptah syncretized with funerary deities. This gave the northerner Ptah both a geographic portfolio here in the south and a spiritual one in the land of the dead. The Ptah-Sokar-Osiris temple must have become a focal point for the annual Festival of Sokar, which took place at the end of every Inundation season and lasted a week or more. It was a festival of renewal and celebrated Osiris's triumph over death, just as the land would arise new and green after the annual flood subsided. Celebrants wore garlands of onions, whose tightly bound white bulbs send up green shoots, just as a wrapped mummy sends up its owner's spirit.

Ptah-Sokar was just the first of the gods to be honored at Kom el Hettan, Amun and the deified king himself becoming the primary beneficiaries, with stelae dedicated to them here and there at the site. Any art historian familiar with religious construction in the Middle Ages might immediately suspect that these varied dedications testify to phases in this vast temple's construction and to related sources of patronage. In medieval Europe, as soon as a cathedral's apse was built and dedicated, it was a functioning church. As each additional portion was completed, that new section was dedicated, often with a mention or image of the patron who had supplied the necessary funds. Applying this concept to Kom el Hettan, as soon as Ptah-Sokar was completed and dedicated, it functioned as a venue for the annual Sokar festival as well as other west bank celebrations, but in a pinch, it could also serve as the king's memorial, should he expire unexpectedly.

No one knows exactly how these temples were funded. Of course, the king decreed the foundation of the temple and endowed it with estates, but where did these lands come from? The decline in importance of previous kings' temples over time suggests that some of their lands were siphoned off to support the current one. The dedications to Ptah and Amun hint that Amenhotep III also diverted funds or lands from their divine estates. Our king and his well-educated officials, in particular, Amenhotep son of Hapu, who bragged on his own monuments about his knowledge of the past, must have known that this was common practice in the Old and Middle Kingdoms. And it continued later on. For example, Dynasty 20's Ramesses III is strongly suspected of having purloined endowments from Ramesses II's Dynasty 19 Ramesseum to build his own temple nearby at Medinet Habu. Other temple inventories show that furnishings and votive instruments were regularly moved from older ones to newer ones over time.

Inscriptions at Kom el Hettan name some of its temple personnel as belonging to Ptah, while others were property of Nebmaatra. Amun also claimed some ownership. One stela, in the words of Swiss archaeologist Gerhard Haeny, who excavated at the site, "invites Amun to take possession of the building prepared for him. Then Amun expresses his gratitude for the temple and his satisfaction with its beauty and perfection. Finally the ennead of minor gods in Amun's retinue chime in," inviting the god to his temple and thanking the king for preparing chapels and statues for them as well. In other words, at Kom el Hettan, as at so many other temples in Egypt, the site was not dedicated to one *or* another, but to one *and* another *and* another.

By the end of his reign, our king had built far more on the west bank than at Karnak. The Third Pylon, the Kha-em-maat temple, and the later Tenth Pylon (Chapter 10) were no match for the memorial complex. Suspicion arises that the tremendous revenues accruing to Amun-Re from his estates up and down the Nile Valley were transferred at least partially to the west bank. During Amenhotep III's reign, both the high priest of the Amun temple and the *sem*-priest (the chief) of his memorial temple were named Meryptah, and they may have been the same person, possibly a close blood relative of our king making the diversion of resources that much easier.

THE ROYAL TOMB AND ITS WORKERS

At the same time as Amenhotep III began work on his memorial temple, he must also have continued work on his tomb in the Valley of the Kings, which was actually founded for him by his father. Most of the Dynasty 18 royal tombs are in the narrow eastern channel of the Kings' Valley, lying in the shadow of the Qurn, the pyramidal mountain peak harkening back to the great monuments of the Old Kingdom. Amenhotep III's tomb, however, tunnels into the soft limestone talus of the broad West Valley, backing up against a massive cliff (Figure 17 and Map 4).

His tomb, Kings' Valley 22, had long passageways with multiple halls and chambers to hold his mummy as well as some of his family members' and their treasures. Its walls were plastered and painted, and the style of the few painting fragments known today belong to the first decade of his reign (Figure 46). These show the king being greeted individually by various deities, iconography similar to his father's. Traps in the tunnels were designed to catch ancient robbers. Unfortunately, these did not work, and only small fragments of his treasure have been found in modern times. When located in 1799, the tomb was in terrible condition, and soon after its discovery, some of the best parts of the extant painted walls were hacked out and taken to France and are now in the Louvre. Since 1989, a team from Japan's Waseda University, headed by Jiro Kondo, has undertaken some conservation work in the tomb, but the geology of the site causes extreme difficulty.

The artisans who painted the royal tombs lived in a tiny village known today as Deir el Medina, in a cul-de-sac on the other side of the mountains from Kings' Valley (Map 4). Foundations of simple row houses remain today, lined up along two or three narrow streets. The entire rectangular village was walled off around its perimeter by the adjoining back walls of the houses. From here the artisans and workers hiked along narrow desert footpaths over the hills, shortcutting the journey to Kings' Valley. The commute was long enough that they often spent ten-day weeks camping out close to their work.

Tomb decorators included wall preparators and plasterers as well as the actual draftsmen, outline painters, and color painters. Their trades were handed down from father to son, and hundreds of documents in the form of practice sketches as well as administrative records of roll calls, team assignments, lists of rations, professional equipment and supplies, and even notations of holidays and sick days have been found at Deir el Medina, written on limestone chips – much cheaper and more readily available than papyrus. Most of these records date from Dynasties 19 and 20, but much of what they tell us must hold true for Amenhotep III's time as well.

From these *ostraca* (sing. *ostracon*), we learned that workmen were divided into gangs, one that worked on the left side and the other on the right, much like rowers on the royal sailing ships. Each gang had a foreman who was responsible for obtaining the materials and tools used

17. View of the Valley of the Kings west valley with entrance to KV 22 at lower right. Photo courtesy Richard H. Wilkinson, University of Arizona Egyptian Expedition.

by his gang. Some of these items could be quite expensive because they were made of bronze, and the pigments contained precious minerals; even gold overlays were occasionally used. Theoretically, they worked about 20 days out of 30, finding plenty of excuses for taking extra time off – anything from the normal festival days to a marital spat to a bad hangover. The latter sometimes required a friend to stay home nursing the afflicted colleague. One worker spent so much time tending to his friends, his friends' friends, and his friends' wives that he seems to have avoided working in the tomb for months. And yet another absented himself for five months because "his wife was away together with the doctor" – whatever that meant.

Piecing together details from the ostraca reveals a relatively middle-class society. Many residents were literate and read Egyptian classics on papyri published by schools of scribes who earnestly copied and recopied the ancient scrolls. Some villagers were wealthy enough to own their own bronze tools, which means that they had small businesses or craft shops of their own. Some were carpenters and made beds and furniture chests not only for the royal tombs but also for sale to private individuals such as officials and wealthy merchants.

Some artisans were so highly regarded that they had their own tombs at Thebes, giving historians rare opportunities to learn their names.

Most venerable of these craftsmen was Kha, chief of the cemetery, who spanned the reigns of Amenhotep II, Thutmose IV, and Amenhotep III. His Deir el Medina tomb, including his and his wife Meryt's mummies and sarcophagi, was found undisturbed in 1906 by Italian archaeologist Ernesto Schiaparelli. Its treasure was acquired by the Museo Egizio in Turin. Among Kha and Meryt's tomb furnishings were a painted storage box for linen, an exceptionally beautiful Book of the Dead papyrus painted with their portraits, a box of glass perfume bottles, a gold measuring stick inscribed with Amenhotep II's name, and an electrum cup with Amenhotep III's. Neither Kha nor Meryt had come from titled families, and so the status achieved in their afterlife came purely by dint of Kha's talent, service, and longevity.

THE GOLDEN AFTERGLOW

Deir el Medina artisans worked not only for the king but also for wealthy officials and courtiers, who were favored by the king with tombs on the desert hillsides facing the floodplain.

Some were military men, such as Horemheb, Nebamun, and so on, who ordered their tombs decorated with scenes of army troops marching in neat files. The color palette in their tombs tended toward browns, ochres, and muted greens. Others were civilians, like the British Museum's Nebamun, grain accountant of Amun, who preferred agricultural scenes and vignettes of the owner and family fishing and fowling in the marshes. These latter tombs share a similar palette with the royal tomb – rich greens, cobalt blues, vibrant reds, brilliant whites, and even costly golden orpiment obtained by international trade. The grain counter Nebamun's even has a spot of gold leaf set into the eye of a hunting cat! Some of the most beautiful scenes in the entire Nile valley were executed by the master painters of this reign, and their oeuvre has to be counted as some of the finest in the history of ancient art, rivaling Lascaux, Pompeii, and the Buddhist caves of Tibet and China.

Depicted in all the tombs from our king's reign was an increased sense of conspicuous consumption undoubtedly a result of the new wealth supplied by Nubia. Army scenes are loaded with overlapping rows of well-equipped soldiers, spirited horses, and the latest design in chariots. Landowners count herds of unusually massive, well-fed cattle and flocks of breast-heavy geese. Offering tables spill over with the freshest, highest-quality fruits and vegetables.

18. Menna's wife in her best finery. Theban Tomb 69. Photo: APK/JSB.

Egypt's increasing wealth after the Nubian campaign – particularly among the elite – was evident in the fashions of the day. Both male and female dress in Amenhotep III's day was much fancier and more voluminous than ever before. The latest fashion in menswear included linen T-shirts; short, pleated opaque kilts; and long overskirts of gossamer thinness and transparency. Women's gowns were made of light, transparent linen formed in tiny cascading pleats, far more delicate than the thick, opaque, starched white dresses of the past (Figure 18). Over their shoulders women often wore fringed and pleated shawls, the more generous, the better.

Pleated gowns required a great deal more cloth to manufacture, which means that more looms and weavers were active in private villa workshops as well as at the palace and its harems. The new accordion pleats also must have required a great deal more maintenance than previous fashions calling on large numbers of washermen and -women to launder the garments and reset the folds. In other words, the new complexities introduced into Egyptian fashion are also signs of increases in the economy in both the manufacturing and service sectors.

Jewelry became extravagant during this reign. Both sexes wore multiple armlets, bracelets, and pectorals of gold, semiprecious stone, glass, and faience. Broad collars made of small, exquisite faience beads extended from two-thirds to full shoulder width, requiring an increase of hundreds of elements as compared to previous styles and, therefore, more materials and more workshops. They were made in every color, from red to deep blue to a pure yellow to brilliant white, the latter two being especially difficult to achieve and being hallmarks of Amenhotep III's superb craftsmen. The beads came from royal workshops and must have been gifts or payments to the officials from a generous king. Earrings were a new fashion for men, and pierced earlobes on statuary are often used as dating criteria. Amenhotep III himself, however, was too conservative to adopt this fashion.

As the amount of linen and jewelry increased after the Nubian campaign, so did the length and thickness of both men's and women's wigs, traditionally worn over shaven heads or closely cropped hair. By the end of the reign, wigs would puff up at least twice the size of that worn, for example, by Queen Tiaa, the mother of Thutmose IV. On some female statues, "big hair" engulfed tiny faces in cascades of long, thick, black tresses tumbling down over the shoulders. The availability of the raw material – long, black human hair – and the manual labor to weave and braid it must also have increased after the war in Nubia.

The golden afterglow of Amenhotep's military success in Nubia lasted throughout his reign as long as the precious metal continued to flow north with the river. It funded his building projects, not only the Third Pylon but the great monuments to come. The increased amounts of linen, jewelry, and even wigs worn by the burgeoning upper class are evidence that the king's new wealth translated into riches for them as well. They benefited as contractors, architects, shippers, traders, provision suppliers, craftsmen, and of course, priests, as their cadres expanded with the size and numbers of temples.

All this must have required an increase in basic labor manpower either via the birthrate, or immigration, or wartime captives, or some combination of the three. No statistics shed light on this aspect of Nile Valley life, but records from Kom el Hettan and elsewhere mention that entire Syrian and Kushite towns were founded there and nearby to serve the temples and probably, to some extent, the rest of the area as well.

THE KING'S FIRST TWO WIVES

(Reign of Amenhotep III, Years 10 and 11, ca. 1382–1381 B.C.)

GREAT ROYAL WIFE, TIY

No Eighteenth Dynasty woman was more lavishly attired than Amenhotep III's Great Royal Wife Tiy. Statues show her wearing exquisitely pleated linen robes, ornate jewelry, and complex headdresses (Figure 19). She was more than a fashion plate, however. She must have been highly intelligent, multilingual, and politically adept to reach the level of international trust and esteem that was hers by the end of the reign. A tiny, naturalistic portrait of her made toward the end of her life depicts a daunting and determined facial expression revealing a woman of indomitable strength of mind and purpose (see Figure 48).

Tiy's husband was devoted to her and introduced her to the world in an unprecedented manner: by commissioning an entire series of commemorative scarabs dedicated solely to her (see Figure 9). They read,

> The Living Horus . . . Amenhotep Ruler of Thebes, given life: the Great Royal Wife Tiy, may she live. The name of her father is Yuya, the name of her mother is Thuya. She is the wife of a mighty king whose southern boundary is to Karoy, whose northern [boundary] is at Naharin (the small, but powerful kingdom of Mitanni in the upper Tigris-Euphrates valley).

This is the only set of commemorative scarabs not dated with a year of Amenhotep's reign, suggesting that Tiy had entered his life while he was still a prince. Rather than date their union to his father's reign, he used no date at all. He then included her in the inscriptions of all of his other great scarabs as though she had been there all the time.

The 56 known Queen Tiy scarabs traveled widely, some as far away as modern Jordan and Syria to the northeast and the Sudan to the south.

19. Fragment of a pair statue: Queen Tiy beside Amenhotep III (arm only), glazed steatite, height 12 inches, Musée du Louvre, E. 25493. Photo APK.

That few people in Egypt or abroad understood hieroglyphic writing did not keep their messages from being appreciated because they were read aloud to assembled masses by local officials or special royal messengers. Tiy's scarab text, according to philologist Edmund Meltzer, is sheer poetry – "a carefully composed and exquisitely balanced proclamation" – designed to get the audience to chime in as a chorus on the rhyming couplet "The name of her father is Yuya. The name of her mother is Thuya."

That her parents' names are known at all, and that they appear so prominently, is utterly remarkable, and it suggests that they were recognizable to a large audience, possibly foreign as well as Egyptian. "Yuya" was an extremely rare name in Egypt and is considered by some scholars to be Semitic, possibly similar to "Yoel." Yuya's mummy, found in 1905 with that of his wife in their nearly undisturbed Kings' Valley tomb (KV 46; see Chapter 9), has aquiline features with a prominent, hooked nose similar to the profiles of eastern foreigners painted on tomb walls in Dynasty 18 and dissimilar from traditional Egyptian faces. Thuya's mummy has wide-set eyes, high cheekbones, a wide, thin-lipped mouth with a long upper lip, and a small, aquiline nose, as does her famous gilded mummy mask (Figure 20). She may have had some foreign blood, but Dimitri Laboury has made a strong case for her name being a perfectly good Dynasty 18 diminutive for Ahhotep. Even so, the names of all three family members confused the royal scribes and scarab carvers, who spelled them in various ways.

Hints about the family's heritage come from the Amarna letters written to the Egyptian court by Tushratta, king of Mitanni (Naharin) in upper Mesopotamia, modern Kurdistan, in an area bisected by the modern-day Syria–Iraq border: what Amenhotep called his "northern boundary." Mitanni was the Kentucky of its day, where some of the ancient world's finest and swiftest horses were bred and trained. Every letter from its king to Pharaoh began with best wishes for the latter's wives, sons, officials, and horses; and every transaction between the two countries included the exchange of Nubian gold for Asiatic horses, chariots, and all of the tack and trappings.

The Amarna correspondence shows that there was a close relationship between Tiy and the Mitanni court (see Chapter 18). Tushratta wrote to Amenhotep IV (Akhenaten) after Amenhotep III's death, pleading with the new pharaoh to check with his mother Tiy about what had been said between her husband and Mitanni's royal messenger, Keliya. Tushratta urged the new king, "Now inquire carefully of your mother about the words that your mother (Tiy herself!) spoke to Keliya." "Tiy, your mother, knows all the words that I spoke with your father. No one else knows them. You must ask Tiy, your mother, about them, so she can tell you."

He wrote one letter directly to Tiy as if he knew her, saying, "You are the one . . . who knows much better than all the others the things we (Tushratta and Amenhotep III) said to one another. No one else knows them as well." Evidently Tiy was Amenhotep III's interpreter and spoke a

20. Funerary mask of Thuya, gilded cartonnage, colored stone, glass, height 16 inches, JE 95254. Egyptian Museum, Cairo. Photo by Andreas Voegelin. Courtesy Dr. Zahi Hawass and Egyptian Museum Cairo.

Near Eastern language, presumably Tushratta's native Hurrian. She also wrote on her own account via her own private messengers to Tushratta's wife, Yuni, as if they were close friends or relatives.

Additional evidence of ties between Tiy's family and western Asia comes from what is thought to have been Tiy's hometown, Akhmim, in Middle Egypt about halfway between Memphis and Thebes. Akhmim, the capital of Egypt's ninth nome, was a major center of linen weaving with a high immigrant population. It was also the seat of worship for the ancient fertility god Min, whose name echoes in the town's modern name. Thutmose III had built a chapel at Akhmim and filled it with images of Min standing erect with his mammoth (nearly equine) phallus thrusting perpendicularly from his groin. Min also had strong associations with the East, being the only Egyptian god depicted with his right arm raised high, a pose traditional to Near Eastern gods.

Yuya was a "priest of Min" and "overseer of cattle of Min, lord of Ipu." Thuya was "chief of the entertainers of Min," "singer of Amun," "singer of Hathor," and "chief of the entertainers of Amun." Perhaps more important, Yuya, whose mummy shows him to have been straight backed and strong, was "master of the horse" for Amenhotep III and "lieutenant commander of chariotry." Considering that true royal princes were proud to bear the title Master of the King's Horses, Yuya's titles placed him very high indeed. The handsome, light chariot found in the couple's tomb is symbolic of his expertise. Perhaps he was one of the princely *maryannu* cavaliers brought into Egypt by Amenhotep's predecessors, or he may have been one of the Naharin blue bloods who traveled to bring gifts, including horses, to Thutmose IV, an event celebrated on the walls of nobles' tombs.

The topography surrounding Akhmim was perfect for the horse industry. The town stands on a peninsula built up from Nile silt, which, along with the broad plains across the river, was well suited for breeding, grazing, and training horses. During World War II, the area served as a holding point for British cavalry stock, and even today, its main agricultural crop is animal fodder. In antiquity, it would have been a likely spot for relocating some of the *maryannu* and for setting up equestrian facilities. Its location in Middle Egypt made access to both ends of the empire relatively easy.

We know nothing about how Tiy and Amenhotep met. She may have been an "ornament" at the royal court like the daughters of military officials mentioned in Chapter 6. We also do not know if Amenhotep and Tiy had a ceremony, but increasing scholarly focus on this subject in general suggests that they probably did. Marriage contracts exist from much later periods, but not from the New Kingdom. Recently, however, scholars have begun to patch together details and innuendos from widely scattered texts to form a sketchy idea of marriage events, including ceremonies drawn out over a period of seven days.

Tiy probably had very little power at first. Official order in harems was kept by individuals like Sebek-hotep and by harem overseers, palace stewards, and queens' stewards, who became increasingly visible and powerful during Dynasty 18. Informal control within the harem rested in the hands of the highest-ranking woman. In Prince Amenhotep's fledgling harem, there were two candidates for alpha female: his mother Mutemwia, who was depicted so prominently in his coronation portrait from Theban tomb 226 (see Figure 8), and his big sister Tiaa, who lived long into his reign, becoming the highest-ranking member of one of his households (see Chapter 11).

By Year 10, Tiy had several children, some of whom must have been born before Amenhotep was crowned king. By now eldest son Thutmose was old enough to be a priest and to officiate at the burial of one of the Apis bulls. His brother Amenhotep, the future Akhenaten, was probably just born or a toddler. A prince named Si-Atum, who produced a daughter by the 20s of the reign, may have been Tiy's son as well. Daughter Sitamen was close to puberty, and her sister Isis was likely born by now; perhaps her two other known sisters, Henut-taneb and Nebetah, were also. Having produced a male heir, a spare, and some lively girls could have clinched Tiy's promotion to Great Royal Wife, in other words, queen.

Great Royal Wife Tiy is mentioned on all of the commemorative scarabs, including the bull hunt scarabs of Year 2 and the lion hunt scarabs of Years 1 through 10, as though she participated during what must have been her prime child-bearing years. Since the Museum of Fine Arts Boston's Lawrence Berman, when at Cleveland, showed that all of these commemorative scarabs were made at about the same time, in Years 10 and 11, Tiy's inclusion in all of them seems more like propaganda aimed at raising her status at that particular moment rather than a record of her actual attendance at each event. The reason for this will soon become clear.

Tiy's earliest portraits (Figure 19), now in the Louvre and elsewhere, are in glazed steatite like most of the commemorative scarabs, and they were probably made in the same workshops at around the same time. Now mostly fragmentary, many of them are halves of pair statuettes showing her standing next to her husband. In these images, the king's crown and jewelry are not adorned with sun disks, which he favored later on, and so they must have been made early in the reign. Many of these statuettes were found at Karnak, probably temple gifts to honor the newly proclaimed queen before the gods, just as the scarabs honored her before the people.

The statuettes show Tiy with a squarish face, high cheekbones, and almond-shaped eyes like her husband's, but with a thinner upper lip. How much of this image is true to her and how much part of the standard idealization that made all contemporaries resemble their king is not clear from studies of the mummy thought to be hers. Clearly she did favor intricately pleated gowns, ornate jewelry, and heavy, long wigs full of tiny braids, as previously mentioned. In her early statuary, she appears more diminutive than ritually necessary next to her husband, and she may, indeed, have been quite petite, for she wore unusually tall headgear, which made up the difference.

As time went on, Tiy's styles and image changed. Her wigs became even heavier, her robes trailing on the ground and becoming more voluminous, while her jewelry grew more complex and, in keeping with the natural aging process, her figure gradually drooped – her later statuary shows her to have gained typical, middle-aged weight around the hips and thighs (see Figure 36).

A SECOND BRIDE: GILUKHEPA, THE MITANNI PRINCESS

The fourth series of scarabs, of which five examples are known, announced the arrival in Year 10 of a new bride, a second official wife for Amenhotep III. She was a Mitanni princess named "Gilukhepa," the daughter of King Shuttarna and sister of one of the major authors of the Amarna letters, his son Tushratta.

Amenhotep III had a hard time winning Gilukhepa's hand, according to her brother Tushratta's account, written some 25 years later and preserved in one of the Amarna letters. He wrote that Amenhotep III had been forced to petition King Shuttarna repeatedly before the latter relinquished his daughter. Allowing for some degree of exaggeration, this Mitanni reluctance appears to have been real and was probably a visceral reaction stemming from the fact that only a century earlier, they had been trampled by Thutmose III in his brutal conquest of Asia as far as the Euphrates. Since Egypt was so much more powerful, playing hard to get was an easy way to tweak Pharaoh.

Tiy's, Yuya's, and Thuya's names are all inscribed on the Gilukhepa scarabs as though they were part of the welcoming party, making it clear that they were above the new girl in pecking order and that she was a guest, albeit official and permanent, in their territory.

Gilukhepa's arrival must have been a factor in Tiy's promotion to queen. Gilukhepa's scarab made it clear that the brilliant and talented Tiy was now the alpha female in the royal harem, that Gilukhepa was a mere consort, and that Tiy's offspring (at least one already in the priesthood) were the heirs to the throne. At the same time, the inclusion of Tiy's and her parents' names on the scarabs must have communicated a comforting sense of protection for the new girl considering the ties between Tiy and Mitanni.

Gilukhepa arrived in Egypt with an entourage of 317 women, "a marvel," say the scarabs. Her dowry must have been no less wondrous, judging from the gift lists that accompanied foreign brides later in the same reign: earrings, bracelets, necklaces, and pins of gold and lapis lazuli; ointment vessels, wash basins, flasks, and mirrors of silver and gold; gilded boots with stone buttons; silver combs; carved mythological plaques overlaid with precious metals; shirts "of many-colored cloth"; blankets for the head and for the feet; and everything in the dozens. The Amarna letters describe a viewing by courtiers and officials of the dowries sent with foreign princesses to the court of Amenhotep III, suggesting that this was part of a larger event, perhaps an actual marriage celebration.

The logistics of housing, clothing, equipping, and feeding such an important woman and her extended household must have been awesome. An official (probably of Thutmose IV) named "Bengai" held the title Great One of the House of the Noble Lady of Mitanni. These few words offer a great deal of information: (1) that an important foreign woman held her own household in Egypt; (2) that she was of foreign royalty but not named queen of Egypt; and (3) that she had a large staff, of which Bengai was head. Gilukhepa must have had her own palace, staff, fields, and workshops; however, the girl remained completely in the shadows of Tiy and her daughters for the rest of the reign.

A MILITARY FORAY IN AID OF THE NEW IN-LAWS?

Tiny bits of evidence here and there suggest that Amenhotep III took brief military action on behalf of his new in-laws at about this time. Amenhotep son of Hapu made an oblique mention of an effort in Asia, but a slightly more specific, though brief, reference occurs in a later Amarna letter from Tushratta to Amenhotep III. This missive seems to recall a moment in Year 11 when Egypt and Mitanni joined together in a battle against the Hittites. Tushratta wrote that after his father gave Gilukhepa to Amenhotep III, "the very next year . . . my brother's (Amenhotep's) . . . all the land of Hatti (the Hittites of Anatolia). The enemy advanced against my country, Tessup (a deity) gave him into my hand, and I defeated him." Then Tushratta listed the Hatti booty sent to

Amenhotep III. The gaps logically fill in as follows: the Hittites invaded Mitanni and Amenhotep's army surprised them from behind and chased them into Mitanni hands led by crown prince Tushratta, who defeated them and sent captured treasure to Egypt.

An amethyst cylinder seal, which came to light in 1992, when it was put up for auction in Paris, may refer to this event. It shows a striding Nebmaatra, fit and youthful, his name in a cartouche, and behind him Queen Tiy in her regalia of double-plumed headdress and lily scepter. With his right hand, the king clutches the scalp of a kneeling Asiatic, and with his left, he raises a *khepesh* sword to brain him. Facing them, an Eastern-costumed, bearded nobleman, his arm poised in greeting, leads a slim, naked woman toward the fray. Whether the scene is symbolic or historical, it conveys the clear quid pro quo of one nubile Asian princess in exchange for mighty Egypt's military support.

QUEEN TIY'S LAKE: A GIFT TO HER HOMETOWN

That same year, Amenhotep III honored Queen Tiy by ordering construction of a huge lake for her at her hometown of Djarukha, a geographic name associated with the Akhmim area. Naming this massive undertaking for Tiy gave her yet another step above Gilukhepa and Amenhotep's other harem ladies. No Egyptian queen had ever received such an honor. Documenting this great event is the fifth and final series of our king's commemorative scarabs, dated Year 11, the third month of Akhet (Inundation), day 1 (around early to mid-September). Eleven are known, and they read, in part:

> His Majesty commanded to make a lake for the Great Royal Wife
> Tiy, may she live, in her town of Djarukha. Its length is 3700
> cubits, its width 700 cubits (roughly 2000 by 400 yards), His
> Majesty celebrated the festival of the "Opening of the Lakes" in
> the third month of Akhet (*Inundation*), day 16, [when] His Majesty
> was rowed in the royal barque "Dazzling Sun Disk" on it.

Taking the king at his word, this vast (about 161 acres) hydraulic project took only two weeks to complete, unbelievable by modern construction methods, but during the Nile flood season and with thousands of otherwise idle hands, the fantastic becomes credible. The speed with which the basin was dug suggests an urgency not normally born from the desire for a pleasant sail. Perhaps the lakes acted as holding tanks to alleviate pressure from a particularly high inundation or as reservoirs for irrigation in case of a low one.

Whereas Amenhotep named his first boat *Kha-em-maat* after his own Horus name, this second craft, *Aten Tjehen* (*Dazzling Sun Disk*) would become the king's own favorite epithet for himself. In this case, the name, not just the image, recalled the sky as a vast expanse of water on which the sun god sailed. Both names merged the king with his ships in a spiritual way, and they tied his travels on earth with the daily journey of the sun god making his outings divine acts with a guarantee of renewal. They did not terminate when the boat docked, but, like the sun, they went into a nocturnal phase until rebirth. The use of the word *Aten* (Sun Disk) is particularly noteworthy, not because it was a first-time use in Dynasty 18 or in Egyptian history but because from now on, it would become increasingly prominent in Amenhotep III's reign and, eventually, the central focus of his son Akhenaten's years on the throne.

The Opening of the Lakes festival for which the great lake was dug probably coincided with the flood's high point. According to Diodorus Siculus, writing centuries later, this was an emotional time for the Egyptian populace. "The entire nation, when it has learned that the river has ceased rising and begun to fall, is relieved of its anxiety, while at the same time all immediately know in advance how large the next harvest will be, since the Egyptians have kept an accurate record of their observations of this kind over a long period."

By Year 11, hundreds, perhaps thousands, of scarabs naming Tiy and her parents had been published, raising Queen Tiy to an unprecedented level of renown not only in the Nile Valley but also abroad. Though the king liked to say for his own achievements that "never the like had occurred" before his time, Tiy could justifiably have borrowed this phrase to describe her own status. No previous Egyptian woman of nonroyal blood had ever achieved such prominence – and this was only the beginning for her.

9

THE LOST YEARS

(Reign of Amenhotep III, Years 12–19, ca. 1380–1373 B.C.)

YEAR 20: BRIDGING THE GAP IN THE RECORD

Suddenly, in Year 12, Amenhotep III's scribes stopped writing, or so it seems, because after more than a decade of chronicling the opening of quarries, the conquest of Nubia, bull hunts, lion hunts, marriages, in-laws, temple projects, sailboats, and even the construction of a "pleasure lake," there are no dated records at all for eight years. Our king is not the only one with a gap in his record. His grandfather Amenhotep II, for example, had a similar one. Our Amenhotep, however, more than any king before him, had made a mission of memorializing his life in unusual detail beginning in his days as a prince. After ravaging the gold fields of Nubia, he had the funds to continue doing so on a grand scale. For him, this lull was completely out of character, and it suggests trouble.

Apparently residing in the north at this point, Amenhotep III broke his silence in Year 20, month 2 of Inundation by sending his messenger, Royal Scribe Khaemhet (TT 57; see also Chapters 10 and 16), south from Memphis to Karnak to announce the promotion of a man named Nebnufer to his father's post as keeper of the measurements of offerings at Karnak's granary. The story is carved onto Nebnufer's small, and rather crude, limestone statue, now in Brussels, in a very long text covering all four sides of his seat. It describes the installation ceremony and names the major officiants: First Prophet of Amun Meryptah (a royal half brother?), Second Prophet of Amun Anen (Queen Tiy's brother), Third Prophet of Amun Amenemhet (the son of Nefer, the previous Third Prophet), Fourth Prophet Simut (promoted to Second Prophet before the end of the reign; see also Chapters 13 and 16), and the steward Sebek-nakht.

Considering the importance of the men attending, this must have been quite a significant event. Perhaps it fit into a larger context that Amenhotep son of Hapu mentioned in his autobiographical text: "The

King has placed me to record the house of Amun, I set priests in [their] places [] back/after [] in the entire land." The square brackets indicate erasures in the text. The gist seems to be that son of Hapu was ordered to take a census of the Amun priesthood (generally in Thebes) and to fill empty ranks after *something* had occurred throughout the Nile Valley. If the word in the gap between "after" and "in the entire land" referred to a positive event, it should be chronicled elsewhere, because it clearly had a major impact on the national religion, but it is not. If the lost word had evil connotations, erasure destroyed its power, according to Egyptian belief, and the traditional Egyptian distaste for recording unfavorable events prevented any further elaboration.

WHAT HAPPENED?

There is no evidence of a major foreign invasion during Amenhotep III's reign; therefore the culprit was most probably something such as a natural disaster like an earthquake or a major disease outbreak.

Earthquakes are fairly common in Egypt because it lies at the juncture of the Eurasian, African, and Arabic tectonic plates, and one earthquake, in A.D. 1211, is considered to have been one of the deadliest in world history. A quake centered at Thebes could have caused a great many deaths not only from stone structures collapsing on scores of priests and temple staff within them but also by the spread of fires in closely concentrated workshops and habitats within the temple precincts or at the artists' colony Deir el Medina, for example. Modern seismic studies have identified quakes a bit later in date, but not yet within Amenhotep III's years, although research in this area for Dynasty 18 is still in its infancy.

On the other hand, there are many texts and inscriptions from the fourteenth century B.C. that imply or actually state the presence of infectious disease, of plagues, during this period. Our king's son and successor, Akhenaten, railed against a terrible thing ("it") that had occurred during his father's reign, and he reported to Babylonian king Burna-buriash that one of his father's wives had died of the "plague." During the reign of Tutankhamen, Hittite king Mursilis II wrote the following prayer to the Sun Goddess: "What is this, O gods, that you have done? A plague you have let into the land, the land of Hatti, all of it is dying: so no one prepares sacrificial loaves and libations for you. The plowmen who used to work the fields of the god are dead. To mankind, our wisdom has been lost, and whatever we do right comes to nothing."

The biblical book of Exodus and the Jewish Haggadah (the Rabbinic account of the Hebrew liberation from Egypt as celebrated in the Passover festival) enumerate a series of plagues that had victimized Egypt over a period of time and had caused great devastation in terms of human disease and the destruction of crops and animals. The Exodus is thought to have occurred in Dynasty 19, and so the general time frame fits. It is impossible to take these references as certifiable history, but the coincidence is striking.

A thousand years after Amenhotep III, there was a foggy and muddled memory of some disease event during his reign. Third-century B.C. Egyptian historian Manetho wrote that King "Amenophis" (the Greek form of Amenhotep) wanted to see the living gods and told his namesake Amenophis, Paapis' son (presumably Amenhotep Son of Hapu),

> who in virtue of his wisdom and knowledge of the future, was reputed to be a partaker in the divine nature. This namesake, then, replied that he (the king) would be able to see the gods if he cleansed the whole land of lepers and other polluted persons. The king was delighted, and assembled all those in Egypt whose bodies were wasted by disease: they numbered 80,000 persons. These he cast into the stone-quarries to the east of the Nile, there to work segregated from the rest of the Egyptians.

The story of cleansing the land is what Canadian Egyptologist Donald Redford called a "floating" plot, "but the tradition of 'seeing the gods' is peculiar to . . . Amenophis III alone."

The most concrete testimony to serious disease events are the hundreds of twice-human-size, granodiorite statues of Sekhmet, the lion-headed goddess of war and pestilence, commissioned by Amenhotep III and placed in his memorial temple and possibly also in temples on the east bank. He had more statues made for Sekhmet than for himself and all of the other deities combined. Never had the like occurred, truly! Weighing nearly a ton each, they depict Sekhmet with a human female body sheathed in a tight-fitting gown and a lion's head often wearing a crown on a sun disk (see Figure 24). Many of the Sekhmets bear unique mentions of otherwise undocumented towns or villages that seem to have mysteriously vanished from the face of the earth, like many in Europe during the Black Death. Their names on the goddess's statues are the only records of their existence.

Most of the other evidence is very sketchy. A brief, partially hacked-out passage on the west side of the back of Luxor Temple seems to refer to difficulties and hardships encountered during construction. This may refer to a loss in workforce or an interruption between the early phase of the building (the birth room and back section) and the second phase (the great columned courtyard) but whether this resulted from an earthquake or a loss of workforce due to disease is unknown.

In addition to glazed steatite, some other luxury domestic and ritual goods declined in number. For example, bronze mirrors, vessels, vessel stands, and ceremonial axe heads remain from the reigns of Amenhotep's predecessors, but few bronze objects can be dated to his own reign, one of the rare exceptions being an exquisite bronze object in the form of a priest's cheetah skin with its spots, its collar, and the king's cartouche inlaid with gold. The reason for this decline may have been a shortfall in the supply of copper when all of the men in Cyprus's copper mines died of "plague," according to an apologetic letter from the king of Cyprus. The letter's date is not known.

The number of diseases known or suspected to have existed in the Late Bronze Age is fairly significant, and it includes polio, smallpox, malaria, and bubonic plague. Anthrax has also been a recurring problem for hoofed animals in the Nile Valley, but it seems less likely to have caused great immediate devastation in the human population because, while humans can contract it, they cannot pass it to each other. On the other hand, loss of large number of cattle leads to starvation in a population.

First on the list of human diseases, polio, the diagnosis by sight of a gatekeeper named Roma, whose stela in the Ny Carlsberg Glyptotek, Copenhagen, shows him with a withered leg. This disease has a relatively high survival rate compared to some of the others on this list, and it could fit Manetho's scenario of persons with "wasted bodies" being sent off to work in the quarries.

Smallpox has a spotty record in antiquity. It is known to have existed in China at least by the twelfth century B.C. and has been detected in Egyptian mummies of a later date but not yet identified in Amenhotep III's time. The Athenian plague, recorded by the fifth-century B.C. writer Thucydides, has been pinpointed as typhoid fever by DNA testing of human remains, although some question has been raised about this diagnosis, and the symptoms described by Thucydides, who suffered through and survived the disease himself, sound like smallpox. He wrote that the Athenian plague "first began, it is said, in the parts of Ethiopia above (upriver from) Egypt, and thence descended into Egypt and Libya, and into most of the King's country." Thucydides also noted that one of the Athenian commanders lost 1,500 out of 4,000 hoplites in 40 days to this plague.

Malaria tropica, the most severe form of malaria, was certainly a torment in ancient Egypt. The mosquito carrying the disease from human to human thrives in marshes and swamps, which were naturally a fact of Egypt's geography. Apparently it does not affect animals; however, some reports differ. Especially successful in Africa, malaria kills nearly one million people worldwide every year, mostly children and pregnant women, recalling one of the plagues in the Haggadah and the book of Exodus, a curse on the firstborn. One or two severe outbreaks affecting large numbers of pregnant women and children would have been a serious blow to Egypt's workforce, if not immediately, then within at least a decade, as fewer children went to work in the fields and the army. Adults residing in malaria-infested regions usually build up a tolerance to the disease and are able to live with it, unless their health is already compromised. *Malaria tropica* has been found in the mummies of Tutankhamen and Tiy's parents Thuya and Yuya, and the scientists involved in the study suspect it as their cause of death.

Archaeological evidence has recently been found to substantiate the presence of bubonic plague at Amarna, in particular, and infectious disease experts who specialize in the study of bubonic plague are sure that it has existed in the Nile Valley for the past 20,000 years. *Yersinia pestis*, which causes bubonic plague, according to biologists, is endemic in the Nile rat, a swamp dweller, which has built up an immunity to it. They report that during periods of heightened international trade, such as the reign of Amenhotep III, new rats arriving on ships from other lands were highly susceptible to plague and, once on land, would catch it and spread it either directly to humans or to cats, which are also quite vulnerable, and they would spread it by means of their fleas or sputum to humans, who would continue the contagion among themselves. It has been estimated that 20 infected rats could lead to the deaths of several thousands of humans.

Plague is extremely deadly, killing 90 percent of all who catch it. Tightly clustered populations are very quickly wiped out. During the European Black Death, English and European monasteries were easy targets. Temple priesthoods and workshops in ancient Egypt would have suffered similar fates. Thus the sudden cessation of commemorative scarabs and small glazed steatite statuettes of Amenhotep and Tiy at Karnak Temple may be, like the dead canary in the coal mine, a sign of unlivable conditions at Thebes. Armies were also susceptible to contagion; for example, the Hundred Years' War in Europe was repeatedly interrupted by plague. If Amenhotep's army as well as his enemies' were decimated by disease, this lauded period of peace and tranquility may have come about as much by destiny as by desire.

Ancient remains of *Yersinia pestis* are extremely fragile and difficult to identify. For example, specialists studying fourteenth-century European bodies suspected of having died of bubonic plague have found that only well-protected dental pulp harbors traces of *Yersinia pestis* when other parts of the same body, including the marrow of long bones, show no signs. Researchers who sampled the royal mummies in the Cairo Museum found no traces of bubonic plague, but they sampled long bones and not dental pulp, according to a personal communication from Dr. Zahi Hawass. Thus, their cause of death may still be unresolved.

RITUAL OFFERING SPOONS

The shortage of copper mentioned in the Cypriote king's Amarna letter may have been an impetus for an extremely beautiful new class of small objects made of boxwood, a material imported from Mitanni and Cyprus. These are exquisitely carved spoons, sometimes enhanced with ivory or other inlays. For more than a century, they have been called "cosmetic spoons" by most Egyptologists, even though only one of the hundreds known was found with a lump of perfumed resin in its bowl, and almost all of them are so wafer thin that they would snap in two if used to dispense heavy ointments. More likely, in this writer's opinion, they were used sparingly and with a delicate touch during funeral rites to offer a few drops of water to the mummy according to the "chapter of drinking water" in Theban funerary papyri, where the deceased drinks water from a tree called "the sycamore of [the goddess] Nut." Illustrations on papyri and stelae show Nut, her body superimposed on a tree trunk, extending spoons or vessels from among the branches out to the deceased.

The spoons' handle designs are often water related, such as swimming girls, ducks, girls playing music in the marshes, and even water carriers, while their overall shape is patterned after the hieroglyph *ankh* (life), with the shallow bowl forming the loop of the *ankh* and the decorated handle forming the vertical element. The combination of these two themes is appropriate for the "chapter of drinking water."

No two spoons are exactly alike, and the decoration of each one is replete with complex symbolism. The most dramatic design is of three-dimensional nude swimming girls stretched out horizontally, each one holding a goose or duck in front of her (Figure 21). The girls represent Nut in her other form as the sky goddess, an avatar of the Milky Way.

She stretched nude across the nighttime sky, swallowing the sun at dusk and giving (re-)birth to it on the horizon the following morning, an eternal story of death and resurrection. The goose was the avatar of the earth god Geb, Nut's husband, and the duck is the hieroglyph for the word "son," Nut and Geb's son being Osiris, the god of the dead, and especially of the dead king. Floating on the arms of the nude girl, the bird resembles very closely the constellation of stars now called Cygnus (the swan), which appears to float in the nighttime sky in a space between two branches of the Milky Way, just as the geese or ducks float in the arms of the swimming girls.

Prayers of late Dynasty 18, such as those on a shrine of Tutankhamen, speak to the deceased in the following words; "Oh, son of Geb . . . Nut has lifted thee up and thou hast seen the gods." In other words, the Milky Way, personified by the goddess, has raised the deceased, her husband–son, into the sky among the stars. Since Tut resurrected prayers of his grandfather that had been abandoned during the Amarna period, his invocation echoes Amenhotep III's own desire to see and be placed among the gods, a desire strong enough to resound a thousand years later in the writings of the historian Manetho quoted earlier.

Many of the spoons are decorated with scenes of *neferut* riding in skiffs in the marshes while playing instruments or gathering reeds. These are activities related to the goddess Hathor, the sacred cow, who sometimes hid in the marshes or, alternatively, according to some theologies, also stretched across the evening sky as the Milky (!) Way, serving as a vessel for the nighttime journey of the sun. Other motifs carved on the spoons or their handles refer directly or indirectly to astronomical phenomena.

In sum, the spoons, which seemed to early Egyptologists to be merely pretty, decorative objects, enhancements for the luxurious life of an effete king, are likely items of intense and deep spiritual content. The figure styles of the decorative details are almost identical to those of the best Theban tomb painters, which means they date to the first half of the reign. Many of these spoons were found at Thebes. One in the form of a goose was made and inscribed for Mutemwia, who apparently survived into the third decade (see Chapter 10).

THE BURIAL OF YUYA AND THUYA

If Yuya and Thuya died of malaria, as the scientists who tested their DNA concluded, their sudden deaths would explain why they were buried

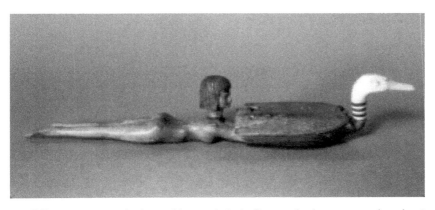

21. Offering spoon with sky goddess and duck. Boxwood, ebony, ivory, length 12 inches, E. 218. Courtesy Musée du Louvre, Réunion des Musées Nationaux.

together in a poorly planned tomb, hastily carved and undecorated. Burials of two or more individuals together in the same tomb, except in the case of reuse or usurpation, were not very common in Dynasty 18, but there are several examples in Amenhotep's reign. Located in the Valley of the Kings, an extremely rare honor for nonroyals, the in-laws' tomb was discovered by American amateur archaeologist Theodore Davis in 1905. The tomb's furnishings made it the richest find of any in Egypt before Howard Carter located King Tut's burial in 1922.

Two of the most charming objects from this tomb are chairs featuring images of Princess Sitamen, Amenhotep's oldest daughter. The smaller, child-size chair shows her as a budding adolescent 10 to 12 years old, wearing the tiara of a Royal Ornament and reaching toward her enthroned mother, Queen Tiy, with a bouquet of flowers. The larger chair shows her enthroned, around 14 or 15 years old, receiving "gold of the lands of the South" from a maiden wearing foreign dress (Figure 22). Since Sitamen was likely born during her grandfather's reign, this scene may symbolize activities of Years 12–14 of Amenhotep III's. Her maternal grandparents' death and burial, it would follow, likely took place later in the second decade, by which time Sitamen had outgrown her childhood furniture.

The royal in-laws' mummies and coffins were intact, the latter encrusted with glass and gold. Thuya's gilded mask with its fine glass inlaid eyes is one of the most beautiful in existence (see Figure 20). Thuya's coffin mentions son Anen, who attended granary official Nebnufer's promotion, and Anen's title, Second Prophet of Amun, a title he may have received after his sister became queen in Year 10. Thuya's coffin does not mention Anen's titles in relation to the king's memorial temple, which he would have by the third decade of the reign, so she probably died before Year 20.

Scientists guess that Yuya and Thuya were about 50 years of age at death, which would fit the age of their daughter, who was probably about 35 late in her husband's second decade. Yuya's mummy is one of three of the fifteen mummies studied by the Supreme Council of Antiquities that show no skeletal malformations. He stood tall and straight backed until his death. Poor Thuya, however, was very bent over with severe kyphoscoliosis and must have walked with great difficulty. In modern times, with good nutrition, this degree of malformation usually does not occur until quite a bit later in life.

PRINCE THUTMOSE'S MONUMENTS

Crown Prince Thutmose, Amenhotep's oldest son and stated heir, who appeared on a relief with his father at the Apis bull cemetery at Sakkara, seems also to have died in this period. He had attained the high positions of Director of Prophets of the North and South, High Priest of Ptah, and *sem*-priest, the latter probably having to do with his father's other memorial temple at Memphis. Therefore Thutmose must have been in his late teens or early twenties when he died, likely before Year 20. That his career centered around Memphis means that either his death was a unique event or whatever trouble brewed down south in Thebes also affected the northern capital.

Like his father, and unlike most Egyptian crown princes, Thutmose did not languish in the shadows during his life. A number of monuments are known for him, in addition to those related to the Apis cemetery (see Chapter 5). A small stone figure shows Thutmose wearing the garb of a *sem*-priest kneeling at a mortar and grinding ingredients for incense for the temple. His facial features compare with those of statuettes from early in his father's reign. His last personal depiction is a small, schist sculpture showing him lying dead on a bier. The location of his tomb is not known.

Thutmose's best-known monument is an enormous stone sarcophagus he commissioned for his beloved female cat, "Ta-mit" ("The Kitty"), whose elegant and alert profile sitting image is carved on the box's sides. Its inscriptions unite her with Osiris as if she were human. Now in the Cairo museum, Ta-mit's coffin was found at nearby Memphis,

22. Chair of Sitamen from tomb of Yuya and Thuya, gilded wood, height 40 inches. Egyptian Museum, Cairo, JE 95342. Photo by Andreas Voegelin. Courtesy Dr. Zahi Hawass and Egyptian Museum Cairo.

and it may have spiritual associations to the Memphite god Ptah via his consort Sekhmet, also a feline, although a very large and ferocious one.

For now the precipitous rise of Sekhmet's importance, the sudden appearance and disappearance of artists' workshops, and the refilling of the ranks of priests are mute testimony to a period of upheaval in Egypt so devastating it was expunged from the record, leaving generations of historians to fill the void with a period of indolence, peace, and tranquility. Obviously Amenhotep himself, Queen Tiy, and some of their children survived. Amenhotep III would eventually move south again to Thebes but as far away from Karnak as possible, building a palace on relatively clean desert soil at the edge of the western mountains miles away from the marshes and the dense population of Thebes.

BRINGING HEAVEN TO EARTH TO SEE THE LIVING GODS

Building the King's Religious Monuments at Thebes
(Reign of Amenhotep III, Years 20–29, ca. 1372–1363 B.C.)

"NEVER BEFORE HAD THE LIKE BEEN DONE"

The second half of Amenhotep III's reign was markedly different from the first. The days of mere earthly heroics were now irrelevant because the king had survived mortal combat with the forces of nature – with the very gods themselves. Triumph manifested itself in a grand building program the length of the Nile Valley, especially at its fulcrum, Thebes (Maps 4 and 5). Euphoria inspired this work, and divine justification fueled it.

Like many other pharaohs, Amenhotep III claimed that "never before had the like been done," but in this king's case, it was true. On the east bank of Thebes, Luxor Temple blossomed from a small shrine into a magnificent edifice. A mile away, grand Karnak turned away from the river and began to stretch out along a new axis running parallel to it. Neighboring Mut Temple, the royal alma mater, gained beautiful statuary. Processional ways leading to and from the temples unrolled between rows of great ram-headed sphinxes with images of the king held firmly in their forelegs' embrace. Across the river, the project at Kom el Hettan continued to unfold ever larger. In Lower and Middle Egypt, old shrines at sites such as Athribis, Bubastis, Heliopolis, and Hermopolis were augmented either architecturally or sculpturally or both. In Upper Egypt and the Sudan, sanctuaries were revised and redecorated, while new ones were conceived and built from scratch, complete with beautifully carved, enormous sculptures.

Statue after statue portrays Amenhotep III as one god or another. He came to be represented repeatedly as Amun, who was now at the apogee of his power, and as Re or Horus, as well as Montu and the rest. As he wrote on a wall at Karnak, "His every image is in accord with the forms of the Majesty of Re. His divine image is beautiful." It has become a rule of thumb in modern Egyptology that statues of gods bear the faces of the rulers who commissioned them, but it is little recognized that Amenhotep III's reign was the springboard for this phenomenon, which was infrequent in sculpture in the round before his time and commonplace thereafter.

A new approach to inscriptions backed up his ideology. Amenhotep III was not just king but king of kings (as compared with king of the gods, Amun) or even "Re of kings." Amenhotep's titles repeatedly call him "the good god" with an insistence never before seen in royal inscriptions. As French Egyptologist Susanne Bickel suggests, these signs, which seem rather subtle and uncertain to modern minds, were clear markers of deification for the ancient viewer, and she adds that the diversity of Amenhotep III's linguistic and artistic expression far surpasses anything we know of his predecessors.'

A new doctrine formed the framework for the scope and breadth of the building campaign as well. It revolved around Amenhotep III's emerging solar ideology, which emphasized all Egypt's sun gods, such as Re and Horus, the deities associated with them, and their creative powers. Amenhotep III aimed his program at re-creating the heavens on earth in the form of dazzling temples filled with divine statues so that the gods might be "seen existing upon earth." Among them was to be the central figure, Amenhotep III himself, not just the son of the sun but the very sun itself, often portrayed in ancient imagery as a golden disk with raptor's wings.

Even Egypt's vassal states in western Asia spoke of Pharaoh as a celestial falcon. Abi-Milku, who ruled Tyre during Amenhotep's last years, expressed it best: "The (Egyptian) king is the Sun who comes forth over all lands day by day according to the way of being the Sun, who gives life by his sweet breath and returns with his north wind. Who gives forth his cry like Baal and all the land is frightened by his cry," like a hawk soaring high on the thermals of a cloudless day, invisible against the blinding sun, its shriek seeming to come from the orb itself. "Seen from the mile-high bird's eye view," wrote Johns Hopkins's Betsy Bryan, "the falcon's wings would appear to stretch up and down the Nile Valley," just as Amenhotep's building program extended from wing tip to wing tip, from the Delta to Nubia, with its nexus at Thebes.

While every pharaoh was inherently a god, clearly Amenhotep III desired a superdivinity beyond anything since the Old and Middle Kingdoms. He placed himself squarely in the center of religious thought and practice like the kings of the Pyramid Age. Whereas most New Kingdom temple construction until this point had focused on the traditional gods themselves, now, in addition, a great percentage of the national resources was lavished on temples and statuary devoted to Amenhotep III himself, his divinity, and his centrality within the universe of gods. By bringing all of them to his own temples, he stood among the gods, not just as their representative on earth but as one of them, the pivotal one.

Key to the planning and implementation of our king's program, especially as it was manifested at Thebes, was Amenhotep son of Hapu, who proved himself to be a "Renaissance man" (see Figure 40). The intellectual and administrative match this wise priest made with his brilliant and ambitious pharaoh was one of the great ones in world history. Egypt's own past had only one precedent for such a phenomenon, that of Djoser, the builder of the Step Pyramid, and his architect–physician–adviser Imhotep, who, like Hapu's son, was later deified, the two being held almost as twin deities in Roman times. Some scholars might also cite Senenmut, Hatshepsut's right-hand man, confidant, and presumed lover, but Hapu's son easily trumps him.

With his early foundation in scholarship, Amenhotep son of Hapu searched through the halls of records and libraries for "strange things like that which is unintelligible," and he deciphered damaged and destroyed texts when others failed in order to guide the king. One of his statues bears the words, "I have seen the spirits of Thoth and I am supplied with their secrets . . . so that [the king] takes advice from me in all of their deeds." As Amenhotep III began to envision, plan, and eventually execute his grand scheme, he relied heavily on the son of Hapu's ability to supply answers to profound questions, work out solutions to complex theological problems, and cause the solutions to materialize in the form of monumental temples and colossal sculpture from one end of the realm to the other.

FURNISHING AND EXPANDING "PHARAOH'S TEMPLE"

Memorial temples allowed each pharaoh to lay out his sense of *ma'at* – the right order of things – as it pertained to Egypt, the exterior world, and indeed, the cosmos. For Amenhotep III, the linchpin was the original unification of Egypt some 1,600 years earlier, and Thebes's location was crucial to this concept, especially considering its role in Egypt's recovery from the Second Intermediate Period. Dedicating the temple to both northern and southern gods was symbolic of this union, and the centrality of Amenhotep III himself at the temple meant that the two lands were unified under his unique power and grace. Materially this concept was expressed in the materials used: granite and granodiorite from Elephantine and Aswan in the south, quartzite from a quarry near Heliopolis in the north, sandstone from Gebel el Silsilla near Thebes, and fine limestone very likely quarried from nearby tombs (see Chapter 11).

During Amenhotep's third decade, the memorial temple, his "mansion of millions of years," or "Pharaoh's Temple," as it was called in some contemporary inscriptions, grew in the following way. At the back of the temple was the previously mentioned Ptah-Sokar-Osiris shrine, and at its entrance stood two 30-foot-tall quartzite statues of the striding king. A processional route led north from Ptah-Sokar. This route is now camouflaged by the Dynasty 19 temple of Merneptah, which British archaeologist Sir Flinders Petrie described as being "constructed out of the materials of [the temple] of Amenophis III." Colossal statues originally made for our king remain in fragments in Merneptah's foundations. Sphinxes of both the king and Tiy as well as additional Sekhmets have been found in this area, and Benoît Lurson believes that they were part of a processional way leading to a great court with a sandstone architrave.

The avenue continued northward to the temple of grandfather Amenhotep II, which our king seems to have restored for his ancestor. Many faience kohl (eye paint) tubes bearing Amenhotep III's name were found there. In addition, according to Petrie, "probably to this time, or a little later, belong the many pieces of limestone with trial sculptures of some students, who seem to have used the temple as a school." Beyond that, the route aimed toward Hatshepsut's memorial temple at Deir el Bahri and, beyond that, to the entrance to the Valley of the Kings.

Two seated statues of the king in black granodiorite now in the British Museum come from a spot near Ptah-Sokar, and examples now in the Metropolitan Museum (Figure 23) were usurped by Merneptah and perhaps relocated by him to Luxor Temple where they were found. Ramesses II also stole his share, in some cases recarving the face in his image. These are some of the dozens of similars from half life-size to three times life-size that depict the king wearing his nemes headdress, short kilt with bull tail, thick beard, broad collar, and no sandals, while he sits enthroned on a block with a short back pillar. The striped nemes headdress, made famous by the blue and gold version on the funerary mask of Tutankhamen, is the headgear most commonly worn by Amenhotep III on his sculpture in the round, despite the array of official crowns at his disposal. Other than that the stripes resembled solar rays, the reason for this may have been purely practical; that is, the pyramidal shape of the nemes and its pendant tail in the back supported the statue's neck, making it less likely to snap during manufacture, transport, or even later, if it happened to topple over.

At right angles to the preceding avenue and southeast of the Ptah-Sokar building, toward the middle of the tract stretching toward the Nile, was a hypostyle hall – a forest of columns – followed to the east by a large (100 yards square) peristyle sun court with 166 stone columns arranged in rows around its perimeter, a new feature in Egyptian architectural vocabulary but reminiscent of Old Kingdom models, particularly the small columned courts in some Old Kingdom pyramid temples. Amenhotep son of Hapu wrote, "I have not merely copied what was done before," as though he copied, but not exactly, and then finished his statement by implying that what he did was more and larger. A similar structure would appear across the river at Luxor.

The sun court was divided into two halves, north and south, along its axis, and its intercolumnar spaces were filled with exquisitely carved, monumental statues of both the king and the gods, the ones on the northern side in brown quartzite from Lower Egypt and the southern ones in red granite from Aswan, representing Upper Egypt. Around eight yards tall, they stood with feet pressed together and arms crossed over the chest, holding the shepherd's crook and flail of divine kingship (compare Figure 50).

The starched pose of these statues is usually called "Osiride," after the god of the dead, whose presence is natural in a funerary temple. The figures do not wear Osiris's usual long cloak but an elaborate kilt with a highly decorated belt and buckle and a bull's tail visible between the king's bare legs. Archaeologist Hourig Sourouzian interpreted this image of the king as one of Amenhotep III's innovations in pharaonic imagery, not funerary but celebratory, in fact, jubilant. Perhaps it was a merger of Osiris in his resurrection mode with the aspect of the king as a mighty and fertile bull ready to spread his seed far and wide.

Behind the rows of columns, against the walls of the peristyle, were placed hundreds of monumental granodiorite Sekhmet statues

23. Two statues of Amenhotep III usurped by Merneptah, granodiorite, (left) height 100 inches, (right) height 89.5 inches. Metropolitan Museum of Art, 22.5.1, 22.5.2. Photo: APK.

(see Figure 24). Here the moody goddess was put into a totally controlled, rigid environment where she could not create chaos. *Ma'at* prevailed. It was suggested some decades ago that there were originally 730 Sekhmets: one for each day of the year and one for each night. In the 2005–2006 season alone, Sourouzian's team unearthed 41 more, bringing to 62 the number of new ones found in just the first several seasons of excavation. Who knows where the final count might end!

There were monumental statues of other divine creatures as well: a lion–crocodile sphinx, jackals, serpents, scarab beetles, and even a huge white alabaster hippopotamus. Hippos' viciousness is legendary, and they had a reputation for brutally slaying sailors who came too close, including one of Egypt's earliest rulers. The bane of agriculture, they commonly rose out of the depths of the Nile at night to forage

24. Sekhmet statues formerly in the Mut Temple precincts, Karnak. Photo courtesy John Ross.

in the fields, each one able to eat more than 85 pounds of vegetation before morning. Representing these beasts in the great temple helped to appease them, thereby giving Pharaoh control over them both in the real world and in the afterlife. Certain of these creatures, like the lion–crocodile sphinx, had no purpose in mythology, except as part of the ancient Egyptian sky map, and Betsy Bryan suggests that Amenhotep III organized all the faunal statuary, along with the Sekhmets, into maps of the heavens, truly bringing the heavens to earth and placing the king among the stars as he passed through the temple during his festivals (see Chapter 13).

THE MEMNON COLOSSI

East of Kom el Hettan's peristyle were three pylons arranged about 110 yards apart. As on the east bank at Karnak, that the pylons were built sequentially from west to east – a new one for each jubilee according to Sourouzian – may be evidence that the temple was creeping forward in an attempt to keep up with a shrinking Nile during a period of low inundations.

The pylons' doorways were flanked by truly colossal portraits of the king enthroned and surrounded by relatively diminutive (about

25. View of Colossi of Memnon from a distance of one-fifth mile. Photo: APK/JSB.

one-third scale) figures of royal women. Each of these grand monuments is more than five storeys tall and estimated to weigh 700 tons. There had been no statuary on this scale since Middle Kingdom pharaoh Amenemhet III set up two great portraits of himself overlooking the lake in the Faiyum, the birthplace and early home of Amenhotep III. Placing colossal statuary in front of the temple gates, according to Susanne Bickel, made them accessible to the great unwashed public, allowing even the lowliest humans to interact spiritually with the king and the gods, who otherwise remained hidden away from all but the royals and elite. Anyone could address the statues, pray to them, and beg assistance from them, even from a great distance. This was consistent with Amenhotep III's practices in other spheres: his enlargement of festivals and his nationwide building program in general, which engaged such a broad populace in the physical construction, decoration, and maintenance of new temples and their priesthoods.

The pair of gigantic statues flanking the first pylon closest to the river are known today as the Colossi of Memnon (Figures 25 and 26). The Greeks named them "Memnon" after the mythical king of Ethiopia and son of the goddess of the Dawn, who came to the aid of Troy in its war with Greece but was slain by Achilles. The entire area behind the statues became known as the "Memnonium." The Colossi were considered deities in their own right in antiquity, and they had their own cults. In 27 B.C., an earthquake created fissures in the northern one. Every morning at daybreak, it emitted a moaning or groaning sound as the night's accumulation of moisture began to evaporate and the rock began to heat up and readjust along the cracks. Roman emperors and other visitors came to hear the statue's voice, believing it had oracular powers, but Emperor Septimius Severus, in A.D. 199, patched the cracks, and the Memnon has remained silent ever since.

Amenhotep III wrote that the temple had a lake that lay in front of the Memnons and filled with the annual inundation. This lake was likely a water retention reservoir that prevented the temple from flooding during high inundations, saved water during droughts, and served as an artificial harbor connected by a canal to the river. Some scholars suggest that Amenhotep purposely built his temple in the floodplain so that the Nile would wash through it annually, as shown in nineteenth- and early-twentieth-century photographs. Sourouzian feels, however, that he did not plan for the site to flood. Both the presence of the lake and the fact that the temple's walls were made of mud brick (faced in stone) tend to substantiate her position.

In 2008, at the second and third pylons of the memorial temple, Sourouzian and her team began exhuming previously unknown colossi that had apparently jumped from their spots, fallen, and shattered during ancient earthquakes. While the Memnon Colossi, exposed to the air and wind-blown sand for millennia, are now terribly weathered, the recently unearthed colossi from the second pylon retain areas of such an incredibly fine polish that they feel like glass to the touch, despite brown quartzite's coarse and pebbly appearance. This is testimony to the painstaking workmanship demanded by Amenhotep III and produced by his sculptors and workshops. In the sunlight, the fine finish of the golden-brown skin areas glows brilliantly. The surfaces of beard and crown were left a bit rough, perhaps to hold gesso and paint or overlays of precious metal. As on the Memnon Colossi a remarkably preserved, 12-foot-tall, standing image of Queen Tiy is attached to the leg below the knee of one of the seated colossi.

Mutemwia seems to be one of the other females attached to the Colossi, suggesting that she was still alive in the years leading up to the First Jubilee, and indeed, a jar label from her was found at Amenhotep's nearby palace, which was also constructed in this third decade and is described later (see Chapter 11). A life-size seated, headless portrait of her in granodiorite, probably originally meant for Kom el Hettan but last

26. View of Kom el Hettan and Colossi of Memnon from summit of nobles' cemetery. Photo: APK/JSB.

seen openly at the Ramesseum in the 1980s, is carved in a conservative style, suggesting a date no later than the third decade of the reign.

Among the individuals who may have worked here at Kom el Hettan was Minemheb, "army scribe" and "chief of works in the jubilee temple," known from his beautiful granodiorite statue now in the Cleveland Museum of Art. He claimed Amun of Thebes as his city god, and his name, "Min Is in His Festival," may be a reflection of Min's rise in importance at Thebes during this reign, or it may indicate that this official was from Akhmim, Min's cult center. Another inscription on his statue is dedicated to Re-Harakhte of Heliopolis in the north. The statue shows Minemheb holding an altar, on which is perched a baboon sacred to Thoth of "Hesret" (a cemetery in Middle Egypt at Hermopolis). Minemheb clearly wanted to cover all the geographic and divine possibilities, but his mention of "the jubilee temple" with no modifier or other designation most likely means the great one here at Thebes.

THE QUARRIES AND THE SCULPTORS

Black granodiorite, finely speckled charcoal gray stone, one of the hardest nonprecious stones known, came from Aswan at the edge of Nubia. Crews worked at several sites in this area, one being very close to the modern-day Kalabsha Hotel. Not far from this site is a rock stela honoring a father and son who managed the production at Aswan. The elder was named "Men," "chief of sculptors in the very great monuments of the king." His son Bak followed into service working for Amenhotep IV, becoming chief sculptor and claiming the king himself as his instructor. A brown quartzite stela depicting Bak and his wife was discovered at Amarna.

According to geologists, the quarrymen's and sculptors' careful workmanship helped the statuary to resist millennia of erosion. The process started with wedges driven into holes in the rock to force the blocks to fracture from the mother vein. Dolerite and granite hammers were used to chip away slowly and carefully at the surface of the block without damaging its interior structure. The outer layer of weathered stone was sliced away much like a cucumber's outer rind, then the image was sculpted to about 90 percent of its final appearance, lightening the monument for transport. Any superficial damage that might occur would be fixed later at the final location, where delicate lines, details, and polishing were completed after the statue was set up.

Ancient texts state that the glinting brown quartzite (called "wondrous" in ancient Egyptian) used for the Memnon Colossi was quarried at "Red Mountain," normally identified as a quarry southeast of modern-day Cairo, today called "Gebel Ahmar," the same name in Arabic. Petrographic and geochemical analyses by scientists have shown that the main bodies of the Memnons did indeed come from that site, while Septimius Severus's Roman repair patches, perhaps opportunistically salvaged from broken pieces of nearby statuary like the colossi at the other pylons, came from brown quartzite quarries down south near Aswan. This information recalls that Bak's father, Men, was also "overseer of works in the Red Mountain," where he claimed to have managed the production of a colossus for Amenhotep III. In this case, "Red Mountain" probably refers not to Gebel Ahmar, near Heliopolis, but to a second site with the same name across the river from Aswan at the edge of the western desert. Perhaps one or more of the other colossi came from there.

"PHARAOH'S TEMPLE" AT FESTIVAL TIME

"Pharaoh's Temple," Amenhotep's "mansion of millions of years," and other royal temples on the west bank were venues for a colorful, joyful celebration called the "Beautiful Festival of the Valley." In honor of this holiday, the king gave a very specific appellation to his temple: "Receiving-Amun, Extolling-His-Beauty." He wrote that he made it as "the resting place of the Lord of the Gods when he celebrates the Valley Festival at Amun's western river-procession to see the Gods of the West." This feast may have been the only time that the temple fully belonged to Amun.

The new moon in the second month of summer (*shemu*) signaled the beginning of this annual event, the Theban version of a popular Hathor festival celebrated throughout Egypt from at least the Old Kingdom. Here, however, the major role was played by Amun-Re. During the festival performance, his Karnak temple cult statue was carried in its portable bark shrine on poles on the shoulders of files of priests, then on his splendidly decorated, gilded barge to the west bank of the Nile. As was true during all festivals, those who lined the processional routes never saw the god himself because Amun was the "Hidden One," but they watched every jiggle and torque of his shrine on the priests' swaying shoulders in the hope that some magical movement might indicate an answer to fervent prayers.

During our king's reign, the festival's west bank trek may have started and ended at Kom el Hettan, making use of its relative proximity to the river and its artificial harbor. Amun's cult statue was off-loaded there and then carried westward through Kom el Hettan, turning northward via the processional way from Ptah-Sokar and along the desert's edge to Deir el Bahri, the site of Hatshepsut's dramatic funerary temple and a shrine of the bovine goddess Hathor, who was associated at Thebes with the western mountains and was a protector of the cemeteries nestled into the ridges and valleys there. For the rest of the festival period, her chapel in the spectacular limestone bay of the sacred mountain at Deir el Bahri was Amun's home base, from which he paid visits to the various royal temples of the west bank.

The citizenry of ancient Luxor participated by traveling to the west bank and visiting family tombs, where they prayed and partied with the spirits of the dead. It was a sort of annual reunion, according to University of Chicago's Lanny Bell, during which the ancestors were reintegrated into the family and bonds between the living and dead were strengthened. The festival and its rituals, he wrote, helped to confirm the priority of the family over the individual within Egypt's social and political organization. Those who could afford it wore the usual festive garb of fine white linen garments and perfumed ointment cones atop their heads. In addition, especially for this event, they donned beautiful *wah* collars, tiered necklaces composed of petals of fresh flowers so fragrant their perfume was thought to wake the dead. Thus the *wah* symbolized regeneration and was distributed to all participants, both living and deceased.

Camping at their family tombs, the residents of Thebes prepared for encountering the returning spirits by feasting and drinking heavily throughout an all-night vigil, until a huge sacrificial offering was torched and consumed entirely by flames. Priests poured heavy, myrrh-scented oil over the pyre so that thick, sweet-smelling smoke rose skyward, filling the valley with its aroma and establishing a link between heaven and earth. Hypnotic rhythms of music and dance heightened the effect and summoned the ancestors' spirits, allowing the ecstatic (read inebriated) participants to communicate with them, according to Bell.

While the god's cult image rested overnight in the holy grotto of Deir el Bahri, elaborate bouquets worked in the shape of the sign of life, *ankh*, were stacked around it to receive its regenerative power. At dawn, a lighted torch was extinguished in a bowl of cow's milk (itself a symbol of rebirth) to signify the successful return of the dead to Hathor, who resided inside the sacred mountain. Then the large *ankh* bouquets, pungent with Amun-Re's might, were purchased from priests and distributed to the dead in the offering chapels of their Theban tombs. The presentation of the bouquets and other offerings was typically introduced by the toast, "To your *ka!*" At the end of the festival, the god returned inside his portable bark on his great gilded barge to the Holy of Holies at Karnak.

Courtiers' tomb sites provided their owners with a grandstand view of the events (see Figure 26). From there they could make out the royal and divine barges and a flotilla of privately owned crafts as they crossed the river. Their eyes could catch sight of the scores, if not hundreds, of priests, dancers, and acrobats, and their ears could take in the rising strains from specially trained choruses of women and musicians. The visual feast of processions and bonfires, the troops of chanting priests and ululating women, the symphony of wind instruments and beaten drums, all suffused with the aromas of flowers and burnt offerings wafting up the hillside, made these tombs prime real estate during the Valley Festival.

Queen Tiy's brother, Second Priest of Amun Anen, owned a tomb at the top of the hill with a panoramic view of both the landscape below and the sky above. At night the skies were luminous. As Gustave Flaubert wrote in 1850 about Theban nights, "the air is warm, the sky streams with stars; tonight they take the form of semi-circles, like half-necklaces of diamonds with here and there a few stones missing. What wretched poverty of language! To compare stars to diamonds!"

Anen's specialty was astronomy because he knew "the procession of the sky" and was "chief of sightings in the great house (i.e., the palace)." His greatest surviving monument, now in Turin, shows him wearing a garment virtually covered in stars. One of the most elegant and beautiful private portraits of its day, this granodiorite figure is sculpted as if wearing a priestly cheetah skin, the cat's spots covered over with large, five-pointed stars probably sewn on in gold. A cheetah face looking much like the gilded and jeweled one from Tutankhamen's tomb hangs near his waist. Another of Anen's titles, priest in the "Southern Heliopolis," means that he worked at Amenhotep III's memorial temple, and he was likely involved in organizing Bryan's star map of statuary as well as being one of the major officiants at the annual Valley Festival.

The view from his tomb would have been enjoyed by his wife, who is portrayed sitting next to him on a small limestone pair statue likely made before he became so important at Thebes. Amenhotep III and Queen Tiy, Anen's sister, are represented inside the tomb, but the relationship is not mentioned there. The only record of their kinship is the previously mentioned inscription on proud mother Thuya's coffin.

THE TEMPLES OF THE EAST BANK

Amenhotep III and his officials memorialized his east bank constructions in texts and imagery, but he and his men failed to explain anywhere, so far as we now know – perhaps it was too obvious – why he altered the entire gestalt of the east bank of Thebes, virtually turning Karnak Temple on its ear by enhancing and emphasizing the perpendicular axis started by Hatshepsut. At the other end of town, he continued to advance Luxor Temple northward toward Karnak and created sphinx-lined avenues as links. To quote Elizabeth Blyth, "despite their having been usurped, reworked and repositioned many times by later kings, these paved alleyways, linking the various temples of Karnak with one another and with Luxor temple, were to remain very much as he envisioned them." By the end of his reign, the east bank, like the west, was thematically unified, and the entire region was a religious metroplex far beyond the scope of any other on earth.

The starting point of this new northeast–southwest orientation at Karnak was the ornate Kha-em-maat temple, which seems to have had some continuous work during our king's reign. Behind it and leaning up against it is a small temple to the goddess Ma'at, which, in its present form, is a later construct; however, reliefs and stelae of Amenhotep III claim his original ownership of the site.

The procession south toward Luxor passes the Third Pylon with its great nautical panorama, which was revised, in this author's opinion, during the years leading up to Amenhotep III's jubilee. This involved erasing small images of himself carved at the time of construction in normal scale vis-à-vis the ships (Figures 14 and 15). These diminutive figures wear blue crowns with the proportions and crown shape used early in his reign and not later. The erased figures, now visible as ghosts, were at the time of revision covered with plaster and paint (with an image of Tiy, perhaps?), which has worn away over the millennia.

Leading up to his jubilee, in keeping with his recently acquired penchant for the colossal, he added figures of superhuman size on either side of the barge. The back lines of these new figures are formed in exquisite, shallow, S-shaped curves. These are hallmarks of the art in his later years and cannot be found earlier, in the Amarna period, or later. His kilt is held by a sharply angled waistband, quite high in the back. This same style of waistband appears on other late images of him like the red quartzite statue found in the Luxor cachette (see Figure 45). The high waistband continues to expand higher in the next reign, and of course, the abdominal shape changes dramatically. The uraei with sun disks on the kilts of these new figures were shown by Ray Johnson to have been added to the king's costume leading up to the jubilee. The depth of carving of these later images suggests they were inlaid with colored stone.

Some other details, such as an offering table and a ribbon-bedecked fan, were added to the scene in a hasty, scratchy, and superficial bit of carving perhaps at the end of Dynasty 18, perhaps by Tutankhamen or by Horemheb, and they make a complete art historical analysis, including the one given here, open to reassessment as time and further study go on. French archaeologists and other Egyptologists continue to study this monument, and a great deal of ink will continue to spill in the search for a final judgment on the Third Pylon's construction and decoration.

Images of the Third Pylon's finished grandeur at its completion are preserved in ancient tomb and temple depictions of only slightly later date. The great gateway was fronted by flagstaffs so tall they rose above the pylon's roof, their pennants flapping in the breeze. Each pole was the trunk of a gigantic cedar tree, mottled with knots where hundreds of branches had been sawn off. On either side of the doorjambs, carved panels illustrated the king offering to Amun or to Min. At their feet were guardian sphinxes. The jambs themselves were topped off by a row of uraei wearing sun disks. Perfectly shaped trees were planted in rows within sunken pots in front, and clumps of papyrus and shady sycamore trees flanked a small harbor with a canal leading to the river.

THE GRANARY

On the southern side of Karnak, continuing the northeast–southwest path in the direction of Luxor, the modern numbering of pylons proceeds from inside out, starting with the Thutmoside Seventh, followed by Hatshepsut's Eighth, Horemheb's Ninth, and Amenhotep III's Tenth. During our king's reign, there was a fairly large blank space between what are now the Eighth and Tenth, because the Ninth did not yet exist.

Geoarchaeologists feel that a branch of the river reached into this area, and a quay has been found somewhat to the west. It is not beyond reason that this waterway operated as a service entrance to Karnak Temple, in particular, to the priests' villages and to a large granary for storing mostly emmer wheat and barley – a combination of the produce of Amun's estates and income from taxes. Both wheat and barley were made into bread, and the barley into beer, to the benefit of daily offerings as well as for the upkeep of the priests, their families, the flocks kept inside the temple walls, and beyond that, for the public at festival times.

Amenhotep III either built or expanded Karnak's granary late in the third decade of the reign. It is depicted prominently in the tombs of Anen and Scribe and Counter of the Grain Khnummose, who are thought to have died before Year 30 because neither of them sent a gift to the king for his jubilee or mentioned it in their tombs. When the granary was finished, an important event was held – a dedication or a harvest festival, presided over by the king himself.

Overseer of Fields of Amun Amenemhet Surer, whose later tomb also contains scenes of Amenhotep III offering inside the granary, took an official stake in reckoning the amounts of grain to be paid in taxes there. Surer's portrait sculptures depict him holding coils of measuring cord, and 13 of them, topped off with sculpted heads of rams sacred to Amun, are pictured in his tomb. Since fields changed in size and shape each year due to the Inundation, the annual measurement was crucial to determining the amount of offerings and taxes to be expected from each farmer and landowner. Taxpayers who came up short in their payments were beaten.

The granary was destroyed by Akhenaten, rebuilt by Tutankhamen, and then razed by Horemheb at the end of the dynasty. He used the rubble from it to fill and stabilize the walls of his Second Pylon, along with some blocks from Akhenaten's Gem-pa-Aten temple (dedicated to the sun disk as god), which stretched out behind the granary and behind the Amun-Re temple.

Fifty-five painted sandstone blocks belonging to the granary had been identified by 2006, including fragments of its three gateways. Many of these relief carvings show the king wearing multiple sun disk decorations, which he began to affect in the third decade of his reign. Among the granary blocks are the only mentions of Queen Tiy at Karnak, and this argues for locating the granary within view of the temple of Amun's consort, the goddess Mut. Additional blocks from the Second Pylon have recently been identified as belonging to another building that must have stood near the granary – a workshop for preparing and consecrating temple offerings. Its long and complicated name was "The Workshop of Nebmaatra – Image of Re – 'Amun Is Rich in Provisions.'"

The Tenth Pylon, the southernmost extent of Amun-Re's temple, was begun by Amenhotep III but left unfinished. It was originally meant to have two nearly 70-foot-tall, brown quartzite colossi flanking the door, but only one was managed until the end of Dynasty 18, when Horemheb finished the structure and added the second colossus. Only the base and one foot are left of the first.

Amenhotep son of Hapu proudly organized transport of one colossus. He wrote on his limestone block statue,

> My Lord placed me as overseer of every work and I have made the name of the King enduring forever. I have not merely copied what was done formerly. I have created for him a mountain of gritstone (brown quartzite), for he is indeed the heir of Atum. I have acted according as my heart desires, dedicating his likeness in this his great temple, with every costly and hard stone like the sky. But there is none who can do it since the time that his Two Lands were founded. I have undertaken a work for his statues, great in width, and taller than his pillar. Its beauty has eclipsed the pylon, and its length is 40 cubits (around 67 feet) from the august mountain of gritstone in the presence of Re and Atum. I constructed

"Eight"-boats that may take it southward. My testimony is among you, and those who shall come after us. The whole army is all together under my oversight, they being joyful and rejoicing, shouting and applauding the Good God. They moored at Thebes in joy and the monuments are resting in their place for eternity.

None of the huge stone-laden barges, called "Eight"-boats by Amenhotep son of Hapu, survives, and so we can only judge from two-dimensional images of the transport of Hatshepsut's obelisks from the Aswan quarry to Thebes that they were special crafts with multiple decks and a system of hogging trusses giving tension reinforcement. They seem not to have had masts or space for oars, so they must have been towed and guided by other vessels. How they were loaded and unloaded can only be guessed, but possibly the ancient channel of the Nile, which once came nearby the Tenth Pylon, was involved. This was probably the son of Hapu's last major works project, since in Year 30, he moved on to another, more sedentary job. It was here at the Tenth Pylon that Amenhotep son of Hapu's most famous portrait statues were found (see Figure 40).

MUT TEMPLE

This completely female sanctuary, harboring the royal alma mater, stands a few steps from Karnak's Tenth Pylon and backs up onto a promontory surrounded by an oxbow lake, an artifact of the ancient eastern branch of the Nile. Mut's avatar was the white vulture, protectress of kings, and from the bird's-eye view, the temple and its lake look for all the world like the body of a vulture framed by its half-spread wings as if protecting her nestlings, an image repeatedly used in Egyptian art of the time, richly produced as a gold and jeweled pectoral for Tutankhamen, and recalling Mutemwia's rebus statue (Figure 3). The oxbow lake was also the shape of the arching Milky Way, personified by other mother goddesses, especially Nut and Hathor, whose bodies gave the sun safe passage through the night. Perhaps being too obvious to mention, these symbols in Mut's landscape design are not recorded in ancient writings.

Quays along the bank show that the lake was actually sailed on, and a drawing in a later tomb depicts a vessel as it departs the western end of the lake and docks at the eastern end, as if mimicking the sun's nighttime subterranean journey. Priests burn offerings and incense, while musicians beat their tambourines. A flock of animals gambols on the bank. A woman and children race hand in hand through a pylon flanked by colossal seated statues of a queen. In front of the temple is a row of potted trees, and in front of that a processional way flanked with recumbent rams wearing sun disks. These connect Mut with Karnak Temple, where a figure of Amun-Re resides enthroned within his sanctuary behind a statue of Min.

During Hatshepsut's reign, a Festival of Drunkenness, a religiously sanctioned orgy, was held at Mut Temple during the first month of the New Year after Inundation. The aim was to drink until falling-down, vomiting drunk and to engage in limitless sex. Barley beer was the favored beverage, Karnak's granary being conveniently close. The religious genesis for this madness was the ancient story of leonine Sekhmet, who tried to kill all of humanity but was tricked by father Re into slaking her bloodthirst with red-tinged beer, which put her to sleep. She arose the next morning in a much better mood as bovine Hathor, who also wore a sun disk on her head. It is not clear if this festival was observed during Amenhotep III's reign, but certainly its spawn carried on centuries later because Herodotus wrote that similar events drew 700,000 people, with inebriated women exposing themselves to onlookers. This is not to say that drunkenness, though officially and culturally frowned on in daily life, was unique to the Mut Temple festival because in actual fact, it was associated with many religious celebrations, including the Opet and the Valley festivals.

Our king added a prodigious amount of statuary to Mut Temple. Best known in modern times is the field of Sekhmet statues (Figure 24), which have recently been cleared away, but they do not appear in the ancient drawing of the temple. According to Brooklyn Museum's Richard Fazzini, who excavates the precinct around the temple, the Sekhmets may have been brought in later from Kom el Hettan or from another site across the river.

Two monumental granite sphinxes with lion bodies and Amenhotep's beneficently smiling face were found here in modern times but are also absent from the drawing. In 1820, the statues were removed to the quay of the Neva River in front of the National Academy of the Arts in St. Petersburg, Russia, where they stand guard today (Figure 27). Hieroglyphs had not yet been deciphered when the sphinxes were brought there, and so their new owners were blissfully unaware of the inscribed warning that Amenhotep III "strikes fear in every foreign land . . . crushes the tribesmen and seizes their land." A colossal red

27. Amenhotep III sphinx from Karnak on the quay of the Neva River, St. Petersburg, Russia. Photo: APK.

granite striding image of the king usurped by Ramesses II lies today in the Mut's precinct, and pieces of another, the head of which is now in the British Museum, were found nearby.

The two colossal queen statues shown in front of the pylon in the drawing have not yet been found, and so their date is not known, but considering our king's penchant for the colossal, it would not be surprising if they represented Tiy. A beautiful lifesize granodiorite statue wearing a crown decorated for the *heb-sed* and probably representing Tiy, or perhaps her daughter Sitamen, was unearthed at Mut Temple by Bryan's Johns Hopkins University expedition. The back pillar was reinscribed for a queen of Dynasty 21.

West of the Tenth Pylon and Mut Temple, backing up to the Amun-Re temple, stands Karnak's nearly intact shrine to the moon god Khonsu, son of Amun and Mut. This structure's earlier incarnation, perhaps closer to the Tenth Pylon, may have been founded by our king, but the present one (possibly resituated westward on account of the Nile) was built by Ramesside kings, and not a trace of Amenhotep III's original work can be seen, except for a few inscribed blocks raised from the foundations. An avenue of sphinxes belonging to Amenhotep III, and likely resituated there with the temple, leads from its south-facing pylon toward Luxor or, more specifically, toward a quay in that direction.

LUXOR

Karnak's Tenth Pylon was united with Luxor Temple into one cosmological scheme by a processional avenue founded by Amenhotep III. At the same time, the king "widened, greatly magnified and made [Luxor Temple] surpassing in its beauty. Its walls were of electrum, its floors were of silver, and all its doors wrought with shining stone. . . . Its pylons drew near to heaven and the flagstaffs up to the stars."

Some dramatic finds of exquisite more-or-less lifesize statuary have been made at Luxor temple in modern times. In 1989, an accidental discovery unearthed an entire cache of monumental royal and divine sculptures toward the western side of Luxor's sun court, which included statues commissioned under Amenhotep III (see Chapters 13 and 17, Figures 38 and 45). Sourouzian has discovered even more of Amenhotep III's statuary out in the open at Luxor, but hiding behind inscriptions for Ramesses II, just as the Metropolitan Museum's portraits of Amenhotep III from this same temple were re-inscribed for Merneptah (Figure 23).

Some of these sculptures surely filled Amenhotep III's famous peristyle court at Luxor Temple, arguably the most pleasing architectural space in all Egypt (Figure 28). Framed by rows of beautifully proportioned columns in the shape of bundled papyri, this plaza is completely open to the sky. Admired by twenty-first-century eyes for its spare elegance, Luxor's sun court, in its creator's day, must have been stocked cheek by jowl with statuary, in keeping with Amenhotep III's rococo taste, just like its mirror image at the memorial temple on the west bank. Very likely, some of the hundreds of Sekhmet statues known from his reign were posed against the back walls at Luxor, as they were in the memorial

28. Amenhotep III's temple at Luxor, sun court. Photo courtesy John Ross.

temple's peristyle court. In line with Bryan's idea of sky maps at Kom el Hettan, 365 Sekhmets at Luxor might have worked as daytime figures, while ones on the west bank served the night. Perhaps Luxor's are the ones that ended up at the other end of the processional way at Mut Temple.

In addition to the Sekhmets, there may have been Osiride-type statues of Amenhotep III similar to those in the peristyle of the memorial temple. Monumental sandstone statues found in Amenhotep IV's Gempa-Aten temple at Karnak are actually originals of Amenhotep III recut by Amenhotep IV in the earliest years of his reign. One of the best preserved, now in the Cairo museum (see Figure 50), retains in places the subtly detailed carving of Amenhotep III's sculptors beneath and beside the crude, rough-shod reworkings of his son. In their original condition, they represented the king wearing the striped nemes head cloth, the double crown, a finely pleated kilt, and an ornate apron. His arms were crossed over his chest, the crook and flail held in his hands, and his feet were together in the stance of Osiris, almost exactly like the Osiride statues directly across the river at the memorial temple (see Chapter 18).

There are at least 36 spaces for intercolumnar statues in Luxor's sun court, and remains of about 30 of these sandstone portraits are known.

They appear to have fallen and been damaged, and were then gathered up and reconstituted, some of the recarving extending past the breaks. None are complete today, and most are known only as heads. The largest number survive in Egyptian museums, but a few are elsewhere, for example, in Copenhagen and Paris.

The image of Osiris is appropriate for Luxor Temple. Osiris's mother, Ipet, had a cult center at Thebes from the middle of Dynasty 18. Luxor Temple is the home of her homonym and bore the name "Ipet-resyt," translated as "the Southern harem." Furthermore, in the annual Opet Festival, the king's *ka* was thought to die and then come back to life at this site, making Osiris's presence appropriate.

As University of Arizona's Richard Wilkinson has noted,

> by New Kingdom times [Osiris's] stature as an independent god was considerable, as is seen in the titles which were applied to him such as 'lord of the universe.'... Osiris' position became, in fact, comparable to that of the sun god himself. He came to be regarded not only as the counterpart of Re in the netherworld, but also in some cases as the sun god's own body – so that Osiris and Re came to be considered as representing the body and soul, respectively, of a single great god. The solar cycle was thus imagined as the *ba* (soul) of Re descending into the underworld to unite with Osiris as his own corpse.

In the back of Luxor Temple, there is a long hall on the traditional east–west line (perpendicular to the temple's main axis) that has been interpreted as connecting the king with the voyage of the sun god along the traditional east–west line. What may be more important is that this line points over the Nile, across the memorial temple, over the western mountain ridge, and across the bend in the Nile north of Thebes directly to the burial place of Osiris at Abydos, reinforcing the concept of the unification of Osiris and Re (Map 3).

The ancient Egyptians, especially Amenhotep III, as evidenced in the British Museum portrait of his mother on her sailing bark (Figure 3), loved interlocking rebuses and layers of meaning in their iconography. It would certainly not have been beyond his or Amenhotep son of Hapu's imagination to create a rebus or combination of them in the temple's ground plan. From the bird's-eye view, the three sides of double columns surrounding Luxor's sun court appear to form the outstretched arms of the hieroglyph *ka*, appropriate for a temple where the rebirth of the royal *ka* was celebrated.

Yet another image can be conjured up if one thinks of the long back temple as the outstretched figure of the sky goddess Nut with the column rows of the solar court (the *ka*) stretching out like her arms to gather in the sun as it travels toward her on its path from Medamud to Armant. Inscriptions on the temple walls repeatedly refer to Luxor as a resting place for the Lord of the Gods and compare it to "his horizon in the sky." Amenhotep III's repeated use of the feathered dress of the solar god Horus in Luxor Temple reliefs and on his red quartzite statue found here (see Figure 45, side view) coincides with this idea.

This iconography, in which Luxor Temple acts as the divine receptacle for the setting sun, would tie Luxor Temple directionally and symbolically with Karnak via the processional way and Karnak's new axis through the Kha-em-maat temple in north Karnak to Medamud, the site sacred to Nut's husband, the earth god Geb, and the site of the rising sun. Furthermore, it would emphasize the distinctively feminine ancient name of Luxor Temple.

The iconography of the relief sculpture on the walls of Luxor Temple is even more complex than the three-dimensional design and imagery. Once again, we turn to Lanny Bell, former director of the Oriental Institute's Chicago House, which was responsible for recording all the relief decoration on Luxor Temple. He sees Luxor Temple as

> two temples in one, serving two different manifestations of the god. The small Opet temple proper [the earliest part in the back] was the dwelling place for the mysterious [god] Amenemopet of Luxor, and the much larger Opet-festival Annex – all of Luxor Temple north of the Hidden Sanctuary – was, in essence, an elaborate bark shrine for accommodating Amun-Re of Karnak and his full entourage during his annual visit to Luxor. The two temples at Luxor and the two forms of Amun were physically united once a year during the Opet festival, when the annual ritual rebirth of the royal *ka*, the immortal creative spirit of divine kingship, miraculously restored the worlds of the gods and of humankind.

The temple's statuary and architecture reinforce these concepts.

The most mysterious of Amenhotep III's Theban buildings was the *maru* (viewing place), which he described on one of his stelae. The *maru* included a temple and gardens "facing," "in front of," "next to," or "opposite" Luxor Temple, depending on how one interprets the inscription. It was "a place of recreation" for Amun-Re "at his beautiful festival" and "a place for receiving the revenue of every foreign country, the presentation of much tribute before [Amun] from out of the dues of all lands."

Foreign tribute is mentioned repeatedly in inscriptions at Luxor Temple. For example, "the Syrians who do not know Egypt come bearing their tribute on their backs in order to see the monument of the Lord of the Two Lands, Nebmare." Although the monument in question is undoubtedly the memorial temple, the most remarkable edifice of its day, it would not have been inappropriate for the offerings to be brought to the east bank and piled up where the citizenry could see them. Therefore a *maru* may have faced the entrance to Luxor Temple, which, in Amenhotep III's day, was nearly 145 yards from where it is today, on the same ground where Ramesses II's pylon now stands. Possibly the *maru* was dismantled by Ramesses and used to pack the foundations of his pylon, as Horemheb did with the granary and Gempa-Aten temple at Karnak, but the interior of Luxor's first pylon has not yet been explored. Another *maru* has been identified on the west bank, near the royal palace (see Chapter 11).

ARCHITECTS AND CONTRACTORS ON THE EAST BANK

Though Amenhotep son of Hapu was overseer of every project, three additional men are linked to work on the east bank. They are the twin brothers Suty and Hor and the treasurer (Overseer of the House of Silver and Gold) Sebek-mose, the son of Min, the old mayor of Thinis, and royal grandfather Amenhotep II's archery master. Min eventually became royal treasurer and passed on the job to Sebek-mose at his death.

Sebek-mose was architect and overseer of works at Luxor. He did not live in his father's Middle Egyptian town of Thinis but, perhaps because of his work at Thebes, in a town up and across the river from Luxor, near Armant at ancient Sumenu, modern Dahamsha (El Mahamid Qibly). Sumenu was yet another town sacred to the crocodilian Sobek, Amenhotep's childhood god at Ghurob. Amenhotep built a temple at Sumenu, probably within Sebek-mose's portfolio; however, the area has not been well excavated, and little is known about it. The Greek writer Strabo visited the shrine in the late first century B.C. and reported that the temple housed a sanctuary for crocodiles.

Sebek-mose's tomb at nearby Er Rizeiqat was lined with sandstone sheets, perhaps remainders from Luxor Temple. They are carved in sunk

29. Amenhotep III with god Sobek. From Dahamsha. Egyptian alabaster, height 103 inches. The Luxor Museum of Ancient Egyptian Art, J. 155. Full view photo by Gerard Ducher, details by APK.

relief with scenes of the official's funeral and procession and presentation to gods of the underworld. There are prayers to several gods, but in particular to the Moon, whose color was always portrayed as silver (Sebek-mose's jurisdiction), in contrast with the sun's gold. These carved reliefs were sold by the Egyptian government to the Metropolitan Museum in 1908, and two sections were transferred to the Museum of Fine Arts, Boston, in 1954.

A majestic and colossal alabaster statue of Sobek seated with human body and crocodile head embracing Amenhotep III at his side was found at the bottom of a canal at Dahamsha in 1967. It is now one of the masterpieces of the Luxor Museum (Figure 29). Sobek wears a tall *atef* crown with ram's horns, plumes, and a solar disk, the latter tying him to the sun god Re. The composition, quality of carving, and fleshlike surface of the stone render the king's portrait ineffably sweet, human, and almost vulnerable compared to the monstrous, reptilian Sobek, in whose protective grasp he stands. Alternate stripes of the nemes headdress are left rough as though to hold gesso and gilding, perhaps in contrast to the other stripes originally in blue paint.

This great sculpture may have been one of Sebek-mose's projects because his tomb inscriptions relate that he "drew forth monuments for the King of his time from the pure alabaster of Hatnub" in Middle Egypt, the principal alabaster quarry used by the ancient Egyptians, also a likely source for the great white hippo at Kom el Hettan. Sobek's solar affinity, Sumenu's proximity to Thebes, and its position on the new northeast–southwest axis suggest that Sumenu, like Medamud, may have played some part in the grander Theban festivals.

Twin brothers Suty and Hor were a rare pair because, acting as one, they seem to have survived an ancient taboo against twins. Two identical black granodiorite cube statues were made for them, showing them crouching, wrapped in cloaks, only their feet and heads visible, and the surface of the cloaks providing a flat surface for inscription. Hor's complete, 22-inch-tall image is in New York, and Suty's is in scattered fragments. Each text names its owner as chief of works in Karnak, in Luxor, and in the "Southern Heliopolis" (the memorial temple) across the river.

Their most important monument is a large brown quartzite stela from Karnak, now in the British Museum. There they spoke in one voice: "I was in charge of your (Amun's) private quarters, overseer of works in your shrine itself. . . . The Overseers of the Herds of Amun in the Southern Harim, Suty and Hor, I in charge of the western side and he of the eastern side, both being in charge of the great monuments in Ipet-Sut (Karnak), foremost of Thebes, the City of Amun."

Remarkably, two-thirds of the main text is devoted to the sun in various forms. It begins, "adoring Amun when he rises as Harakhte" and continues, "Suty and Hor . . . say, 'Hail to you, O Re, the goodness of every day, who shines continually without ceasing.'" And to Khepri, the sun in the form of the sacred beetle, they say, "Your brightness opens the eyes of the livestock." In particular, they greet the future solo-god of the Amarna period, the Aten, "Hail to you, O sun-disk of the day, one who fashions everyone, and who makes them live, the great falcon, many-colored of plumage."

The twins' attention to solar deities suggests that they worked in the second half of the reign. Sebek-mose is also thought to have worked during that period and before Year 36, by when his son replaced him (see Chapter 16). If and how much Sebek-mose and the twins overlapped is not known. As treasurer, however, and because of his association with the sandstone quarries, Sebek-mose may have had more responsibility for materials and supplies and the twins for supervising the physical labor. The prayers on their stela mention hard work and tired limbs.

A redesign of Thebes and its monuments would have been accomplishments enough to stand out in history, but Amenhotep III readjusted theology and ritual practice as well. His emphasis on both the sun and the moon as deities, and as visible, palpable, physical presences, was downright contradictory to the traditional essence of Amun, the "Hidden One." It was a move away from darkness and toward light, away from the unseen to the overpoweringly visible. It suggests a sublimation of Amun and of the Amun priesthood to a greater power long before the Amarna "revolution" of Akhenaten. The degree to which "dazzling," radiant Nebmaatra became conjoined with the sun himself equals the degree to which all of these ideological and sculptural programs and their treasures were aimed not just away from Amun but toward the king. Amenhotep son of Hapu made these radical changes appear conservative, derived directly from the purest form of primeval worship.

PER HAI ("THE HOUSE OF REJOICING") AT MALKATA

(Reign of Amenhotep III, Years 25–29, ca. 1367–1363 B.C.)

THE PALACE, ITS INHABITANTS, AND ITS STAFF

Traveling south from the memorial temple toward Armant and Sumenu, the sloping foothills of the nobles' cemeteries give way to the sheer rock face of the western mountains. Nearby, on a flat, sandy bay of nearly virgin soil, Amenhotep III built a new palace-city. In ancient Egyptian, the word for *palace* was *per-aa*, literally the "great house," a phrase already in use since the time of Thutmose III to indicate the king himself, much the way the "White House" indicates the U.S. president or "Buckingham Palace" suggests the British monarch. *Per-aa* eventually mutated through Hebrew and Greek into the modern word *pharaoh*.

Amenhotep named his new *per-aa* "Per Hai" ('The House of Rejoicing'). The name was no understatement, judging from the superabundant potsherd gift labels found there, many inscribed with year dates. Some were noted as coming from the east bank "Dazzling Sun Disk" palace, which obviously remained in use. Per Hai or Per Haa also applied to a temple of the god Anubis, the sleek, black, canine guardian of the cemetery, and one cannot help but wonder if our king's choice of names took some inspiration there since his palace stands at the foot of the Theban burial grounds.

Per Hai is now known as "Malkata," coming from the Arabic meaning "the place where (ancient) things are picked up," because it has provided thousands of finds, including some predynastic, for scavengers and archaeologists alike. It is one of the few ancient Egyptian palaces known and excavated today, but the site is so vast – covering at least seven acres – that only a small fraction of it has been examined.

148

Malkata was a royal village with all the accoutrements: a compound of residential and administrative buildings, a festival hall, a small temple, and beyond that a workers' village, villas for courtiers, artisans' workshops, and doubtless stables abutting a vast artificial lake. No one knows when the first shovel was thrown, but like most of our king's projects, Malkata was a continuous work in progress likely beginning sometime in the 20s. Judging from the dated storage jar labels found there, he resided at Malkata virtually full-time from about Year 29 as plans geared up for his Year 30 jubilee.

The main palace is situated at the southwest corner of a walled enclosure. It was a rambling edifice with thick mud brick walls to insulate it from extreme temperatures. The entrance led up a side ramp to a series of labyrinthine corridors and courts, some with raised daises and throne bases. Visitors with any hope of a royal audience had first to pass and be approved by the phalanx of courtiers and stewards manning these stations.

Perpendicular to the axis of the building was a hall with two rows of eight columns and a throne base at the end. The throne base was decorated with images of bound captives and nine (archery) bows of vassal nations, symbolic of Egypt's traditional enemies lying underfoot eternally conquered. A canopy was painted on the ceiling above, and the rear wall held a scene of hunting in the desert. Colored plaster wall fragments of a large female figure have also been found. This may have been the room where the king received reports from his vizier, nominally the most powerful official at court. He informed the king daily on the state of the treasury, and he was the chief operating officer of the palace in charge of security, protocol, and external relations. He also acted as the king's deputy, when necessary.

Central to the palace and forming its axis was a columned hall much larger than the first, this one decorated with a portrait of the king seated on his throne; the floor was painted with a pond and marsh full of swimming fish and quacking, flapping ducks. The hall was flanked on each of its two long sides by four nearly identical apartments with en suite bathrooms, one with the tub still in place at the time of excavation. Called "Harim suites" by the first excavators, they were lavishly decorated with painted images of flying birds and grape arbors, and their storage rooms' walls were decked with depictions of overflowing offering tables, papyrus plants, and leaping calves. Scattered fragments of plaster, wood, and faience architectural decoration conjure up images of colorful crown moldings, dados, and wainscoting.

This area may have served larger receptions and ceremonies, and if the flanking rooms were indeed harem apartments, they may have been dayrooms or even permanent quarters for favorite princesses – like the female royal children of Sinuhe's tale – who came to the doorway and greeted visitors before ushering them onward, and later entering the grand audience chamber to hear the royal pronouncements.

On the ceiling of Amenhotep III's supposed bedroom, at the back of the structure, Mut's vultures hovered, their wings spread wide protecting their "son." Lower parts of the walls bore colored wainscoting panels, above which stood painted, paired figures of the domestic god Bes, a dwarf with a leonine face, who was viewed as a protector of homes. The ancient Egyptians loved puns, and one may have been at work here, because two representations of Bes together were *BesBes*, a word for "goose," the bird symbolic of the procreator god Geb, who was frequently depicted with a large phallus, perhaps meant to be an inspiration to the king in his bedroom. The word *bsbs* also denotes a medicinal plant or fruit, but what it cured is not known.

West of the main palace were villas, one as grand as the "King's House" of Akhenaten at Amarna. The Malkata version had duplicate suites of rooms, perhaps Amenhotep's and Tiy's true living quarters, but attempts at identifying the ownership of these various structures is still mostly at the guesswork stage.

THE KING'S PRIMARY OFFICIALS AT MALKATA

During Amenhotep III's reign, there were two vizierates: one for the north and one for the south. During part of the third decade of Amenhotep's reign, the southern vizier was likely a man named Ptahmose, who was also mayor of Thebes. At some point, he seems to have been transferred to his last high office, that of High Priest of Amun, a post not generally known to have been held concurrently with the vizierate. His most famous and beautiful artifact is a votive *shawabti* donated at Abydos, the traditional burial place of Osiris, and now in the Cairo museum. This is not a worker *shawabti* – one of the normal complement of 401 meant to take on agricultural labor in the afterlife – but a special amulet type. Like old schoolmaster Hekareshu's group, Ptahmose's special *shawabti* was meant to be donated at Abydos, which actually lies, as the birds fly, directly across the western mountains from Malkata (see Map 3, Chapter 10 and later in this chapter). The brilliant white, yellow, turquoise, and cobalt blue colors of this superlative object, its composition, and its figure style fit the second half of our king's reign.

30. Interior of Tomb of Ramose (TT 55). Photo by David Schmid.

Sometime in the third decade, a new southern vizier and mayor of Thebes came onto the scene: Ramose, younger son of Memphite mayor Neferhabef (from the Year 5 Nubian campaign) and half brother of Amenhotep Huy, the wealthy steward of Memphis (see Chapter 12). These were some of the most important offices in Egypt, a concentration of power that made this family nearly equal to royalty.

Ramose's tomb at Sheikh Abd el Gurna (TT 55), world famous even today for its grandiosity and the quality of its art, is testimony to the prestige he held at court (Figure 30). Carved into a vein of Tura-quality limestone, unusually fine and white for Thebes, its main room is like a temple's columned hall, with two rows of pillars cut out of the living rock. The stone removed was likely used for statuary, canopic jars, and stelae.

The east and west walls are carved in relief of exquisite workmanship and artistry by the best sculptors of the day, while the south wall is just beyond the limits of the good vein and is painted on plaster, one of the last Eighteenth-Dynasty painted tomb scenes in the Theban necropolis. Banquet scenes on the east walls include portraits of Ramose's nearest and dearest – his parents, wife Royal Ornament Merytptah (who may also have been his niece), half-brother Amenhotep Huy, Amenhotep son of Hapu (with long, wavy white hair), Commander of Chariotry and Royal Messenger to All Lands May, and a huntsman named Keshy.

It is not known if the last three of these individuals, including Hapu's son, were actually blood relatives.

Ramose did not mention children, but the painted scene on the south wall shows his eventual funeral presided over by Fourth Priest of Amun Simut (known from granary accountant Nebnufer's promotion in Year 20), normally the honor of the eldest son. A fragmentary inscription on a stela formerly in a French private collection apparently names (Si)-mut, dressed in late Amenhotep III style, "son of (Ra)-mose" (Figure 49). By Year 30, Simut became second priest, and he is represented at Soleb with that title (see Chapters 13 and 16). Therefore Ramose's tomb must have been quarried out and the south wall painted before Year 30. The walls with relief decoration appear to have been carved later in at least two stages (see Chapter 18).

Ramose and his family aside, the most powerful individual at the Malkata court of Amenhotep III was the septuagenarian Amenhotep son of Hapu, and he probably resided close to his liege in one of Malkata's villas. Hapu's son had become indispensable and was likely by his monarch's side on an almost daily basis. Because of his ability to decipher ancient, revered, and recondite texts, when administrative or political questions arose, he was ready with solutions based on historical, legal, and religious precedent. His self-described oratorical ability ("skilled of speech, pleasing of phrase") must also have made him stand out at court, impressing both king and nobility with his silver tongue. Testimony to the degree this talent was prized in ancient Egypt is the Middle Kingdom *Tale of the Eloquent Peasant*, which recounts the story of a poor, provincial farmer who argues his own legal case so articulately that he wins settlement by dint of his forceful and critical appeals.

In addition to being unmatched in academic knowledge and rhetoric, one of Hapu's son's other important traits was his political savvy. He never aspired to a single particular high office, and would have had a difficult time achieving it because he came from lowly parents, but his officially unimposing status made him a nebulous target for upwardly aspiring youngsters and jealous peers. At the same time, his favorite titles, Royal Scribe and Army Scribe, allowed him great freedom of movement in court and military venues, and his old post, Priest of Horus Khenty-Khety, made him a peer of the religious realm.

The king's chief steward, Amenemhet Surer, whom we already met in his previous capacity as an official surveyor (Chapter 10), was related to the king in a sense because his mother, Mut-tuwy, had been a royal concubine, probably one of Thutmose IV's or even Amenhotep II's harem leftovers, turned over in marriage to an overseer of the cattle of Amun, Ith-taui. The old man was barely mentioned in Surer's tomb (TT 48), as if he were the steward's father in name only. Mut-tuwy, on the other hand, figured prominently where ordinarily a wife would have been, and so Surer is assumed to have been nominally a bachelor. Surer's brother Setau was also well situated as second priest of the goddess Neith.

Surer's tomb walls portray two events that were obviously high points of his life. One depicts him as a fan bearer for the king as the latter burns incense at Karnak's granary (Chapter 10). The other shows him at the king's reception for New Year's gifts – the output of his royal workshops, which had more recently come under his supervision as steward. Surer now had the honor of marshaling the (annual?) parade of ornate jewelry and beautiful statuary to the king. Among this panoply were several statues of the king himself, some being dragged by gangs of laborers, and three of Queen Tiy wearing her huge wig and a vulture headdress. One female statue wearing the tall plumes of a queen sports a new hairdo, short in the back and tapering downward in the front to shoulder length. Perhaps this represents Gilukhepa or even Sitamen, who would become a queen by Year 30.

One of Surer's other titles, Elder of the Common Folk, suggests that he reached old age. His jobs as Chief in the Royal Robing Room and palace steward may have been the last ones he held, when the efforts of traveling to Amun's fields and overseeing their measurements were physically beyond him. He apparently lived to see the First Jubilee because he sent the king a gift that year and, in his tomb, portrayed Amenhotep III wearing regalia for that event, perhaps robed by Surer himself. That would have been an especially touching and proud personal moment!

Surer's tomb was purposely damaged in two bouts of sanctioned vandalism. For some unknown reason, this was a common occurrence for royal stewards. Was the aim to destroy all of the palace secrets along with the men's images? Was it because a steward's position made him exceedingly vulnerable to graft and theft in office, only to have been found out after his death? The second attack on Surer's tomb was during the Amarna period, when Atenists attempted to expunge all mention of the god Amun, which was unfair because Surer actually emphasized their sun disk god in his tomb, placing a prayer to the rising sun at the entrance and praising Nut as the mother of Aten on a wall inside.

As for a pharaoh's personal servants, Diodorus Siculus many centuries later wrote that "not one was a slave, such as had been purchased or born in the home, but all were sons of the most distinguished priests, over twenty years old and the best educated of their countrymen, in order that the king, by virtue of his having the noblest men to care for his person and to attend him throughout both day and night, might follow no low practices." While Diodorus's view may be too romanticized, what we do know about the upper level Malkata palace staff confirms their virtuousness. The royal butler of the king's chamber, Neferronpet, like all good butlers, claimed on a portrait statue to be "pure of hands." He must also have been greatly respected by his monarch because he was given a good-size chunk of expensive brown quartzite for his statue.

The Amarna letters suggest that domestic staff from Kush were also highly prized during the Late Bronze Age and that medical doctors attended the king full-time. In this vein, a Syrian ruler specifically requested that the pharaoh send him "two palace attendants . . . from Kush. Give me, too, a palace attendant that is a physician." These requests were turned over to the Egyptian messenger Haaramassi (see Chapter 14) for transmittal to Pharaoh.

Finally, adding to the colorful personalities at Malkata were the foreign messengers, who brought royal letters many hundreds of miles from Anatolia, the Tigris-Euphrates Valley, and the northern Mediterranean rim to the Theban valley. Their months-long voyages necessitated stays of some duration as guests at Malkata to rest, carry out their duties, and reprovision for the return trips. This normally took weeks or months, but the king of Babylon at one point complained that one of his messengers had been "detained" there for years. Or was the visitor just having too good a time to return to his difficult boss?

How the foreigners were housed at Malkata is not known, but it would not be surprising if they were assigned to special, well-equipped, and beautifully furnished quarters, as happened during old Hammurabi's days in Babylon, the idea being that the guests would return home lauding the comforts and delights of the (friendly) rival's standard of living.

QUEEN TIY AND HER STAFF

Tiy had her own palace stewards. Mery and his under steward, Ihuy, have burials at Thebes, known only from terracotta cone-shaped doorway markers. Her most famous steward was Kheruef, who claimed to have been reared and educated by the king himself at the royal palace. Kheruef's mother, Ruiu, depicted in his tomb in place of a wife, had multiple titles, including Royal Ornament, Singer of Isis, God's Mother, and Chantress of Amun. His father was an army scribe, Seqedu (called "Nebked"), and, like Surer's father, seems of negligible importance compared to his mother. As the queen's palace steward, Kheruef was in charge of Tiy's workshops, which probably supplied her immediate needs for linen and other furnishings. His monuments suggest that he was absolutely devoted to her and to Amenhotep III as well.

Kheruef's tomb (TT 192) was even larger than Ramose's and was also carved into a rare Theban vein of nearly Tura-quality limestone, a huge section of which was removed to create an open courtyard with a gateway. The stone is of such high quality that the amount pulled out to create the open court and the tomb should have been used for sculpture – something, perhaps, like the enormous, two-storey-tall image of the king and queen seated side by side with their daughters at their feet that is now in the atrium of the Cairo museum (see Chapter 13). There was enough stone removed from this courtyard to have formed four such monuments.

The age of the girls on this group sculpture, especially the second oldest, Henut-taneb, who wears the full wig of a grown woman, suggests that it was carved during the third decade, likely around the time of the groundbreaking for Kheruef's tomb. The tomb walls were later carved with scenes depicting Amenhotep's First and Third Jubilees in Years 30 and 37 (see Chapters 13 and 17), and some walls were decorated in the following reign (Chapter 18), but the greater part of the tomb was never finished.

Tiy and some of the other high-status women had their own messengers, who transported abroad correspondence on clay tablets, for example, the letters that Tiy wrote to Mitanni. Messengers must have been quite a large item on the queen's expense sheet because they had to be well mannered, multilingual, and courageous men, and they needed to be equipped with horses, chariots, weaponry, food, appropriate clothing, servants, and other provisions for their voyages. Likely the funds for supporting such individuals and other expenses came from agricultural estates assigned to her.

The steward of (presumably) Malkata's harem, probably a separate structure with its own workshops, was a man named "Userhet." He was also important enough to have a fine limestone tomb at Thebes (TT 47), not far from Surer's. He was still alive in Year 30, judging from a jar label found at Malkata.

THE MYSTERY OF THE MASS BURIAL
OF ROYAL CHILDREN

The remains of several female royal children were found by mid-nineteenth century Scottish Egyptologist A. Henry Rhind in a mass burial at the foot of Sheikh abd el Gurna behind the memorial temple and below the tombs of some of Amenhotep III's most important officials. An inscription identifies them as belonging to the "House of (female) Royal Children," as though this were a discrete structure. Some of the names recorded there are familiar: royal sister Tiaa; Princess Py-ihi, whose name appears on a papyrus from Ghurob, probably a half sister or sister of Tiaa and/or Amenhotep III; and Amenemopet, perhaps the young princess pictured in a tomb painting sitting on the lap of the venerable military man, Horemheb.

A fourth princess was Nebetia, the daughter of Prince Si-Atum, he being known from his childhood portrait on the lap of his tutor (previously his father's *kap* supervisor), the treasurer Meryra, whose tomb reliefs are in Leiden (see Chapters 8 and 17). Assuming that Si-Atum was one of the older true royal sons, Nebetia was likely born in the second decade of the reign and, when she was old enough, moved into a household of royal women headed by her aunt Tiaa. She was given the title of King's Daughter, despite being one generation removed.

None of the Rhind tomb inscriptions makes any reference to spouses or children, and so all the women seem to be spinsters, perhaps literally, considering the association between linen workshops and harems. In any case, it looks as though this group comprised members of three generations of royal women: one or two maiden aunts, a likely niece, and a nephew's daughter, all living in the same residence, making the phrase "(female) royal children," as it was applied to participants at royal audiences and other events such as the upcoming jubilees, much more broadly inclusive than we might have guessed.

The designation of this mass burial is not without controversy. The tomb was closed with a possible seal of Amenhotep III, but even so, it had been disturbed many times throughout antiquity. A document inside bears a date of Year 27, the fourth month of Peret, day 11, but Dodson and Janssen do not believe this is an Amenhotep III date. They are sure that the hieratic writing style on that document dates to Dynasty 21, when the tomb was reused and reorganized. Further complicating the matter, the space was recycled in classical times, leaving the disarray found by Rhind. Yet the coincidence of so many palace women from one reign in one place suggests that they were all originally buried together, their remains repeatedly disturbed, looted, reorganized, and finally abandoned until modern rediscovery.

Since the burial is at Thebes, not Sakkara, this "House of the Royal Children" stood either at Karnak or at Malkata, not Memphis. If all these women died at the same time, along with some of their servants and an embalmer mentioned in the labels, the culprit may have been a bout of contagion wiping out the entire residence (even its undertaker), requiring its demolition. Traces of a painted brick building were found by Kemp in a nearby mound, suggesting that such demolition and revision of Malkata structures was an ongoing process for one reason or another.

SUBSIDIARY BUILDINGS AND WORKSHOPS

Adjacent to and south of the main palace is a smaller building sometimes associated with Queen Tiy but which Lacovara sees as a records office for the magazines and storerooms clustered nearby. If he is right, then somewhere in or near these administrative chambers must have been a school for scribes like the one at Amarna. This was something of a graduate school for scribes who needed to learn to write a second language. Whether these were Egyptians learning the Near Eastern languages and cuneiform or whether they were foreigners learning Egyptian is not exactly clear. What they left behind at Amarna are school exercises in translation. They are not dated, but even if none of them actually originated at Malkata, they at least represent a tradition of academic training in language that must have existed there as well.

Some workshops and a small workers' village were just to the west of the main compound, and a larger "South Village" of small factories and workmen's houses stood 300 yards to the south of the main palace enclosure. Here is where some of the most tantalizing objects were made. These were the items of jewelry, amulets, vessels, and statues the likes of which Surer presented to his king at New Year's. The name of one of the palace artisans is known from part of a small limestone shrine inscribed for him and found at Deir el Bahri. This man, Anu, was titled Chief Artificer in the House of Nebmaatra in Western Thebes.

Colorful finger rings were made of faience, an ancient forerunner of porcelain, glazed in rich hues of lapis blue, turquoise, bright yellow, green, and violet. They were handed out in great number by the king and his family as gifts to courtiers, perhaps, but more probably, because of the rings' small sizes and their fragility, to Royal Ornaments, Songstresses of Amun, and members of various harems. Intact ones are rare. Most of the remaining bezels are inscribed with royal names, and the molds for some of them were taken from sturdier bronze rings probably made for the officials. Around 500 bezels were recorded by Hayes at Malkata, 90 percent of them inscribed with the king's names, most of the rest for Tiy, and two for Sitamen.

The word for faience was *tjehen* ("dazzling," like Amenhotep III's epithet), and during his reign, it lived up to its name. During these later years, the art of producing brilliant faience in the purest colors reached its climax, never to be repeated in Egypt's history, perhaps because of the technical demands. Rich, pure yellows and reds and stark whites were extremely difficult to achieve because they required perfect control over the kiln temperature and other aspects of faience production. Malkata's artisans were able to create single objects with multiple colors, each at its optimal hue. The masterpiece is a lemon-yellow cosmetic jar in the Louvre with cobalt blue, bright red, and pure white decoration. The panel of cartouches on the side of the vessel names both the king and Tiy. A fragment of a brilliant white faience box lid found at Karnak is inscribed in blue and red for the First Jubilee.

The most famous faience object from the reign is the Metropolitan Museum's turquoise blue sphinx, the size of a house cat, with the nemes-dressed head of Amenhotep III and, instead of feline paws, his hands outstretched holding offering jars (Figure 31).

Blue and yellow (gold) – the colors of the gods – were used in combination most often for objects naming Tiy, or Amenhotep III with Tiy, or Amenhotep III alone. This pairing of colors must have been so identified with the royal couple that it was almost never used in the next reign. The combination of deep cobalt blue with sky blue was the favorite combination for objects named either for the king or for Tiy alone. The next king almost never used this combination either, although his wife did. The two colors used most often when Amenhotep's name was joined to another female of his family were bright white and cobalt blue. The Amarna-period color combination of sky blue with blue-green was almost never used by Amenhotep III.

Glassmaking reached its zenith at Malkata. The technique, today called core-form, required wrapping molten glass around a core (mostly dung), shaping and decorating it while hot, and removing the core later. Most of the vessels are small, less than four inches tall, but their shapes are elegant, some copying the forms of "palm-topped" capitals like those we will see at Amenhotep III's temple at Soleb in Nubia (see Figure 34).

31. Faience sphinx of Amenhotep III (front view), height 5 1/2 inches. Metropolitan Museum of Art, 1972.125. Photo APK.

Their exterior surfaces, 70 percent being cobalt blue, are festooned with trails of white and yellow glass in intricate patterns (Figure 32). These tall, thin bottles held eye paint (kohl), and sometimes the applicator sticks have been found with them.

THE MAN-MADE LAKE AND THE CHARIOTRY VENUES

East of the South Village is the largest and most astonishing element of the entire Malkata complex: a vast, rectangular man-made lake, now called "Birket Habu" ("Hapu's Lake"), the north-western corner of which abuts the royal town, the two having been laid out according to a master city plan. The lake itself, now under cultivation, is about one and a half miles long by three-fourths of a mile wide. Knowing where to look, it is easy to see on Google Earth from an eye altitude of 10 miles and higher because the earth removed to create the basin was set in a series of tall mounds around all four sides. Another such *birket* visible on Google Earth exists on the east bank southwest of Luxor's modern airport. This site has not yet been excavated or dated and seems not to be mentioned in any ancient texts.

Birket Habu must have had myriad uses aside from being a western reservoir. Connected by a canal to the Nile, it provided a superhighway between eastern Thebes and the new mini-capital, making the commute exponentially faster and more comfortable than going overland by chariot or foot to and from the river's edge, and it acted as a harbor for goods to be brought to Malkata. Its most famous role, however, would be played out in the king's jubilee of Year 30 and described in Kheruef's tomb (Chapter 13). Its hillocks were likely planted with desert flowers and shrubs, carpeting them with color in the spring, their roots keeping the mounds from eroding year-round. These mounds could also have served as viewing areas for thousands of spectators who came to attend the king's jubilee and other festivals held on the west bank. Kemp and O'Connor showed that the *birket*, with its artificial terrace, was a *maru*, or viewing place, where foreigners brought their gifts to Pharaoh. Some of the mounds may even have been foundations for dwellings within easy reach of farmland but standing safely high and dry, even during Inundation.

Napoleon's followers thought the site's scale was fitting for a hippodrome for chariot racing or a *champs de Mars* for training military troops, but those theories were quickly discarded when the *birket*'s basin turned out to be a lake. The latter identification, however, does not negate the first because the basin's perimeter, an artificial terrace of hard-packed sand and earth, is a perfect base for exercising horses. Meticulous maintenance and grooming of the surface would have kept it free of injury-producing debris and ruts from the chariot wheels.

Packed sand was the footing of choice for ancient Roman hippodromes, where chariot races were held, the modern word *arena* arising naturally from this Latin base. Sand or sand in combination with artificial materials is today the footing of choice for modern equestrian competitions such as show jumping and dressage. The surfaces of the *birket*'s sand banks have the appearance of fastidious maintenance similar to the footing prepared for fine horses in modern times. But can we imagine that such an effort went into the training grounds of ancient horses?

32. Glass kohl (cosmetic eye paint) tube, height 4 inches, EA. 2589. Courtesy the British Museum.

The short answer is a resounding yes. After all, throughout history, horses have been among monarchs' most precious possessions, a claim Shakespeare immortalized in *Richard III*, and horses and their trappings often topped the list of dowry items sent from foreign kings to Late Bronze Age Egypt. Why else would so many of them open their correspondence to Pharaoh with salutations like, "For your household, your wives, your sons, your horses, your chariots, and in your country, may all go very well"? Amenhotep III, according to a Malkata jar label, was "rich in horses." His family history included both his chariot-racing father and his "master of horses" father-in-law, and there was a workshop for chariots within the precincts of Karnak temple (see Figure 11). Therefore it is not surprising that so much effort would have been put forth on behalf of the royal stables.

The earliest known texts for training horses, preceding Xenophon by several centuries, are the writings of a Mitanni stable master named "Kikkuli," that have been preserved for decades in Berlin but have only recently been translated and published in their entirety. Kikkuli's instructions are written in the Hittite language (with specific terms in Indic dialect) on large clay tablets (the same grand size as the Amarna letter tablets, a testimony to their importance) found at the Anatolian capital of Hattusha. Dated to around 1400 B.C., they, their principles, and their practices must have been widely known to the likes of Yuya and his colleagues. Copies of them probably traveled from Anatolia to Egypt just as readily as did the horses and chariots themselves.

These cuneiform texts call for a series of workouts gradually increasing in length and difficulty over a period of more than five months. The in-harness workouts included trotting longer distances (*dannas*) and then galloping shorter ones (*ikus*). Modern translations of *dannas* and *ikus* vary slightly from author to author, but the length of the *birket* is about three *dannas*. The eastern lake mentioned earlier is two *dannas*.

The *birket*'s carefully configured spoil heaps, 40–50 yards in diameter, would also have fit Kikkuli's method of horse training. These might have served two purposes: (1) to mark off the *dannas* as drivers worked their teams the length of the terrace and (2) as barriers around which to serpentine their horses, as prescribed by the master. For the serpentines and an exercise called *wasanna*, Kikkuli called for an artificial pen bounded by a wood fence or wall; however, in Egypt, where wood was at a premium, the row of mounds would have given drivers obstacles of a suitable size around which to turn their horses. Furthermore, driving the horses up and over the mounds would have conditioned them for traversing the sort of hilly country they would encounter elsewhere. The village at the northern edge of the *birket* is one of the few areas where riding horses are kept for sport in Egypt today, and the owners ride and train their horses on and around the mounds of the *birket*.

Horses imported from Asia were revenue of foreign lands. To the extent that the Birket Habu may be where they were off-loaded from ships traveling south from Memphis or Akhmim, taken to nearby stables, and trained, this was indeed a *maru* for Asiatic revenue (Figure 33). When the king of Babylon complained in a letter to Amenhotep III about

33. Chariots on parade, Dynasty 19 relief on west exterior wall, Luxor temple. Photo: APK.

his horses being paraded together with horses of much less important rulers, the *birket* may have been the show arena. Of course, Amenhotep III replied that they were all his horses now, and he could exhibit them in any order he wanted!

A break in the mound rows at just about the middle of Birket Habu's western long side leads back toward the ancient South Village behind Malkata. The contiguous area would have been a logical place for the royal stables, nearby enough for easy access but separated from the palace and its central buildings by a wall to fend off the dirt, odor, insects, noise, and other detractions of a stable site. The lake itself was the perfect water supply for large animals, each of which would have consumed a dozen gallons of water or more per day, and for the regular postworkout baths prescribed by Kikkuli's texts. Moreover, the areas north, south, and east of the *birket* were prime agricultural lands for growing the enormous amounts of feed necessary for a large stable. The small ancient Egyptian horses probably ate about 20 pounds of hay per day, in addition to grain, which was measured in handfuls – several for each horse – the feeding plan being customized to each animal's needs, according to Kikkuli. Furthermore, the resulting measure, when dried, would have made perfect fuel for the kilns of the South Village's workshops and core materials for glass vessels.

If the area around the *birket* served for training horses, then it follows that nearby Kom el Abd, with its almost 13-foot-tall, landscaped, mud brick platform and its adjacent cleared, three-mile strip of desert (Kola el Hamra), may have been a royal grandstand and racetrack, as Barry Kemp suggested. The width of the main part of the cleared strip at Kola el Hamra is about 130 yards, plenty wide enough to allow chariots to start at Kom el Abd, turn near the western end, and race back to the grandstand, turning once again as they gradually pulled up after the finish. The hills at the opposite end of the strip would have served for additional viewing areas, if not for the royals and courtiers, at least for the hoi polloi. The track was never entirely finished, however, and it gives the appearance of not having been raced on because its western end peters out roughly into the cliffs, and the surface was apparently never picked clean of small rocks, as the *birket's* western bank was.

Many scholars maintain that there are no records of chariot races in ancient Egypt, although, as Kemp wrote, "this is perhaps too natural a thing to do for them to have avoided it." There are actually several mentions of kings racing their chariots, not the least of which is Thutmose IV. Chariot races were a staple of contemporary Mycenean funeral celebrations, and Homer rhapsodized about the one Achilles held in honor of Patroclus after he died in battle during the Trojan War. If chariot races existed among Egypt's Bronze Age allies and correspondents, can we imagine that Egypt had none? Racing was, in fact, necessary to determine the relative merit of individual horses, teams, trainers, and drivers to assign the best to the king and his highest officials. If Kola el Hamra was not designed for racing, then we should search for a site that was.

Catharine Roehrig has shown that Kola el Hamra also aligns with the movement of the sun at Thebes in the winter as the sun seems to rise from and set into mountains whose shapes resemble ancient Egyptian imagery of the horizon. This, of course, given Amenhotep III's solar bent in every aspect of his realm, does not contradict the Kola's use as a racing venue but only enhances it. Full sunlight the length of the strip from sunrise to sunset would have made gilded chariots much easier to follow.

There is another rather eerie point that should be made in regard to the Kola el Hamra. Because of the great bend in the Nile just north of Thebes, Osiris's traditional burial site, Abydos, downriver and nominally north of Thebes, is actually more west than north (Map 3). Therefore the line of the Kola can be seen from Google Earth to point straight over the mountains to Abydos. Certainly Amenhotep III and his wise men were well aware of this, and one can only fantasize about the implications this fact of geography might have in regard to the landmarks built and the ceremonies held in the last years of our king's reign or even at his death.

Along the road from Malkata and from the southern end of the *birket* to Kom el Abd is a desert altar at Kom el Samak. This is assumed to have been used during the king's jubilee, and its placement between the *birket* and Kom el Abd may have been designed for the king and his horses and chariots before the dangerous, even life-threatening competition. It recalls Kikkuli's preparations before a sacred rite involving the horses: "On the tenth day, at the moment of the last watch of the night, as the day is rising and it is not yet completely light . . . in the stable I make a libation and I invoke the gods Pirinkar and Ishtar. In Hurrian I pronounce these words: 'For the horses. . . . O Pirinkar and Ishtar.' And in Luvian I pronounce the words, 'For the horses! May all go well' . . . and then with a bit of mutton fat I anoint the horses." Kom el Samak is a dream location to serve as an altar for blessing the horses before a race.

BENEATH THE DIVINE FALCON'S WINGS A NEW WORLD TAKES SHAPE

(Reign of Amenhotep III, Years 26–29, ca. 1366–1363 B.C.)

THE SECOND NUBIAN CAMPAIGN IN YEAR 26

Twenty-one years had passed since Amenhotep III sailed home from Nubia with boatloads of gold and caravans of slaves. Now in Year 26, an ambitious building program was in progress, and lavish jubilee celebrations were on the drawing board. It was time once again to boost the treasury and increase the labor force, so Amenhotep III ordered his military south, somewhat disingenuously, to quell a rebellion.

Having reached his late 40s, Amenhotep III turned the campaign over to his viceroy of Nubia, King's Son of Kush Merymose. Like his predecessor, Merymose carried royal emblems, and many of his lesser titles – Overseer of the Cattle of Amun, Director of All Works of the King, and Overseer of the Gold Lands of Amun – were princely. Part of an inscription on one of his royal-quality, nested granodiorite sarcophagi suggests that he was a true prince indeed. After Merymose's name on the coffin is part of the hieroglyphic sign *ms* (born of), followed by signs that possibly stand for "Mut." According to philologist Edmund Meltzer, the phrase could be read "born of Mutemwia," making Merymose Amenhotep III's (younger) brother.

A modest, youthful statue of him found in Middle Egypt and now in Vienna bears the following titles: King's Son, Royal Scribe, Fan Bearer on the Right of the King, and Judge. Though King's Son in this case is taken by Egyptologists as an abbreviation of Merymose's full vice-regent's title, the statue is very conservative in style and may, in fact, date to the very end of Thutmose IV's reign.

166

The cream of officialdom associated themselves with Viceroy Merymose. Graffiti in southern Egypt and Nubia dating to the time of his vice-regency show Merymose in close contact with Malkata palace insiders such as southern vizier Ramose and treasurer Sebek-mose. Tiy's chief steward, Kheruef, accompanied Merymose on trips as an escort, advisor, or, perhaps, watchdog. In one rock-cut memorial near Aswan, the queen's steward appears flanked by two mirror-image Merymoses — the one being our viceroy and the other being a completely unknown treasurer with the same name. The design of the scene — Kheruef sandwiched between two Merymoses — could be interpreted to mean that both Merymoses were actually one and the same, adding yet another title to the viceroy's string. Since one of Merymose's responsibilities was to secure the income from Nubian gold mines (Overseer of the Gold Lands of Amun), the title of Treasurer fits his portfolio well.

As for the battle of Year 26, Merymose's victory text tells us that "the army of the Pharaoh . . . which was under the authority of the viceroy was mustered, and companies (of troops) were formed, commanded by commanders — every man (assigned) according to his village." Staging took place outside of Egypt proper in northern Nubia, at the fortress of Baky at the mouth of the Wadi el Allaqi, where Amenhotep III had built a bark sanctuary. From there the troops made their way south 52 *iteru* (about 300 river miles) to the now unknown fortress of Tery, apparently close to Ibhet, located by scholars such as Karola Zibelius-Chen in the eastern desert, a spot that nevertheless must have been moist enough to support agriculture. The battle took the enemy by surprise at harvest time (some rebellion!), and it was over "in one day, in a single hour, and a great slaughter was made." Plunder consisted of cattle and 740 human captives, two-thirds of whom were women, children, and their servants, and 312 hands of the dead were taken as trophies (see Figure 13).

These seem like small numbers compared to the tens of thousands of the Year 5 campaign. Perhaps this rebellion was smaller or, on the other hand, the decrease may have been the result of the known decline in Nubia's population in late Dynasty 18. This is often blamed on Egypt's having siphoned off manpower for labor; however, after Amenhotep III's first campaign, he claimed to have left behind enough locals to continue to reproduce, sounding a bit like good animal husbandry. Therefore diseases and other natural disasters rise up as possible causes.

Despite the momentary unrest, or because of Merymose's success, Egypt's frictional relations with Nubia seem to have settled into mutually beneficial trade in these last years of the third decade. A vignette in the tomb of granary overseer Khaemhet, who had at least part of his tomb decorated in or after Year 30, has been identified by Cristina Pino as illustrating the royal fleet arriving at a bustling Sudanese market town, where the king's sailors off-load grain and negotiate for local produce with Nubian shop owners in front of kiosks set in rows dockside.

AMENHOTEP III'S NUBIAN TEMPLES: ASWAN, WADI ES SEBUA, SAI, SOLEB, AND SEDEINGA

Having made his mark and secured the necessary flow of gold, goods, and manpower, Merymose likely remained in the south managing royal projects as "overseer of works." As such he would have supervised renovations and new construction at a number of sites from the First Cataract at Aswan to well below the Second (Map 2). One of his titles, King's Confidant in the Southern Cities, also gave him responsibilities as far north as Edfu and Kom Ombo, and he seems to have had some jurisdiction over the quarries at Silsilla (see Chapter 17).

Under Merymose's broad aegis was a small chapel on rocky Elephantine Island in the middle of the Nile at Aswan. Known from drawings made by Napoleon's artists in 1800, soon after that it became a convenient quarry and was picked clean by 1822. As preserved in the French renderings, it was an architectural jewel with a central chamber and a surrounding porch standing on three or four courses of stone risers, protecting it from a high Nile, and a staircase leading up to the eastern doorway. The porch's columns were the same shape as those at Luxor's sun court, so this structure probably dates to the second half of our king's reign. What Napoleon's draftsmen indicated of Amenhotep III's ornate costume and the importance given to a figure of Queen Tiy substantiate this dating.

The previously mentioned (see Chapter 7) tiny, cavelike shrine at Wadi es Sebua seems to have undergone some renovation at this point in time. According to Martina Ullmann, just before the First Jubilee, Amenhotep changed the Amun figure painted on an interior wall to a new falcon-headed deity with the king's own facial features. This little amendment was the harbinger of new ideas in temple decoration farther south where, at the time of his jubilee, Amenhotep III would become a god in his own right.

Evidence of work from around this time also crops up 200 miles farther south at Sai Island, where he had done some work around the time of his first campaign. In a beautiful low relief image on one face of

34. Soleb as it appeared in the late nineteenth century, watercolor by Ernst Weidenbach. After Lepsius.

a sandstone pillar, the king wears the aerodynamic blue *khepresh* crown, a kilt with a long transparent skirt over it, and a bull's tail. The pair of long ribbons trailing from the back of the crown were a late affectation, pinning this monument to the last decade of his reign. An excavation on Sai in 1974 uncovered the wreck of a beautiful small portrait of Queen Tiy in hard serpentinite stone, likely also dating to this period.

Soleb

Soleb Temple, lying 15 miles south of Sai Island, is the best preserved ancient Egyptian temple in the Sudan (Figure 34). It was the first Egyptian temple dedicated not to a long-standing, venerable god but to a specific king as a deity. It is the only one built during Amenhotep III's lifetime in which the king is clearly and unequivocally deified, although it seems very strongly implied elsewhere, as discussed at the beginning of Chapter 10. At Soleb Temple, Amenhotep III actually became the moon god Khonsu, the son of Amun and Mut. Khonsu was equated with Horus, the son of Re (or of Osiris, depending on one's allegiance). Horus's left eye was the moon, and when the moon waned to nothingness, it was considered damaged. If it did not come back to full strength, chaos ensued. According to images in Soleb, the damaged eye of Horus fled to that actual site, recovered there, and returned to the sky as the full moon, as Amenhotep III himself.

Reference to physical renewal had been a theme central to pharaonic jubilee festivals since "primeval time," but the imagery of waning strength and ill health may have had some personal resonance for our king, who was now close to 50 years old. No one knows what physical ailments he might have had other than the clubfoot. His mummy shows terrible, surely painful, dental deterioration, but whether this was already a problem a decade earlier is not known. The healing aspect of Soleb's mythology may also have pertained to disease in general during Amenhotep III's reign. Since communicable diseases throughout northern Africa's history generally traveled from south to north (see Thucydides' comment in Chapter 9), the temple may have had an additional purpose – as a spiritual bulwark against infection.

Soleb was "a noble temple out of fine white sandstone, all of its doors being made with electrum, their rays in faces, the figure [of the God being ram-headed]," according to hieroglyphs on a monumental ram statue from there. The temple's name was "Kha-em-maat," "Risen in Truth," like the little, ornately decorated northern one at Karnak, which naturally has caused a great deal of confusion among Egyptologists. Soleb, however, was not "a resting place for the god" like the Theban Kha-em-maat. Instead, it was "an excellent fortress, which is surrounded by a great rampart, the portals shining more than Heaven," and elements of its high, crenellated wall are still in place.

The stronghold aspect of Soleb is typical of pharaonic edifices in Nubia, for good reason, considering its strategic importance to gold shipments and the vulnerability of Egyptian emissaries and mercenaries far from home. In addition, the phrase "fortress of the gods" had rich historical and religious symbolism. These Nubian fortresses were venues for the display and ritual killing of war prisoners and animals, both types of victims being pertinent to Soleb's location. The carved decoration on some of Soleb's walls and columns includes the names of all of Egypt's captured and subservient nations and peoples. Likely the indigenous population was well aware of the temple's symbolism.

Soleb also recalls elements from both Kom el Hettan and Luxor. It may not be a coincidence that its final length of 190 yards is almost exactly the final length of Luxor Temple as planned by Amenhotep III and that its architecture has many similar elements. Sanctuaries at the back of Soleb are fronted by a hypostyle hall and two peristyle courts with grand pylons. The columns of the peristyle courts are papyrus bundles like those at Luxor (and the small temple on Elephantine), but our king revived an ancient form of column used in Old Kingdom pyramid temples for the hypostyle hall. Here the capitals are in the form of palm fronds or, perhaps, ostrich feathers, the abstracted version of both being nearly identical.

Palm-frond capitals, as they are called today, were a feature of King Unas's Fifth-Dynasty pyramid temple, which means they were an attractive bit of archaism for Amenhotep III. Their exact meaning is unclear. The notched, naked palm branch was traditionally associated with Heh, the god of infinity, but Soleb's are the fully leafed frond like that historically carried in Christian and Jewish festivals. In the Late Bronze Age Middle East, "the voluted palmette . . . appears [to] be related to . . . symbols of royal strength and legitimation," according to art historian Marian Feldman, which is certainly appropriate symbolism at Soleb. Ostrich plumes were the symbol of Re's daughter Ma'at and of the god of the air, Shu. Both Ma'at and Shu remained in favor during the early years of Akhenaten's Amarna religious revolution, even when other gods were banished, because they were considered part of the solar cult.

Palm-frond capitals became a favorite of Amenhotep III for other artistic media as well, and he had elegant glass and faience versions made as kohl vessels in his Malkata palace workshops (see Chapter 11 and Figure 32). Kohl, usually black, blue or green, was both a cosmetic and a medicinal eye paint, and placing it inside bottles shaped like Soleb's columns, where Horus's eye was restored, must have augmented its magical and healing properties. During these later years of his reign, the king affected kohl lines extending from his eyes nearly back to his hairline, with his eyebrows painted to match, perhaps in reference to the dramatic facial markings of a Horus falcon.

Early in its conception, a canal led from Soleb's front gate to the river, but as the temple stretched itself eastward toward the (retreating?) Nile, the canal was replaced by a harbor connected to the temple by an avenue bordered with pairs of over-life-size, inward-facing recumbent rams, the animal sacred to Amun, each with a little figure of Amenhotep III tucked under its chin. They are carved from a particularly rare and hard granite gneiss stone quarried farther south by the Third Cataract at Tombos, where Merymose left two rock-cut inscriptions and likely oversaw their production. Ram's horns became a new feature of Amenhotep III's crowns here at Soleb, "the figure [of the God being ram-headed]" (see also Chapter 13).

Four colossal statues were set up by the door of the eastern pylon, which was named "the Great Gateway of Amenhotep, Ruler of Thebes, Nebmaatra-Who-Hears-Petitions." Worshipers spoke directly to these kindly statues, and they in turn transmitted petitioners' requests to the god. To approach the colossi, however, visitors had first to pass between a pair of red granite guardian lions, one named "Living Image on Earth, Nebmaatra, Lord of Nubia, Who Resides within the Fortress of Soleb." The lions' bodies are stretched out as though at rest, but their heads have raised up at the visitor's approach. Their ears fold low against their heads, a sign of deep distrust, and one can imagine a low, warning growl rumbling in the beasts' throats.

The pharaonic love-hate relationship with lions is apparent at Soleb. The beast served as a guardian in the red granite statues but as prey in the area behind the temple in a fenced wild game park, where Schiff Giorgini, who excavated Soleb, felt that royal hunting parties shot these noble creatures for sport. Many spent arrow heads still lie in the sand there. In the nearby cemetery, a horse is lovingly interred on its right side on a bed of clean sand, its head to the east and its haunches near the door of its owners' chamber. Its skeleton bears the bite marks of a large predator, the hunter and the hunted having reversed their roles.

Soleb was attacked during the religious extremism of the Amarna period, when the god Amun was out of favor and his name was erased wherever it could be found. An inscription on one of the red granite lions records Tutankhamen's restoration of the temple when he succeeded to the throne at the end of this period. The site continued to be a magnet for destruction, however. In the third century B.C., two of the red granite lions (now in the British Museum) and some gray gneiss rams (one in Berlin) were moved by a Nubian king to Gebel Barkal by the Fourth Cataract, and a third red granite lion was moved in postantique times to the citadel in Cairo.

Sedeinga

About halfway between Soleb and Sai Island stands what is left of the temple at Sedeinga (Figure 35), the first temple dedicated to a reigning queen, setting a precedent for Ramesses II's pair of rock-cut temples at Abu Simbel for himself and Queen Nefertari. Queen Tiy's temple was named "Hat-Tiy" ("the House of Tiy"), echoing in the name of the nearby modern village "Adaya".

35. Sedeinga. Photo courtesy Lawrence M. Berman.

Today it is barely more than a rock pile having been built in local, poor-quality sandstone that has suffered greatly from both human and natural destruction. A lone column with a capital in the form of the goddess Hathor's cow-eared head stands tall and erect amid the rubble like the biblical Lot's wife turned to a pillar of salt. Eight similarly decorated columns, now lying in fragments, formed a vestibule with a doorway leading to a hypostyle hall decorated with more Hathor-headed columns. The doorway's carved lintel gives a schematic representation of the building's architecture decorated with sphinxes named for Tiy. The other face of the lintel shows the king performing temple rituals.

A fine black stone portrait of the queen found nearby is inscribed "beloved of Amun who resides at Sedeinga," however, his presence was secondary to Hathor's. Queen Tiy was worshiped at this temple as Hathor, whose mythology was complex, and many layers of her personality were at play at Sedeinga. More than the other divine doyennes of sky and motherhood, Hathor was considered the goddess of love and sexuality to the extent that in Greek times, she was equated with Aphrodite. This aspect is particularly appropriate for Tiy, Amenhotep's great love, in light of the upcoming jubilee festival, which will include a renewal of his sexual prowess as well as his other strengths.

Hathor was also the god Re's daughter, his solar "eye." This made Sedeinga the perfect complement to Soleb, where Amenhotep III was worshiped as Re's lunar "eye." The connection between the two temples is so compelling that if the two royals, Amenhotep III and Queen Tiy, did not actually travel to Nubia, they should have, because the return of both the solar and lunar "eyes" healthy and whole from there to Egypt would have guaranteed or restored *ma'at* to the entire land.

The spirit of the Nubian temples, particularly at Soleb and Sedeinga, was the opposite of the tone of those in Egypt proper. Normally, in Egypt, the gods were in equilibrium within their temples. They abided in a relatively happy state, being served by the cult, receiving requests for favors, and sometimes granting them. The deities of the Nubian temples, on the other hand, were in a continuous state of disequilibrium, requiring repeated efforts at pacification. This was obviously a reflection of New Kingdom Egypt's contentious history in the Sudan. The deification of himself and his queen was Amenhotep III's trump card. In Nubia, the great Nebmaatra Amenhotep Ruler of Thebes was more than an earthly ruler against whom the disenchanted might occasionally rebel. Now he was a god and his principal wife a goddess. They were forces of nature, invincible and omnipotent.

THE DELTA TEMPLES AT ATHRIBIS AND BUBASTIS AND THE OFFICIALS WHO BUILT THEM

At the other geographic extreme of the empire was the Delta north of Memphis, where the Nile fanned out into several branches before emptying into the Mediterranean Sea. Its northernmost parts were marshy, and centuries worth of alluvial deposits needed to settle before the land would become firm enough to support a city like Alexandria. Therefore the towns of Athribis, Amenhotep son of Hapu's home, and Bubastis, where the royal nurse left a statue of herself, were just about as far north as a town could be in Dynasty 18 (Map 1). Amenhotep III renewed or enhanced temples to Horus Khenty-Khety at the former and to the goddess Bastet at the latter.

In Athribis, Amenhotep son of Hapu was given permission to rebuild the temple, bury his mother, Mistress of the House Itu, and rebury his father, Hapu, perhaps in a tomb more suited to the parents of the magnate he had become. According to his inscriptions, the scope of the temple renovation went beyond simple repair and restitution to expansion, refinement, and beautification with two lakes, a northern one and a southern one, planted with flowers, probably the blue lily (*Nymphaea cerulea*), which opens daily during peak sunlight hours and was a favorite temple offering in antiquity.

Why the temple needed such drastic work is not known, but it may have come about at least partly as a result of changes in theology. The falcon-headed sun deity Khenty-Khety, whom Amenhotep son of Hapu served as priest early in his career, underwent a transformation during Dynasty 18, likely during Amenhotep III's reign, according to Bryan. Khenty-Khety became equated with the healing eye of Horus, the polar opposite to the eye that had fled south to Soleb. In this transformation, he represented the diurnal sun, especially the rising sun.

Unlike the sandstone temples in the south, northern temples were built of limestone, and Hapu's son was probably able to commandeer Tura-quality limestone for his hometown. Scraps of the New Kingdom temple's sculptural decoration are known today. One is a large granite statue of a snake slithering along a *hm* sign (a hieroglyph for "Majesty") inscribed with the words "the good god, Nebmaatra, the son of Re of his body, Amenhotep, Ruler of Thebes, beloved of the good (guardian) serpent of the House of Horus Khenty-Khety." Another statue, the lower half of a figure of Amenhotep son of Hapu, is inscribed with promises to recite hymns every day, refill the granaries and the treasury, and fill the chapel with offerings.

Just 20 miles northeast of Athribis in the eastern Delta is modern Zagazig, ancient Bubastis. In Dynasty 18, this was the last major city inside Egyptian territory before travelers and traders exited their home-land heading east to Canaan or north along the Mediterranean rim. Likewise, it was the first real taste of home on the return trip. The temple at Tell Basta was dedicated to a peaceful and reassuring mani-festation of the maternal goddess Bastet, and it was for this reason that the statue of the nurse with the four royal children had been donated here decades earlier. Best known in her form of a cat, Bastet was a some-what more benign and tractable counterpoise to her cousin, the bipolar Sekhmet.

Remnants of our king's stone structures were found at Tell Basta long ago. Those bits and the significant statues found more recently by Polish excavations suggest he must have built something yet to be located. A colossal red granite portrait of Queen Tiy was unearthed more recently and has been reerected in recent times on a high base (Figure 36). It was carved late in the reign, judging from her middle-aged figure and fashions – a trailing gown and enormous wig nearly enveloping her small, round face. Centuries later, the statue's back pillar was inscribed by Osorkon II, but he did not touch the rest of the statue, either out of economy or respect.

Two fine black granite statues were left there by northern vizier Amenhotep (a very popular name), whose administrative portfolio included the regions of Egyptian imperial control reaching from Memphis far into western Asia. Another of his titles, Head of All Works of the King, may refer to buildings whose construction he supervised in this region, including these at Bubastis.

The climate and geography of the Delta was obviously the extreme opposite of that in Nubia. One of northern vizier Amenhotep's Bubastis statues tells us that he was head of all the provinces of pasture marshes. This is a good description of the eastern Delta landscape at the time, a flat expanse of lagoons and marshes filled with wildlife, quite different from the parched, rocky tracts of Nubia. The word *pasture* also suggests a certain amount of herd farming, as in cattle and horses, which continues there today.

The deities at Athribis and Bubastis were generally content, and they formed a perfect counterweight to those in Nubia, who were always on the edge of temper tantrums. In terms of gender, Athribis's male Horus Khenty-Khety and Bubastis's female Bastet also made good counter-points to Soleb's divine Amenhotep III–Khonsu and Sedeinga's Tiy–Hathor. It follows, then, that Thebes served as a geographic fulcrum between these two antipodal entities. Recalling Karnak's new northeast–southwest axis, one can not help but wonder if all three pairs of male–female temples – Athribis–Bubastis, Soleb–Sedeinga, and Karnak–Luxor – were tied into an overall scheme that was very clear at the time and governed by the movement of celestial bodies.

POWER BROKERS AT MEMPHIS: HIGH STEWARD AMENHOTEP AND HIGH PRIEST PTAHMOSE

Only traces of Amenhotep III remain at Memphis, either because little space was left after earlier kings had built there, or because his work was masked by later kings, or because it has not yet been found under modern dwellings and agriculture. Yet it is known that Amenhotep III founded another "mansion of millions of years" in the irrigation area west of Memphis, as though he intended to recelebrate his jubilee in the north, just as he had likely repeated his coronation there 30 years earlier.

36. Colossal statue of Queen Tiy usurped by Osorkon, Bubastis. Photo: APK.

He named it "Nebmaatra-United-with-Ptah," and evidence shows that it existed, at least in part, by Year 26.

Like the earliest structure at the memorial temple at Kom el Hettan in western Thebes, the Memphite temple was dedicated to Ptah, or as the inscription goes,

> given as a monument for [the king's] father Ptah, in excellent works of eternity out of [Tura] limestone, its beauty being like the horizon of the sky, all its doors from the cedar of Lebanon . . . they

being worked with real gold of the foreign countries and electrum and every costly and noble stone.... A lake was dug, and trees were planted and made bright with every august wood from the choice of God's land. The offering tables were of silver and gold, turquoise and every costly and hard stone.

Work at Memphis was overseen by High Steward Amenhotep "Huy," Ramose's elder half brother. He recorded his life and career in an extremely self-serving account on a statue now in the Ashmolean Museum. Through his court service as a youth, Steward Amenhotep claimed to have become so intimate with and trusted by Pharaoh that all his life, he was allowed to enter the palace even while "other nobles proceeded out." His position as High Steward also gave him control of the treasury, the granary, and the regional workshops. He acknowledged that he benefited enormously from his governmental position. As High Steward, his staff "being over the heads of the common folk," he was "enriched with servants, bulls, and everything without limit, and there was no saying, 'Oh for this or that.'"

In turn, Amenhotep "Huy" was personally generous to the Ptah temple. At some point, apparently while he still had some years ahead of himself, he donated to the temple a large alabaster slab for grilling burnt offerings. He inscribed it to Ptah and Sekhmet, calling the former "King of the Gods" (which Amun thought *he* was) and asking the god for a "happy lifetime." He also donated an apparently enormous statue of the king to the Memphite temple in return for service and offerings for his tomb after his death.

The statue had a long name, "Nebmaatra, the Strong One, Which His Majesty Made for His Father Ptah in This Temple," as though the king had given it himself, but the steward made it clear on his own statue that was not the case. He claimed it cost him 210 arourae (about 140 acres) of land in the northern region, 220 arourae of land from holdings he had formerly been given by the king, in addition to 24 servants, 10 female servants, 1,000 laying fowl, 1,000 pigs, and 1,000 piglets, but does not mention whom he paid. Since he did not identify the great statue's material, we can only guess that it was carved either in brown quartzite from nearby Gebel Ahmar, like his own statue, or else from Tura limestone, like the temple itself and like the tumbled-down colossus of Ramesses II now lying nearby in the village of Mit Rahineh.

Private endowments of royal statuary were extremely rare in ancient Egypt because the system usually worked the other way around. Statuary of officials and their families were traditionally "boons" the king gave. Steward Amenhotep's gift suggests that the official and merchant classes had become so wealthy that they were able to buy favor with their gods and king by privately funding and furnishing sanctuaries, as did the Medicis during the Italian Renaissance, for example. In Egypt, this would happen increasingly in Ramesside times, but for Dynasty 18, the scale of the steward's remarkable donation seems unprecedented.

What the steward Amenhotep asked in return was that his tomb at Sakkara, an important cemetery since archaic times, would receive in perpetuity a daily share of the god's offerings, namely, 200 loaves of bread, ten jars of beer, one jar of wine, a container of fat, the foreleg of every calf that comes to the temple, a jar of milk, two cakes, one duck, six bundles of vegetables, and one plate of fruit, as well as bunches of flowers. Presumably this was a major means of support for the steward's *wab* priest, probably his eldest son and his descendants, who would eventually tend to the old man's burial and the maintenance of his tomb.

Did other officials also pay for some temple construction and embellishment out of their own pockets? When Amenhotep son of Hapu wrote that he had been given "permission" to restore his home temple, should we read between the lines that he used at least some of his own funds, thus buying his own proverbial staircase to heaven? After all, his own statue promised to maintain the temple and its granaries. This sounds every bit like a private endowment, not a royal one.

Another Memphite official who needs to be mentioned, if only because of the exceptional quality of his monuments, is the High Priest of Ptah, Ptahmose, who probably rose to this position after the untimely death of Prince Thutmose. His exquisitely carved, large brown quartzite statue, now in Florence, originally resided in the Ptah temple at Memphis or perhaps in "Nebmaatra-United-with-Ptah" but appeared in the Uffizi inventories by 1753. Ptahmose sits on a pillow on the floor, heels drawn up to his buttocks, arms folded atop his knees, and his round face peering upward over them as if listening intently. He pulls his kilt over his knees and wears all the elaborate jewels of his office as well as the short wig with a heavy braid to one side that indicates his affiliation with Ptah. His torso is quite thick with folds of fat, and his eyelids are creased like the king's in his later years.

Ptahmose also appears on a superbly carved brown quartzite stela with several major officials. Most important of this group is Meryptah, the steward of Amenhotep III's memorial temple, previously the High Priest of the Ptah cult at Thebes. Two other extremely important and highborn officials imaged here are a second High Priest of Ptah named "Ptahmose" (who probably preceded Prince Thutmose as high priest) and his father, a vizier named "Thutmose", who probably straddled the reigns of Thutmose IV and Amenhotep III. In their midst is Meryptah's mother, Tawy, whose title is simply Lady of the House. Her presence as the only female suggests that she is a crucial linchpin in the lineup and very well connected, but how and to whom other than her son? It must have been obvious to all viewers at the time. Her name is the same as that of a suspected sister or half sister of Amenhotep III (see Chapter 1), but it is impossible to tell if they are one and the same.

What this stela does tell us is that one family or closely allied group of individuals controlled major priesthoods in Egypt at this time, again rather like the Medicis in Renaissance Italy. Except for the brief period of time when Prince Thutmose was high priest, the individuals on Ptahmose's stela held that seat. Simultaneously, their close friend and/or blood relative, Meryptah, had become High Steward of Amenhotep III's memorial temple at Thebes after being High Priest of the Ptah cult at Thebes. He may also have been the same Meryptah who was High Priest of Amun at Karnak in Year 20, the three positions creating a network of power and influence of great service to the king if they were loyal, or the opposite if not.

MIDDLE EGYPT BEGINS TO RISE IN IMPORTANCE

Between Thebes and Memphis lies Middle Egypt. This is where Akhenaten would eventually found his new city, Akhetaten, at what is now called Tell el Amarna. Amenhotep III had been busy here from early in the reign (see Chapter 5), acquiring stone for Thoth's temple at Hermopolis not far from Amarna's eventual site. Now in these later years, in preparation for his jubilee, he placed enormous brown quartzite statues of baboons sacred to Thoth at the temple. They are positioned standing with the palms of their paws raised in the traditional pose of adoration, as if they are hailing the sun, which they encouraged to rise with their alarming shrieks.

Not far from Hermopolis was Hebenu. In antiquity, Hebenu was the capital of the oryx (gazelle) nome, one of the 22 provincial divisions of Upper Egypt. According to tradition, this is where Horus defeated his father's murderer, evil Uncle Seth, who had disguised himself as a gazelle to fight Horus. During the battle, Horus's eye was wounded and then restored, obviously a favorite theme of Amenhotep III. The Horus temple at Hebenu was constructed of limestone like Hermopolis and the northern temples. Brilliantly painted reliefs of nome gods bringing offerings, led by the god of the oryx nome, like those in Cleveland, may have come from such a temple here or elsewhere.

Hebenu's high priest, Taitai, is the subject of an exquisite stone statuette now in Berlin. Thick waisted and almond eyed like the aging Amenhotep III, the figure can be dated by both style and inscriptions to the time of the jubilees. Taitai is "the hereditary noble and Mayor, the Controller of the Double Thrones (during the *sed* festival), Overseer of Priests, Greatest of the Five in the Temple of Thoth, sole one of the heart of the king, whose failing there is not, the High Priest of Horus, Lord of Hebenu, Taitai."

There are very few periods in the entire history of Egypt when the priest of such a small temple would be memorialized by a portrait of such masterpiece quality. Yet he is just one of scores of Amenhotep III's officials, high and low, with important private monuments, and their statuary far outnumbers that of the courtiers of previous reigns. The number, quality of workmanship, and richness of materials of these sculptures are not equaled in any other period of Egypt's history. Thus, as public works projects go, Amenhotep III's building program created enormous wealth for the officials involved in seeing it through, many of whom were lifelong friends of the king, and some of whom may have been blood relatives. They shared his vision, they helped him to realize his dreams, and many of them became as rich and powerful as kings themselves.

In sum, it was not only at Thebes but throughout Egypt and the Sudan that Amenhotep III carried out his grand construction plan of enormous scope, imagination, and complexity, all aimed at promoting himself from mortal to immortal, from human to divine. The central theme of this building program concentrated on appeasing the two eyes of Re, the sun and the moon, two great cosmic forces that began to be emphasized in personal prayers during the second half of this reign. The spiritual concepts are quite complex, but the pacification of these elements prevented chaos, such as that which had occurred before Creation, and perhaps like that which occurred during the lost years of Amenhotep's reign. It was gold that supported this plan to ensure *ma'at*, the right order of things, and reciprocally, *ma'at* kept the gold coming.

THE FIRST JUBILEE FESTIVAL (HEB=SED)

(Reign of Amenhotep III, Year 30, ca. 1362 B.C.)

TRADITION

The royal jubilee, or *heb-sed*, was a festival of renewal rooted in Egypt's most ancient history. One of its iconic images comes from Dynasty 3, a scene in Djoser's Step Pyramid complex at Sakkara. It shows Djoser in full stride running a footrace to demonstrate his fitness to rule, an important feature of the jubilee because the kingdom's own strength, health, and fertility depended on that of the ruler himself. The *sed* festival traditionally took place during the thirtieth year of the reign. Most kings, of course, died long before reaching this goal, and some celebrated early. Amenhotep III was one of a small percentage who survived to celebrate as prescribed.

Considering the amount of treasure spent in preparation, Amenhotep III's *heb-sed* must have been the most lavish in history. Temples and colossal sculptures had been erected the length of the Nile Valley; jewelry and ornaments were produced in the thousands at the royal workshops; and the new palace compound, the "House of Rejoicing," with its huge, gleaming lake, was readied on the west bank of Thebes. The main celebration would occur here at Malkata and in its surrounding area, including the vast memorial temple nearby at Kom el Hettan.

In charge of planning every aspect of this jubilee was Amenhotep son of Hapu, one of the few courtiers who actually remembered the last full-blown one (Amenhotep II's), lending him an air of exceptional expertise. He and his scribes scoured the ancient libraries, most of which were inside the temples. They studied inscriptions and images on archaic monuments to prepare the protocol, organize the correct regalia and costumes, and find clues to the most ancient and authentic rites. They examined 1500-year-old predynastic palettes (archaic ritual objects), one of which was updated with the image of Queen Tiy carved on its back as a votive gift or memento. They toured Old Kingdom sun temples, the scribe May leaving his graffito at the pyramid of the Fourth Dynasty king Sneferu in Year 30. The resulting ceremonies and costumes would tie Amenhotep III irrevocably and undeniably to the ancestral kings.

Amenhotep III's *sed* festival lasted some weeks, months, or even longer, its length and timing having been discussed in numerous modern Egyptological articles. Tableaux of some of the ceremonies appear on ancient temple and tomb walls in Egypt and in the Sudan, and these allow the festival to be glimpsed in pieces. The records left behind of Amenhotep's three jubilees are the wellspring of a great deal of what we know today about the ancient Egyptian *sed* festival in general, but much of it is still a mystery.

The most extensive scenes are on the walls of Soleb temple. These carvings not only describe many of the rituals but also document the individuals – royal family members and courtiers – involved. The tomb of Queen's Steward Kheruef (TT 192), one of the largest at Thebes, contains exquisitely carved depictions of some of the public and private events of the First and Third jubilees, some starring Kheruef himself, as does the tomb of granary official Khaemhet (TT 57), focusing on himself, of course. A centuries-later rendition of jubilee rites appears on the walls of a granite gateway at Bubastis built by the Libyan king Osorkon II, the usurper of the colossal red granite statue of Queen Tiy at that same site. The Bubastis rendition of the jubilee is so close to Soleb's that many scholars think Osorkon copied his scenes either from those at Soleb or from an undiscovered Bubastite monument of Amenhotep III.

The most interesting documentation for the secular and personal side of the First Jubilee comes from the trash heaps of Malkata palace. Great numbers of large jars (see Figure 43) were sent, many labeled with the contents, the title and/or name of the donor, and sometimes the date of the gift in black pigment on the vessels' shoulders. The jar labels are an equalizing, almost democratizing factor since the donors ranged from extremely rich officials to small servants, from native sons to foreign immigrants, yet all the jars were generally of equal quality in terms of material and workmanship, and all seem to have been accepted, stored, and used with no discrimination toward their origins.

For, the First Jubilee, the most common gift was ale. Donors named on the labels range from the highly important southern vizier Ramose to the lowliest butchers, like Henu, who worked for the high priest Meryptah, who also sent a gift. In addition, Ramose's half brother, Steward Amenhotep, the northern vizier Amenhotep, Theban surveyor and steward Amenemhet Surer, and royal harem steward Userhet sent gifts in Year 30. So did Paser, who had by now succeeded his father Sebekhotep, our king's childhood mentor, to the post of mayor of the Faiyum. The untitled name "Meryra" also appears among the labels. Is he the former *kap* supervisor of the king and nurse of Prince Si-Atum? Viceroy Merymose is missing from this list, but he is shown participating in the ceremonies in reliefs at Soleb temple.

Scribe Roma, the "gatekeeper" appearing with his wife on the so-called Polio stela (see Chapter 9), gave potted food gifts to the king in Year 30. The couple are thought to have been foreigners at the court both because of his unusual name and because he and his wife worship Ishtar on their stela. He may have been a son of a Canaanite or other eastern ruler brought to Egypt to serve Pharaoh, a practice often recorded in the Amarna letters (see Chapter 15). Making these boys palace gatekeepers, in particular, is reminiscent of the Ottoman practice of kidnapping young boys in foreign countries and bringing them hundreds of miles to the royal court, where they had no one to depend on but the king. With no other local loyalties, they made true and fierce guardians.

EVENTS AT THE PALACE AND HONORED PARTICIPANTS

The festivities probably started on the twenty-seventh day of the second month of summer (around late April). Kheruef recounted that "the king appeared gloriously at the great double doors of his palace," possibly a balcony above one of his throne rooms. An ebony statuette of the king in Brooklyn, inscribed "Lord of *Sed* festivals in the House of Rejoicing," represents the king as he might have looked that day, wearing his blue *khepresh* war crown with its gold brow band and gold uraeus, a beautifully pleated gold kilt, a wide beaded belt, and an elaborate apron draped in front of his thighs, the gold sparkling against the rich, brown color of his skin (Figure 37).

He ushered in his officials, friends, acquaintances, the "crew of the bark," and other dignitaries. They stood in order of their rank (Kheruef

37. Amenhotep III at his jubilee, ebony, gilded and inlaid, height 103/8 inches. 48.28. Courtesy the Brooklyn Museum (http://www.brooklynmuseum.org/opencollections).

shows himself in front) and were given awards, some as important as British knighthoods, for example. These included the Gold of Honor (one or more choker-length necklaces of large gold beads), gold ducks and fish, and ribbons of green linen. A fragment of Amenhotep son of Hapu's mortuary temple relief shows him wearing such a ribbon as a headband. Khaemhet's tomb also contains a scene of officials receiving rewards, with himself in front, of course. Afterward, a reception was held at the palace, with bread, oxen, fowl, and beer all in great quantity.

This was followed by the king and queen sailing across the "Lake of His Majesty" (Birket Habu) in their special boats. Officials, according to Kheruef, "grasped the tow-ropes of the evening bark and the prow rope of the morning bark and they towed the bark at the great place," imagery conjoining the king and Tiy with both the sun and the moon. The lake's northeast to southwest orientation is precisely parallel to the angle of the processional way between Luxor and Karnak temples, which cannot be coincidental. In order for this to happen they must have been oriented to celestial and/or solar movements.

By now it is apparent that Amenhotep III designed many of his processions to be waterborne rather than traditional marches, considering the Festival of the Lakes, his two-way sail during the Opet Festival, and now his cruise on the Birket Habu being made, for the first time, as far as we know, a major element of the jubilee. For longer-distance, over-land jubilee travel, he rode aloft in a sedan chair, wearing his blue crown. Did he plan his ceremonial transportation thus because his clubfoot made walking too difficult or because the accompanying limp rendered him less than divine? There is no evidence that he ever ran the traditional footrace illustrated by King Djoser. How this was explained away or substituted is not known.

Queen Tiy, in her crown of tall plumes, followed the sedan chair on foot, as did the princesses, who wore short, round wigs with cascading braids and platform-shaped crowns (Figure 39). In the Soleb reliefs, Sitamen, the eldest, was given a place of honor alone behind her mother. Sisters Henut-taneb and Isis were nearby and, in smaller scale, six or eight additional young women, "(female) royal children," accompanied by an unnamed Chief of the Royal Harem. Elsewhere, "royal children boys and girls" make "acclamations four times." Therefore the king's sons were not excluded from the ceremonies, even though they appear in smaller size and at a greater distance from the king himself. Some of them may actually have been grandchildren since, as we learned from the Rhind labels, Prince Si-Atum's daughter, Nebetia, Amenhotep III's granddaughter, bore the title King's Daughter. At age 50, having reared several sons and daughters, Amenhotep III must have had numerous grandchildren.

In Kheruef's representations, a row of girls, dressed and coiffed like Egyptian princesses, pour water from gold ewers and electrum libation flasks. They are the "children of the great ones," the latter probably being foreign rulers. One girl is captioned "daughter of the Mentiu," thought to have been a foreign tribe living northeast of Egypt, perhaps in the

38. Statue of goddess Yunet from Luxor Cachette, height 55 inches. Photo: APK.

Sinai or around Canaan. This scene and its captions recall Amarna letter 369, in which Amenhotep III petitioned the king of Gezer in Canaan to "send extremely beautiful female cupbearers in whom there is no defect" for 40 shekels each (eight times the price of a good ox).

Amenhotep III's officials also joined the retinue. One of these, who appears in almost every scene at Soleb, in the blocks from Karnak, and in Kheruef's tomb, was Chief Lector Priest Nebmerutef, often shown holding a papyrus roll in his hand. He was apparently the grand marshal of these hopelessly complex ceremonies, a task requiring energy, memory, and organization as well as diplomacy, considering that he was herding both royalty and high officials. It would have helped to have royal blood himself.

Nebmerutef is also known from two Malkata jar labels, one dated to the First Jubilee, and two tiny statuette groups (now in the Louvre) showing him seated in front of a shrine with the god Thoth's baboon perched on top. An inscription on one of these little monuments refers to the propitiation of the lunar eye of Amun-Re, one of the raisons d'être of Soleb. In Kheruef's tomb, Nebmerutef's name was inscribed once and then erased and replaced with just the title Chief Lector Priest. This seems like an act of *damnatio memoriae*, so maybe he was not so diplomatic.

Another official depicted at Soleb was Ramose's son Simut, the former Fourth Priest of Amun in Year 20, now Second Priest, succeeding Amenhotep III's brother-in-law Anen, who must have died since his name is not among the Malkata labels, nor does he appear at Soleb. Simut is often depicted at Soleb with a *sem* priest named "Meryra" (?), the highest-level priest of a royal memorial temple, notwithstanding High Priest Meryptah, who was still alive at this time and sent gifts to the jubilee. The rest of the officials in the entourage are mostly identified by title only. Appearing often, though small in size, are the two viziers, one of which is Ramose, the southern vizier and governor of Thebes. The northern vizier is unnamed in the Soleb scenes, but northern vizier Amenhotep, whose statues are at Bubastis, sent a gift to the king dated Year 30. Both viziers traveled a great deal, and there is some confusion about who belonged where (see Chapter 14).

On the Soleb reliefs, an unnamed King's Son (the future Amenhotep IV/Akhenaten?) marches in front of the viziers at one point, and King's Son Merymose marches behind the viziers in another scene. His title elsewhere, Controller of the Two Thrones in Nubia, referred to his participation in these jubilee festival celebrations. The phrase "Two Thrones" refers to a specific jubilee event described later in this chapter.

One of the most interesting individuals in the procession is an anonymous chief of artisans. He wears the special wig and side lock sacred to Ptah, the god of craftsmen, and the priestly cheetah skin, its head resting in front at hip level, the haunches and tail draping over his back. This is how the technology, the tortuous expeditions to acquire the raw materials, not to speak of sheer creativity and artistic skills, were officially recognized during the jubilee.

The procession of king, family, harem, and officials, all in their perfumed wigs, crowns, ribbons, jewelry, fine linen, and regalia, was public. Ordinary subjects could line the avenue, as royals and officials approached the temple; however, outrunners surged ahead and shouted "to the ground," sending all on the sidelines to prostrate themselves in the dirt, stealing furtive glances no doubt, but never having direct eye contact with the passing royals.

RITUALS AT THE MEMORIAL TEMPLE

Amenhotep III announced his arrival at the temple and requested entry by rapping on one side of the double-leafed door with a stone mace head mounted on a rod. This action was mimicked symmetrically by his favorite and most powerful courtier, Amenhotep son of Hapu, who knocked on the opposite door leaf with his own mace, essentially acting as a shadow-royal himself. Grand marshal Nebmerutef orchestrated every movement from nearby.

The scenes inside the temple must have been magical, with the glitter of jewels and the swish of linen sweeping across silver floors as king and family crossed the threshold of a doorway covered with gold and inlaid with semiprecious stones. Heightening the atmosphere were the aroma of burning incense, the intonations of chanting priests, and the scent of perfumed wigs and gowns. The royal daughters carried *menats*, bronze implements with multiple strings of tiny beads which, when shaken, produced a subtle, soft rustling sound, evoking the reeds and rushes in which the bovine goddess Hathor dwelled and the marshes from which the earth rose at creation.

As the king moved from one venue to another, he was preceded by the standard of the svelte jackal god Wepwawet, who was always shown standing erect on all fours rather than recumbent like Anubis. Wepwawet's name meant "Opener of Ways." He was at the heart of the *sed* festival because his name was originally an epithet of the archaic jackal god Sed. This animal was a great guardian, who ceaselessly prowled the borders of his territory, defending it against all interlopers. Thus the *Sed* festival honored this ancient canid, actually two of them – one for Upper Egypt and one for Lower – and the original footrace recalled the dog's eternal patrol.

Each jubilee activity required the king to wear a distinctive costume including robe or kilt, various crowns, type of beard (or none), and footwear (or none). The king changed his garb often enough during the events that there was a special "house of clothing" devoted to keeping his gear in order and providing him a place to change. Queen Tiy's appurtenances changed from one event to another, but not her gown. At Soleb, she is shown mostly wearing her two tall plumes and two uraei (cobras) at her forehead and carrying an *ankh* (life) in one hand, sometimes a flower. Sometimes she carries a baton in the other hand and sometimes her flail with its long handle and drooping pendants, the accoutrement most characteristic of her sculpture in the round. In one scene at Soleb, she is shown inside the palace not wearing a crown. Throughout the jubilee she wears sandals or not, in concert with her husband.

A second iconic moment other than the footrace involved the king being twice enthroned, once as ruler of Upper Egypt and once as ruler of Lower Egypt. Since the beginning of recorded history, this ritual was illustrated as a mirror image of Pharaoh seated within back-to-back shrines, wearing the white crown in one, the red crown in the other, and in both a long, heavy, wrap-around mantle, an item of clothing uniquely associated with this festival and illustrated on one of a set of cornelian bracelet plaques in the Metropolitan Museum (Figure 39 right). Before him were the appropriate gods of each locale, who had left their home shrines to attend the festival. They sat in individual wooden booths set up in two groups, northern and southern, while offerings were brought and incense burned for them.

Amenhotep III had commissioned a whole new series of statues of the gods and goddesses in black granodiorite for this occasion at his "mansion of millions of years." Some of them bear the name of the god and the title Lord of the Jubilee. Many were later moved to other locations, gifted to their home cult centers still bearing their original inscriptions. Some, like the mummiform statue of Isis unearthed by the Italian mission at Antinoe, were reinscribed by Ramesses II and perhaps moved more than once.

Leonine goddesses were put in charge of the temple's water clock (*clepsydra*), according to Soleb temple relief carvings which depict the king handing over the clock in the form of a hieroglyphic symbol. The earliest one known – basically a huge, stone bucket with pierced sides – dates to the reign of Amenhotep III and is now in the Cairo museum. It was filled with water which drained slowly, allowing time to be tracked as signs indicating the hours revealed themselves. Since the *clepsydra* could measure time in the dark, unlike sun markers, the moment of transfer was probably sundown, after which the divine felines theoretically guarded time itself, thus guaranteeing the king and the entire country safe passage through the vulnerable period of darkness until the arrival of the coming day.

Timing was crucial for the climax of the festival deep inside the royal tomb. There Pharaoh faced the images of the gods represented on his tomb walls and remained for a period of time before going to his funeral bed, where he "died" and was "reborn" in a series of rituals, incantations, and offerings, not to speak of changes of costume, all of which had to be carried out in the appropriate order and within a span of a certain number of hours before daylight.

This resurrection was the culmination of a process of deification that had begun with Amenhotep III's coronation. At that time, like all Egyptian kings, he was the representative and high priest of each

39. Three cornelian bracelet plaques from bracelets, average length 2 inches. Tiy as sphinx, 26.7.1342; Tiy and Amenhotep III enthroned before princesses, 26.7.1340; mirror-image jubilee scene, 26.7.1339. Courtesy Metropolitan Museum of Art.

god on earth (son of Re, heir of Geb, and Horus incarnate) and was treated as nearly divine. He had his own cult statue, like a god, and in his palace, he was approached with great ceremony – prostrations and bowed heads – like a god in a temple. Over the decades, however, and passing through difficult times, Amenhotep III's own divinity had intensified. Substantial amounts of statuary and stelae identified him, as mentioned in Chapter 10, not just as the deities' representative, but as the gods themselves: as Amun, Min, Montu, Horus, Thoth, even the Aten. One of his inscriptions on Karnak's Third Pylon states that the statues of himself he has placed there are actually images of Re, "divine and beautiful."

Now at the time of his jubilee, Nebmaatra himself became a god in his own right. In Nubia, he was the god Nebmaatra of Soleb, receiving a new form of headgear, including the special downward-curling horns of a breed of rams husbanded there. This crown he brought back to Thebes and wore in scenes at Luxor Temple. The ram's horns became such a powerful symbol of divine kingship that Alexander III of Macedon adopted them a millennium later, after being deified at Siwa oasis. That image, perhaps originating with court sculptor Lysippos, was not only used on issues of Alexander the Great's own coins but also influenced the coin portraits of many later rulers.

Amenhotep may have repeated the jubilee rites at various other "mansions of millions of years," particularly at Memphis, and possibly also at Bubastis and Soleb. The queen's steward Kheruef left indications of having traveled with the king to celebrations at both ends of the empire, which means that Tiy probably did as well. Kheruef was portrayed on the walls of Soleb Temple, and he left a statue base inscribed for the jubilee at Bubastis. Judging from the known dates for various parts of the celebration, it officially lasted somewhere between two and a half to eight months, but there are jubilee gift labels at Malkata dating to Years 31 and 32, perhaps reflecting the time it took to re-create the ceremonies elsewhere.

Reports of the jubilee spread throughout the relevant world. Gifts were sent to rulers far and wide, and according to Kheruef, a number of foreign chiefs actually attended the extravaganza. However, one foreign ruler, the king of Babylon, was miffed at not having been invited, and years later, he complained of this perceived insult in writing. His hurt feelings were eventually salved with gifts of gold, ebony, and ivory sent to him from Egypt in exchange for the promise of one of his daughters in marriage to Amenhotep III (see Chapter 16).

A GOOD YEAR FOR WOMEN: THE QUEENS OF YEAR 30 – TIY AND SITAMEN – AND REDUCTION OF TAXES

By Year 30, Amenhotep III had three official wives: Tiy; his daughter Sitamen, whom he promoted to queen at the time of his jubilee; and Gilukhepa, the Mitannian princess, whose whereabouts and activities at this point are not known but whose name turns up in royal correspondence around this time (see Chapter 14). In addition, there must have been a stable of other harem women he never officially married.

Tiy was still the most important of the royal women. In addition to her divine presence at Sedeinga, she is one of the rare Egyptian queens depicted as a sphinx, and larger than any before her, a colossal brown quartzite sphinx in her name having been found at the memorial temple. She also appears as a sphinx guarding her husband's precious cartouche on mirror-image reliefs at Sedeinga and on another of the small, carved cornelian plaques in the Metropolitan Museum (Figure 39 top). The previously mentioned plaque with the *heb-sed* booths scene shows mirror images of Queen Tiy handing a notched palm rib with a tadpole and circle at its base, representing "dominion for hundreds of thousands of years," to her seated husband. A mere mortal cannot give such a gift, only a divinity. The colossal standing statue of her now at Bubastis must also have been an implicit message about her status. Therefore Tiy, too, had risen above mere mortals to the divine realm.

Cairo's gargantuan (23-foot-tall) limestone statue group (possibly carved in limestone from Kheruef's courtyard) shows Tiy enthroned in equal scale beside her husband and is further testimony to her prominence. It must have been made around the time of the First Jubilee because her wig is at its most developed, nearly shrouding her face. Three daughters stand in miniature beside their parents' legs. In the middle, Henut-taneb wears the full wig of a woman. Two of her sisters are in front of the throne's corners. One is labeled "Nebetah" – the only image known of her, although her name is also preserved on a few small objects dating in style to the fourth decade. The other girl, whose name is destroyed, is probably Isis because she is shown with a young girl's coiffure: a wide, braided mass of hair falling over her right shoulder like the hairstyles of the princesses on the walls of Soleb Temple.

Sitamen is notably absent from this colossal group, perhaps because by now, she had become queen in her own right. A gift label dated to Year 30 identifies her as both Royal Daughter and Great Royal Wife, a rare combination of titles. A woman thought by many to have been her childhood nurse, Nebet-kebny, had previously left a stela at Abydos (now in the Cairo museum) showing Sitamen sitting on her lap and noting her title at that time, Great One in the Harem of Amun. After the princess's promotion, Nebet-kebny or her family altered the stela, carving a royal cartouche around Sitamen's name and placing a uraeus on her brow.

The young queen had a palace of her own at Malkata, probably what is called the North Palace, the structure across the central courtyard from the main buildings. Judging from gift labels, Sitamen received a great many presents from courtiers at Malkata – twice as many as her mother! Her palace steward was none other than the octogenarian Amenhotep son of Hapu, now given a stationary and sedentary sinecure for his declining years. He was "appointed as an administrator" of Sitamen's household on the second day of the third month of summer, a few days after the other officials had been rewarded, says Hapu's son, at the end of the "first Sed festival of his Majesty." Clothed in the finest linen, Hapu's son "received the adornments of gold and every precious and noble stone [including] the Hathor necklace (!) and pendant [made of] . . . electrum and every precious stone." In deference to his great age, unique position at court, and undoubted frailty, he did not prostrate himself before the king on his dais but was seated on a gold throne directly in front of it.

Sitamen's promotion and the establishment of a palace for her raise the question of sexual intimacy between her and her father-husband. Incest was generally avoided by mere mortals in ancient Egypt, despite that husbands and wives often referred to each other as "brother" and "sister," and despite that sibling marriages occasionally happened among royals such as Hatshepsut and Thutmose II. Incest was normal among deities, however. In fact, the various creation myths depended on it. Primeval Egypt's population increased by way of the first deities, who were siblings, producing offspring together, and the goddess Hathor was magically mother, wife, and daughter of the sun god Re, all three of these aspects being crucial to his daily rebirth. Therefore what was incest among mere mortals was a necessity among deities and very possibly among members of a royal family that now had claims on true divinity.

Maintaining the virginity of a perfectly good queen, through whose body coursed royal blood, ran counterintuitive to the ancient Egyptians' eternal desire for fecundity and reproduction and especially to the requirement that their king be fertile. That was, after all, the essence of his being and an important outcome of the *sed* festival. The renewal of his fertility had repercussions not only for human beings but also for all aspects of an agrarian society, including the beasts and the fields. By Year 30, Tiy was certainly past her child-bearing years, and the only way to continue the pure line was for the king to mate with her (their) daughter(s). Royal incest may have been particularly important if this was a period of plague and the populace was in serious decline. This type of situation is reminiscent of the biblical Lot's daughters, who believed their little family to be the only people left on earth after a catastrophe had struck, and who tricked their father into impregnating them to continue the human race.

There is some evidence that Sitamen actually did bear a son. Remains of relief sculpture from the memorial temple of her great-grandfather Amenhotep II, which was restored by her father, show the young queen wearing a goddess's vulture headdress. Another small fragment contains the head of a young prince wearing one lock of hair braided to the side as a youth. Sitamen must have been around 30 years old or more at the time of the jubilee, certainly mature enough to have borne a number of children, and so this boy may be her child.

In the context of a temple, this little prince might be Ihy, Hathor's son, who leads the deceased along the tortuous and dangerous path to new life and was essential to the king's revitalization during the festival. If Sitamen was Hathor, then her son was Ihy. If Sitamen had a child by her father, she would have been the perfect embodiment of Hathor. She was the daughter and the wife and now had borne the king's future self, making her his mother as well. The question begs to be asked: was Nebmerutef, who led the king through every element of his jubilee festival, Sitamen's son?

Sitamen's face may have been used as the archetype for other goddesses in other venues as well, for example, on the goddess statues from the Luxor cachette. The facial features on the large granodiorite portrait of the goddess Yunet (Figure 38) from this group, now in the Luxor Museum, clearly differ from those of Queen Tiy. It has a stronger, squarer chin, a longer nose, and smaller eyes – still recognizable as belonging to the reign of Amenhotep III and inscribed for him, but just different enough from Tiy's portraits to suggest another woman.

In Year 30, Amenhotep III made a decree that benefited Theban women in general, and those working for the Amun temple in particular. Carved on a wall at Soleb Temple and repeated in Osorkon's Bubastis texts (presumed copies of Amenhotep III's inscriptions), the decree declared the following individuals exempt from special taxes: (1) harem women and chantresses of the estate of Amun; (2) Theban women "who have been servants since the time of his forefathers;" and (3) Thebes and her inhabitants in general. Amenhotep son of Hapu brought the good news to Karnak, "bringing to him the people of Thebes who were subordinates in the king's house, so that they might be exempt, serving as priests unto eternity for Amun, Lord of the Thrones of the Two Lands, in the first *sed*-festival of His Majesty."

Throughout history, the typical result of sparing women from the burdens of paying taxes was that marriage and raising families suddenly became more affordable. If that was indeed the reason behind these decrees, then Thebes, particularly the Amun priesthood, must have needed an increase in population, perhaps because the corps of priests at Karnak had been siphoned off to work across the river or because the population had been decimated by tragedy, or both.

These two important events of Year 30, the promotion of Amenhotep III as a divinity and the promotion of women, both individuals and groups, recall Millard Meiss's seminal work on the art of Florence and Siena following the Black Death, where he described a sea change in the religion after the disaster. The focus in fourteenth-century Italy was not away from Christianity, of course, but from the image of the adult Christ to the infant Christ and his young mother, Mary, who became regarded as a spiritual queen. Similarly, in the second half of Amenhotep III's reign, Egypt's religion began its metamorphosis away from its previous form – a diversified portfolio of aged gods – to a more singular focus on the son of those gods, who had become divine in his own right. He was no longer just the son of the sun but was the earthly sun itself. At the same time, the status and appreciation of women – especially queens – increased in both symbolic and real terms.

RAISING UP OLD OFFICIALS AND BUYING A NEW BRIDE

(Reign of Amenhotep III, Years 30 and 31, ca. 1362–1361 B.C.)

AMENHOTEP SON OF HAPU'S MONUMENTS

Amenhotep III's deification created a nebulous and unstated vacuum between himself and members of his court because he was now a step above mere king. Therefore, as a result of his becoming a god, his officials rose up a notch, not in title per se, but certainly in terms of eternal real estate and statuary. One was endowed with a temple of his own, others acquired tombs of a size and opulence just a step away from temples themselves. Their statuary was carved in the finest, hardest, most intractable stones, none of it colossal but a great deal of it larger than life.

Amenhotep son of Hapu received the nearly unprecedented gift of his own memorial temple, behind his king's and beside those built for Thutmoses II and III in the kings' row of royal cult temples. Royal workshops associated with Amenhotep III's monument had apparently been razed and relocated in favor of the great official's shrine. A bird's-eye view places Amenhotep son of Hapu's memorial at the hub of a circle encompassing Kom el Hettan, Malkata palace, the Valley of the Nobles, and the Valley of the Kings. In Amenhotep son of Hapu's afterlife, his spirit could view all that he had accomplished and join in on the various festivals parading right past his front pylon. Two centuries later, Ramesses III built his own temple just a few paces away to the south. Its modern name, Medinet Habu ("Hapu's Town"), does homage to its neighbor.

Given the scale of all-things-Nebmaatra, Amenhotep son of Hapu's structure was more the size of a chapel, like the Sistine as compared to the entire Vatican, but even so, it outshone the other officials' monuments by virtue of its location, its complexity, and its free-standing architecture. A plaza lay in front of the first pylon, behind which was an exquisitely landscaped courtyard with a rectangular pool set longitudinally between two rows of ten trees each. Deep wells were dug into the rocky, sandy desert to a depth of ten feet or more and lined with bricks, then filled with potting soil. Young trees were planted in pots, then set into the wells. This shady courtyard must have made a wonderful small oasis for birds, ducks, fish, and lilies as well as human visitors.

The second pylon led to a paved court lined with delicately fluted columns fronting chapels on each side. At the back was a dark sanctuary bordered by storage rooms. The temple's main walls were sheathed with sandstone, some carved in relief. Columns were inscribed in sunk relief, the hieroglyphs filled in with blue paint.

A large stela in the British Museum bears the royal dedication decree (probably recopied at a later date) dated to day 6, fourth month of Inundation, Year 31, and lists those present at the ceremony: the northern vizier Amenhotep (Ramose was absent), the treasurer Meryptah (possibly the same man as the steward of the king's memorial temple), and all of the royal scribes of the army. This last group is perhaps the best indication of where Amenhotep son of Hapu's career allegiance lay and how he was perceived by king and country – as a man who could marshal an entire army to accomplish his king's enormous projects.

No important statuary was found in the excavations at Amenhotep son of Hapu's temple, but seven major stone portraits of him – six granite and one limestone – all carved by the best sculptors of the day, were found across the river at Karnak: five in the Amun temple, one in Mut Temple, and one in Khonsu Temple. Another two were found up north at Athribis (see Chapter 12).

Two of the Karnak figures show the royal scribe in exactly the same form and pose as those of Mentuhotep, vizier and overseer of works under Dynasty 12's Senwosret I, builder of some of the earliest structures at Karnak. Mentuhotep had a series of statues at Karnak, at least ten, which were still in place when Amenhotep son of Hapu oversaw construction there. One of Mentuhotep's portraits may have been recut for Amenhotep son of Hapu. It represents him as an elderly man with a lined, sagging face, and it bears signs of rework, new carving over old. Economy in a reign as rich as Amenhotep III's seems an unlikely reason. More likely atavism, a deliberate attempt to connect with and absorb the traditions of Egypt's past, was Amenhotep son of Hapu's motive.

His two finest, and original, statues show Hapu's son sitting in the scribe's position on a cushion with his legs crossed in front of him, stretching his linen skirt across his thighs to act as a writing table (Figure 40, first and second from right). His upper body leans slightly forward, his serene face tilted slightly downward, yet his eyes look toward the observer as if listening for dictation. One hand holds the reed pen, and his ink well hangs from a strap over his shoulder. His face is symmetrical, with large, intelligent eyes and a full mouth. Each feature is beautifully sculpted, from the arching eyebrows to the individual locks of hair on his wig to the undulating rolls of flesh on his torso as he bends forward over his scroll.

The limestone statue, now in the Luxor Museum, bears his autobiography, quoted throughout this book. Found in two pieces in the court between Karnak's Third and Fourth pylons, the statue is a blocky shape. The subject sits on a cushion with his knees drawn up toward his chin, his legs and torso enveloped in one mass of drapery, providing large, flat fields for inscriptions. All of Amenhotep son of Hapu's titles were inscribed on these statues, including his favorite, Royal Scribe, as well as Overseer of Works in the Mountain of Gritstone (quartzite), Overseer of all the Works of the King, Seal Bearer of the King of Lower Egypt, and Hereditary Prince. Some titles and epithets testify to his close personal and confidential relationship with Amenhotep III: "sole friend," "his (the king's) beloved," and Fan-Bearer on the Right of the King.

RAMOSE'S LOST PORTRAITS FOUND

Vizier Ramose had one of the most beautiful tomb chapels in all of ancient Egypt, decorated over several years' span (see Figure 30 and Chapters 11, 16, and 18). But what about his statuary? Generations of Egyptologists have lamented that these monuments no longer exist or have never been found, when in fact two major ones were resting in disguise under our noses in the Cairo museum at the foot of the colossal limestone pair statue of Amenhotep III and Tiy. They were missed because they were usurped and reinscribed for Horemheb's vizier, Pa-Ramessu, who became Ramesses I of Dynasty 19.

Pa-Ramessu's two scribe statues were found right next to Amenhotep son of Hapu's at the Tenth Pylon (Figure 40, first and second from left). The composition and style of carving are unmistakably by the same workshop. Pa-Ramessu's statues wear the chest-high vizier's dress, with shoulder straps identical to Ramose's costume on a doorjamb at the back of his tomb. Pa-Ramessu's wig style is also exactly the same shape and length as Ramose's doorjamb image. Coiffures at the cusp of Dynasties 18–19 were much longer. The figure style was also different, very late Dynasty 18 and early Dynasty 19 chests being more sunken and bellies distended. The Pa-Ramessu body type is similar to Amenhotep son of Hapu's.

The statues' bases, which should have been straight up and down and must have borne inscriptions for Ramose, were hacked away. As a result the bottom of each base is narrower than the top and the edges are rough, completely out of character with the fine finish of the statue. Where Ramose's name already existed, it was easy to revise as Pa-Ramessu. The cartouches of Horemheb on the shoulders have ragged edges, like scratches on dry skin, because the "skin" of the statue had been exposed to the elements and had dried out before these new elements were added.

We do not know if Ramose paid for his own statues, where they were originally set up (not necessarily at the Tenth Pylon), what their original inscriptions said, and how they were originally dedicated. What is clear, however, is that Ramose and Amenhotep son of Hapu both rated statuary of royal quality and of a size greater than portraits of many kings, for example, about twice the scale of Thutmose IV's famous statue where he sits next to his mother. Obviously, old Hapu's son had earned his statuary over the past 30 years in all areas of the king's life – military, spiritual, architectural construction, and family – but what did vizier Ramose do that was so special? The answer may be in the Amarna letters, and it's a long story.

NEGOTIATING FOR A SECOND MITANNI BRIDE

Sometime around Year 31, Amenhotep III turned his thoughts to acquiring another Mitanni princess. Twenty years had passed since Gilukhepa's arrival, and it will soon be apparent that she was still around. She probably provided Amenhotep III with offspring in the intervening years, but we do not know their names. In any case, by Year 31, she must have passed her child-bearing years, and the king needed a viable replacement for her.

Amenhotep III had dealt with her father, Shuttarna, in the past, and there seems to have been some lapse in relations after the old Mitanni king's death. Gilukhepa's brother Tushratta was, according to his own

40. Statues of Amenhotep son of Hapu (right) and Pa-Ramessu (left), the latter usurped from Ramose found at Karnak's Tenth Pylon. After Legrain.

recollection, "young" (a child or youth) when he succeeded Shuttarna in about Year 12 of Amenhotep III's reign. Tushratta's earliest surviving letter to Amenhotep III, probably written about 16 years or more later, was a bid to rekindle their countries' alliance. His motives were twofold. First of all, the Hittites were always threatening him, and he must have wanted Egypt's army on standby. Second, he wished to encourage trade between his own country and Egypt.

As a show of good faith, Tushratta sent a cover letter with the ancient equivalent of a squadron of fighter jets: at least three dozen (18 pair

of) horses with chariots, silver snaffle bits, bridles, blankets, other orna-
mented tack, and grooms. Some gold jewelry and perfume were included
for his sister Gilukhepa, which is how we know that she was still alive.
In return, he expected Nubian gold, and plenty of it.

Tushratta entrusted this batch of correspondence and chattel to his
chief minister, Keliya, and to a man named "Tunip-ibri." The latter
never again returned to the records, but Keliya became a mainstay of
Tushratta's missions to Egypt. His integrity must have been unassailable
and his diplomatic skills unexcelled because he is the likely recipient of
a gift made by the best of Amenhotep III's own artisans: a white faience
shawabti with red face and hands, periwinkle blue inscriptions, yellow
eyelids, and a blue-striped headdress (Figure 41). Now in Leiden, it is
inscribed for "Ker" or "Kel," since the hieroglyph for *r* could be either an
r or an *l*. This was a foreign name otherwise unknown in Egypt, and the
red skin and yellow eyelids suggest a sun-burned, light-skinned Indo-
European face rather than the usual golden brown Egyptian face. Instead
of holding traditional *shawabti* agricultural implements, each hand grasps
an *ankh*. An exquisite *ba* bird is drawn in blue across its chest.

This *shawabti* was left at Osiris's burial place, Abydos, like those of
Hekareshu and vizier and High Priest of Amun Ptahmose. Kel's and
Ptahmose's are so close in quality and workmanship that they seem to
have been made in the same atelier, but Ptahmose's may have been
made slightly earlier, judging from the shape of the necklace, which
is not nearly as wide as Kel's, an extravagantly broad model dating to
the end of the reign. This shop had previously produced (presumably
under an earlier master) at least one *shawabti* for Thutmose IV, in a less
pure white with a cobalt blue inscription, of which only the lower half
remains.

Keliya returned home to Mitanni from this trip with an Egyptian
messenger named "Mane" (likely pronounced in two syllables) bearing a
request from Pharaoh to Tushratta: "Send your daughter here to be my
wife and the mistress of Egypt." The child, named "Tadu-Hepa," must
have been just nearing puberty if her father was now somewhere in his
late 20s or early 30s. Obviously Tadu-Hepa was the niece of Gilukhepa,
since the latter was Tushratta's sister. Where Gilukhepa now lived or
what titles she may have held other than something like "the foreign
lady" are not known. Therefore Amenhotep's offer to make the new girl
his wife and the mistress of Egypt seems, at best, insincere. Nevertheless,
there was not the slightest sense of aversion from either side of the deal

41. Multicolored faience *shawabti* of Kel, height 8 inches, 3.3.1.25. Courtesy Rijksmuseum von Oudeheden, Leiden.

at the thought of this young girl joining her aunt in the same man's harem, and Tushratta was ready to negotiate.

Via Keliya and Mane, Tushratta let it be known that Tadu-Hepa's bride price was gold, "much more" than Amenhotep had sent Shuttarna in Year 11 for Gilukhepa. And he wanted "unworked" (pure) gold, none of those statuettes and other knickknacks made from gold alloys that the Egyptian king liked to send. After all, as Tushratta wrote, "in my brother's country, gold is as plentiful as dirt," a sentiment echoed in exactly those words throughout the Amarna correspondence from other western Asiatic kings, as if it were a catchphrase of Middle Eastern royal gossip. Hiding behind atavism, Tushratta claimed in the letter illustrated as Figure 42 that he wanted to build a mausoleum for his grandfather, in other words, a man with whom Amenhotep III's father, Thutmose IV, had done (bride) business.

Keliya was supposed to head back to Egypt with this response and with a gift of ten more teams of horses, jewelry made of lapis lazuli, and 30 women and men. The next letter from Tushratta, however, reports that Mane and Keliya were detained in Mitanni, possibly because Mane had become ill and was close to death, which Tushratta went to great and suspicious lengths to deny. Amenhotep III sent troops to investigate under the command of a man named "Haaramassi" or "Nahrammassi" or "Haramassa" or "Haamassi" (depending on which letter one reads), an official who would live on into the reign of Amenhotep IV.

Tushratta gave Haaramassi a tablet stating that Mane and Keliya would bring Tadu-Hepa to Egypt within six months or, he waffled, this year. On one hand, he may have been holding out for more treasure because he was extremely unhappy with what had just arrived. He reported having gathered all his foreign guests and opened the crates in front of them, and everyone wept (!), saying, "Are all of these gold? They do not look like gold!" On the other hand, he may have been waiting for his daughter to come of age because Amarna letter 20 suggests that she was still developing, and it was not until Year 36 that she was actually recorded as being present at Amenhotep III's court (see Chapter 16).

WHO WAS HAARAMASSI?

This name in all its various spellings crops up at various sites in western Asia during these years and at the beginning of the next reign. Apparently he was a major royal ambassador, or negotiator, or envoy but bore a name that was difficult for foreigners to pronounce in their own native tongues, much less transliterate into the more universal cuneiform. The name and its variants have been equated with the Egyptian name "Harmose" (or "Hormose"), which is nearly nonexistent before Dynasty 19, and there is no official of this name known in the reign of Amenhotep III. Tushratta mentioned that this Haaramassi was a magnate, an official of such power that he was above other officials, just below the king himself. If he was so important, how could he have escaped our notice? The answer most likely is that he, like his statues, has been there all the time – the southern vizier and mayor of Thebes, Ramose.

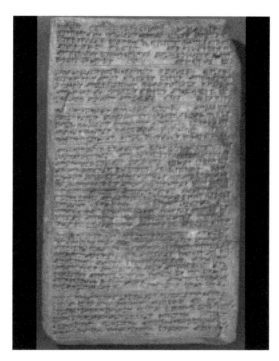

42. Amarna letter EA19, from Tushratta to Amenhotep III, announcing the dispatch of gifts and requesting his daughter's bride price, 8-3/4 by 5 inches, EA 29191. Courtesy the British Museum.

Tushratta and/or his scribes had a history of trouble spelling Egyptian names. Early on, Tushratta spelled his brother-in-law's name "Nibmuareya," later changing it to "Nimmureya," and eventually to "Mimmureya." The variant spellings of "Haaramassi," therefore, are consistent with the foreigners' inability to grasp the correct Egyptian pronunciation of a name and to transliterate it. The letter *R*, in particular, caused trouble then, as it does today. The modern linguistic term *rhotacism* refers to this problem. In modern times, almost every language has a different take on that letter, from the guttural to the rolled, or even no take at all. The same problem must have existed in antiquity (see earlier in relation to the spelling of Kel's name). Therefore, if Mimmureya was Nebmaatra, then Haaramassi was likely Ramose, the vizier, the magnate above other officials.

Considering that these negotiations transpired over a number of years, and consumed a great deal of time, what with all the travel and illnesses involved, it is quite possible that one of Ramose's trips abroad took place over a period of months in Year 31, which would explain his absence from the dedication ceremony for Amenhotep son of Hapu's memorial temple. Ramose's lengthy stints abroad would also explain why northern vizier Amenhotep was often recorded in the south during these years.

The messenger Mane is the subject of one of the most beautiful limestone nonroyal portraits remaining from the reign of Amenhotep III. It was hidden at the Louvre for 80 years underneath some terrible restoration and overpaint to the extent that it looked like a modern reproduction. At the suggestion of Élisabeth Delange this situation has been reversed, and the quality of the original is now apparent. The style of the work of art, the shape of the wig, the thickness of the torso, and the length of his necklace all conform to the art style and beauty of the later years of Amenhotep III's reign.

The portrait is inscribed for Real Royal Scribe Meniu, and allowing for the fact that Mane is transliterated from Akkadian and Meniu from Egyptian hieroglyphs, Christophe Barbotin believes that this appears to be our man. Few men bore the title Royal Messenger during Amenhotep III's reign, possibly because he sent individuals who already held more meaningful titles within Egypt. Real Royal Scribe is also a less-than-common title, but at least one other royal messenger uses it. One of the hieroglyphs used to spell Meniu's name is actually the figure of a shepherd – an appropriate spelling for the official escort of a royal mission. An undated jar label from Malkata may be his, as well as a *shawabti* in Cairo. The latter, a double *shawabti* of "Meny" with his wife, Henutiunu, is inscribed with prayers to Anubis "that he may give a coming forth of the horizon to see the sun disk, to sniff the gentle breeze of the northern wind," phrases that came into use in the last years of Amenhotep III's reign.

INTERNATIONAL TRADE IN PRINCESSES AND OTHER GOODS

(Reign of Amenhotep III, Years 32–33, ca. 1360–1359 B.C.)

EGYPT'S TRADING PARTNERS BY LAND

All Egypt's missions abroad, both the peaceful ones and the battle-ready, journeyed through the eastern wing of the Nile Delta on a coastal road called the "Ways of Horus." The route was studded with forts and customs houses controlling access to the Near Eastern lands beyond. One of these was a fort at Tell el Borg near what is now the Suez Canal. A cartouche of Queen Tiy has been found there as well as ceramics dating to this period. Another six miles to the west was the fortress at Tjel (Tjaru) by modern Qantara. Its commandant, Thutmose, gained enough wealth to afford sending eight signed gift jars to Malkata during the jubilee years.

The Ways of Horus led across the northern part of the Sinai Peninsula to Palestine and Canaan, not a unified nation but a series of city-states, some in the lowlands along the Mediterranean Sea (Ashdod) and some in the highlands (Jerusalem), with large areas of unsettled and undesirable land between them. Each city-state had its own governor or mayor, but there was no overall ruler during the fourteenth century B.C., except for Egypt's pharaoh, who was represented here not by a viceroy, as in Nubia, but by overseers with military backgrounds who maintained Egyptian authority with the assistance of manpower from Egyptian garrison towns.

Two Egyptians, Khaemwaset and Penhet, both military men, were essentially governors of Egypt's northern foreign territories, "overseers of the hill country," as they were called in Egyptian. Penhet is known from his tomb at Thebes, which depicts Syrians arriving in Egypt with gifts for the king. Khaemwaset, buried at Bubastis, had himself portrayed separately in two small, exquisitely carved statuettes, each with one of two wives: Khebunes was a "great one of the harem of Bastet," and Manana was a musician of Bastet.

Khaemwaset wears a long, pleated linen kilt and a fine linen shirt with flared sleeves, the latest fashion for men and not yet portrayed on larger, more conservative portraits. The amount of textile involved testifies to his wealth and prestige. His wives wear luxurious robes, adornments, and overabundant wigs rivaling Queen Tiy's styles at the end of the reign. The soft green-black stone in which these little masterpieces are carved and the style of carving suggest that they were made at the royal workshops in Thebes, the same origin as a set of statuettes for the royal family and other courtiers appearing in the next few years.

The system of overseers worked well much of the time because many of the local chiefs in Canaan and farther north in Kumidu and Amurru (modern Lebanon) had been educated in Egypt and considered themselves fully Egyptian. One of them, Yahtiru, wrote, "When I was young, [Pharaoh] brought me to Egypt. I served the king my lord and I stood at the city gate of the king, my lord." Now grown up, they took their places as multilingual, literate, politically and socially polished heads of vassal states as loyal to their *alma pater* as he was to them. The governor of Kumidu in the Beqa Valley gave hospitality to Ramose on a journey abroad and sent a son back to Egypt with him. Another governor, Aziru of Amurru, wrote to Pharaoh, "I here give my sons as two attendants and they are to do what the king, my lord, orders." This multigenerational mutual loyalty guaranteed the governors' longevity, and stabilized the routes of Pharaoh's far-flung trading ventures. They were egregiously subservient in their letters to the king, characteristically including phrases like "I prostrate myself at the feet of my lord seven times and seven times on the back and on the stomach."

Unfortunately, Egypt's control over Canaan began to disintegrate toward the end of Amenhotep III's life. The downturn started with the murder of the king of Tyre, around Year 33. The alleged culprit was Abdi-Ashirta, a vassal of Egypt in Amurru. His accuser was Rib-Hadda, the mayor of Byblos and one of the most prolific authors of the Amarna correspondence. Rib-Hadda waxed hysterical about this "dog" Abdi-Ashirta stealing grain shipments from him and other Egyptian vassal states and towns, and he begged repeatedly for military aid and food from Egypt.

This created a conflict of interest for Pharaoh, however, because meanwhile, the cool and confident Abdi-Ashirta was sending Amenhotep III the most earnest of letters with warm attestations of loyalty. In addition, he sent women, not necessarily highborn, but they must have been as comely as he could manage. This was about the same time that Amenhotep was writing to Milkilu of nearby Gezer for "extremely beautiful cup bearers in whom there is no defect," for whom he was willing to pay 40 shekels apiece. So Abdi-Ashirta had clearly used the right bait, and it would be some years before our king would face up to dealing with him.

THE LITTLE KINGDOM OF ARZAWA

During the last years of his life, Amenhotep III began to extend his reach to Arzawa in western Anatolia (the Asian part of modern Turkey), now thought to have lain along the Aegean coast. Politically, Arzawa was an independent kingdom, something of a buffer state between Mycenae on mainland Greece and the Hittites in Anatolia. Marriage with an Arzawan princess would secure trade routes to the West, and therefore Amenhotep III requested a daughter from Arzawa's king, Tarhundaradu. Amenhotep sent his royal messenger, Irshappa, with greeting presents of a sack of gold, some linen garments, ebony, and other treasures, quite a bit less than he had sent to Mitanni. Irshappa's mission was to meet the prospective bride – probably checking her age, health, and beauty – and to pour oil on her head, consecrating her to his king.

Tarhundaradu's response to Amenhotep's letter was that of a true businessman who took nothing for granted the way blue-blooded Tushratta did. He wanted a clearly stated contract in Hittite (which he apparently could read himself), signed by the scribe who wrote the tablet, and stating the exact same terms as those spoken by Egypt's messenger. He did not trust a previous messenger because what he had stated was "not confirmed on the tablet." It is not known if this marriage was ever consummated. It is easy to imagine the divine Amenhotep III taking offense at Tarhundaradu's abrupt tactlessness and deciding as a result to leave commerce to the merchants.

EGYPT'S TRADING PARTNERS BY SEA

Foreign trade was open to all who had the goods to sell and the wherewithal to bring product to market. This meant that both Egyptian temples and wealthy officials with their large, grain-producing estates and their linen-manufacturing workshops could trade abroad and muster their own fleets of ships or lease space on others. In Egypt, a sign of one's favor with the god, Redford has written, was health, wealth, a house, servants, and a ship coming home from Asia. The Nile Valley became familiar with distant places and valued them for their best products: Amurru for its wine, Mitanni for its oil, Palestine for its grapes and figs, and Ashkelon for its silverware.

The famous Ulu Burun shipwreck discovered in 1982 just off the southern coast of Turkey (Arzawa?) gives a glimpse into commodities exchange of late Dynasty 18. It is thought that this vessel was on a counterclockwise route circling the eastern Mediterranean rim before it crashed against a cliff in a storm and sank. The craft was nearly 60 feet long, built of cedar, and capable of carrying 20 tons of cargo, including ten tons of copper ingots; unworked glass ingots; faience; gold; resins for perfumes; food (olives, figs, and pomegranates); finished vessels in ivory, faience, and gold; and, among many other treasures, a ring engraved for Nefertiti, the wife of Akhenaten.

Much of the copper was probably eventually destined for Egypt because there were many requests for it in the Amarna letters, including one to the mayor of Byblos, Rib-Hadda, from an Egyptian official named Amanappa. At first, Rib Hadda claimed to be out of copper, but a fully laden ship must have arrived eventually, because Amanappa left Byblos with his order filled. Amanappa and Rib-Hadda wrote to each other as "father" and "son." These titles were honorific ("paternalistic?") but suggest that Amanappa was an official of very high standing. The name "Amanappa" is usually equated with the Egyptian name "Amenemopet." A military scribe of that name sent a jar to Malkata in Year 30, and a statue of perhaps the same man is known, but he gives no sign of having risen to such high esteem, at least under this name. Another possibility arises at the end of the reign.

THE AEGEAN

The Myceneans, framed in time between the gold-laden shaft graves of the sixteenth-century B.C. and the Trojan War of the twelfth century, and populated with legendary names like "Agamemnon," "Helen," "Ajax," and "Achilles," owed Egypt a cultural, or at least a mythological, debt. Mycenae was said to have been founded by Perseus, a descendant of Aegyptus, who, with his brother Danaus, had emigrated generations earlier from the Nile Valley. An early name for the Myceneans is "Danaoi" or "Danaia," which is similar to the Egyptian name for them: "Tanaja" or "Tinay."

The Aegean peoples had commanded quite a bit of attention during the reigns of Thutmose III and Amenhotep II. Tomb paintings of important officials depicted legions of them bringing gifts to the Egyptian court, and Mycenean ceramics of that period are frequently found in Egypt. A palace of Thutmose III-date not far from Bubastis had wall paintings of Minoan bull fighting painted in Minoan style. Many new ideas entered the Egyptian wall painting repertoire inspired by those scenes such as frontal faces of animals and humans, certain types of ceiling patterns (probably copied from textiles), naturalism in the depiction of certain animals such as birds in flight, and more, some of this being visible in the decorations of Malkata palace.

Evidence of Aegeans in Egypt diminished, however, during the reigns of Thutmose IV and Amenhotep III, and correspondence with Mycenae and Minoan Crete does not appear in the Amarna archive. In fact, the names of "Tanaja" and "Keftiu" are categorized as "all secret/difficult countries of the North of Asia" on a statue base at Amenhotep III's memorial temple, where each foreign country's or city's name is inscribed within an oval ring marked at regular intervals with sharp projections like a stockade or crenellated wall. The head and torso of a foreign prisoner with arms bound behind his back rise from each name ring, as though the cities and ports were conquests of Amenhotep III. This cannot be taken too literally, however, because names of Egypt's allies – Babylon, Mitanni, and Arzawa, among others – also appear in this traditional form of depicting foreign lands in pharaonic contexts.

Other names on the "Aegean list" are thought by many scholars to refer either to a diplomatic or a trading mission sent by Amenhotep III to that part of the world (Map 1). The list reads like the itinerary of a modern archaeological cruise: first to Crete, stopping at Amnisos, Phaistos, and Kydonia; then to Mycenae, Boeotian Thebes, the Argolid (Nauplion) before heading to the island of Kythera; then to the west coast of Anatolia, presumably to Ilios (Troy); then back to Crete, stopping at Knossos and again at Amnisos and Lyktos before sailing home via other sites whose names are now lost.

It is hard to imagine Amenhotep sending an embassy anywhere without demanding a bride to add to his string. Yet no such woman is known in terms of either Crete, Mycenae, or Cyprus (Alashiya), the one sea-bound country with which there is Amarna correspondence. Letters from the Cypriote king (he did not give his name) to Amenhotep IV indicate that he had corresponded frequently with Amenhotep III over a number of years ("the messenger that your father used to send to me I let go immediately"). Talk of exports to Egypt was restricted to copper and timber. In return, Cyprus requested silver and an expert in vulture augury.

At Crete and Mycenae, Egyptian items, such as faience scarabs and plaques with the names of "Nebmaatra" and "Tiy," have been found. These are not the finest output of the royal workshops, but they were souvenirs so important to their owners that they took them to their graves, and some of the plaques were found in Mycenae's cult center. Exactly when or if the Mediterranean tour(s) occurred is not known, but that the items found at these sites were made of faience rather than glazed steatite, which Amenhotep favored in his early years, and that they emphasize himself equally with Tiy suggest that they were sent around the time of his first *heb-sed*, when he was sending multiple missions to kingdoms in the East.

Trade in women from the Near East and commodities from there and the Aegean continued throughout the middle of the fourth decade of our king's reign, despite the gathering storm among the Canaanite vassals, which would eventually obstruct travel by land and trade by sea. As long as he could, Amenhotep III turned a deaf ear to the Levantine squabbles, and in Year 34, energies and attention turned to a second jubilee.

A MIXED FORECAST

Dazzling Sun and Dark Clouds
(Reign of Amenhotep III, Years 34–36, ca 1358–1356 B.C.)

THE SECOND JUBILEE AND PLANS FOR A THIRD

Amenhotep III's Second Jubilee, held in Year 34, would be lost to history had it not been for all the rubbish left at Malkata (see Figure 43). The royal trash heap contained 404 jar labels, more for that event than for any other. Tiy's steward, Kheruef, who carefully documented and dated scenes from the First and Third jubilees in his tomb, depicted nothing of the Second, although he did present food to the palace that year. Granary official Khaemhet, now known to us for 14 years since his days as royal scribe attending Nebnufer's promotion in Year 20, illustrated the First Jubilee in his tomb and sent gifts in Year 34 but did not actually mention this Second Jubilee by name in his tomb. Old Amenhotep son of Hapu was still alive and sent gift jars of wine, meat, and fat.

Eighty-three percent of the jars from the Second Jubilee held meat, as distinct from the First Jubilee, when the theme was ale. Some of the meat came from the private stockyards of an Egyptian official and are specified as the product of a breed of bulls named for the "Meshwesh" tribe of Libya, the earliest mention of a relationship with these people. The prominence of ale at the First Jubilee and beef at the Second may have resulted from the successful harvests of the late 20s, which had apparently forced the enlargement of Karnak's granary, and which would have provided plenty of barley for the ale and plenty of feed for Egypt's cattle.

The discarded jars marked "Year 34" and "for the repetition of the *heb-sed*" were all found beside an important Amun temple on the northern edge of the palace city. The design of the sanctuary recalls Old Kingdom architecture such as the pyramid temples of Neferirkara and Sahura at Abusir. Inserting Amun into the ancient architectural forms

214 / Amenhotep III: Egypt's Radiant Pharaoh

gave this relatively new god an antiquarian patina he otherwise lacked, as did the mention of the early dynastic goddess Shesmetet (a form of Bastet) at the entrance of the temple. There are three central chambers inside the temple, probably dedicated to the cult of Amun, with another 24 arranged in various clusters, possibly relating to the gods and goddesses representing each hour of the day and night and to astronomical formations.

The location of this temple made it perfectly situated as a "royal peculiar" something like St. George's at Windsor, available to serve in the procedures of daily official protocol since Karnak was at such a distance across the river. Every morning, the treasurer was supposed to emerge from Karnak's Amun-Re temple and give his report to the vizier, and the vizier, in turn, would report to Pharaoh on the condition of the treasury. Having an Amun temple at Malkata followed *ma'at*, and it made observing protocol much more convenient for both an aging king and his officials.

An inscription on the doorway states that construction of Malkata's Amun temple was overseen by Simut, who, like Khaemhet, has been known to us since Year 20, when he also attended Nebnufer's promotion. Now, 14 years later, Simut had succeeded Anen to the post of Second Prophet of Amun, and he had accumulated additional titles: Treasurer of the King of Egypt, Sealer of Every Contract in Karnak, and Official of Min-Amun. This seems to be the last record of his career, but other monuments are known for him: a painted tomb, two statues (one of which bears the title First King's Son of Amun), two *shawabtis*, and the fragment of a painted limestone stela (Figure 49 and Chapter 11).

NEW CONSTRUCTION AT THEBES

It is not clear whether the Second Jubilee was considered a success or a failure, but the king began planning for yet another a short time later. In "Year 35, first month of summer, day 1 . . . His Majesty . . . in order to renew his noble temple sailed upstream" to Silsilla, where he had a rock stela inscribed commemorating the startup or rejoining of work at the quarries there.

That same year, the northern vizier Amenhotep, "eyes of the king in the whole land," was also down south at Silsilla, where he dedicated a shrine to his king, suggesting that he was overseeing work there. Normally this work would have been managed by one of a number of other individuals with portfolios in this area. Viceroy Merymose,

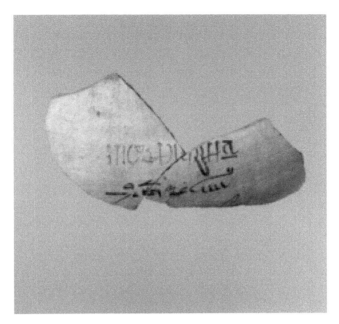

43. Honey jar fragment (ink label from a jubilee pottery gift jar), from Malkata, height 3 3/8 inches, width 6 inches. The Metropolitan Museum of Art, Rogers Fund, 1917 (17.10.12). Image copyright the Metropolitan Museum of Art. Inscribed, "That which has been brought (from the house of) the King's Wife, May She Live! Red honey of . . . (?)."

whose bailiwick included Silsilla, may have been busy farther south in Nubia. Treasurer Sebek-mose, overseer of work at Luxor Temple, may already have been "repeating life" because he was succeeded as treasurer by his son Sebek-hotep (Panehesy) by Year 36, if not earlier. Panehesy was likely also away, assigned to difficult royal missions abroad (see later in this chapter). Amenhotep son of Hapu, if still alive, no longer supervised monumental projects, now being semiretired, serving Queen Sitamen at her Malkata villa. Finally, Ramose, whose portfolio was southern Egypt, was back and forth to Mitanni with royal marriage negotiations. Therefore northern vizier Amenhotep may have been saddled with responsibility for new construction at Thebes by default.

Amenhotep III's last architectural stroke at both Karnak and Luxor temples included the design of long colonnades leading away from the front pylons. The columns were a new shape, each built up into the form of a single papyrus stalk, re-creating in stone and on Bunyanesque scale the marsh from which the world (and Thebes) had arisen.

Karnak's colonnade, for which only the foundations were laid, eventually became the center aisle of a daunting hypostyle court built in Dynasty 19. At Luxor, construction of the colonnade was actually completed by Amenhotep III, but it was not decorated until two reigns later, during the post-Amarna restoration of Tutankhamen.

If Karnak's Third Pylon was built to accommodate the westward movement of the Nile's eastern flank, which Angus Graham has suggested is a very clear possibility, then Karnak's newly planned colonnade may have been necessitated by the eastern flank's continued western movement of nearly 60 yards in some 15 to 20 years. Simultaneously, across the river, the memorial temple's pylons marched eastward toward Luxor, perhaps to keep up with the eastern movement of the river's western bank. If this is the case, then the river had shrunken dramatically in volume at Thebes. At Soleb, too, a marsh had originally stood between the front of the temple and the river's free-flowing water, but gradually this filled in so that a large court was built on the new, dry land.

At each of these sites, was the land purposely filled in to allow more construction, or had the river's volume decreased? Were the inundations substantially less productive than they had been in the past? How did Amenhotep III's gigantic lakes affect the Nile's volume? Were they built to respond to a need for better water conservation? Was Egypt's agricultural economy, especially in the Theban area, on the road to some very bad years? These are all questions that will take years, if not decades, to answer because geoarchaeologists are just in the early stages of their studies of the river and its movements.

FETCHING TURQUOISE FROM SINAI

The most intriguing effort made in anticipation of the Third Jubilee was an expedition to fetch turquoise from Serabit el Khadim in Sinai. Turquoise, especially its greener shades, was a symbol of rebirth. Leading this campaign was treasurer Sebek-mose's son and successor, Panehesy. According to an inscription left at Sinai by Panehesy's scribe, Amen-mose, on the ninth day of the second month of winter, Year 36, "His Majesty was in the southern city [in his palace of the West] of Thebes. Then the royal scribe, overseer of the treasury Sebek-hotep, who is called Panehesy, was commanded to bring turquoise when His Majesty was planning the *sed*-festival."

Mountainous Serabit el Khadim was sacred primarily to the goddess Hathor and tangentially to the god Sopdu, Lord of the East, who represented the scorching heat of the sun. As such, Sopdu was a worthy guardian of the eastern borders, of Sinai, and of its mines. Pilgrims who managed to make the difficult climb up the mountain to the plateau at some 2,800 feet above sea level were doubtless grateful that Sopdu had not killed them. The kings who sent missions there were rewarded with large amounts of turquoise, copper, hematite, and other minerals. Men who carried out successful missions, like Panehesy, were richly recompensed. For his trouble on this mission, he received the Gold of Honor.

Sinai's temple to Hathor, Lady of Turquoise, backs up into a cave within a cliff where the first sanctuary was built many centuries earlier by Amenemhet I in the Middle Kingdom. Subsequent pharaohs added to the temple, stretching it out beyond the cave and following a narrow, curving channel between two flanking rises. By Panehesy's time, the axis of the temple was some 130 to 165 feet long. He supervised the construction of the next three small chambers from local sandstone, his stela being placed in the first one and two for Amenhotep III being placed in the last chamber closest to the entrance.

Naturally, statuary was added as well: a series of diminutive statuettes of the king, queen, and even Panehesy, himself, carved in soft black or very dark green steatite. Fragments belonging to this series are now scattered from Cairo to England, and there are doubtless many more still to be unearthed at Sinai. Best known is the tiny but charismatic head of elderly Queen Tiy in the Cairo museum. Her face, drawn by the years, and her voluptuous lips, down-turned with age, are framed by her trademark heavy wig and modius headdress. Perhaps related to this group is an exquisitely carved, now headless statuette of Princess Isis, once part of a group with her father to her left, and possibly Tiy on his left: a triad something like those of Giza's Menkaure, where the king is flanked by a goddess and a queen. The inscription on Isis's back refers to her as "King's Wife," and so she, too, had been promoted to queen.

This series of statuettes was probably made at Thebes, Panehesy's starting point, their diminutive size allowing them to be carried easily. A number of other officials with ties to Thebes had small statuettes made in the same stone and in very similar workmanship. These include the northern overseer Khaemwaset and his wives, mentioned previously; Hebenu's high priest, Taitai; and Nebmerutef, the grand marshal of the First Jubilee. Another statuette from this group belonged to a second Khaemwaset, he being chief of works at Karnak Temple. Its inscription tells us, he was previously fan bearer of the troop named "The Recruits

Are Perfect," and he was "one of good character, friendly, not negligent and evasive." Perhaps he accompanied Panehesy to Sinai, to help him with construction there.

The Sinai expedition was not Panehesy's first. His scribe recorded in the same inscription that his boss had "gone forth by the shore of the sea in order to make known the wonders of Punt and to receive the gum-resin for the perfume, which the chiefs brought in Eight-boats, as the produce of foreign countries, without the (Egyptian) people even knowing." The ancient land of Punt was located in east Africa in the region of Ethiopia and Eritrea (Map 2). It was home to giraffes, baboons, and rhinoceros and was especially known for its aromatic resins and for gold as well. Hatshepsut famously illustrated a voyage there on the walls of her temple at Deir el Bahri. The means of getting there involved carrying partially constructed boats across the Eastern Desert to the Red Sea, putting them together, and then sailing off. Panehesy likely used the same overland route to embark on his trips both to Punt and to Serabit el Khadim.

THE ARRIVAL OF TADU-HEPA, GILUKHEPA'S NIECE

The acquisition of foreign brides was still a top priority for Amenhotep III during these last jubilee years. There is no telling exactly how many times he sent his envoys to finalize negotiations for his new Mitanni bride, but at last, Ramose traveled to the court of Tushratta to retrieve Princess Tadu-Hepa and the cartloads of wedding gifts and dowry, not to speak of hundreds of attendants, she would bring with her to Thebes. Facilitating the movement of so many goods and chattel and tending to their welfare, physical needs, and security during travel required the skills and patience of an extraordinary official, which Ramose certainly seems to have been. Simultaneously, the vassal states along the Levantine coast must have stopped squabbling – or at least agreed to cooperate – long enough to aid, house, and supply such an enormous caravan as it made its way south and west to the Nile Valley.

We can only imagine how they traveled. Probably the princess herself was carried on a litter shouldered by several strong, sure-footed men, while others of the highborn may have been seated in decorated oxcarts. Assuming that methods did not change much since antiquity and well into later, Islamic times, these travelers must have spent many nights in tents that were carried ahead and set up at each way station in time for their arrival. Medieval travel tents, while often rather plain on the outside, could be highly decorated inside and composed of several rooms, and it would not be surprising if something like this served Tadu-Hepa on her journey.

Tadu-Hepa arrived around Year 36. We do not know if Gilukhepa, who had been welcomed with so much hoopla decades earlier, was there to greet her niece. The good wishes and gifts occasionally sent to her with her brother's previous letters ceased as Tadu-Hepa's betrothal drew near.

Amenhotep III made his new bride feel at home by establishing special quarters for her. This makes her the fifth of our king's women, including Gilukhepa, Mutemwia, Tiy, and Sitamen, to have her own establishment, the last three being documented by Malkata jar labels. Clearly the status of women had improved during the reign of Amenhotep III. Though Egyptian women historically had the same rights to own, buy, and sell land as did men, the evidence of occasions when they actually did is fairly rare. Amenhotep's women must also have received allowances to fund their domiciles, which were administered by stewards such as Bengai (of the foreign lady), Kheruef, and Amenhotep son of Hapu.

The king held an audience in Tadu-Hepa's new quarters, where he received all of the Mitanni messengers and gifted them. To Keliya, Tushratta's most trusted messenger, went an ingot of gold weighing 1,000 shekels (more than 20 pounds) and, to the young princess, sacks of gold. All of it, including the princess's sacks, was carried back home to Mitanni.

The inventory of wedding gifts sent from Tushratta to his brother-in-law comprises four very long lists in the Amarna letters, with a total of about 250 groups of items, each group containing many multiples. Of course, at the top of the first list are "four beautiful horses that run swiftly," followed by a gold-plated chariot with all of the fittings, and bridles and horse necklaces overlaid with gold and inlaid with lapis lazuli. The second and third lists contain items of personal adornment and clothing such as jewelry and shoes of blue-purple wool adorned with gold and lapis lazuli as well as shirts "for the city" and others of "many-colored cloth." On both lists, there are plenty of weapons: daggers, bows, bronze helmets, and helmets for the horses as well.

The fourth list specializes in housewares such as kettles, braziers, lock bolts, wash basins, and water dippers, all made of bronze, in addition to some additional chariot fittings. The mention of so much bronze is especially remarkable because hardly any survives from the reign of Amenhotep III, probably having been melted down at some later time. A second inventory mentions toiletry items such as silver combs and ointment jars of alabaster and gold. And all Tushratta wanted in return was "very large quantities [of] gold that has not been worked."

All of this was just a preamble to Tadu-Hepa's dowry, which included jewelry, vessels, mirrors, garments, and cooking pots. Mixed in among all the durable and soft goods were personnel – 270 women and 30 men, in addition to two principal ladies in waiting, probably noblewomen themselves, who would help Tadu-Hepa feel more comfortable in her new surroundings. These women were provided with their own jewelry in the dowry list.

Tushratta's most touching gift of all was the loan of his favorite goddess, Sauska, to Amenhotep III. Sauska was the Hurrian–Hittite goddess of love, and Tushratta had called on her previously to make Tadu-Hepa attractive to her new husband. This was not the first time an eastern goddess had been honored by royalty in Egypt. Astarte, the Near Eastern fertility goddess, was first worshipped there under Amenhotep II. In the mortuary temple of his son, a relief now in London shows Thutmose IV offering to Astarte on horseback.

But Sauska was also similar to Mut and had some responsibility for both healing and war. It seems the salutary aspect of Sauska suddenly became more important. In a letter to Amenhotep III, apparently accompanying the Sauska idol, Tushratta asked not for her erotic inspiration but for her protection. He wrote,

> Thus Sauska of Nineveh, mistress of all lands [says]: 'I wish to go to Egypt, a country that I love, and then return.' Now I herewith send her, and she is on her way. Now in the time, too, of my father, . . . went to this country and just as earlier she dwelt there and they honored her, may my brother now honor her 10 times more than before. May my brother honor her, [then] at [his] pleasure let her go so that she may come back. May Sauska, the mistress of heaven, protect us, my brother and me, 100,000 years, and may our mistress grant both of us great joy.

This letter was marked as received by Amenhotep in Year 36, fourth month of winter, day 1, in the southern villa of the House of Rejoicing.

CANAAN AND BABYLON – RECRIMINATIONS

Meanwhile, the war in Canaan had been allowed to fester, despite the mounting number of baleful letters from Rib-Hadda, the mayor of Byblos, complaining to Amenhotep III about Abdi-Ashirta of Amurru stealing his grain shipments. Finally, after three years of strife, in Year 36, Abdi-Ashirta was murdered. It is not clear exactly who carried out the deed. In one letter, Rib-Hadda implied it was the archers Amenhotep III sent into Canaan. In another, however, he wrote that Mitanni had become annoyed with this villain and had sent down forces. Perhaps the need to transfer Tadu-Hepa to Egypt and her bride price to Mitanni forced both Amenhotep III and Tushratta to stabilize the area. Within a very short time, however, Abdi-Ashirta's sons, yet another group under suspicion, took their father's place and proceeded to make life even more miserable for Rib-Hadda well into the reign of the next pharaoh.

At about this same time, Amenhotep III began negotiations with Kadashman Enlil I, the Kassite king of Babylon, for one of his daughters. The Kassites had conquered the ancient kingdom of Hammurabi and, after a murky two centuries, had begun to emerge as major players in the Near East. They were skilled horsemen – breeders and charioteers – and expert cart and wheelwrights. They were not particularly cultivated, but were tolerant, and they absorbed the ancient Babylonian deities, architecture, and rites as their own and presided over a period of prolific Babylonian literary activity. Thus the Kassites in Babylon, the Hatti or Hittites in Anatolia, the Mitanni in upper Mesopotamia, and Egypt were the four major international powers of their day, and they wrote to each other respectfully as "brothers," but of course, Amenhotep III must have flared his nostrils at the thought of equality with a Kassite hayseed.

Kadashman Enlil wrote to Amenhotep III that he was insulted at not having been invited to the *heb-sed*. "When you celebrated a great festival," he wrote, "you did not send me your messenger saying, 'Come, and eat and drink.' And you did not send me a complimentary gift in accordance with the festival." As if it were possible to make an Egyptian king feel guilty, Kadashman continued that *he* would certainly invite Pharaoh to the housewarming of *his* new palace, for which, by the way, he needed to be sent a great deal of gold to finish construction before summer.

Kadashman Enlil further complained that his messenger had been detained at Pharaoh's court for six years (presumably since the First Jubilee) and was then sent back with a paltry 30 minas of gold "that looked like silver!" – an amount less than what Kadashman Enlil claimed to have sent to Egypt every year. Kadashman was so suspicious of the gift that he melted it down in front of the Egyptian messenger, a young man he called "Kashi," possibly the huntsman "Keshy" on Ramose's tomb wall. Did Amenhotep send electrum, which occurs naturally in Egypt, or was it poor-quality gold? Or was it indeed silver, which Egypt most likely would have obtained by trade because it rarely occurs there naturally?

Kadashman Enlil had still more bones to pick with the king of Egypt. He complained that when Amenhotep reviewed all the chariots and teams of horses sent to Egypt from abroad, Kadashman Enlil's, in his own mind the superior examples, were simply mixed in among "the chariots of the mayors," probably Canaanite vassals of a lesser grade than he, and were not reviewed separately. Thus the Babylonian drivers and their teams were humiliated in his eyes. Of course, Pharaoh slapped back that Egypt was his country, and the horses were all his, and he could put them in any order he wanted (see Chapter 11).

THE BABYLONIAN BRIDES AND MORE TROUBLE

The more important theme of this correspondence centered on Amenhotep III's request for a Babylonian princess to add to his harem – in exchange for more gold, of course. And there lay another point of contention. In Babylon's words, "here you are asking for my daughter in marriage, but my sister whom my father [Kurigalzu] gave you was (already) there with you, and no one has seen her so as to know if she is alive or if she is dead." Kadashman Enlil claimed that Amenhotep had shown his men not his actual sister but a substitute, who stood silently so they could not judge her from her speech. Pharaoh retorted that Babylon had sent "nobodies," "an ass-herder," who would not have recognized her in any case. This was certainly an ethnic slur on the Kassites' pastoral past and the garb they continued to wear, an insult that required Kadashman either to sever relations or to swallow the obvious bluff and accept that his sister was likely dead. In the end, gold mattered more, and Kadashman Enlil agreed to send his daughter to Egypt for adequate recompense.

Kadashman Enlil was so thoroughly deluded about his own importance that he had the gall to ask Amenhotep III to send one of his own daughters to Babylon as a bride for himself. Pharaoh responded, "From time immemorial no daughter of the king of Egypt is given to anyone." Of course, the Babylonian would not let go, and he counseled Amenhotep to send any pretty girl and just say that she was a princess. There is no reply on record, although one can imagine that our king was furious.

In advance of the Babylonian girl's arrival, Amenhotep sent furniture made of ebony and ivory overlaid with gold and an unknown amount of solid gold, promising more gifts after receiving her. Once again, it seemed of no moral discomfort to anyone that the young girl would be joining the same harem as had her aunt. According to the last preserved letter from Amenhotep III to Kadashman, the former was busy preparing bride price gifts to send to Babylon with the messenger who would return with the girl. The young woman, whose name was not recorded, was escorted to Egypt by 3,000 soldiers, necessary because of the unrest in the intervening territories. Tragically, she "died in a plague," which Amenhotep IV revealed a few years later in a letter to her brother, Kadashman's successor.

That the Babylonian princess eventually "died in a plague" foreshadows a problem that would become widespread in the Near East over the next decades. A newcomer like this eastern girl would have had no built-in immunities to whatever diseases existed in the Nile Valley. In any case, disease was now rampant throughout the Near East. The Keftiu (Cretans) called one illness the "Asiatic disease," perhaps because that is where they came into contact with it through trade. A medical papyrus, the original dating to the time of Amenhotep III, contains a spell against this disease in the Keftiu language. This new recrudescence of the disease and its spread may have been due in some measure to the number of missions traveling back and forth through western Asia.

AMENHOTEP III'S DARK CLOUDS

By now, 30 years had passed since our pharaoh had been the conqueror of Nubians, lions, and wild bulls. The Amenhotep III of Year 36 was a very different man from the one of Year 5 or even Year 26. Aside from the obvious, his age and physique, his mind-set was also radically changed. The Amenhotep III we once knew would have dealt with Abdi-Ashirta within the first few months of difficulties, and he would have sent an army, not just a small force of archers, ordering them to dispense with the man's sons and deputies and bring home their severed hands. He would have recorded his triumph for all to read and/or hear recitations of them.

The king's building projects had also dwindled in number and size. Was he too old to care? Had his beloved courtier Amenhotep son of Hapu finally died, leaving him bereft of inspiration? Was he short of funds or manpower? We know from Amarna letters written from foreign kings to his son Amenhotep IV that the intrinsic value of the gifts sent from Egypt to them had declined rather sharply, and so when we read that Tushratta and Kadashman Enlil felt cheated, or at least let down, by the value of the presents they received from Amenhotep III, we have to give their complaints some weight. It looks as though Amenhotep III's financial resources were indeed drying up.

If the Nile banks were receding both from the right and from the left, which admittedly has yet to be proven, the annual floods must have been much lower than normally expected or desired, and they neither fertilized the fields nor supplied irrigation water to the extent necessary to fill Egypt's granaries. An inscription from Amarna, spread across four fragmentary tablets, bears some unsettling words and phrases. The first sounds as though the Inundation, along with its life-giving effluvium, had diminished: "The king of Egypt . . . why your messenger . . . is lost . . . months and seven years the lands . . . not pouring from the rivers." A second reports, "Inhabitants . . . not harvesting." A third has a phrase that may be read as "go for help."

These tablets are undated, but they are among the cache found in 1887 with the Amarna letters, and so they can just as easily date to the reign of Amenhotep III as later. In the early years of Amenhotep IV, reliefs from Karnak show men in processions carrying bare branches where once they would have carried bouquets. One cannot help but wonder if all this points to a sudden deterioration in climate and agriculture, perhaps beginning in the later years of Amenhotep III's reign and continuing on to the next.

The presence of disease and its effects on closely quartered populations such as armies would have made the king reticent to send troops abroad. It would have stalled his building projects and diminished his ability to revamp irrigation systems or build new retaining lakes. A disease event caused by or coupled with a number of years of unfavorable Inundations would have created a perfect storm for Egypt, sending the agrarian economy into deep depression.

17

THE LAST HURRAH

(Reign of Amenhotep III, Years 37–38, ca. 1355–1354/3 B.C.)

THE THIRD JUBILEE

Amenhotep III's Third (and last) Jubilee, held in Year 37, paled in comparison with the first two. Only 78 jar labels were found at Malkata, mostly for wine, one-fifth as many as Year 34's total. In addition to donors' names and dates, the vintages and estate names of the vineyards were written on the jars, testimony to the sophistication of ancient viniculture. Documented in royal records from Dynasty 1, Egyptian wine was manufactured in much the same way as it has been throughout history. Scenes of men picking grapes from arbors and stomping grapes in vats, producing purple, red, and pink juices, abound in painted tomb scenes from Amenhotep III's reign. In addition to the carefully recorded varieties of red wines at Malkata, there is also evidence of "blended wines," but not white.

Kheruef commemorated the Third Jubilee in his tomb with vignettes of one of the closing rites, the raising of the *djed* pillar. This monument resembled the backbone-shaped hieroglyph meaning "stability," a representation of the spinal column of Osiris. The ceremony may reach back to the Isis-Osiris myth, when Osiris's corpse was set adrift in a simple wooden coffin by his fratricide, Seth. Washed ashore in Byblos (Lebanon), the coffin took root and grew as a tall tree, then was summarily chopped down and used as a pillar in a local king's palace. By trickery and magic, Osiris's cunning wife, Isis, rescued and repatriated the pillar to the Nile Valley. Perhaps based on a primeval Egyptian tree cult, this myth echoes through New Kingdom prayers in which Osiris is likened to a ship's keel or a depth-sounding pole made of Lebanese cedar.

Apparently as large as an obelisk, the huge *djed* pillar was traditionally hoisted at dawn at the close of the festival of Ptah-Sokar-Osiris, whose

225

shrine, it may be remembered, was at the back of Amenhotep III's memorial temple. This exercise required great effort and many ropes as well as the participation of "women of the oases," who were skilled at both magic and tree husbandry. It was preceded by a night-long vigil during which dancers, gymnasts, jugglers, and musicians performed. Women chanted, sang, and ululated in the presence of the king, warming up the magic associated with the pillar. A small statuette in serpentinite in the Metropolitan Museum shows the king with a back pillar in the form of a *djed* column (Figure 44), referring to the jubilee event and to the king's anticipated resurrection like, with, and as Osiris.

In his tomb scenes, Kheruef portrayed his monarch's physique as somewhat thick waisted but muscular and fit; however, the Metropolitan's and other royal statuettes of this late date depict the old man as quite obese. Lacking the waistline necessary to keep up a kilt, he wore a pleated, floor-length gown. A rare large granite image from Kom el Hettan, now in Cairo, also shows a paunchy Amenhotep in a long robe with his arms stretched forward in an embrace of his own ample girth. A limestone domestic shrine found at El Amarna, in the house of Panehesy, the captain of the turquoise expedition, shows the old ruler (with Tiy beside him) hunchbacked and dressed in the same comfortable, though somewhat effeminate, dress. Never before had an Egyptian king been portrayed so informally.

In ancient Egypt, obesity was not a bad thing. It was a sign of plenty, robustness, and fecundity. The Nile gods who annually brought fertility to Egypt had large bellies and pendulous breasts. Therefore Amenhotep III's rotund portraits, in addition to probably being rather realistic, may have been propaganda showing that the jubilees had been successful in renewing Pharaoh as both a source and a sign of burgeoning abundance and fruitfulness for the land and its people. That this body type runs absolutely contrary to the fighting trim paradigm for two millennia of pharaonic images suggests that external military threats to the homeland had dwindled, which is confirmed by Amarna correspondence.

An astonishing sculpture in red quartzite, found in the Luxor Temple cachette in 1989, shows Amenhotep III very thick waisted when viewed from the side but, from the front, more nipped in at the hips, at least enough to carry a kilt (Figure 45). And what a kilt it was, intricately pleated with a complex jointed metal apron hanging down in front and a feather pattern wrap showing in the back! At the bottom of this was a row of disk-topped uraei above jeweled cartouches, details dating late in the reign. A broad, pleated sash wrapped around his waist, tied with

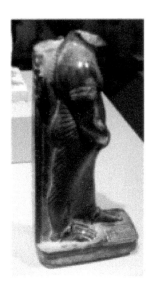

44. Statuette of an elderly, obese Amenhotep III with *djed* pillar at back, serpentinite, height 9 inches, Metropolitan Museum of Art, 30.8.74. Photos: APK.

a perfect square knot below his navel. This sash is three times the width of those he wore in his youth and may have acted less as a belt than as a girdle, or even a lumbar support, because his spine is shown in these later years with a pronounced lordosis (inward curvature). This defect was portrayed as a beautiful S curve in his late sculpture and reliefs and is one of the reasons his colossal relief figures on Karnak's Third Pylon must date to these late years of his reign.

His jewelry is equally ornate – an expansive broad collar with an inlaid pectoral suspended below it, extra-wide wrist bands, and upper armlets – all fitting the style of his last years. The old man's slightly stooped shoulders and the forward pitch of his neck, like his large girth, are visible only in profile. From the front, the king is the image of the svelte, muscular warrior, but from the side, he is a somewhat overfed, underexercised elder.

To be precise, this image is actually a statue of a statue, its base resting on a sledge of the type used to transport heavy sculpture. At 100 inches tall, including the double crown and base, the figure itself is eerily close to what must have been the actual height of Amenhotep III – just over five feet. The matte surface of the red quartzite skin is mysteriously life-like. There is no other statue like it from the reign, and it radiates magic like a true *ka* statue of the king, a unique and highly charged effigy standing effectively in his stead. Perhaps it was made for Luxor Temple at a time when the king was too old and infirm to participate in its festivals. Its inscriptions mention Amun-Re, Re-Harakhte, and the Dazzling Aten.

The statue's red color was symbolic of the setting sun, making the choice of this stone appropriate for a radiant Dazzling Aten in his last years, months, or days. It coincided with the fervent belief that the sun, as it set, was gathered into the protective embrace of one or another mother goddesses and would be reborn the following morning. As we have seen, this theme is illustrated in royal tombs, coffins, funerary papyri, and small luxury objects of the day. It instilled the statue, and indeed, true believers, with hope and uplifting spirituality rather than regret and resignation. This is the only known Amenhotep III image in red quartzite (one also exists for Kheruef), a material usually associated with the Amarna period.

THE DEATH OF AMENHOTEP III

He died in the thirty-eighth year of his reign, about 1353 B.C., the richest, most powerful, and longest-ruling emperor in the world of his time. The mummy identified as his seems to have lost a huge amount of weight toward the end because his skin was so loose that packets of materials had to be inserted to plump it up. His teeth and jaws were in disastrous condition, with caries and dental granuloma (a disease mass forming at the root of the tooth inside the jawbone). He may not have been able to eat, and he certainly must have been in great pain, with nothing but opium and magical spells to dull the suffering. Recent studies also show erosions of part of his skull, a condition that can be caused by, among other things, a meningioma, a common, usually benign, brain tumor. Clearly his last weeks or months of life were hellish.

Amenhotep III's funeral rituals probably followed tradition, like his father's. As far as we know, chariot races were never a part of traditional Egyptian funerary practice, despite being a mainstay of funerary celebrations in the northern Mediterranean region and western Asia. As mentioned previously, the Greek poet Homer rhapsodized about the

45. Red quartzite statue of Amenhotep III from Luxor Temple, total height 100 inches, including base and crowns. Luxor cachette, the Luxor Museum of Ancient Egyptian Art. Photos: APK.

one held for Achilles' comrade Patroclus at Troy. One wonders, considering the amount of energy and resources that went into the maintenance of royal stables, the amount of influence from Asiatic trainers, breeders, and so on, and the number of foreigners present at the court and even married into the royal family, if Amenhotep III might have ordained such an event for himself.

Chariot races or not, after all of the exterior rites were performed, Nebmaatra's coffins and burial equipment were placed inside his tomb (KV 22) in the western valley ("tombeau isolé de l'ouest," according to Napoleon's scribes; Figures 17 and 46), and the last spells were chanted. If we can extrapolate from grandson Tutankhamen's burial, Amenhotep

III's must have comprised room after room of gilded furniture and statues, gold jewelry, silver trumpets, ornately sculpted alabaster vases, and beautifully crafted chariots. The tomb was carefully sealed, and its corridors were designed with special traps, but our king did not rest in peace. The royal tombs were robbed throughout the New Kingdom (see Chapter 4), and at the end of that period, the scattered mummies were gathered by priests, labeled, and stashed away in new locations. All that is left in Amenhotep III's tomb is the red granite lid from his outermost sarcophagus, the lid from one of the others having been usurped by Sety II in Dynasty 19.

Small objects, including a few of Tiy's, continued to be found in the rubbish heaps and environs of the tomb as early as Napoleon's expedition and until very recently. As a result, many *shawabtis* or fragments thereof in black granodiorite, red granite, and white Egyptian alabaster, these three colors being of primal ritual and spiritual significance, entered museum collections in Egypt, Europe, and the United States. The cornelian bracelet plaques from the collection of the Fifth Earl of Carnarvon and now in the Metropolitan Museum could be imagined as having come from the tomb (Figure 39). Necklace elements inscribed with our king's cartouches entered various European and American collections at least by the early twentieth century. The largest and most beautiful of these is a broad terminal, one of two originally, in the form of a lily blossom in white, blue, red, yellow, and green faience, now in the British Museum.

The single most important element of Amenhotep III's burial decorates his sarcophagus chamber: the *Amduat*, the Book of the Hidden Chamber, which was meant to guide him in his journey on the solar bark as it disappeared under the earth at the end of each day and sailed through the dangerous, nocturnal darkness. The *Amduat*, almost entirely restricted to kings' tombs, is divided into 12 chapters – standing for the 12 hours of the night – each one headed with an image of the solar bark as it travels through the night. The sailing is smooth for the first few hours, but soon the ship runs into trouble and has to be towed (remember the First Jubilee event). The journey becomes a nightmare. There are evil serpents, caverns, crypts, strange noises, and far-off animal howls to deal with or tolerate, but there are also friendly goddesses, oarsmen, uraei, and scarab beetles to assist.

At the deepest point of the journey, in the presence of various gods and all of the kings of Upper and Lower Egypt, the sun god Re and the god of the dead Osiris unite, and the deceased pharaoh is resurrected.

46. Interior of Tomb of Amenhotep III, corridor G (KV 22). The king before various deities. Photo courtesy Institute of Egyptology, Waseda University.

There are still many dangers, but at last, at dawn, the solar bark sails clear, and the god Shu seals off the Netherworld, the scary nighttime passage having been safely negotiated. The Dazzling Nebmaatra himself is not specifically illustrated or inscribed as having arisen from this dark night, but all one has to do is step outside the tomb to find proof.

WHERE DID ALL THE THEBAN COURTIERS GO?

The number of long-standing, familiar officials had diminished by now. Amenhotep son of Hapu was gone by the time of the Third Jubilee, the cult at his temple receiving regular service supplied by the estates with which it was endowed. The next most powerful courtier, Ramose, lived on at least into the first few years of Amenhotep IV's reign.

Viceroy of Nubia Merymose was buried at Qurnet Murai, a relatively undeveloped part of the Theban cemetery not far from Malkata, between Deir el Medina and Amenhotep III's memorial temple. The only tomb there at the time, as far as we know, was that of Amenemopet, Overseer

of the Treasury of Gold and Silver and Judge, titles that partially overlapped with Merymose's. The former's tomb-painting style and subject
matter suggest that he lived earlier in the reign of Amenhotep III. The
only other nearby tomb of this time period is that of Merymose's successor as viceroy, yet another Amenhotep Huy. Merymose's undecorated
tomb was plundered in antiquity, and one of his canopic jars – perhaps
his mummy as well – was reburied in Dynasty 21 with royal mummies
that had been similarly desecrated. It is worth remembering Meltzer's
suggestion that Merymose was royal.

All three of Merymose's granite, royal-quality nested coffins are dis-
persed in various museums. A shrine was started for him at Gebel el
Silsilla, the location of the great sandstone quarries, an Upper Egyptian site over which he must have had some general jurisdiction. The
monument was left unfinished, "no more than a cave with rough curving walls and ceiling," according to Egyptologists T. G. H. James and
Ricardo Caminos, as though the owner had died before it could be
completed. However, an inscription at Silsilla calls Merymose "God's
Father, Beloved of the God," a title usually applied by a younger king to
an older, intimate official. Tiy's father, Yuya, held this title, for example,
in regard to Amenhotep III. Could it mean that Merymose lived on into
the early years of the reign of Amenhotep IV?

Treasurer Sebek-mose was buried a few miles upriver from Thebes at
Er Rizeiqat, downstream from where he had overseen the production of
statuary made from "pure alabaster," perhaps referring to the great statue
of Amenhotep III and Sobek (Figure 29). His burial chamber, sheathed
in sandstone from the nearby quarries, has a figure of the goddess Nut
on the ceiling and a prayer to the moon on one side: "Oh Moon, who
are in the day of your first appearance, brilliant of luster, be bright in
the face of . . . [the treasurer] Sebek-mose that he may gaze upon your
beauty, that he may rejoice over you, that he may worship your beams."
Certainly Sebek-mose was aware of his monarch's deification as the
moon in Nubia, which happened before Sebek-mose died, and so this
prayer may have held double meaning.

Downriver in Middle Egypt, a scribe of recruits named "Senu," who
probably mustered human resources for the acquisition and installation of the colossal quartzite baboons at Hermopolis in Middle Egypt,
commissioned two large limestone stelae showing himself in the latest
fashions of the reign. These were placed near Hermopolis at neighboring Tuna el Gebel, close to the site that became Tell el Amarna. They
are now in the Metropolitan Museum.

AND THE MEMPHITE OFFICIALS?

Some of the northern officials were buried at Thebes. For example, Ramose and Amenhotep's father Heby, mayor of Memphis, may have been buried at Thebes in a tomb since destroyed, if the wall fragment and other items with his name and similar titles are indeed his. Menkheper, another Memphite mayor, also had a tomb at Thebes. On his limestone doorjamb in the Metropolitan Museum, he wears a wide sash around his waist and a long wig of late Amenhotep III style. Northern vizier Amenhotep had an important and large tomb at Thebes adjacent to Kheruef's, but it was largely undecorated and mostly destroyed, leaving very little information about its owner, including his family connections.

By the end of the reign, Sakkara once again became an important cemetery. Probably from there are the monuments of a third Memphite mayor, Tjenuro, and his wife, Ipay. These are rare, nearly four-foot-tall *shawabti*-shaped, limestone *sah* figures, depicting the couple as mummified, purged of their perishable parts, and magically transformed into divine images. Ipay's identifies her as "Nurse of the King," presumably meaning Amenhotep III. Perhaps she and the Bubastis nurse were one and the same.

The last well-known high priest of Ptah, the younger of the Ptahmoses discussed in Chapter 12, died late in this reign. His beautiful statue, now in Florence, was commissioned by his son Pahemnetjer, who succeeded him as high priest at Memphis. The stela on which Ptahmose is represented along with other "family" members is carved with all of the figures shown frontally in high relief, which is rare in Egyptian art, like the stela of the Chief of Works and Chief Sculptor at Amarna, Bak. Both Ptahmose's and Bak's stelae are carved in brown quartzite and must have come from the same workshop.

The treasurer Meryra's tomb was found in the nineteenth century. Its reliefs were removed (now in Leiden), then the tomb was lost for a century beneath Sakkara's wind-blown sands. Fortuitously, it has been rediscovered by French archaeologist Alain Zivie. Meryra died quite late in the reign judging from his wife's wig styles and length, the draped effect of her broad collar, the width of Meryra's waistband, and his paunch. The relief showing Prince Si-Atum on Meryra's lap does not bear a memorial phrase like "true of voice," and so it seems that Si-Atum, too, was still alive late in Amenhotep III's reign.

The discovery of a few unusually fine veins of limestone in the nobles' cemeteries at Thebes (e.g., Ramose's, Kheruef's, Khaemhet's, and Surer's) toward the end of Amenhotep III's reign meant that the richest tomb decorating commissions at Thebes were going to sculptors rather than painters. There are very few painted tombs, if any, that can be surely dated to these last years. Which happened first, the decline in the number of painters or the decline in the amount of work for them, is not known. In any case, habitation at their village of Deir el Medina was interrupted, and some painters may have moved north.

The tomb of two artists, father and son, the elder being Director of Painters, Amenemwia, and the younger, Thutmose, was found at Sakkara. The older man's thick torso, with its fat folds, and a kilt waistband hitched quite high in the back are signs of a late Amenhotep III date. Amenemwia carries in his hand an artist's palette inscribed with our king's cartouche and containing an exceptionally large number of color daubs. The style of painting in this tomb equals that in the finest tombs at Thebes, and so it is possible that this father-and-son team had emigrated north to Memphis from Deir el Medina.

Memphite steward Amenhotep Huy's burial was discovered at Sakkara in the nineteenth century and then lost again. His ponderous and costly brown quartzite canopic chest holding the jars with the steward's internal organs is now in Leiden, while a number of his small treasures are in Cairo, Florence, London, and New York. A stela from his tomb had been used as a doorsill in a monastery, until it was recognized and put in the Cairo museum. His elegant white alabaster scribal palette is in the Metropolitan Museum. Recently, a granodiorite *shawabti* of the steward appeared in a French private collection. The face has the same somewhat haggard appearance as the small Queen Tiy portrait from Serabit el Khadim, and therefore must date quite late in the reign. His granite sarcophagus was so huge that the early explorers could neither extract it through the doorway nor figure out how it had been inserted there to begin with.

Arguably the most important piece of equipment for these officials, the *Book of the Dead*, served essentially the same purpose as the *Amduat* did for the king. As John Taylor has written, "The Book of the Dead was a book of magic – a collection of spells to empower, protect, and guide the dead on their perilous journey [to the Afterlife]. Those who knew these spells, or had them written on a papyrus scroll or inscribed on their coffin, believed that they could escape the clutches of death and reach eternal paradise." A number of beautiful *Book of the Dead* papyri are known from the Eighteenth Dynasty, not the least of which is that of Tiy's father, Yuya.

According to Irmtraut Munro, such papyri were quite expensive, about one *deben* (around three ounces) of silver, which was equal to the value of three donkeys. But for those who could afford a *Book of the Dead*, here was the guidance to transition through gateways guarded by monsters and the power to overcome weird mounds and caverns and proclaim lifelong integrity as one's heart was weighed against the feather of truth, hopefully being found just as light, innocent, and pure.

As noted previously, records from just a couple of hundred years later in Ramesside times show that individuals actually paid for their own monuments, contrary to the standard phrase "a boon which the king gives" on everything from *shawabtis* to bronze statuary. Furthermore, Kathlyn Cooney has shown that they appreciated and paid more for the highest-quality work. One cannot help but wonder if this practice had not started already in Amenhotep III's reign. If individuals like Steward Amenhotep paid for royal statuary in temples, then why not for their own? These men had become rich and powerful beyond the imaginings of their predecessors. They were probably both richer and more powerful than many of the kings of other nations. Their wealth was a dazzling reflection of Amenhotep III's own.

AMENHOTEP III'S LAST NORTHERN VIZIER

Little was known about the end-reign administrative officials up north until Alain Zivie's surprise discovery at Sakkara in 1989, of an important tomb stuffed with hundreds of Late Period cat mummies at a site called the Bubasteion, after Bastet, to whom the cat was sacred. The human burial located under the debris should have been safe because it was cut into the rock cliff in four stages, the first two split-level, the third and fourth separated from the previous by long, dangerous vertical shafts, but it was not. The tomb was robbed in antiquity and was almost totally incinerated in a fire of unknown date. It belonged to Aper-el or Aperia, a formerly unknown vizier, originally a "child of the *kap*," probably closer in age to Amenhotep III's children, like princes Thutmose, Si-Atum, and Amenhotep IV–Akhenaten. Buried with Aper-el were his wife, Taweret, and son Huy, a commander of the horse, commander of chariotry, and scribe of recruits of the Lord of the Two Lands.

The tomb's ancient robbers left behind as scrap a number of objects valuable to Egyptologists today, including a wooden chest with cartouches of Amenhotep III and Tiy, some imported Aegean vessels, an exquisite red-tinted ivory dish in the form of a fish, and nicely carved canopic jars for holding the internal organs of the deceased. The family's wooden coffins, opulently inlaid with colored glass, survived the fire heavily damaged but have been restored as close to their original splendor as possible. Clay seals with the name of Amenhotep IV show that Aper-el's career continued after Amenhotep III's death (see Chapter 18).

LOOKING BACK AT AMENHOTEP III'S REIGN

In the last years of the fifteenth century B.C., Egypt was the greatest military power in the world and had a strong economy based on agriculture nearly guaranteed by the annual inundations of the Nile River. The level of sophistication of Egypt's literature, architecture, art, and even warfare was unsurpassed. Though inventions often germinated in the East, they were refined in the Nile Valley, and the products of these inventions were manufactured in enormous quantity in Egyptian palace and temple workshops. The prince who became Amenhotep III was born at a time and in a place when the best of everything was attainable and achievable. He styled himself as the Dazzling Sun Disk, not too bold a statement, considering that he outradiated all other rulers, and they knew it.

His reign had started out well. He stabilized the Delta and affirmed Egypt's control over Nubia and its wealth in all its forms, especially gold. At the end of his first decade, he raised his favorite wife, Tiy, a match for his own brilliance, to queen, and they already had several healthy children. He and his talented courtiers, most notably Amenhotep son of Hapu, planned and achieved an almost unimaginably complex program of architecture and sculpture from the Delta to beyond the Second Cataract in Nubia, leading up to his First Jubilee.

Hardly any foreign power or overconfident rebels challenged him. The minor scuffles he had early on with unnamed "bulls" and "lions," a limited foray he may have made in the aid of Mitanni, two brief campaigns in Nubia, and perhaps a final mission sent into Canaan in his last years were the extent of his military efforts, as far as we know, for all of his 38 or so years on the throne. This is quite a remarkable record for any king, indeed, any empire in history.

Amenhotep III's achievements and his peaceful reign masked problems beyond even a pharaoh's control, however. Disease was rampant throughout the ancient world, attested time and time again in ancient texts. His eldest son died prematurely, his parents-in-law suspiciously close together in time, as well as several women in a royal house.

His second campaign to Nubia brought back far fewer slaves and a great deal less gold than 21 years earlier. Foreign kings raised objections about the quality of goods sent to them. A few years after the king had enlarged Karnak's granary, complaints rolled in from Canaanite governors over dwindling shipments of grain from Egypt, and the king told them to look elsewhere, as if there had been a reversal of agricultural fortune. Normally subservient, well-controlled Canaanite city-states began to brutalize each other, causing turmoil in international trade. The hayseed Babylonian king bridled at being dunned for a daughter when it was not clear what had happened to her predecessor, his sister. Piling on the insults with unprecedented audacity, he arrogantly demanded quid pro quo from Pharaoh.

Things were no longer going well, but the king continued to celebrate one jubilee festival after another. The reinvigoration, rejuvenation, and reinvention transforming him would also bring new life to Egypt. Amenhotep III was sure of it. Amenhotep son of Hapu had researched everything and helped him create *ma'at* throughout the land. The king had deified himself and Queen Tiy and affected appropriate new emblems, in particular, multiple sun disks on his clothing. His courtiers increasingly included prayers to the Aten, the Sun Disk, on their stelae and in their tombs, perhaps directed as much at the king, the self-proclaimed Dazzling Sun Disk, as at the god.

Amenhotep III's jubilees may have veiled Egypt's decline for a few years, but the charade did not last. The last two festivals sputtered and contracted. The building program ceased; its masterminds and overseers died. Even though Amenhotep III could rightfully claim that what he accomplished on earth had never been done before, it was a hollow triumph because Egypt was about to descend into one of the darkest periods of its history – ironically, when the sun god, the Aten, ruled supreme.

18

WHOSE HEAVEN IS IT?

The Reign of Akhenaten and Beyond

Amenhotep IV was probably in his late twenties when he was crowned. Mitanni king Tushratta sent his condolences on the death of Amenhotep III, addressing the new king for the first time as an equal. This letter was in response to one from Tiy (now queen mother), in which she requested that Tushratta write to her son in the same manner as he had to her late husband and he obliged. Tushratta later wrote the following to the new king, whose throne name, "Nefer-khepru-ra," as usual, was mangled:

> When my brother Nimmureya (Amenhotep III), went to his fate it was reported. When I heard what was reported, nothing was allowed to be cooked in a pot. On that day I myself wept, and I sat. On that day I took neither food nor water. I grieved saying, "Let even me be dead, or let 10,000 be dead in my country, and in my brother's country 10,000 as well, but let my brother whom I love and who loves me, be alive as long as heaven and earth. . . . But when they said, "Naphureya, the oldest son of Nimmureya and Tiy, his principal wife, is exercising the kingship in his place," then I spoke as follows: "Nimmureya is not dead. Naphureya, his oldest son, now exercises the kingship in his place. Nothing whatsoever is going to be changed from the way it was before."

Interesting questions crop up with Tushratta's mention of Amenhotep IV as the "oldest" son. What were the names of the remaining princes? Is the mention of "Naphureya" as son of Tiy indirect evidence of the existence of sons by other wives? Could one of them have been a son of Sitamen or one of her sisters and Amenhotep III? Or even of Gilukhepa? Did any of them have official posts in their father's or brother's administration?

Transition to the new king was seamless, judging from representations in officials' tombs. Carved on a back wall of Ramose's tomb is an enthroned king, with the goddess Ma'at standing behind him, receiving offerings from the tomb owner. The king's chunky figure style and elaborate jewelry are identifiable as those of Amenhotep III, even though the elements were only blocked in, with no details of facial features or jewelry before the sculptors stopped in the midst of their work, either because of the king's death or Ramose's absence. When work resumed, the details of the figures and jewelry were not finished, but the inscription, normally the last thing added to a scene *after* the fine details, was filled in, and it included the cartouche of Amenhotep IV. There was no need to change the image itself for the new king, as long as the name in the cartouche belonged to him.

Kheruef also moved quickly into Amenhotep IV's good graces by placing the latter's youthful images on the doorway and the entrance gate to his tomb, spots either undecorated or left until last to keep them undamaged. One scene shows Amenhotep IV and Tiy standing before several gods; another depicts the new pharaoh offering to his parents, and another shows him offering to Re-Harakhte. Accompanying these scenes are three lengthy texts. The first is written in a grid like a crossword and can be read either vertically or horizontally to hail the arrival of the new king, a paean to him.

The other two texts are hymns, one to the rising sun and one to the setting sun. These hymns are couched in liturgically correct phrases, but the choice of words, their location, the timing, and the emotion barely hidden between the lines reveal the deep sense of loss Kheruef felt at the demise of his greatly adored sovereign, the man who had raised him. In both prayers, he begs to be allowed to "grasp the tow-rope of the evening bark and the mooring post of the morning bark," referring to one of his favorite memories, probably the high point of his life, when he participated in the event at Birket Habu during the First Jubilee eight years earlier. Of course, this also referred to the king's travels on the solar bark through the night, as outlined in the *Amduat*. In Kheruef's mind, Nebmaatra Amenhotep Ruler of Thebes, the Dazzling Sun Disk, had indeed become one with the sun itself.

THE ROYAL WOMEN

According to Tushratta, Tadu-Hepa had immediately become Amenhotep IV's wife because the Mitanni king referred to her in his letter

47. Limestone votive stela with image of Akhenaten, Nefertiti, and three daughters, height 12 3/4 inches, 14145. Courtesy Ägyptisches Museum und Papyrussammlung, Staatliche Museen zu Berlin – SPK.

to Tiy as her "daughter-in-law," and he addressed Amenhotep IV as his "son-in-law." Most scholars believe that Tadu-Hepa changed her name to Kiya, a woman who played active roles in both ritual and secular ceremonies at Amarna. She had at least one child, and she may be the woman shown on a relief dying in childbirth (?) and leaving behind an infant.

Amenhotep IV's principal wife was the famous Nefertiti, who, if her mummy is correctly identified, has been proven by DNA tests to be his full sister. Which sister was she? "Nefertiti" is currently unknown among Amenhotep III's daughters, but a name change, as with Kiya, cannot be ruled out. Sitamen was probably too old. Henut–taneb's and Nebe-tah's whereabouts are unknown. Isis became a queen late in her father's reign and may have been transferred to her brother at his accession. On the other hand, the royal couple's early images show them with a handful of wiggly, affectionate (female) children (Figure 47), suggesting that their marriage was well established by the time he ascended the throne. Whoever she was, Nefertiti became a constant force during her

48. Portrait of the elderly Queen Tiy from Medinet Ghurob (without feathered head-dress), yew wood with silver, gold and glass, height 3 1/2 inches, no. 21834. Courtesy Ägyptisches Museum und Papyrussammlung, Staatliche Museen zu Berlin – SPK.

consort's reign, having sanctuaries dedicated to her and being frequently portrayed in his company.

The Amarna letters addressed to Queen Tiy and to Amenhotep IV suggest that the dowager queen mother remained close by her son's side at Thebes, at least in the early days of his reign. At some point, she and/or some of her daughters and/or closest courtiers may have moved briefly up north to Medinet Ghurob, Amenhotep III's birthplace. No new palace was built for her in the Faiyum, but small wood statuettes of noble or royal women were found there, including Berlin's famous fist-sized portrait head presumably of Tiy as a drained and aged woman with sad eyes, a furrowed brow, and a down-turned mouth appearing, perhaps, ten years older than her Sinai portrait (Figure 48). Her headpiece with double plumes was found with the portrait.

After all these decades, even centuries of depicting kings and queens at their best, Tiy's realistic portrayals as an old lady seem to be out of royal character. On the other hand, the Metropolitan Museum's Dorothea Arnold sees the representation of age not as an image of weakness but of strength – venerable and experienced. Time-worn facial features like Tiy's became fairly common in female representations of the time, even for younger women, perhaps to honor Tiy in the same way that the faces of courtiers' statuary usually mimicked portraits of their king.

One of the most touching items found at Ghurob was a small stela addressed by Tiy to her beloved Nebmaatra, perhaps evidence of a center for the cult of the deceased king at the site. One other little known statuette of an elderly courtier with haggard features like Tiy's carved in ebony, set onto a body of another material, and wearing the colorful, patterned "dress of life" looks as though it, too, must have been carved by the same hand as the Ghurob statuettes. It is tempting to identify this startling image, now in southern France, as beloved steward Kheruef or, perhaps, as Ramose.

THE NEW AESTHETIC AND A NEW FACE

The new king had viewed his country's problems first hand as prince and must have recognized its decline. In his first couple years on the throne, he tried to reverse the trend and jump-start a recovery by celebrating a jubilee, obviously well before the traditional thirtieth regnal year. In Amenhotep IV's defense, Redford has pointed out that "mythologically pharaoh had been designated king while still 'in the egg,' [therefore] the thirty years could conceivably be counted from the king's birth."

Amenhotep IV hastily built a huge new temple complex to the Aten behind Karnak Temple and moved colossal sandstone statues of Amenhotep III, which had fallen and broken, to this new site possibly from Luxor Temple (see Chapter 10). He drastically revised these statues in his own state image, shaving down Amenhotep III's pudgy, round, beneficent face into a narrow and dour one with sunken cheeks and eye sockets and a chin so long that the root of the royal beard had to be cut away to accommodate it. The old man's wide hips were left nearly as they were, but his thick chest and upper abdomen were hollowed to a shallower form. Some of the new tool marks continue past areas where these sculptures had been damaged, evidence that the breaks preceded the recarving (Figure 50).

49. Fragment of a stela of "(Si)-mut, son of (Ra)-mose," painted limestone, height 9 inches. Private collection, USA. Photo: APK/JSB.

Amenhotep IV's odd, rather misshapen physique would become the archetype for his portraits for the first half of his reign. His appearance is so strange that generations of medical specialists have suspected a physical cause, offering diagnoses from acromegaly to Marfan's syndrome, now ruled out by the previously mentioned scientific analyses. The mummy rather definitely identified as Akhenaten's did have a cleft palate and scoliosis, however. The cleft palate was easy to disguise in statuary, and the lateral malformation of the spine is not depicted. Considering Arnold's previous suggestion that Tiy's haggard look portrayed a sense of wisdom, can it be that this was also Amenhotep IV's aim in his bizarre new imagery? Whatever the reason, as the reign progressed,

Akhenaten's portraiture became more traditional in appearance, suggesting that the early, extreme representations were formed by aesthetic choice rather than adherence to realism.

The early style, according to a stela at Aswan, was the work of quarry master Men's son Bak, who claimed to have been personally instructed by the new king. Some writers do not take this literally because there was in Egypt a tradition of artists claiming royal inspiration; however, the kings must have had complete control and approval of their imagery, so this declaration should not be so easily discounted.

The weird aesthetic of the colossal sculptures bounced back across the river to Ramose's tomb. On the other side of the doorway from the scene where the figure of Amenhotep III is titled as Amenhotep IV and receives offerings, Ramose placed a scene of the actual Amenhotep IV and Queen Nefertiti (or possibly Tiy, since the image is too hacked to tell for sure) adhering to the new aesthetic with gaunt bodies, long necks, long chins, and thin arms. Their sashes and ribbons flutter in the breeze, a sign of the presence of Shu, the air or atmosphere, which was new to Egyptian art. The royal couple stands in a palace "window of appearances," presumably at Malkata, with the Aten, the Dazzling Sun Disk, casting its rays down on them. This depiction of the sun did not come into use until the end of Year 2 or early in Year 3 of his reign, according to Redford.

If that is indeed Nefertiti, shown so early in the reign on a nearly equal par with her husband, it should have been a tip-off that she was of royal blood, considering what great-grandmother Tiaa and grandmother Mutemwia had to go through to be recognized as royalty, not to speak of the propaganda campaign Amenhotep III had waged for Tiy. It makes such a romantic story, however, considering Nefertiti's name, meaning "the beautiful one has come," and her incredibly elegant portrait in the Berlin Egyptian Museum (in contrast to Amenhotep IV's extreme ugliness), that she was a fair-skinned and enigmatic foreigner from a far-away land.

In the "window of appearances" scene, Ramose stands below, showered with multiple strands of the Gold of Honor. His figure, too, adheres to the extreme aesthetic of the early years. Nearby he transmits a royal speech to Near Eastern emissaries, identified by their long, bound-up hair, big beards, and un-Egyptian outfits, who have gathered together near the palace as if to attend his awards ceremony. This may be the final sign of his career as a traveling ambassador. Did Ramose translate the young pharaoh's speech for them? Or considering the king's cleft

50. Colossal statue of Amenhotep IV in Osiride pose recut from a statue of Amenhotep III, sandstone, height 117 inches. The Egyptian Museum, Cairo, JE 49529. Photo: APK.

palate, which must have made his speech indistinct, perhaps Ramose had become the royal mouthpiece.

During his father's reign, when he was still just a King's Son, Amenhotep IV already had his own palace at Malkata, recorded on at least one jar label. In his own regnal Year 5, his name changed to "Akhenaten" ("Effective for the Aten"), and he decided to abandon Thebes for a site he had under construction on sterile soil halfway between Akhmim and Memphis a few miles upstream from Thoth's cult center at Hermopolis. He called it "Akhetaten" ("Horizon of Aten"), known today as Tell el

Amarna. This was not the location Nefertiti wanted. Even so, Akhenaten quarantined himself and his family there, never leaving its borders and marking them with special boundary stelae. One silenced his queen with the words, "Nor shall the King's Chief Wife say to me: 'Look, there is a nice place for Akhetaten someplace else.'" Like Ghurob, perhaps?

Why he moved away from Thebes is not known. As the late Egyptologist William Murnane of the University of Memphis (Tennessee) once said to an interviewer, "Akhenaten can't bring himself to say what actually occurred, but it really ticked him off. He rants about 'it' in an inscription at Amarna, saying, 'it' was worse than anything he or his ancestors had experienced." Murnane was referring to phrases on one of the Amarna boundary stelae warning about what would happen if the burials of his body, his wife, the Mnevis bull, and his officials did not occur at Akhetaten: "It shall be worse than what I heard in Year 4; it shall be worse than what I heard in Year 3; it shall be worse than what I heard in Year 1, it shall be worse than what [Amenhotep III] heard; it shall be worse than what [Thutmose IV] heard . . .", phrases of a type rarely used in Egyptian royal texts because avoidance of mentioning unfortunate events was normally the rule.

There is a strong possibility that "it" was bubonic plague because Kemp found traces of it at Amarna. On the other hand, an inscription at Karnak suggests earthquakes. Fragments of a speech recorded on the remains of a wall of Amenhotep IV's earliest building at Karnak mention temples falling in ruin and divine statues "cease, one after another," as if a series of statues had toppled sequentially. He might have been referring to statues set up in rows like the sandstone statues of his father set up at Luxor Temple, which, this author suggests, Amenhotep IV salvaged and recarved. They would have been easy victims for an earthquake because their Osiride pose – feet together rather than stretched out in stride – gave them only a narrow base of support.

Whatever his reasons, Akhenaten allowed hardly anyone at the new capital to carry a name referring to any gods but the solar ones. The sculptor Thutmose retained his name based on the god of wisdom, Thoth, and a name like Ramose was acceptable for its solar reference, but the name Amun, as in Amenhotep, was totally disallowed and systematically expunged from all inscriptions throughout the entire country, even in his father's cartouches. Courtiers formerly named Amenhotep used the nickname "Huy" instead. This moniker appears often in the Amarna letters as "Haya," referring to any number of individuals, one of whom was distinguished from the others as the son of "Miyara," perhaps Meryra. Another may have been the northern vizier, Amenhotep.

A powerful official named Amanappa was ubiquitous in the Amarna correspondence at the end of Amenhotep III's reign and beginning of Amenhotep IV's. This Amanappa was addressed with tremendous deference by Byblos's mayor, Rib-Hadda, and Amanappa seems to be someone who would have left a significant mark in terms of monuments inside Egypt. Could he have changed his name from Amanappa to Aper-el in Year 5, thereby losing his former identity? A charioteer named "Huy" accompanied both Amanappa through Canaan and Ramose to Babylon. Was he Aper-el's son, the chariotry commander Huy, who was interred in his father's tomb around or after Year 10 of Akhenaten's reign?

EGYPT'S DAZZLING SUN DISK

Akhenaten's religious "revolution" was the culmination of the gradual solarization of the "Hidden One," Amun, and his juncture with the sun god, Re, which had begun in the Middle Kingdom and continued and increased during Dynasty 18. Sun prayers and royal references to the sun, especially its physical disk, the Aten, had become frequent during the reign of Amenhotep III, as has been shown. When crowned, Amenhotep IV–Akhenaten chose the throne name "Nefer-kheperu-ra" ("Beautiful Are the Forms of Re"), and in his early years, he promoted a form of Re-Harakhte as the light of the sun disk. Gradually, he focused the cult solely on the light that is in the disk, the Aten. The hieroglyph for the Aten took the form of a disk with long rays reaching toward earth. In art, this icon was a disk with rays terminating in small hands, those closest to royal family members extending *ankhs* ("life" signs) to their nostrils.

Akhenaten's most extreme act was to close all the temples not associated with his new religion. If the temples possessed their full cohorts of priests at that moment, there would have been tens of thousands of priests, chantresses, and temple workers out of jobs all over Egypt with nowhere to go. There certainly was not enough room for them all at Amarna, and while he also built temples at Memphis and Sesebi (Nubia) and added new elements to existing structures elsewhere, Akhenaten had not gone on such a comprehensive building campaign to provide enough royally sanctioned venues for all the individuals who would have been displaced if they were alive and well. There should have been massive riots or evidence of mass emigration, but there are no signs of this. The implication is that the personnel no longer existed and perhaps had died from whatever was/were the subject(s) of Akhenaten's rant and the aftermath.

Steward Amenhotep's son Ipy, the new steward of Memphis, sent a letter to Akhenaten at Amarna reporting that all was well with Memphis's Ptah temple, one of the oldest and largest in the empire. Soon thereafter, he locked its doors and moved to Amarna to become Akhenaten's steward, forsaking Ptah. This means that Ipy was not summarily dismissed as the keeper of an unapproved cult. Instead, he was gathered into the royal bunker like the rare survivor of a lost cause. The Memphite temple's closure and the shuttering of other temples as well, therefore, were likely due to a shortfall in personnel and funds to maintain them, similar to what happened to monasteries in Europe in the fourteenth century A.D. Because Ipy's father's tomb and its caretakers were supposed to receive a percentage of the offerings brought to the Ptah temple, the old steward's burial and its staff were now out of luck. His carefully laid and expensively endowed plans had come to nothing.

Artistic production saw a sharp drop, despite that some of the most beautiful masterpieces in Egypt's history were made during these years, Berlin's bust of Nefertiti, carved by the royal sculptor Thutmose, to name just one. Thutmose likely started his career in the reign of Amenhotep III. Ramose's exquisitely carved banquet panorama on the front walls of his tomb may be his work because of one idiosyncratic detail; that is, the sculptor softly modeled the hollows above and below the eyes, the so-called blind eye, without any of the rich, carved detail evident in the rest of his work. Then he painted eyebrows, cosmetic lines, and pupils in thick, black pigment – the only paint on these stark, white walls – to bring the figures to life. This was a startling innovation, and it would crop up again in the royal portraits of Akhenaten's female relatives found in Thutmose's workshop at Amarna. It is unlikely that this was a meaningless stylistic invention. It must have been related to the iconography of eyes – the solar and lunar eyes of Re and Horus – that were so important to the First Jubilee and to Amenhotep III's deification.

Thutmose's high standards did not extend far beyond his workshop, unfortunately, and the number of exceptional sculptures from Akhenaten's reign is quite small, considering its length of 17 years. Much of the artistic production of the Amarna period is downright crude, in particular, the tomb decoration in the nobles' cemetery at Amarna and the awkward reliefs of the Gem-pa-Aten at Karnak. The only series of colossal statuary for Amenhotep IV–Akhenaten were not even originals but were just the 30-some sandstone colossi usurped from his father, a tiny fraction of the numbers quarried and carved in the previous reign of 38 years. It appears that there was a dearth of trained quarrymen, outline draftsmen, and sculptors, and life in their Workmen's Village was extremely unpleasant. Barry Kemp's excavation, one of the few to examine insect and small rodent remains, identified a high frequency of bed bugs, maggots, fleas, and rats indicating squallid living conditions.

RAMOSE REDUX

As for Ramose, himself, who had demonstrated complete allegiance to the new king on his tomb walls, did he, too, move to Amarna? The General Ramose known there is thought to have changed his name from Ptahmose, and another Ramose, a steward and granary official starting in the reign of Amenhotep III, became steward of the Aten temple at Amarna. Our Ramose seems to be lost without a trace.

No burial was found for Ramose at Thebes, and at least one of his granodiorite coffins – its carved images, no longer suitable during the Amarna period, seems to have been cast off. Whereas the first Pa-Ramessu had usurped Ramose's statuary (see Chapter 14), Ramesses II absconded with Ramose's burial equipment for his son, another Pa-Ramessu. A granodiorite inner sarcophagus, inscribed for this Prince Pa-Ramessu, was found at Medinet Habu, and an outer one was found at Medinet Ghurob. The inner coffin lid is anthropoid, a portrait of its owner wearing the costume of a late Dynasty 18 vizier and with imagery that would have been unsuitable during the Amarna period.

The basic form of the face and its coiffure are Amenhotep III style. Among the closest comparisons for the Paramessu–Ramose coffins are the set of three nested sarcophagi in red granite and black granodiorite made for the viceroy of Nubia, Merymose. Probably both Merymose's and Ramose's coffins were commissioned at about the same time. Their imagery – the usual funerary gods and prayers to the sky goddess Nut – exclude the possibility that they might have been made during the Amarna period, nor are they post-Amarna in style. Therefore they were commissioned and produced during Amenhotep III's reign at the height of his power; however, small nips and tucks were later made around the mouth and the eye and eyelid area of Ramose's to fit Ramesside facial physiognomy.

THE QUEEN MOTHER AT AMARNA

Like the rest of the extended royal family, Tiy eventually moved into her own household at Amarna with a new steward named "Huya" (a superannuated northern official?). Tiy's son endowed her with a Sun-shade temple of her own, and a relief shows him escorting her to it. International correspondence records that "King's Mother, King's Chief Wife Queen Tiy," as she was called during her son's reign, had great influence on him, but how much? Did she encourage him in his new direction? Was the new religion actually devoted to the worship of her deceased husband transformed into the light of the Aten? This would have been a logical step because the deceased Amenhotep III had styled himself as the earthly sun, and Kheruef's prayers seemed to equate the postmortem king with the solar orb itself. Certainly Amenhotep III's own epithets did! The deceased Amenhotep III's centrality in the transformed state religion would have been reassuring to a people who had lost their long-standing king, and it would have assured Tiy of continued primacy during the reign of her children.

Scientific analyses show that the body thought to be Tiy's had mild scoliosis as well as thyroid disease, but the cause of her death is unknown. She may have died at Amarna and been interred initially in the Royal Tomb, but the mummy was later moved to Thebes (KV 55), along with the mummy of a younger woman now identified as Nefertiti. Some of her burial items have been found there as well, as in KV 22. A group burial of women dated to late Dynasty 18 was found in 2005 and is being excavated by Otto Schaden. One of the women in this tomb, numbered KV 63, was a nurse named "Iny," generally a late Dynasty 18 or early Dynasty 19 unisex name. The others await identification.

THE ECLIPSE

The end of the reign, the line of accession, and the identities of the players are shrouded in mystery and confusion. Akhenaten died (reason unknown) after a brief coregency with Nefertiti and/or, perhaps more likely, their son Smenkh-kara. The latter seems, according to Dodson and Hilton, to have predeceased his father and was replaced by his widow and half sister, Meritaten, who changed her name to

Nefer–neferu–aten. The gap created by Smenkh-kara's demise left the throne after Akhenaten's death to Tutankhaten (later Tutankhamen), identified by Dr. Zahi Hawass's DNA study group as a son of Akhenaten and Nefertiti.

According to recent studies of Tut's mummy, he was a frail boy with a left clubfoot like his grandfather and painful Kohler II disease in the right foot, which is probably why artistic representations show him hunting with bow and arrow from a chair instead of standing and occasionally using crutchlike walking sticks when he was upright. He was never depicted in his parents' company, which was normal for princes.

Tutankhaten returned the capital from Amarna to Thebes, changed his name to Tutankhamen, and began to restore the temples of old, including Karnak and Luxor temples, the latter of which he called "my father's" monument, referring to Amenhotep III. The Dazzling Sun Disk, whose light was uniquely hailed as supremely divine by Akhenaten, began to fade. It did not die out immediately, however, its image remaining on some important areas of Tut's burial equipment, for example, his shrines.

At some point, just as Akhenaten had done to Amun, Akhenaten's image and name were erased wherever they could be found, and the sun disk's rays were severed, destroying its power. If Amenhotep III was the Aten, it was a secret that died with Akhenaten, for no matter how successive generations blamed Akhenaten for their country's problems, they did not exact revenge on Amenhotep III. They revered his monuments and restored them – often adopting them for their own use – and they maintained his temple estates.

Tut lasted fewer than ten years on the throne, leaving no heirs. Like Yuya and Thuya, he was a victim of malaria tropica, which possibly contributed to his death at around age 19. He was buried in King's Valley 62, along with two stillborn female fetuses (both clubfooted).

His widow and blood relative, Queen Ankhesenamen, the third oldest and last living of Akhenaten and Nefertiti's eight daughters, was left to swallow her and Egypt's pride. Contrary to her grandfather Amenhotep III's sentiments only 30 some years earlier, she wrote abroad to the Hittite (!) king looking for a suitable prince to marry. One was found, but he never survived the journey to Egypt, apparently caught up in the chaos of Canaan.

Ankhesenamen was unwilling, unable, or not allowed to assume the throne herself, and she finally married an elderly courtier named Ay, who may have been another of Queen Tiy's brothers. In her letter cited earlier, however, the recently widowed queen wrote that she was trying to avoid marrying a "servant," an unkind term for a great-uncle, so he may have been unrelated. Ay's reign was brief, and at his demise, there was no one left with direct royal connections. Ay's son-in-law, a military general named Horemheb, assumed the throne and added uraei to his images in his previously prepared tomb in the officials' cemetery at Sakkara. He petitioned the deceased Amenhotep III's blessing by offering to his cult and bridged the gap to the Nineteenth Dynasty.

At his death, Horemheb's vizier, the previously mentioned Pa-Ramessu, became Ramesses I, ruling for only a year or two and founding the bloodlines for a new dynasty. The kings and princes of early Dynasty 19 started at rock bottom, with little international power and less treasure. Just as Horemheb had taken the short route to preparing a royal monument for himself at Sakkara by adding uraei to his images as a mere general, the early kings of Dynasty 19 were forced by economics to usurp earlier monuments. As has been mentioned previously, Pa-Ramessu as vizier, before becoming Ramesses I, usurped Ramose's statuary (see Chapter 14), and this practice continued even in better times two generations later, during the reigns of Ramesses II (the Great) and Merenptah, as has been illustrated in the reinscribed statues of Amenhotep III (Figure 23) and in Ramose's coffins.

The grand alabaster coffin of Sety I (son of Ramesses I), now in the Sir John Soane's Museum in London, was also usurped from an earlier owner, its walls having been greatly thinned down and left rather rough, with column after column of inscription scratchily cut into the desiccated skin of the outer walls of the sarcophagus box. Its origins are not yet identified.

IDEALISM, MADNESS, OR TERROR?

If war was not siphoning off Egypt's manpower, and access to gold was unrestricted, why did the building program suffer so much in the last years of Amenhotep III's reign? Why did the jubilees dwindle and his son feel the necessity for calling an early one? If everything was going so well, why did Amenhotep IV–Akhenaten flee to Amarna, refusing to leave its limited boundaries for the rest of his reign? How is it that royal wealth disintegrated so badly by the end of Tutankhamen's reign that he was buried in a comparatively tiny tomb? How is it that with all of the possible marriages available inside and outside Egypt, there were no viable children of royal blood, and rule was left to an aged courtier, who passed it on to a mature army general, who passed it on to his vizier, who started a new, but impoverished, dynasty?

All these events are signs of the devolution of Egyptian culture, power, wealth, health, and society over a period of decades, something like – if not a decline and fall of the empire – a great recession. Archaeologists, such as a group meeting at Cambridge, have begun to examine the phenomenon of decline in civilizations, many of them coming to the conclusion that the great empires in history did not fall precipitously and completely but that the process was more complicated and slow moving. This seems to be what was happening in Egypt in late Dynasty 18, starting partway through the reign of Amenhotep III, reaching a nadir or two during the Amarna period and after Tutankhamen, and then haltingly recovering with most traditions and practices intact in Dynasty 19.

Exactly why it happened is not clear. Undoubtedly, no one thing was the cause, but as many at the Cambridge meeting agreed, natural phenomena could have sped along whatever was happening politically as a result of the redistribution of wealth and power in society.

Akhenaten has been seen by historians as everything from a madman and a heretic to a hero and an idealist. Likely, he was none of these. Instead, it appears very possible that Akhenaten was a terrified ruler on the throne of an empire that was in deep trouble, almost disintegrating around him. In his mind, the classical pantheon had failed, and he made the courageous move of trying to thwart chaos and restore order by reversing centuries of tradition. He turned to a different type of worship, monotheism, concentrating on the light of the sun's orb, with which his father had recently been amalgamated.

Then, because of problems against which Akhenaten railed but did not name, he left Thebes and tried to reinvent his own new cosmos at Tell el Amarna, with the desperate hope of saving himself and his people. Sadly, none of this worked. It took the great empire a century to regain its strength under Ramesses II.

EPILOGUE
ONE GOD LEFT STANDING

Out of all these decades of triumph and disaster, one new god did manage to rise up and survive for centuries. Two thousand years after the collapse of the ancient Egyptian empire and culture, traces of his influence survive today. The god's name is "Amenhotep son of Hapu," the once-humble priest, and his divinity was by his own design.

Normally the king was the only intermediary between ordinary folk and the deities as high priest of all the cults. However, at Karnak's Tenth Pylon, Amenhotep son of Hapu's statues, which he placed there himself, claimed special powers to convey prayers to Amun in return for offerings of food and drink. One of the inscriptions reads,

> Oh, people of Upper and Lower Egypt, every eye that beholds the sun disk, who come upstream or downstream to Thebes to pray to the Lord of the gods, come to me and I shall relay your words to Amun of Karnak. And make an offering formula and a libation to me with what you have, for I am the spokesman appointed by the king to hear your words of supplication and to promote the affairs of the two lands.

On the west bank, Amenhotep son of Hapu was venerated at his memorial temple until at least the end of the Twenty-First Dynasty, but his worship declined over the next several centuries, and his cult center moved to a series of rock-cut chambers on the upper terrace of Hatshepsut's temple at Deir el Bahri. There Amenhotep son of Hapu became an oracle and a healing god similar to the Greek god Asklepios. Another extremely highly regarded commoner, Imhotep, the architect of the Third Dynasty ruler Djoser, was eventually inserted into this shrine, and Hapu's son was forced to share space with him, despite some apparent resentment on the part of the local populace toward this northern interloper. Imhotep's move, however, resulted in Amenhotep's promotion, and the latter was now fully considered a god in his own

255

right. The spirits and prescriptions of both Amenhotep and Imhotep were sought out for all sorts of healing miracles, especially treatments for infertility.

Bronze votive statuettes of Amenhotep son of Hapu and Imhotep were donated on the east bank at Karnak Temple during the last centuries of the first millennium B.C., and they ended up in the Karnak cachette, a treasure of statues and statuettes of all periods buried by priests during a spate of ancient housecleaning.

Well into the fourth century A.D., in other words, toward the end of the Roman empire, Amenhotep son of Hapu's cult no longer existed, but echoes of it remained in sacrifices to an unnamed god at Deir el Bahri. Eventually, the Amenhotep–Imhotep shrine was turned into a Christian monastery named for St. Phoib-amon, and the site continued to be venerated for its healing properties. In modern times, the local Muslim saint of the mountain, Sheikh Abd el Gurna, has been petitioned by women wishing to become pregnant. Thus the deified Amenhotep son of Hapu, who had left no records of any children of his own flesh during his lifetime, and his holy successors have been responsible for the births of generation on generation of children at Thebes over the past 3,300 years.

NOTES AND REFERENCES

INTRODUCTION

Malkata jar labels: Hayes 1951.

The Amarna letters: Sayce 1908, 187–188 (discovery); Campbell 1964, 134–135 (chronology); Moran 1992 (translation and background); Feldman 2006, 147–148. **The language of the Amarna letters:** Moran 1992, xix (identifies them mostly as Babylonian, many in "good" Middle Babylonian); Spar 2008, 169 (as Babylonian Akkadian); Feldman 2006, 147 (as mainly Middle Babylonian Akkadian).

Amenhotep III crowned as a child: Aldred 1988,146.

Coregency: Campbell 1964; D. B. Redford 1967, 88–169; Murnane 1977, 123–160, 231–233; Aldred 1988, 169–182; Yoyotte 1993, 24–25; Hornung 1999, 18, 28, 30; Dorman 2009; Laboury 2010, 87–92.

Egyptian religion: Morenz 1973; Quirke 1992; Assmann 1995.

Karnak's geoarchaeology: Graham and Bunbury 2005, 17–19; Bunbury et al. 2008, 351–373. **Anthem to Thebes:** Leiden Hymn x (Papyrus Leiden I 350 recto) Foster 1995, 70; O'Connor 1998b, 155, and n. 66; Nims 1965, 69.

Herodotus: Book 2, 148 = Waterfield 1998, 154–155.

Kamose's ("Carnarvon") stela: Gardiner 1961, 166.

PROLOGUE. THE BIRTHPLACE OF AMENHOTEP III

The Faiyum and ancient Saharan lakes: Baedeker 1902, 174–188; Lane 1985; White and Mattingly 2006, 58–65. **Herodotus:** Book 2, 149 = Waterfield 1998, 155.

Medinet Ghurob: Petrie 1890, 40–44; Petrie 1891, 21; Gardiner and Bell 1943, 37–46; D. Arnold 1977; Thomas 1981; Lacovara 1997, 297–306; D. A. Aston 1997; I. Shaw 2008.

257

Mi-wer as a harem town, palace harems in general, related terminology: Gardiner 1953a, 145–149; Reiser 1972; Nord 1975, 142–145; Kemp 1976; Seipel 1977; Kemp 1978, 132; Ward 1983, 67–74; Robins 1993, 38–40; Málek 2000, 115; Meskell 2002, 37; Haslauer 2001, 76–80; S. Redford 2002, 49–71. Bryan 1982, 35–54, points out the relationship of *ippet* with the word "to bake" along the lines that a young girl would be turned from a raw lump of dough into a finished product, but as a reason against the harem–prison similarity. **For *khener* as a parallel to *kap* (the royal boys' school; see Chapter 1):** Whale 1989, 278. **Harem conspiracies:** S. Redford 2002, esp. 117–132 (punishment for conspirators). **Childbirth:** Robins 1993, 82–85; see also M. Yoyotte 2008a.

Textile manufacture in the Bronze Age: R. M. Hall 1986; Barber 1991, 97–123, 145–162, who places the invention of the vertical loom in the Near East; Barber 1994, 185–207; Kemp 2001, 54, 145–146, who believes that wool was used commonly in Egypt and that the vertical loom was invented in Egypt. **Textiles and the economy:** Meskell 2002, 109–110; Eyre 1998, 173–189; see also Roehrig 1996, 19–24, and J. J. Janssen 2008.

CHAPTER 1. AN HEIR UNAPPARENT

Amenhotep's clubfoot: Hawass et al. 2010, 645, table 3; Hawass 2010. Grandson Tutankhamen also had a clubfoot as did the two stillborn children buried with him.

Thutmose IV: Bryan 1991. Pair statue with Tiaa (Cairo Museum CG 42080): Ibid., 99–103, plate 3. For the title "prince" used for a royal grandchild, see Chapter 13.

Mutemwia: Erman 1890, 112; Aling 1977, 23–39; Gundlach 1982, 251–252; Bryan 1991, 113–118; Berman 1992a, 36. **Rebus portrait:** (British Museum EA 43): British Museum 2007, 95, figure 56; additional references in Chapter 2. **Head from rebus sculpture:** Robins 1995, 53–55, no. 26 (British Museum EA 43A). **Mut:** te Velde 1982, 246–248; idem. 1997, 455–462.

Luxor Temple birth scene: PM 2, 2: 326–327; Berman 1992a, 36; B. G. Davies 1992, 28–31 (573 = Urk. 1713–1721).

Possible siblings: Bryan 1991, 50–55 (Aakheperura), 55 (Amenemhet), 55 and plate 2 (Amenemopet, male), 67–69 (Ahmose), 120–122 (Tiaa), 122–123 (Amenemopet, female), 123 (Tentamen, Penttepihu/Petpuy?),

Tawy, Meryt-ptah, Sathor, Neferamen, Wiay, Hentiunu, Khatnesu); Meltzer 1974 (Merymose, see also Chapter 12); Gabolde 2004 (Pent-tepihu); Robins 1995, 28–29, no. 14 (British Museum EA 35400, statuette of prince Temy on the lap of official Tjanunna). **Tjannuna's career:** Bryan 1991, 256–257. **Amenemhet's and Tentamen's canopic jars:** Reeves and Wilkinson 1996, 107. **Life expectancy of children:** Nunn 1996, 22. See also Dodson and Hilton 2010, 134–141.

Zagazig nurse statue (Cairo, JE 98831): Saleh 1998, 353–361; Hawass 2004, 174–175; M. Yoyotte 2008, 293, no. 110. **Royal nurses:** Roehrig 1996, 17–18. **Births, infants, early childhood:** Meskell 2002, 69, 79–87.

The *kap* and its inhabitants: Glanville, 1932 (British Museum EA 1332, Inena dated by style to reign of Amenhotep III); Bryan, 1991, 261–263, 316n166; Meltzer 2001, 20–26. **Further education:** Simpson, 2003, 431–437; Janssen and Janssen 1990, 71–79; Callaghan 1992, 7–10. Meryra: Bryan 1992e; A.-P. Zivie 1985, 228; Berg 1987. **Schools in temples,** see Chapters 2 and 10. **Inpu:** A.-P. Zivie 1985, 228; Bryan 1991, 42; Laboury 2010, 81.

Classic Egyptian literature: Parkinson 1997, 21–53 (Tale of Sinuhe), 54–88 (Tale of the Eloquent Peasant); Lichtheim 1975, 1: 184–192 (Satire of the Trades).

Min's tomb (TT 109): PM 1,1: 226–227; Laboury 2010, 83, figure 2–13.

Amenhotep III's prophecy: B. G. Davies 1992, 29 (573.5.3 = Urk. 1715).

CHAPTER 2. THE MAKING OF AN HEIR APPARENT

Pathologists, radiologists, and other physicians have suggested to me that twentieth-century estimates based on various anatomical details of X-rays of adult mummies are likely to be accurate only in the most general terms. Indeed, it seems to this author that many of the early studies were prejudiced by Egyptologists' estimates based on the meager historical evidence known at the time. Bryan also seemed to have serious questions about these early studies and, perhaps as a result, assigned Thutmose IV the nebulous age of "at least adolescent" when he came onto the throne (Bryan 1991, 43).

Thutmose IV's accession and the Dream Stela: Hassan 1949, 189–193; Bryan 1991, 38–49, 145–149; Meltzer 2000, 15. **The princes' stelae:** Bryan 1991, 57–66; Reeves and Wilkinson 1996, 105.

Amenhotep II's mummy: Harris 1999; G. E. Smith 1912, 36–38, no. 61069; Partridge 1994, 82–83; Harris and Weeks 1973, 138–139. **Life-span estimates:** Filer 1995, 25; Nunn 1996, 22.

Elder Tiaa's monuments: C. M. Zivie 1983, 40–56; idem. 1986, 551–555; Bryan 1991, 93–107, and plate 3, figures 8, 9. **Reuse of ancient titles:** Zivie-Coche 2002, 50–51.

Statue of Prince Amenhotep on Sebek-hotep's lap: Capart 1938, 83–86, no. 8; Bryan 1989, 85–86; idem. 1991, 70–71. For the phrase *ma'a kheru* used exceptionally in a "prospective, anticipatory sense," see Murnane 1977, 270–272. **Sebek-hotep and Meryt:** Bryan 1989, 81–88; idem. 1991, 244–246; PM 8, 2: 55. **Administrative relationship between Mi-wer and Shedet:** Thomas 1981, 1:17, n. iii; Gardiner 1948, 43–47.

City dwellings: Desroches 1938.

Mut's history, mythology, symbolism, and roles: Wilkinson 2003, 153–156; te Velde 1982, idem. 1985. **Mut Temple, its location and surroundings:** Cabrol 2001, plate 4. Mut Temple and its precinct are still actively excavated by the Brooklyn Museum and the Johns Hopkins University, and remnants of the school, like those found at the Ramesseum, have not yet appeared. See Leblanc 2005, 80–81, for 130 inscribed and figurative ostraca apparently from a school in the Ramesseum.

Circumcision: Janssen and Janssen 1990, 90–94; Meskell 2002, 87–90; Bailey 1996, 15–28. **Bakenkhons statue:** Schoske and Wildung 1995, 19, 73.

Hekarneheh and Hekareshu: Newberry 1928, 82–85; Bryan 1991, 41–42, 53–55, 259–261. **Tomb of Hekarneheh (TT 64):** PM 1, 1: 128–129. **Hekareshu's** *shawabtis:* Schneider 1977, 1: 269–270. **Hekarneheh's tomb cones:** Hayes 1959, 155. **A second school in Amenhotep II's memorial temple on the west bank:** Sesana and Nelson 1998; see also Chapter 10.

Sebek-hotep's tomb (TT 63): Dziobek and Abdel Raziq 1989; PM 1, 1:124–128. Meryt's title Royal Ornament is probably best translated as "lady in waiting." Holders of this title are thought to have been chosen from a small circle for their looks and perhaps disposition. Numerous girls and women of this title are found among the daughters and wives of well-known officials. See Whale 1989, 277–278n20. **Female literacy:** Bryan 1985, 17–32; Wente 1990, 9.

CHAPTER 3. THUTMOSE IV AND KING'S SON
AMENHOTEP IN NUBIA

Medamud stela: Bigler and Geiger 1994; Meltzer and Bianchi 2009. Montu is also depicted on an ivory bracelet from Amarna, now in Berlin, with an image of Thutmose IV braining an Asiatic, see Borchardt 1914; Wilkinson 2003, 203.

Name of Nubia: Meltzer 1996, 123–129. **Gold-mining and gold-working centers in Dynasty 18 Egypt and Nubia:** Klemm et al. 2002, 215–231; Castiglioni and Castiglioni 2004, 121–131. **Egypt's contact with Kush through the New Kingdom:** Valbelle 2004, 92–99; Vercouter 1956, 1959; Edwards 2004, 101–111.

Sociology and archaeology of Nubia: Säve-Söderbergh 1964; Trigger 1976, 131; O'Connor 1993; F. Hassan 1993; Morkot 2000, 69–90; S. T. Smith 2003, 94–96, 138, 150; Welsby 1996, 2–10; Welsby and Sjöström 2007. **Dynastic Egyptian racial views:** Lobban 2004; Cheal 2004; O'Connor 2003.

Thutmose IV's Year 7 stela: Bryan 1991, 6, 111, 198.

Prince Amenhotep's inscriptions at Konosso: Newberry 1928, 85; Bryan 1991, 50–52 (additional references). **Herald Re'a's tomb and role of the royal herald:** Redford and Redford 1994.

Thutmose IV's Victory Stela, descriptions of the region, and possible locations of the battle: Bryan 1991, 332–336 (largely paraphrased here); R. O. Collins 2002, 111–112; Trigger 1976, 111. Bryan suggested that Thutmose traveled east from Edfu to encounter the enemy in the desert, which was an important source of gold. The eastern mines, however, were never fortified and seem not to have been subject to attack according to Klemm et al. 2002, 216.

Viceroy of Nubia: Reisner 1920, 28–34, 78–83, plate 9; Wolf 1924, 157–158; Habachi 1957, 13–25, plates 6–7; idem. 1980. **Viceroy Amenhotep:** Bryan 1991, 250–254; Kozloff 2004. **Buhen stela:** Crum 1893, 17–18; Urk. IV, 1636; Alliott 1932 (a statue possibly of this viceroy). **Sinuhe:** Parkinson 1997, 30, 36, 48n47.

Thutmose IV's *heb-sed* and self-deification: Bryan 1991, 20–21, 351; Hartwig 2008. **Reason for early jubilee:** D. B. Redford 1967, 180n108; see also Chapter 18.

Thutmose IV's constructions in Nubia: Bryan 1991, 199–205; Török 2009, 229–230. **Amada:** Baedeker 1929, 426; Borchardt 1938, 99–100, plate 22. **Dokki Gel:** Bonnet and Valbelle 2004, 109–112. **Tabo:** Jacquet-Gordon 1999, 257–258. **Gebel Barkal:** Kendall n.d.; idem. 2001; McRae 2005, 46.

CHAPTER 4. LE ROI EST MORT, VIVE LE ROI!

Thutmose IV deification: Hartwig 2008.

Mummification: Shore 1992.

Tomb of Thutmose IV (KV 43): PM 1, 2: 559–562; Reeves and Wilkinson 1996, 74–75, 104–108, 124 (Tutankhamen's scene).

Accession and coronation timing: Frankfort 1948, 102, 178, 193–195; D. B. Redford 1967, 3–27; Van Siclen 1973; Bryce 1990, 97–105. **Sedeinga reliefs:** Schiff Giorgini 1965a, 129. **Possible dates for Amenhotep III's coronation day:** Borchardt 1936, 54–55, 58–59; Hayes 1951, 84; Van Siclen 1973, 290–300 (around the vernal equinox); Breasted 2001, 335 and note d (third month of Inundation – end of August or beginning of September).

Descriptions of coronations of Hatshepsut and Horemheb: Moret 1902, 76–113; Matthiew 1930, 31–32, plate 11; Gardiner 1953, 13–31. **Amun's statue and procession:** Bennett 1939, 8–15. **Miho statue:** Roehrig 1997. **Masking:** DuQuesne 2001, 5–31. **Crowns:** Goebs 2001; Hardwick 2003.

Gold of Honor: Binder 2008.

Royal titulary and other designations: Gardiner 1969, 71–76; Allen 2001, 64–66. Amenhotep's names: Berman 1992a, 34–35. **Ma'at:** Hornung 1992, 131–145.

Private tombs: PM 1, 1: 185–187 (TT 91, captain of the troops), 327 (TT 226 royal scribe, overseer of royal nurses). See also N. de G. Davies 1925, 50–56; Romano et al. 1979, 78–79 (no. 101), plate 7.

Royal audiences and Sinuhe's tale: Gnirs 2009; N. de G. Davies 1925; Parkinson 1997, 40.

Diodorus Siculus: Oldfather 1933, 245 (Book 1, 70.10–11; 71.5).

CHAPTER 5. ESTABLISHING DIVINE MIGHT
AND DIVINE RIGHT

Menwy ("monument man"): D. B. Redford 1986, 178.

Amenhotep's early years: Berman 1992a, 36–37 (limestone quarries), 116–117 (the Tura stela, a piece of which is in the Toledo (Ohio)

Museum of Art, 1925.522). **Bersheh:** B. G. Davies 1992, 13 (570 = Urk. 1678). **Tura:** ibid. 14–15 (571b = Urk. 1681). **Ashmunein:** Spencer 1989, 33–34, 63–64, plates 39–35, 92–97; Bailey et al. 1982; Breasted 2001, 351, notes e and f. **Tura limestone:** Aston et al. 2000, 42; Meyer 1986, 807.

Apis cult: Kessler 2001, 210–212; Dodson 1999; Berlandini-Keller 1993, 20; Berman 1992c, 324; Dodson 1990, 88; Mariette 1857, esp. plate 1. **Herodotus:** Waterfield 1998, 110 (Book 2: 38), 181 (Book 3:28). A fragment of the relief showing Prince Thutmose is in Munich, Staatliche Sammlung Ägyptischer Kunst, Gl. 93.

Commemorative scarabs: Blankenberg-van Delden 1969; Berman 1992b, 67–72 (with bibliography). The latter notes that the names of five of Kha-em-maat's crew are known from stelae and other belongings: Battalion Commander and Standard-Bearer Nebenkemet, Standard-Bearers Siese and Meryptah, Chief of Equipment Nakht, and Sailor Inpu. See idem. 70–71n5.

Amenhotep son of Hapu: Robichon and Varille 1936; Varille 1968; Wildung 1977; Murnane 1991. **Biographical inscription related to Amenhotep III's early years:** B. G. Davies 1994,18 (658: 14–15 = Urk. 1821).

El Kab: von Bissing 1904; Tylor et al. 1895–1900; Clarke 1922, 28; D. Arnold 2003, 83; Bryan 1992b, 79–82. **Sandstone:** Aston et al. 2000, 54–56. **The possibility of a coregency between Thutmose IV and Amenhotep III based on the El Kab reliefs:** Bryan 1991, 349. See also Reeves 2001, 79, on the basis that Thutmose IV had founded two tombs, the second eventually becoming that of Amenhotep III.

Karnak: Phillips 2002, 102–103, figure 197; Bryan 1991, 172–174; idem. 1992, 93–104. **Alabaster shrine:** Carlotti 2003, 241n36; Larché and Letellier 1979; Blyth 2006, 100–101. **Enlarged processional bark:** Karlshausen 1995, 125–137; Carlotti 2003.

Luxor: Bryan 1991, 184–188; idem. 1992b, 82–90; Johnson 1990, 28; Wilkinson 2000, 166–171.

CHAPTER 6. "THE FIRST CAMPAIGN OF VICTORY":
AMENHOTEP III'S RIVER WAR

Amenhotep III's Nubian campaigns: Topozada 1988; O'Connor 1998; Welsby 2004; G. J. Shaw 2008, 112–114.

Officials' inscriptions at Aswan: De Morgan 1894, 28; Murnane 1998, 194–195. **Military officials at Thebes and related tombs:** Bryan 1991, 280, 282, 284–289; PM 1, 1, 152–156 (Horemheb TT 78), 175–178 (Menkheperra-seneb TT 86), 181–183 (Amenmose TT 89), 183–185 (Nebamun TT 90), 185–187 (unnamed officer TT 91), 430–431 (Paser TT 367). Amenhotep son of Heby left a graffito at Biggeh Island near Aswan, noting his title, Army General of the Lord of the Two Lands. If this dates to a known campaign, it is likely Year 5's, because he seems to be settled in Memphis later on. See Topozada 1988, 156; Habachi 1974, 30–33, plate 2.

Organization of the Egyptian army: Schulman 1964, 14–16, 19–25, 30, 58, 62–79; Healy 1992; Darnell and Manassa 2007, 58–90; Spalinger 2005; B. G. Davies 1992, 5–6; D. B. Redford 1992, 219–220. **Medjay:** Murnane 1998, 199–200; Bianchi 1994, 102–103. **Munitions and armor:** Partridge 2002, 36–59; McDermott 2004, 52–81, 127–128, 137, figure 87, 138–179.

Amenhotep III stelae: De Morgan 1894, 3–5, 68; **Konosso stela:** B. G. Davies 1992, 6–7 (565). Second victory stela between Aswan and Philae: ibid., 8–9 (567 = Urk. 1666); Gundlach 1987. **Sai Island fragment:** Vercoutter 1956, 81. The Bubastis stela (B. G. Davies 1992, 35–36 (577 = Urk. 1734–1736), considered by many scholars to refer to this campaign, is written in a style very different from all of Amenhotep III's texts; therefore it may record the campaign of a different king. Furthermore, fewer captives were taken, suggesting that it occurred toward the end of Dynasty 18, by which time Lower Nubia had suffered a major drop in population. **Buhen text:** Randall-MacIver and Woolley 1911, 81; B. G. Davies 1992, 47 (605). This completely conserved stela in the University of Pennsylvania Museum (E. 10995) contains few words carved large and seems more like a welcome sign made for the king's arrival than a record of events left by him. **Sai Island statue:** Vercoutter 1956, 79–81.

Thutmose III at Soleb: Schiff Giorgini 1961, 182–185, 197; idem. 1962, 162, 169.

Tombos: S. T. Smith 2003, 136–166; Edwards 2004, 103; Edwards and Osman 2001; Harrell 1999.

People and place-names: Darnell and Manassa 2007, 91–110; Kitchen 1999, 173–178 (Punt); Vercoutter 1980, 157–178 (Irem); W. V. Davies 2001, 46–58; idem. 2003 (Miw); Gardiner 1937, 118–120 (Terek);

Zibelius 1972, 177–178 (Terek and Irem); Vercoutter 1980 (Irem); Harrell 1999, 239–250 (Tombos). The name of Ikheny should not be confused with 'Ikn (Iken), one of two fortresses south of Buhen: Gardiner 1916, 189–190.

Gakdul Wells: Hough and Paget 1895, chapter 19, whose description is quoted; Churchill 1899, 62. The "Pool of Horus" is named in an inscription on a granite ram Amenhotep III placed at his temple at Soleb much later in the reign. It reads, "He made it as his monument for his father, Amun, lord of the thrones of the two lands, who appointed for him victory against all foreign countries causing that he should seize the 'Pool of Horus' as far as the 'Pool of Set.'" See Randall-MacIver and Woolley 1911, 29. Again, this suggests water features to the south. If the Gakdul Wells were the Pool of Horus, then the Pool of Set may have been another one of the several water features in a line crossing the Bayuda desert. See Crawford 1953, 19–23 and plate 9; Chittick 1955, 86–87.

Sai Island statue: Vercoutter 1956, 79–81.

Wadi es-Sebua: Firth 1915; Desroches-Noblecourt 1999, 243–252; Ullmann 2009.

Modern travelers' descriptions: Baker n.d., 3–4; R. O. Collins 2002, 108–120; Churchill 1899, 138–244; Shipman 2004, 74–131. Travel duration: Suys 1934; F. L. Griffith 1943, 779; Chittick 1955, 86; Lewis 1983, 143; Shipman 2004, 63, 76–79; Darnell and Manassa 2007, 115; Mahoney 2007 (an American woman who rowed alone downstream from Aswan to Luxor in three days). **Difficulties of travel in Nubia**: Welsby 2004, 287–289.

CHAPTER 7. THE SPOILS OF WAR

Amenhotep III's own descriptions of the Third Pylon and his acknowledgment of the source of its funding come from a list of his Theban monuments on a ten-foot-tall granite stela (Cairo Museum JE 34025) from his memorial temple behind the Colossi of Memnon. The stela was defaced during his son's reign and restored by Seti I at the beginning of Dynasty 19. His grandson Merneptah recorded a victory over the Libyans on its reverse. For the pylon's inscriptions, see B. G. Davies 1992, 31–34 (574 = Urk. 1722–1732). See also, for Karnak, Blyth 2006, 104–118, 127–128. **Third Pylon**: Bryan 1992b, 93–99, 114n74; Aufrère et al. 1997, 96–98.

"First" Nubian Campaign: In Year 5, Memphite mayor Neferhabef left a graffito at Aswan also referring to this as the "first" campaign, even though there had not yet been a second. See Topozada 1988, 156. The presumption was that the enemies of Ma'at would have to be suppressed repeatedly (see Chapter 12 for the second campaign in Year 26).

Homer's description of Thebes: Fagles 1990, 264 (*Iliad*, Book 9:8 and 7).

Amun's barge: Described by Amenhotep III on stela JE 34025, see B. G. Davies 1992, 3 (562 = Urk. 1652–1654). For Cleopatra's "barge with a poop of gold, its purple sails billowing in the wind, while her rowers caressed the water with oars of silver which dipped in time to the music of the flute, accompanied by pipes and lutes," see Scott-Kilvert 1965, 293 (Plutarch's *Lives*, Marc Antony no. 26). **Inena:** Glanville 1932 and Chapter 1.

Opet Festival: Bell 1997, 157–176. **East bank palace:** O'Connor 1995, 270–279.

Destroyed Karnak structure: Phillips 2002, 103, figure 197; Prisse d'Avennes 2000, 16 (right).

Kha-em-maat temple: Bryan 1992b, 99–102; Gabolde and Rondot 1996; Aufrère et al. 1997, 144–146. The king's description again comes from the memorial temple stela, Cairo JE 34025; see Lichtheim 2006, 43–48, esp. 46. B. G. Davies's translation of this monument wrongly identifies this Kha-em-maat temple with the similarly named Soleb temple in Nubia; see B. G. Davies 1992, 4 (562: 24–25 = Urk. 1655), also Haeny 1997, 104–105. **Contra identification as a Montu temple:** Gabolde and Rondot 1996, 27–41. **Dedicatory inscription with list of precious materials used:** B. G. Davies 1992, 9–10 (568 = Urk. 1667–1669).

Medamud and the importance of Montu in Theban nome: Aufrère et al. 1997, 142–147.

Kom el Hettan name: Skeletons of actual prehistoric whales have been excavated at another site named Kom el Hettan in the Faiyum, which was, like much of Egypt, once undersea. See Vivian 2008, 256–257; Mueller 2010.

New Kingdom royal projects on the west bank: Babled 1993–1994, 131–146; Petrie 1897. **Memorial temples:** Stadelmann 1979; Haeny 1982. **Memorial temple of Amenhotep III:** Haeny 1997, 101–102; Sourouzian et al. 2004; idem. 2006; idem. 2006b; idem. 2006–2007.

Described on memorial temple stela, Cairo JE 34025, see B. G. Davies 1992, 2 (562 = Urk.1648–1649). **Jackals and sphinxes:** Cabrol 2001, 319–331. The terms *funerary* and *mortuary* are often applied to the royal temples because of their locations on the west bank, their proximity to the valley cemeteries, and their inclusion in festivals with funerary overtones, but the term *memorial* is gaining favor. The ancient Egyptians called them "mansions of millions of years," a generic name also applied to temples in other cities and towns not associated with the royal funeral but that served as venues for the celebration and recelebration of the king's jubilees as well as for the observance of local festivals. According to inscriptions found at his west bank palace, in its own day, Amenhotep III's great edifice was called simply "Pharaoh's temple." **Symbolism of "temples of millions of years":** Leblanc 1997.

Seven Wonders: Clayton and Price 1988.

"Ozymandias" statue (Amenhotep III usurped and moved to Ramesseum) in later literature: Oldfather 1933, 167–169 (Diodorus Siculus I. 47.1–5); Wellesley n.d., 15 ("Ozymandias" by Shelley).

Festival of Sokar: Gaballa and Kitchen 1969, 19, 28–37, 46.

Memorial temple economy and administration: Haring 1997, esp. 12–43, 60–61, 142–143, 214–217, 273, 382, 390–396; Häggman 2002, 137–138.

Royal tomb (KV 22): PM 1, 2: 547–550. The tomb was founded by Thutmose IV (see Chapter 5 notes). Reeves and Wilkinson 1996, 110–114; Reeves 2001, 79. Additional references in Chapter 17.

Deir el Medina and tomb workers: Bierbrier 1984, Andreu 2002. **The economics of artists' work at Deir el Medina:** Cooney 2007. **Egyptian tomb painting during the reign:** Kozloff 1992a, 291–296. **Kha's tomb (TT 8):** PM 1, 1:16–18; Schiaparelli 1927; Scamuzzi 1965, plates 41–49.

British Museum Nebamun: Parkinson 2008.

CHAPTER 8. THE KING'S FIRST TWO WIVES

Tiy: Ziegler 1994, 1: 531–548; Schoske 2008. Riefstahl 1964, 108, felt that Amenhotep married as a crown prince but considered Tiy "lowly" and of "undistinguished parentage." **Queen Tiy "marriage" scarabs:** Blankenberg-van Delden 1969, 4–8; Berman 1992b, 67–68; Meltzer 1989–1990, and personal communication, January 17, 2006. **Date of scarab production:** Berman 1992b, 68. For additional references for

Amenhotep III commemorative scarabs, see ibid., 69. **Tomb of Queen Tiy (KV 55)**: Davis 1908; Davis et al. 1910; M. Bell 1990.

Yuya as Semitic: Meltzer suggests in a private communication a parallel between "Yuya" and the Semitic "Yo-el." The "iA" (reed-leaf-aleph) as a transcription of Semitic "El" = "God" (aleph-lamedh) is well established and found in the name of the vizier apr-iA, generally understood as "Abdu-El" (or "Aper-el") toward the end of this reign (Chapter 17). See also Hornung 1995, esp. 102. "There was a considerable Hurrian component in the population of Syro-Canaanite areas generally characterized as Semitic in the Late Bronze [Age], and extensive Hurrian influence," according to D. B. Redford 1992, 134–137, 146–148. See also Meskell 2002, 33; Hoch 1994. **Thuya**: Laboury 2010, 46.

Amarna letters: Moran 1992, 95 (EA 29), 90–92 (EA 28), 84–86 (EA 26). **Tiy's private messengers**: Podany 2010, 214. **Read aloud**: Podany 2010, 204–205. See also the introduction.

Akhmim: Herrera 2008; Karig 1975; Baines and Málek 1984, 118. **Min**: Wilkinson 2003, 115–117; Ogdon 1985–1986.

"Master of" or "overseer of horses" title: Aling (with Helck contra Schulman) sees this as an important post. Aling 1977, 167–168. **Ancient Near Eastern horsemanship**: Azzaroli 1985, 27ff.; Masson 1998. See also Chapter 11.

Mummies and tomb of Yuya and Thuya (KV 46): PM 1, 2: 562–563; Davis et al. 1907, iii–xxi, xxiv–xxx; Quibell 1908, i–vii; Reeves and Wilkinson 1996, 174–178, and passim; Berman 1992a, 41–42; Lilyquist 1997. See also Chapter 9.

Marriage and ceremonies: Allam 1981; Robins 1993, 56–74; J. Johnson 1994, 113–132; Gee 2001, 17–25; Hansen 2005.

Glazed steatite portraits of Tiy: Bryan 1992a, 193–203; Wiese and Brodbeck 2004, 174–175 (entry by Wiese). See Berman 1992b, 69n9, for a discussion of dating. Most of these scholars date the statuettes later in the reign. Aldred, with whom this author agrees, suggested an early date.

Middle Eastern kingdoms and their relationships with Dynasty 18 Egypt: D. B. Redford 1992, 129ff. **Diplomatic marriage**: Schulman 1979; Bryan 2000a, 80–83; Feldman 2006, 68–70; Liverani 2008, 163–166; Podany 2010, 217–242. **Gilukhepa scarabs**: Blankenberg-van Delden 1969, 18, 129–133, plate 29. **Bengai**: Van Dijk 1997. Thutmose IV was the first Dynasty 18 king recorded to have wed a Mitanni princess, creating a new bond between former enemies. **Relationship with Mitanni:** Bryan 2000a; Podany 2010, 167–168, 217–231. **Amethyst seal:** Schmidt 1993, 153–160.

Queen Tiy's lake: Blankenberg-Van Delden 1969, 18, 134–135, plate 30–31; Berman 1992b, 71–72. **Effect of flood according to Diodorus Siculus:** Oldfather 1933, 125 (Book 1: 36.11–12).

CHAPTER 9. THE LOST YEARS

Nebnufer's statue (Brussels, Musées Royaux d'Art et d'Histoire, E. 1103): Capart and Spiegelberg 1902. The inscription is translated in B. G. Davies 1994, 44–45 (681 = Urk. 1884–1886). **Third Prophet Nefer:** Gaballa 1970, 50–54. **Egyptian priests and priesthoods:** Sauneron 2000. **Amenhotep son of Hapu inscription:** B. G. Davies 1994, 23 (664 = Urk. 1834). **Power of words in inscriptions:** Lacau 1913; Spencer 1982, 156ff.

Earthquakes: Ambraseys et al. 1994, 81–115. See also notes on Colossi in Chapter 10.

Ancient mentions of plague: Waddell 1964, 120–125 (Manetho); D. B. Redford 1986, 250 (Manetho); Goetze 1955, 396 (Mursilis II's Prayer); Moran 1992, 21 (EA 11 Burna–buriash). See also Chapter 18.

Mythology of Sekhmet: te Velde 1997; idem. 1985; Troy 1997; Germond 1981. **Mut statuary:** Lythgoe 1919. **Inscriptions:** B. G. Davies 1992, 50–52 (613 = Urk. 1763–1767). **Granodiorite:** see B. Aston et al. 2000, 36–37. Dozens of these statues have been found at Mut Temple, perhaps moved there in later times.

Luxor Temple inscription: B. G. Davies 1992, 27 (1710), 75n63, 64.

Bronze in Dynasty 18 Egypt: Hill 2007, 23–37; Christie's 2008, no. 99 (inlaid bronze panther skin); Moran 1992, 107–109 (EA 35 King of Cyprus).

General discussion of diseases in ancient Egypt: Buikstra et al. 1993.

Polio and Roma stela: Madsen 1904; Jørgensen 2007, 39, 214, no. 12; see also Chapter 13.

Smallpox and Thucydides: Strassler 1996, 118–123 (Thucydides 2: 48–59). Smallpox in Egyptian mummies: Fenner 1989.

Malaria: From 2007 to 2009, studies of royal mummies in the Cairo Museum by Dr. Zahi Hawass and colleagues have identified the presence of *Malaria tropica*, the most deadly form of malaria. See Hawass et al.

2010, 643–646. Malaria is carried by the anopheles mosquito. It is not communicable through human-to-human contact but by the mosquito carrying it from victim to victim. Septicemia from an infected bite can be a secondary cause of illness and death. Tutankhamen's mummy was found to have a skin lesion, possibly a mosquito bite.

Yersinia pestis (**bubonic plague**): Panagiotokopulu 2004; Kozloff 2006b discusses the possibility of Amenhotep III's reign being affected by disease events, particularly bubonic plague. The Hawass study found no evidence of bubonic plague in the cases studied, but samples were not taken from dental pulp (confirmed by e-mail from Dr. Hawass, March 20, 2010), the only area likely to show traces of this disease. See Raoult et al. 2000. **Evidence at Amarna:** Kemp at al. 1994.

Spoon iconography: Kozloff 1992b, 331–359 (including references to Tutankhamen's shrines). The "chapter of drinking water" appears in the papyrus of Yuya with a painted vignette of the deceased receiving a cup of water from a sycamore tree: Davis et al. 1907, 11, plate 9. **Identification of the spoons:** Kozloff 2007. **Boxwood:** Gale et al. 2000, 337–338. **Goddesses of tree cult:** Buhl 1947.

Yuya and Thuya's tomb: Davis et al. 1907; Quibell 1908. Sitamen's chairs and some other finds are well illustrated in Wiese and Brodbeck 2004, 180–209, nos. 26–36. **Mummies of Yuya and Thuya:** Hawass et al. 2010, esp. 640, 645, table 3, 646.

Monuments of Prince Thutmose: Wildung 1998; Berlandini-Keller 1993, 20–21; Dodson 1990, 87–96, plate 5; Berman 1992a, 43–44; idem. 1992c, 253–254; El Sabban 2000; M. Gabolde 1993, 29.

CHAPTER 10. BRINGING HEAVEN TO EARTH TO SEE THE LIVING GODS

Egypt's view of its past: Tait 2003; Fischer-Elfert 2003. **Amenhotep III's claims on his memorial temple stela (Cairo JE 34025):** B. G. Davies 1992, 2 (562 = Urk. 1648), 3 (562 = Urk. 1654). **Karnak inscription:** Ibid., 32 (574 = Urk. 1724).

Religion in New Kingdom and reign of Amenhotep III: David 1982, 120–154; Assmann 1989; Baines 1991; J. Yoyotte 1993; Hornung 1999, 19–30; Cabrol 2000, 253–293; Birkstam 1984. **Amenhotep III's deification:** Bickel 2002. **"Re of kings":** Varille 1936. Ramesses II would later adopt this title for himself, which is not surprising because he purloined so many of Amenhotep III's monuments.

Amenhotep III's architectural program: Bryan 1992b, 76, 104, 110–111; O'Connor 1998b, 142–172. **West bank projects**: Babled 1993–1994. **Mortuary temple stela**: B. G. Davies 1992,1–5; Babled 1993–1994; Johnson and Forbes 2007. **Temple as cosmos**: Hornung 1992, 115–129.

Amenhotep III as Horus: D. B. Redford 1986, 248–251, suggests that the historian Manetho's King Hor may have been Amenhotep III. **Abi-Milku**: Moran 1992, 233–235 (EA 147).

Amenhotep son of Hapu on his knowledge and research: B. G. Davies 1994, 17–18 (658 = Urk. 1817–1821).

Ma'at: Hornung 1992,131–145; J. Yoyotte 1993.

Memorial temple, north processional way: Petrie 1897, 4, 9, also lists colossal statues found at Merneptah: eight-foot-long, couchant jackals with images of the king between their paws, limestone sphinxes, brown quartzite statues, and sandstone Osirides, some of which may have lined the processional way. Among the fragments of statuary found, there were parts of three colossal groups in crystalline limestone depicting the king with Amun, the king with Hathor, and the king with either his mother or Tiy. **School at Amenhotep II temple**: Petrie, op. cit.; Sesana and Nelson 1998. **Statue of Amenhotep III as Ptah-Sokar-Osiris**: Johnson 2001. **Some statuary from this site in the British Museum, Louvre, and Cairo and Luxor museums**: Bryan 1992d, 125 (figure 5.1, BM EA 3), 126 (figures 5 and 6, Louvre A 19), 130 (figures 5 and 9, BM EA 4), 143 (figure 5.25, BM EA 5), 146 (figure 5.28, Cairo JE 33901), 154–155, no. 5 (Luxor, J. 133), 156–158, no. 6 (BM EA 7). British Museum EA 6 is mentioned, ibid. 156, 158n6.

Memorial temple peristyle: Sourouzian and Stadelmann 2003, 429–435, plates 71–75; Sourouzian et al. 2006b, 401–414, plates 1–17; Sourouzian 1993. **Elements of statuary**: Berlandini-Keller 1993a; Donadoni 1994. **Peristyle statuary and sky map**: Bryan 1997. The brown quartzite statues of Amenhotep III wore the platform crown of Lower (northern) Egypt, and the red granite ones wore the conical crown of Upper Egypt. Heads from two of the brown quartzite statues are now in the British Museum (EA 6 and 7; see preceding citation); a red granite head is in the Luxor Museum and another is in the Louvre (Louvre A 19 and Luxor J. 133; see preceding citations).

Animal statuary: Bryan 1992f. **Sekhmets**: Kozloff 1992h; J. Yoyotte 1980. Other than the Sekhmets, most famous of all animal sculptures from Kom el Hettan is the great red granite scarab, avatar of Khepri, a solar god associated with resurrection, moved by Taharqa (690–664 B.C.) to the sacred lake at Karnak. A second one is in the British Museum. Sourouzian continues to find colossal statuary at the site in 2010: AOL News, Feburary 28, 2010. http://www.aolnews.com/2010/02/28/huge-scupture-of-pharaohs-head-unearthed-in egypt/.

Additional sculpture from Merneptah Temple and Ramesseum: Partridge 2009, 31–35; Lurson 2004, 2006.

Colossi: Bryan 1992d, 138–139. **Mutemwia**: Hayes 1951, 96–97 (jar label); Robins 1995, 53–55, no. 26 (British Museum EA 43A); Sourouzian 1993, 10–15. **Colossi as deities**: Morkot 1990, 332; Bickel 2002, 73, 78, figures 7–9; Sourouzian 2002; idem. 2006–2007, 22–24. Earthquakes are a common occurrence in Egypt; several are known from antiquity. In 1969, French archaeologists noted that two earthquakes centered in Iraq and Ethiopia were strong enough (4 on the Richter scale) to make waves on Karnak's sacred lake, shaking walls and obelisks and causing stones to fall from some of the pylons. See Lauffray et al. 1970. An alabaster colossus was found between the second and third pylons in spring 2011. See Hawass 2011.

Lake in front of memorial temple: B. G. Davies 1992, 2 (562 = Urk 1649).

Minemheb: Bryan 1992c, 244–246; Berman 1999, 233–235, cat. no. 168.

Aswan quarries, quarrymen, techniques: Bryan 1992d, 139 (colossi); Klemm and Klemm 2008, 233–249. **Quarry overseers, Men and Bak**: B. G. Davies 1994, 71 (731 = Urk. 1942–1943). **Men**: Murnane 1998, 215. **Bak's stela from Amarna (Berlin 1/63)**: Fay 1985, 78. **Stelae and remains of an Amenhotep III colossus in Aswan**: De Morgan 1894, 40, 62, 63; Varille 1936. **Brown quartzite quarries and testing of Memnons**: Heizer et al. 1973; Bowman et al. 1984; Stross et al. 1988; B. Aston et al. 2000, 52; Klemm and Klemm 2008, 227–231. **Limestone quarries**: B. Aston et al. 2000, 40; Klemm and Klemm 2008, 73–75, 120.

Valley Festival: L. Bell 1997, 136–137 (his description is largely paraphrased here).

Anen: Bryan 1992c, 249–250. **Tomb of Anen (TT 120)**: PM 1, 1: 234. **Limestone statue of a man named "Anen" and his wife, dated by style to Amenhotep III**: Corteggiani 1994; Christie's 2003, 64–65, lot 519. **Flaubert**: Steegmuller 1972, 164.

Karnak, processional ways: Blyth 2006, 112; Cabrol 2001. Cabrol feels that nearly 100 ram-headed (crio-)sphinxes now at the First Pylon and previously thought to belong to Ramesses II are actually Amenhotep III's. See also Cabrol 1995a, 1–28, plates 1–4.

Third Pylon: see Chapter 7. Murnane 1979 analyses previous studies of this scene, but as proportion analyses were not yet common at his writing, he misidentified the small figure in the blue crown. See also Muhammad 1966, 143–146; Murnane 1993, 29–31; Pillet 1925; Chevrier 1950, plate 12 (Amenemhat Surer stela). **Hypostyle hall**: Chevrier 1971, 75–78. **Drawing of Third Pylon in Neferhotep's tomb**: Aufrère et al. 1997, 98, 127; Murnane 1993, 28 (after Wreszinski); see also Weeks 2005, 88–89; PM 2: 60–61; Sa'ad 1970, 187–193, where the small erased figure behind Amenhotep III is identified as Amenhotep IV; Sauneron and Vérité 1969, 276. **The back curve as an element of Amenhotep III style**: Kozloff 1992a, 269. **Tutankhamen's restorations**: Bennett 1939; Eaton-Krauss 1993.

Granary: Bryan, 1992b, 102; Kozloff 1992a, 274 (TT 253); Bickel 2006; Pinch-Brock 2006; Blyth 2006, 98, 110–111. **Other Amenhotep III blocks from Karnak**: Schaden 1987. Many blocks of a jubilee temple have also been found at Karnak. Whether these were brought over from the west bank or whether they came from a now unknown jubilee temple of Amenhotep III at Karnak is unknown; see Bickel 2006. **Priests' habitations**: Anus and Sa'ad 1971. Anen, see earlier. **Khnummose tomb (TT 253)**: PM 1, 1: 336–337; Strudwick 1996, 23–55, plates 13–25. **Amenemhat Surer (TT 48)**: PM 1, 1: 87–91; Säve-Söderbergh 1957, 33–49. **Harvest festival**: Pinch-Brock 2006. Overseer of the granaries of Upper and Lower Egypt Khaemhet depicts many harvest-related scenes in his tomb but not the actual granary. PM 1, 1: 113–119 (TT 57). **Ancient bread recipe**: H. Wilson 1988.

Tenth Pylon: Bryan 1992b, 99; Blyth 2006, 109–110; Legrain 1914a. **"Eight"-boats**: Jones 1988, 142. **Amenhotep son of Hapu's work on a quartzite colossus**: B. G. Davies 1994, 19 (658 = Urk. 1822–1823).

Mut Temple and precinct: Fazzini 2002, 2005; PM 2: 255–270; D. Arnold 2003, 156–157; Wilkinson 2000, 163. **Statuary**: Cabrol 1995, plate 5a. **Neva sphinxes**: B. G. Davies 1992, 41 (584); Kozloff 1992g, 223, figure 32a. **Tiy statuary**: Bryan 2008; idem. 1992d; Kozloff 1996, idem. 1997a. **Festival of Drunkenness**: Brunner 1986.

Khonsu temple: Blyth 2006, 115; McClain 2009 (blocks are thought to come from the memorial temple); D. Arnold 2003, 124.

Luxor Temple, Amenhotep III description: B. G. Davies 1992, 2 (562 = Urk. 1650–1651); D. Arnold 2003, 134–135; Bryan 1992b, 82–90; Phillips 2002, 8–13. **1989 statue discovery:** El Saghir 1991. **Luxor wall decoration:** Epigraphic Survey 1994; idem. 1998. **Luxor inscriptions:** B. G. Davies 1992, 27 (572 = Urk. 1710). **Amenhotep III in dress of Horus:** Podgórski 1991. **Luxor as a temple for the cult of the royal** *ka*: L. Bell 1985; idem. 1997, 158–176, 179–180.

Sandstone portraits of Amenhotep III recut for Amenhotep IV: Kozloff 2010. **Other reused statuary:** Sourouzian 1993, 8–10. **Blocks of Amenhotep III reused in quay and Nilometer west of Luxor Temple:** Cabrol 1995a. The emphasis on death as a stage on the path to rebirth would also explain the origin at Luxor Temple of a statue to Anubis, the jackal-headed guardian of the cemeteries. This granodiorite monument, now in Copenhagen, was dedicated to "Anubis in the temple of Luxor"; see Jørgensen 2007, 35, 213, no. 7. **Osiris:** Wilkinson 2003, 120. **Amenhotep's use of rebuses:** Berman 1992b, 72; Bryan 1992d, 126; Kozloff 1992b.

Maru: B. G. Davies 1992, 34 (574 = Urk. 1730). **East bank** *maru*: Stadelmann 1978, 179; Manniche 1982; Kozloff 2009. See Chapter 11 for discussion of the west bank *maru*. **Foreign tribute in Luxor Temple inscriptions:** B. G. Davies 1992, 21 (572 = Urk. 1697), 26 (572 = Urk. 1708).

Sebek-mose: Bryan 1992b, 83–85; idem. 1992c, 255; Murnane 1998, 189–190; Hayes 1939, idem. 1959, 269–271, figure 165; Freed et al. 2003, 156–157. **Sumenu temple:** Bakry 1971, 131–146. **Sobek statue:** Romano et al. 1979, 82–84, figures 62–64. **Hatnub:** B. Aston et al. 2000, 59. **Suty and Hor:** Walle 1971; Baines 1985, 461–482; B. G. Davies 1994, 71–74; de Cenival 1991; Foster 1995, 57–58; Quirke and Spencer 2007, 170–171.

CHAPTER 11. PER HAI ("THE HOUSE OF REJOICING")
AT MALKATA

Per-aa in the reign of Thutmose III: Maruéjol 2007, 118–119. **Per Hai:** O'Connor 1980, 1175; Rössler-Köhler 1982.

New Kingdom royal palaces, especially locations, activities of Amenhotep III: O'Connor 1995, 263–265, 270–276, 280; Lacovara 2009; Stadelmann 1994, esp. 313–314. **Malkata jar labels:** Hayes 1951; Leahy 1978.

General description and individual elements of Malkata: O'Connor 1980; Lacovara 1997b, 25–27 (king's palace) and idem. 2009, 28 (large house), 44 (Tiy's palace as office), 48–49 (workmen's village), 69. **Painted walls:** W. S. Smith 1981, 279–295; Leahy 1978, 1 (destroyed building). **Scribes' school:** Izre'el 1997, 9–13. **Besbes:** Kozloff 1992d, 355–356; Meltzer, personal communication. **Houses at Tell el Amarna:** Spence 2004.

King's officials, Ptahmose: Leblanc 2005a, 69–70; Berman 1992a, 49; Bryan 1992c, 241–242; Lorton 1991. **Objects belonging to Ptahmose:** Hall 1931. **Ramose tomb (TT 55):** PM 1, 1: 105–111; N. de G. Davies 1941. **Duties of the vizier:** Van Den Boorn 1988, 310–331; Faulkner 1955. **Simut:** Hayes 1951, 237–238. **Amenemhet Surer (TT 48):** Säve-Söderbergh 1957, 33–48, plates 30–58, 70; B. G. Davies 1994, 52 (695 = Urk. 1902), 52–53 (696 = Urk. 1903–1904), 53 (697 = Urk. 1905), 54 (698); Murnane 1998, 212–213. **Diodorus Siculus:** Oldfather 1933, 241 (I. 70.2). **Neferronpet:** Bryan 1992c, 242–243, no. 38 (statue, Louvre E 14241). **Servants from Kush:** Moran 1992, 120–121 (EA 48). **Messengers' billets:** Podany 2010, 72. **Messengers:** Valloggia 1976.

Tale of the Eloquent Peasant: Parkinson 1997, 54–88.

Queen's stewards: Hayes 1959, 276 (Mery and Ihuy); see also Epigraphic Survey 1980, plate 88. **Kheruef (TT 192):** Epigraphic Survey 1980; Murnane 1998, 217; B. G. Davies 1994, 40 (675 = Urk. 1875–1876); Berman 1992a, 55, figure 2.12. **Userhet (TT 47):** PM 1, 1: 87; Hayes 1951, 100 (jar label). **Malkata's harem:** O'Connor 2010.

The Rhind tomb: Dodson and Janssen 1989; Dodson 2008–2009, 41–49. **Nebetia is also the name of a pubescent girl represented by a wood statuette found at Gurob:** Bryan 1992c, 260, no. 51; M. Yoyotte 2008a. **The father of Rhind's Nebetia was Prince Si-atum:** Murnane 1998, 214–215; Bryan 1992e.

Malkata's South Village: Tytus 1903; Hayes 1951, 36.

Jewelry, faience, and glass: Kozloff 1992c, idem. 1992d, 398–405, idem. 1992e, 445–451, idem. 1997. **Finger rings:** Hayes 1951, 231–236. **White faience box lid:** B. G. Davies 1992, 41. **Anu the chief artificer (BM 41646):** H. R. Hall 1925, 6, plate 9. The art of glass making seems to have been invented in the East just a few centuries earlier, and a great deal of the technology must have originated there. For example, a cuneiform tablet from Mesopotamia, written in Babylonian, bears a recipe for making glass. Dated to our king's time period, it gives step-by-step directions for how to make what was commonly called "Akkadian-red-stone glass." The Amarna letters document shipments of raw material in the form of thick, discus-shaped glass ingots to Egypt from the Levantine coast; however, the chemical analysis of ingots from a late-fourteenth-century B.C. shipwreck show that raw glass was produced both in Egypt and in Mesopotamia. See Pulak 2008a; Finkel 2008.

Birket Habu: Kemp and O'Connor 1974, 101–136. **As a chariot venue**: Kozloff 2009. Today, the nearby modern village, Nag el Qatar, is the only place in the Theban valley where well-bred horses imported from breeding farms up north in the Delta around Zagazig are still kept for hobby and sport. Their owners train them by riding around and over the mounds at the edge of the *birket*. **The eastern *birket***: Laboury 2010, 69.

Kikkuli: Masson 1998; Beckman 2008. **Ancient horse training, breeding, racing, and arenas**: Hyland 2003, 36–41, 201–207; Cotterell 2005, 129–131; Rommelaere 1991; Schulman 1980. **Kom el Abd and Kom el Samak**: Kemp 1977, 71–82; Yoshimura 1985; Roehrig 2010. **"Rich in horses"**: Leahy 1978, 39.

CHAPTER 12. BENEATH THE DIVINE FALCON'S WINGS
A NEW WORLD TAKES SHAPE

Merymose's career and inscriptions: Murnane 1998, 189; Zába 1950, 513; De Morgan 1894, 39; Mahfouz 2005, 55–78. **Vienna statue of Merymose**: Seipel 1992, 322–323, no. 125. **Merymose's lineage**: Meltzer 1974, 9–11. **Merymose with Kheruef**: De Morgan 1894, 39. **Ramose's inscription**: Ibid. 1894, 90. **Sebek-mose's inscription**: Ibid. 1894, 44. **Merymose at Tombos**: Harrell 1999, 244; Davies and Friedman 1998, 136. **Merymose near Aswan**: Habachi 1957, 23–25, plates 6 and 7.

Second Nubian Campaign: Topozada 1988; O'Connor 1998, 269–270; G. J. Shaw 2008, 114–115.

East Semneh stela recording campaign (British Museum): B. G. Davies 1992, 5–6 (564 = Urk. 1659–1661). **Ibhet**: Zibelius 1972, 74–75.

Khaemhet market scene (TT 57): PM 1, 1: 115; Pino 2005, 95–105.

Building program in the north and south: Bryan 1992b, 104–111; O'Connor 1998b, 147–170.

Nubia, Elephantine chapel: *Desc. de l'Égypte* 2000, 79–83 (A vol. 1, plates 34–38). **Wadi es-Sebua:** Firth 1915, 235–236, plates 31–34; Habachi 1960; Ullmann 2009; Török 2009, 234–235. In 1964, before the new Aswan dam flooded es-Sebua, the painted walls were removed and stored in the basement of the Cairo Museum. **Sai Island:** Vercoutter 1956, 74–75, 79–81; Minault-Gout, 1994, 1996; Vercoutter 1973; idem. 1974; Geus 1994. **Soleb:** Schiff Giorgini 1965, 1971, 2002; Leclant 1996; Morkot 1987, 34; Bryan 1992f; Arnold 1997, 34 and 259n20. **Horse burial:** Schiff Giorgini 1962, 164, 169; Leclant 1977. **Ram inscriptions:** B. G. Davies 1992, 42–43. **Lions and rams from Soleb:** Bryan 1992f. **Palm frond capitals:** Phillips 2002, 17–18, 53, 57, 265, 286 (the last two are probably taken by Ramesside kings from earlier buildings); Feldman 2006, 84–85. **Glass vessels in palm-frond column shape:** Kozloff 1992c, 388–389, nos. 96–97. **Sedeinga:** Labrousse 1994, 1996; Schiff Giorgini 1965a, 112–113, plates 30–32; Prisse d'Avennes 2000, 12 (lower).

Delta, Athribis: Habachi 1974; Bryan 1992b, 104; B. G. Davies 1992, 44 (590 = Urk. 1754); Habachi 1974. **Athribis snake:** Bryan 1997, cat. 30. **Tell Basta statues:** Tietze and Abd el Maksoud 2004, 30–32, 38; Tietze 2003a; idem. 2003b.

Vizier Amenhotep statues: Naville 1891, 32 (British Museum 1068 and Cairo CG 590); Gordon 1989, 15. **Geoarchaeology of the eastern Delta:** Graham and Banbury 2008. **Blue lily:** Ossian 1999.

High Steward Amenhotep's statue inscription: B. G. Davies 1994, 8–9 (642 = Urk. 1794–1801); Gardiner 1913. **Private offerings to gods:** D. B. Redford 1967, 45–54, 179. Another private individual, Khaemhat, the granary official, depicted himself making offerings directly to the gods. **Amenhotep III at Memphis:** Berlandini-Keller 1993; Morkot 1990; Haring 1997, 142–143.

Ptahmose: Murnane 1992 (the clearest explanation of this confusing "family" group); Bryan 1992c, 241–242; Bosse-Griffiths 1955; Anthes 1976, 61. The stela mentioned here is preserved in two pieces, one in Leiden and one in the Petrie Museum, University College, London.

Hebenu: Gomaà 1977. **Cleveland reliefs:** Bryan 1992b, 10–11, plates 4, 118–120; Berman 1999, 227–231, no. 166. **Taitai:** Bryan 1992c, 248–249.

CHAPTER 13. THE FIRST JUBILEE FESTIVAL (*HEB-SED*)

Sed-festival: Uphill 1965 (including Bubastis reliefs); Berman 1992a, 38–41; D. Arnold 1997, 39, 69–83; L. Bell 1997, 130; Haeny 1997,

100–103; Hornung and Staehlin 1974, 33–36, 56–77; Hornung and Staehelin 2006, 25–27, 58–63, 83–95; Wente 1969. **Karnak blocks:** Bickel 2006, 23–32. **Soleb:** Schiff Giorgini 2002; Leclant 1996. **Repetition:** Morkot 1990, 334–335. **Authenticity:** Redford notes that in Hatshepsut's reign was "the first appearance in the Thutmoside clan of the hankering after authenticity . . . which was to characterize Amenophis III's approach to the *sd*-festival." D. B. Redford 1986, 173, 187. **Kheruef** (see later and Chapter 18). **Khaemhet (TT 57):** PM 1, 1: 116–117 (15). **Predynastic palette:** Bothmer 1969–1970. **May's inscription:** Rowe 1931, 45.

Jar labels: Hayes 1951, 88–94 (commodities), 90, 94, 100 (officials); Leahy 1978. **Amenhotep son of Hapu jar labels:** Hayes 1951, 100. **Roma stela:** Madsen 1904; Jørgensen 2007, 39, 214, no. 12.

Specific jubilee events and participants: Habachi 1971. **Kheruef tomb (TT 192):** Epigraphic Survey 1980, 43 (day of gold of honor and sailing); Dorman 1993, 464. **Amenhotep III ebony statuette (Brooklyn Museum 48.28):** Bryan 1992a, 194, figure 6.2, 210n8 (notes that the inscriptions are funerary). **Amenhotep III on sedan chair followed by female family, Tiy:** Schiff Giorgini 2002, plates 94–101, 105, 127, plates 115 (crownless Tiy). **Royal children:** Schiff Giorgini 2002, plate 97 (Sitamen, Henut-taneb, Isis), plate 94 (female children), plate 127 (daughters and chief of royal harem), plate 115a (royal son in front of viziers, including Ramose), plate 117 (royal children, boys and girls). **"Children of the great ones":** Epigraphic Survey 1980, plates 31–32. **"Daughter of the Mentiu":** Epigraphic Survey 1980, 46; Yeivin 1965. **Amarna letter 369 to Gezer:** Moran 1992, 366. **Nebmerutef:** Schiff Giorgini 2002, plates 44, 81, 95. **Nebmerutef's statuettes:** Bryan 1992c, 246–248. **Find spot of statuettes:** Habachi 1972, 22–23. **Nebmerutef jar labels:** Leahy 1978, 21–22. **Mention of Nebmerutef in Kheruef tomb:** Epigraphic Survey 1980, 51, n. c. **Simut:** Schiff Giorgini 2002, plates 37 and 38. **Simut's tomb (A.24):** PM 1, 1: 454. **Meryra:** Schiff Giorgini 2002, plates 37 (see also Chapters 1, 11, and 17). **Other officials:** Schiff Giorgini 2002, plate 42 (Ramose), plate 57 (Merymose), plate 120 (Chief of Seers, Chief of Artisans), plates 41, 42, 58 (two viziers), plates 75 (Greatest of Seers in front of viziers). **Confusion over viziers:** Gordon 1989.

Knocking on doors (King and Amenhotep son of Hapu): Schiff Giorgini 2002, plates 41–44. **Wepwawet:** Wilkinson 2003, 191–192. *Heb-sed* **cloak:** Sourouzian 1994. *Heb-sed* **pavilion:** Bryan 1992b, 105, figure 4.24; Seki 2008. **Deities in booths:** Schiff Giorgini 2002, plate 50. **Granodiorite statues:** Donadoni 1994; Bryan 1992d, 178–184. **Clepsydra:** Handoussa 1979; Schiff Giorgini 2002, plates 74–75; Bryan 1997.

Deification of Amenhotep III: Bickel 2002. **Ram's horns:** Bryan 1992b, 87. **Alexander the Great's image:** Arnold-Biucchi 2006, front cover and 64, no. 20.

Kheruef's Bubastis sculpture: Naville 1891, 33–34, plate 35; Gordon 1989, 18.

Tiy as sphinx: Haeny 1981, plate 11b (memorial temple); Prisse d'Avennes 2000, 12 bottom (Sedeinga); Labrousse 1996, 67 (Sedeinga). **Cornelian bracelet plaques:** Berman and Bryan 1992.

Amenhotep III–Tiy colossus: Trad and Mahmoud 1993, 40–44; Johnson 2006, no. 2.38, 135–137. This behemoth was probably installed as a central focus in the memorial temple. In Dynasty 20, it was moved to Ramesses III's temple at Medinet Habu just a few hundred yards to the south. It was found there in 1892, shattered and lying in pieces. Over the next 20 years, it was moved and reconstructed in the central court of the Cairo Museum. One important piece escaped – the head of Princess Nebetah, now in a Dutch private collection, a cast having been donated and placed on the statue in Cairo.

Sitamen: Gabolde 1993, 30–31; Meyer 1984, 485–486; Green 1996, 8. **Sitamen's temple:** Petrie 1897, 9. **Relief fragments from temple in London:** Stewart 1976, 4–5, plates 3.3 and 3.4. **Luxor cachette statue:** El Saghir 1989; El-Shahawy and Atiya 2007, 41–43; see also the goddess Yunet, 38–40. **Gift labels:** Hayes 1951, 98.

Royal incest: Desroches-Noblecourt 1986, 44–47; Dobbs 2010; Wilfong 2001, 343–344.

Amenhotep son of Hapu's appointment: B. G. Davies 1994, 24 (666 = Urk. 1837–1838).

Tax decree: Galán 2000, 255–258. This was the first of several such decrees aimed at Thebes in late Dynasty 18 and early Dynasty 19, the second coming during Tutankhamen's restoration and the third during the reign of Sety I at the beginning of Dynasty 19. Apparently this was some sort of grand restructuring, likely for economic reasons.

CHAPTER 14. RAISING UP OLD OFFICIALS AND BUYING A NEW BRIDE

Amenhotep son of Hapu: Wildung 1977; Murnane 1991; Laurent 1993; Legrain 1914a. **His temple:** Robichon and Varille 1936; Bidoli

1970 (lake in front of temple). **Dedication stela (BM EA 138)**: Varille 1968, 66–85 (this stela, based on its language, probably dates to the Twenty-first Dynasty but appears copied from a document contemporary with the temple). **Son of Hapu's statuary**: Varille 1968. **Compared with Mentuhotep statues**: Berman 1992d.

Northern and southern viziers: Gordon 1989.

Pa-Ramessu statues: Legrain 1914a, 29–38; Delvaux 1992; Kozloff/Meltzer 2010 (recutting of these monuments from Ramose). **Palette of Ramose probably recut for Amenmose**: Glanville 1932a, plate 8.

Amarna letters: Moran 1987, 41–50 (EA 17–21, Tushratta and messenger Keliya). **Diplomatic marriage**: see Chapter 8. "**Foreign Lady**": Van Dijk 1997. **Tadu-Hepa**: Podany 2010, 217–231.

International messengers: Valloggia 1976; Podany 2010, 72, 213–215. **Keliya's name**: Steindorff 1900, 15. *Kel shawabti*: Schneider 1977, 1: 190, 2: 102, plate 112. **Ptahmose** *shawabti*: Trapani 2001, 480. **Thutmose IV** *shawabti*: Carter and Newberry 1904, 45, plate 13.

Mane–Meniu: Barbotin 1997; Hayes 1951, figure 19; Schneider 1977, 1: 304. D. B. Redford 1980, 16, sees Mane as Amenhotep III's "army-scribe, king's scribe, and scribe of recruits, Men," who left a monument at Mut Temple now in the Cairo Museum [901], see B. G. Davies 1994, 62 (714 = Urk. 1922); also Borchardt, Statuen 3: 145. **In Amarna letters**: Moran 1992, 43–99 (EA 19–21, 27–29). Tushratta also mentions the name Nyu, possibly this same man, as a messenger sent by Amenhotep III in letter EA 29; ibid. 93.

Haaramassi (etc.) in Amarna letters, reign of Amenhotep III: Moran 1992, 47–50 (EA 20 Tushratta). **Reign of Amenhotep IV–Akhenaten**: Moran 1992, 21–23 (EA 11 Burna-buriash), 86–90 (EA 27 Tushratta), 92–99 (EA 29 Tushratta), 120–121 (EA 49 Ugarit), 276 (EA 198: Kumidu). D. B. Redford 1980, 13–14, sees one of these writings as Ramose, possibly the "general of the Lord of the Two Lands" at Amarna.

CHAPTER 15. INTERNATIONAL TRADE IN PRINCESSES
AND OTHER GOODS

Egypt and the Levant: Weinstein 1998. **Ways of Horus**: Oren 1987. Tjel became more prominent in Dynasty 19 as Seti I and Ramesses II kicked off major military campaigns from there. **Tjel/Tjaru**: Abd el-Maksoud 1998; idem. 1998a. **Tjel gifts**: Hayes 1951, 91, 101. **Tell el**

Borg: Hoffmeier 2002; idem. 2004, 109, figure 26 (Tiy ring); Hoffmeier and Abd el-Maksoud 2003.

Northern overseers: D. B. Redford 1990, 5–8 (terminology of the title); Gordon 1989; Murnane 1997. **Khaemwaset and Manana:** Saleh and Sourouzian 1987, no. 152. **Khaemwaset and Khebunes:** Habachi 1957a, 95–97, plates 28–29. **Penhet (TT 239):** PM 1, 1: 330; Murnane 1997, 254. **Late Bronze Age Canaan:** Na'aman 2000; idem. 2005, 145–194; D. B. Redford 1992, 123–213.

Northern vassals: James 2000. **Amarna letters from northern vassals:** Moran 1992, 338–339 (EA 296: Yahtiru), 199 (EA 198: Kumidu), 242 (EA 156: Aziru). **Greetings in the Amarna letters:** Morris 2006. **Land disputes:** idem. 2010. **Death of the king of Tyre:** Moran 1992, 162–163 (EA 89). **Conflict in Canaan:** ibid. 137–169 (EA 68–95: Rib-Hadda), 133–136 (EA 61–64: Abdi Ashirta), 366 (EA 369: Milkilu of Gezer). **Chronology of letters concerning Tyre, Rib-Hadda, and Abdi-Ashirta:** Na'aman 2005, 43, 45, 55, 68, 89, 245. **Date of Milkilu letter:** idem. 2005, 245.

Arzawa: Feldman 2006, 140 (location of). **Arzawa's Amarna letters:** Moran 1992, 101–104 (EA 31–32); Feldman 2006, 149–150. The two Arzawan letters actually read as though EA 32 preceded EA 31. **Arzawa and Hatti:** Collins 2008, 56–59; Sayce 1922. In the Amarna correspondence, the Arzawan letters are the only two written in Hittite, suggesting that Arzawa was outside the normal loop of Near Eastern diplomatic correspondence and had some shared cultural history with the Hittites. Letter EA 31 mentions that "the country Hattusha [the capital of the Hittites] is shattered," probably referring to an attack of the Kaska people, who had swept down from their homeland along the Black Sea coast through Hatti, routing the royal family from its capital. The Hittites bounced back, however, and drove off the Kaska, who were subsequently given refuge by Arzawa. Amenhotep asked Tarhundaradu in EA 31: "send to me, too . . . people of Kaska. I have heard that everything is finished."

Egypt's relations with the Aegean: Cline 1998 (including the "Aegean List"); idem. 2001; Duhoux 2003, 234–258; Andreadaki-Vlazaki et al. 2008, 156, no. 121; Hankey 1995 (ceramics); Kemp and Merrillees 1980. **Ulu Burun shipwreck:** Pulak 1998; idem. 2008. **Egyptian seagoing ships in the New Kingdom:** Faulkner 1941, 7–9. **Tell el Dab'a paintings:** Bietak, Marinatos, and Palivou, 2007. **Amenhotep III faience at Mycenae:** Cline 1990.

Letters to or mentioning Amanappa: Moran 1992, 141–194 (EA 73–117 passim). **Statue of Amenemopet**: Sotheby's 1990, no. 415.

Cyprus letters: Moran 1992, 104–110 (EA 33–36).

CHAPTER 16. A MIXED FORECAST: DAZZLING SUN AND DARK CLOUDS

Jar labels: Hayes 1951, 100 (Amenhotep son of Hapu, Kheruef, Khaemhet), 36, 84–85 (404 labels), 86 (meat), 94 (Amenemhet). **Meshwesh**: Ibid. 91. This group of inscriptions, according to Hayes, "constitutes the earliest recorded reference to relations between the Egyptians and this particular Libyan people." **Meat production**: Ikram 1995 (much of her evidence coming from Malkata). **Exports from the Libyan desert**: Giddy 1980.

Malkata Amun temple: Koltsida 2007.

Amenhotep III, Year 35: B. G. Davies 1992, 13–14. **Vizier Amenhotep at Gebel el Silsilla**: PM 5: 220.

Luxor colonnade: Epigraphic Survey 1994, xvii. **Karnak colonnade**: Chevrier 1956, 36. **Soleb**: Schiff Giorgini 2002 (4), 7–23, figures 7a–23.

Serabit el Khadim: Aufrère et al. 1997a, 248–256; Pinch 1993, 49–58; Gardiner and Peet 1995, 37–38. **Deities**: Ibid. 41–44. **Mining methods**: Ibid. 20–21. **Amenhotep III inscriptions at Sinai**: idem. 165–169; PM 7: 350.

Sinai statuettes: Hardwick, unpublished. **Tiy portrait (Cairo JE 38257)**: Saleh and Sourouzian 1987, no. 144. **Isis statuette in the George Ortiz Collection, Geneva (CH)**: Bryan 1992a, 206–208, no. 24; Ortiz 1994, no. 39. **Amarna statuette**: Pendlebury 1933, 117, plates 17–18. **Walters statuette**: Schulz 2008. **Punt expedition**: Kitchen 1999, 173; see also Hall 1928, 75, plates 10, for a statuette of Tutankhamen in the same stone (BM 37639); 75–76, plate 11 (EA 2275) for one of Amenhotep III.

Tadu-Hepa: Moran 1992, 43–21 (EA19–50, negotiations for her), 51–61, 72–84 (EA 22, 25 inventory and dowry lists), 61–71 (EA 23–24, other mentions); Gundlach 1986; Green 1996, 14.

Relations with Mitanni: Moran 1992, 41–84 (EA 17–25), 50 (EA 21, first Sauska letter), 61–62 (EA 23 second Sauska letter); Kitchen 1998b, 256–261; Feldman 2006, 68–70, 105–107, 149–151, 179–180. **Astarte in Egypt**: Stadelmann 1967, 101; Stewart 1976, 50, plate 40, 2.

Death of Abdi-Ashirta: Säve-Söderbergh 1946, 62–67, with references to relevant Amarna letters; Na'aman 2005, 43, 45, 89–90, 245, with references to relevant Amarna letters.

Additional Amarna texts: Izre'el 1997, 9, 32–40, 83–84 (EA 351, 352 + 353, 354, 373).

Babylon: Brinkman 2008; Kitchen 1998a, 253–256; Moran 1992, 1–9 (EA1–4: Kadashman Enlil), 21 (EA 11: Burna-buriash and Amenhotep IV). **Kashi (Keshy)**: N. de G. Davies 1941, 17, plate 8; see also Podany 2010, 234, for another view of the Babylonian bride quandary.

Asiatic disease: Cline 1998, 240; Leitz 1999, 63 and n. 108. Leitz notes that the identification of Asiatic disease as plague was refuted by Bardinet in favor of leprosy. Leprosy, however, does not cause sudden death, as in this princess, the Cypriote queen, and numbers of other recorded cases. See also Chapter 9.

CHAPTER 17. THE LAST HURRAH

Years 36 and 37: Hayes 1949. **Third Jubilee jar labels**: Hayes 1951, 85–86. **Viticulture and viniculture**: James 1996; Lesko 1996. Waseda University archaeologists have found dockets dated to Year 37 and to the Third Jubilee in the royal tomb; see Yoshimura and Kondo 2004. Especially interesting is a docket dated "Year 3, 3rd month of *akhet*-season, day 7," found near the tomb's antechamber (see Reeves and Wilkinson 1996, 111, 113, 115), a date perhaps referring to Amenhotep IV's reign. This could be taken as evidence for many different scenarios, not the least of which is a coregency, or simply that the front room of the tomb remained open.

Kheruef's scenes of raising the djed pillar: Epigraphic Survey 1980, plates 55–57. **Relation to Sokar festival**: Spalinger 2001, 521.

Amenhotep III's obese images: Chassinat 1910, who published the MMA statuette 30.8.74 when it was still in private hands, noted the similarity of this fringed gown to Near Eastern rulers' robes, and others have agreed; see also Bryan 1992a, 204–206, no. 23. However, on Near Eastern statues, those robes appear to be cut from thicker cloth. This one has the thin accordion pleats of fine, light Egyptian linen. **Kom el Hettan statue**: Trad and Mahmoud 1993, 45–47 (JE 33900). **Amarna stela (BM EA 57399)**: Bryan 1992a, 213–214, no. 29. **Luxor cachette red quartzite statue**: El Saghir 1989, 21–27; Bryan 1992d, 132–135, 151n25.

Inscriptions: Murnane 1995, 19–20. **Thick-waisted body habitus in relief sculpture at Luxor:** Johnson 1994, 135, figure 9.1.

Kheruef's red quartzite statue: Epigraphic Survey 1980, plates 86–87. **Head from a second private statue in red quartzite:** Pischikova 2001, 23, no. 12.

Amenhotep III's mummy: Hawass et al. 2010, esp. 645, table 3. **Opium in late Dynasty 18:** Bisset et al. 1996; idem. 1996a.

Chariot races in Bronze Age funerals: Fagles 1990, 559–560 (Homer, *The Iliad* 23: 6–18).

Amenhotep III's tomb, KV 22 (see also Chapter 7): PM 1, 2: 547–550 (tomb), 555 (Sety II usurped lid); Reeves and Wilkinson 1996, 110–115. The tomb is currently under conservation by Waseda University; see Yoshimura and Kondo 2004; Yoshimura et al. 2004.

Amenhotep III *shawabtis*: Bryan 1992h. Note also the *shawabti* of Maya, an artisan of Deir el Medina, who, according to Bryan, may have been the manufacturer of our king's *shawabtis*, ibid. 329–330, no. 71. **Bracelet plaques:** Berman and Bryan 1992. **Necklace terminal and other faience elements:** Kozloff 1992e. **Amduat:** Hornung 1999a, 27–77.

Officials of Upper and Middle Egypt, Merymose (TT 383): PM 1, 1: 436; Caminos and James 1963, 86–88, plate 67 (Silsilla).

Sebek-mose's tomb: Hayes 1939, idem. 1959, 268–270.

Senu's stelae: Hayes 1959, 272–273. **Ptahmose:** Murnane 1994, 192–194.

Officials of Lower Egypt, Heby: Gordon 1989, 17n17.

Menkheper: Hayes 1959, 272, figure 166.

Vizier Amenhotep's tomb: Gordon 1983; Eigner 1983.

Tjenuro and Ipay: Taylor 2010, 24; Schneider 1999, 126.

Ptahmose: see Chapter 12. One might also ask if there is any relationship between this Ptahmose and the priest-son of Nebseny, a scribe and copyist in the temple of Ptah and the temples of Upper and Lower Egypt, who left "one of the longest and most carefully executed Book of the Dead manuscripts of the Eighteenth Dynasty"; see Taylor 2010, 279, no. 148.

Meryra: Bryan 1992e and entry on second relief from same tomb following this (293–294, no. 59); Berlandini-Keller 1993, 22–23; A.-P. Zivie 1985, 228–229, plate 3; PM 3, 2: 706.

Amenemwia: A.-P. Zivie 1989, 34–36.

Steward Amenhotep: Hayes 1938; idem. 1959, 274; PM 3, 2: 702–703.

Book of the Dead: Taylor 2010, 12–13; Munro 2010, 62; Hornung 1999, 13–22. Economic issues of funerary furnishings: Cooney 2007.

Aper-el: A.-P. Zivie 1985, 225–227; idem. 1989; idem. 1990; idem. 2005, 28–29.

CHAPTER 18. WHOSE HEAVEN IS IT?: THE REIGN OF
AKHENATEN AND BEYOND

Amarna letters: Moran 1992, 86–90 (EA 27 = Tushratta's first letter to Amenhotep IV), 84–86 (EA 26 = Tushratta's first letter to Tiy), 92–99 (EA 29, esp. vv. 55–60, Tushratta's account of the historical bilateral relationship); see also Leblanc 2007a.

Dawn of Amarna age: N. de G. Davies 1923; Baines 1998; Hornung 1999, 31–71; Murnane 1999.

Ramose's tomb (TT 55): PM 1, 1: 105–111; N. de G. Davies 1941, plates 29–31 (Amenhotep III–IV in kiosk). Interruptions in New Kingdom Egyptian tomb decoration were common for any number of reasons: the owner's absence, a redeployment of the workers elsewhere, or the king's death, see Kozloff 2008 and forthcoming. Amarna's Ramose: Laboury 2010, 206. Recut coffins: Kozloff and Meltzer 2010.

Kheruef's tomb (TT 57): Epigraphic Survey 1980, plates 11–13 (figures of Amenhotep IV), plates 14–15 (word square), plates 20 and 22 (hymns to the rising and setting suns). Word square and prayers: Murnane 1995, 57–61; idem. 1999. D. B. Redford 1986, 188, notes that Kheruef's prayers to Thoth are thinly veiled addresses to Amenhotep III. Sun hymns in Theban tombs: Assmann 1983.

Amarna women: Green 1996; Do. Arnold 1996; Reeves 1999; Dodson and Hilton 2010, 144–157. Tadu-Hepa as Amenhotep IV's wife: EA 26 (see earlier) refers to Tadu-Hepa as Tiy's daughter-in-law. In EA 27 and following (see earlier), Tushratta calls Amenhotep IV his "son-in-law"; see also Podany 2010, 217–242.

Henut-taneb may be among the individuals represented by fragmentary canopic jars apparently dating to late Amenhotep III–early Amenhotep IV, which were among the chance finds in the Valley of the Queens in 1903 and 1904; see Legrain 1903; idem. 1904 One of these was inscribed for a "Queen Henut." Most of the rest were inscribed for royal governesses, two of them for a woman named "Sati," "of the house of the queen." A lady named "Sati" was also the owner of two polychrome faience *shawabtis*, now in Brooklyn, similar in style to one of Queen Tiy's that was found in Amenhotep III's tomb; see Bryan 1992g. One of the canopics was inscribed for a Prince Menkheperra, perhaps a younger brother or half brother of Amenhotep IV.

Tiy as an old woman: Do. Arnold 1996, 30; Sweeney 2004, 72, 74, 78–79. **Wood statuettes, Tiy portrait, and stela from Medinet Ghurob**: Chassinat 1901; Borchardt 1911; Hayes 1959, 266; Bryan 1992c, 258–260; M. Yoyotte 2008a, 77, 83, 86–87. Markowitz 1999. **Figure in "dress of life"**: Musée Borély 1973.

Amenhotep IV jubilee: Clère 1986; D. B. Redford 1968, 180n108. **Aten Temple at Karnak**: Blyth 2006, 119–126.

Amenhotep III–IV sandstone statues: Kozloff 2010. **Sculptor Bak**: Freed 1999b, 116.

Ramose's "window of appearances" scene: N. de G. Davies 1941, plates 32–34 (window of appearances), plates 34–37 (Ramose receiving foreigners). The "window of appearances" scene shows signs of having been carved over a previous scene that was cut away fairly roughly, but enough so that its original design cannot be discerned. In post-Amarna times, the figures of the two royals were hacked and the rays of the Aten were gashed horizontally. The tool marks of this destruction are different from those made in (re)preparation of the background of the scene. These observations were discussed in a paper presented in a symposium at Montepulciano in August 2008, and currently in production for publication. The queen in this image, as far as one can tell underneath all the damage, looks somewhat similar to the wood portrait of Queen Tiy from Ghurob, hence the lack of secure identification.

Founding of Akhetaten: Lacovara 1999. **Boundary stelae**: Murnane 1995, 73–86; Do. Arnold 1996, 22. **Amenhotep IV–Akhenaten's references to disasters**: Gore 2001, 43 (quoting Murnane); Murnane 1995, 31 (Karnak text); B. G. Davies 1995, 9 (Amarna text: 749 = Urk. 1975). **Earthquakes in Egypt in more recent times**: Lauffray et al. 1970.

Amanappa and Huy: Moran 1992, 140–167, 183, 193 (EA 71–93, 109, 117). Redford 1990, 10, does not identify Amanappa. Ibid. 11–12 discusses possibilities for Huy and Haya. **Haya–Huy in the Amarna letters**: Moran 1992, 140 (EA 71). **Miyara**: Moran 1992, 333 (289: 31).

Amarna religion: Allen 1996; Foster 1999.

Letter of Ipy (Apy): Murnane 1995, 50–51. A Ramesside papyrus tells the tale of an official named "Meryra" who reported to a pharaoh with the fictional name of "Sisebek" ("Son of Sobek") that the temples were prospering and beautifully decorated but that the people were miserable, crying out, and that children were being raised horribly (Posener 1985, 65–67). Amenhotep III's relationship with Sobek and the contrast of his building program with the difficulties of the time make this period a possible source for that legend.

Memphis Aten temple: A.-P. Zivie 2004. **Sesebi:** Spence and Rose 2009.

Amarna artistic production: Freed 1999b. **Thutmose:** Ibid., 122, figure 84, 123–126. **The "blind eye" in Ramose's tomb:** Nims 1973, 183. **Bust of Nefertiti (Berlin 21300):** Fay 1985, 93. Artists' living conditions: Panagiotokopulu 2004, 275.

Tiy's steward Huy at Amarna: D'Auria 1999, 171–173. Huy's tomb at Amarna is decorated with elements of traditional Dynasty 18 funerary rites, which is interesting because it suggests that he was "old school" and that these outdated ideas were tolerated in some instances. **Tiy's physical condition:** see Hawass, cited later. **Tiy's tomb (KV 55):** M. Bell 1990; Davis 1908; Davis et al. 1910.

Mass burial in KV 63: Lawler 2006; Ertman et al. 2006; Wilson 2010.

Succession after Akhenaten: Dodson and Hilton 2010, 143; Allen 2009.

DNA analyses of pathology in the late Eighteenth Dynasty royal mummies: Hawass et al. 2010, 644–645 (Akhenaten). Akhenaten's remains are merely a mummified skeleton, leaving less tissue to analyze than the others. Hawass's team have identified various bone issues in Akhenaten's skeleton, none a definitive cause of death; Ibid. 645 (Tiy), 646 (Tutankhamen). **Familial relationships of the mummies studied:** Ibid. 641, figure 2; see also Gabolde 2002. Harris 1999 had studied and compared jaw shapes of the mummies, concluding contra Hawass that Akhenaten and Kiya were the parents of Tutankhamen and Smenkhkara.

Tutankhamen: Murnane 1999a, Freed 1999a. **Analysis of mummy:** Hawass et al. 2010, 642–646. **Tut's work at Karnak:** Eaton-Krauss 1988; idem. 1993. **Restoration inscriptions:** Murnane 1995, 216–217. **Chronology after Tut's death:** Bryce 1990; Dodson and Hilton 2010, 150–153, 158–175; see also Schulman 1978; Murnane 1990, 22–31.

Malaria tropica: Hawass et al. 2010, 645–646. **Shrines**: Piankoff 1955, 69–70.

Horemheb offering to Amenhotep III cult: Bickel 2002, figure 6; D. B. Redford 1986, 189n178, suggests that during the reign of Sety I, Horemheb's reign was renumbered beginning immediately after Amenhotep III's death and excluding Akhenaten and his family.

Horemheb biography: Booth 2009.

Ramose's funerary equipment usurped: Kozloff and Meltzer 2010. **Pa-ramessu**: Brunton 1943, 133–148 (inner sarcophagus). **Some of Ramesses II's usurpations of Amenhotep III monuments**: Sourouzian 1993; Kozloff 1997a; idem. 1996, idem. 1992f. Reuse and usurpation did not stop with Ramesses the Great, but continued, for example, during the reign of Osorkon, as we saw at Bubastis, and even in Ptolemaic times.

Decline of civilizations: Lawler 2010.

EPILOGUE

Amenhotep son of Hapu: Wildung 1977; Latjar 2006; Bryan 1992c, 251 (statue inscription); Galán 2002.

GLOSSARY OF ANCIENT PERSONAL NAMES

Aakheperura, son of Thutmose IV, full or half brother of Amenhotep III, traveled to Nubia with Prince Amenhotep and predeceased his brother's coronation.

Abdi-Ashirta, headman of Amurru, likely vassal of Egypt, supplied women to Amenhotep III while simultaneously being accused by his neighbors of murder and other activities detrimental to the region. Author of or mentioned in numerous Amarna letters (with few exceptions, 60–107 and 118–137), where his name is spelled several different ways. Succeeded by son Aziru.

Abi-Milku, mayor of Tyre (Lebanese coast), vassal of Egypt, author of Amarna letters 146–155, end of Amenhotep III to early Amenhotep IV.

Ahmose I, first king of Dynasty 18.

Akhenaten, tenth king of Dynasty 18, eldest living son at Amenhotep III's death, inherited the throne as Amenhotep IV, remained in Thebes at first, then changed his name to Akhenaten, founded a new capital at Tell el Amarna and moved there permanently. Insisted on a single god, the sun disk Aten, and outlawed the traditional pantheons.

Alexander III of Macedon, aka "Alexander the Great," warrior king, founder of the Hellenistic Period of Greek culture, who, after conquering western Asia, conquered Egypt in 332 B.C., making way for the Ptolemaic Period (304–30 B.C.) of rule. Adopted Amenhotep III's (Amun's) ram's horns as royal–divine headgear.

Amanappa (= Amenemopet?), named in the Amarna letters as a major official who acted as an Egyptian royal messenger and ambassador at the end of Amenhotep III's reign and the beginning of Amenhotep IV's, possibly to be equated with vizier Aper-el (Aper-ia).

Amenemhet I, founder of Dynasty 12, father of Senwosret I (*see* Sinuhe).

Amenemhet III, sixth king of Dynasty 12, prodigious builder, especially in the Faiyum, Amenhotep III's birthplace.

Amenemhet, a son of Thutmose IV, died in infancy or early childhood, canopic jars in father's tomb (*see also* Tentamen).

Amenemhet, Third Prophet of Amun in Year 20, recorded on Nebnufer's statuette.

Amenemhet Surer, Overseer of the Fields of Amun, chief steward of Amenhotep III, owner of Theban tomb 48.

Amenemopet (f.), a daughter of Thutmose IV.

Amenemopet (m.), a student in Amenhotep III's nursery school (*kap*) who became chief of a rope and hammock workshop.

Amenemwia, Director of Painters, joint owner with son Thutmose of a tomb, apparently bearing his self-portrait, found at Sakkara by Alain Zivie.

Amenhotep I, second king of Dynasty 18.

Amenhotep II, seventh king of Dynasty 18, grandfather of Amenhotep III. King's Valley 35 is his tomb.

Amenhotep III, the subject of this biography, ninth king of Dynasty 18, son of Thutmose IV and Mutemwia, father of Akhenaten and Nefertiti, grandfather of Tutankhamen. King's Valley 22 is his tomb.

Amenhotep IV (*see above* Akhenaten).

Amenhotep, army general, not clearly identifiable, possibly overlapping with one of the many other Amenhoteps.

Amenhotep, northern vizier active during the second half of the reign.

Amenhotep Huy (steward), son of the mayor of Memphis, Neferhabef (aka Neby, Heby) and half brother of the southern vizier Ramose. "Huy" was a common nickname for "Amenhotep" but is most often applied to this steward, who had an important tomb at Sakkara and who commissioned with his own funds a major statue for the Ptah temple at Memphis, of which he was steward.

Amenhotep son of Hapu, a priest of modest birth in the Delta who seems to have signed on to the king's entourage in its earliest years at the age of 50, eventually becoming his most trusted, productive, beloved, and powerful official. Stuck to modest titles such as Scribe of Recruits, which allowed him to harness huge labor forces in the service of royal building projects. He died in his eighties, serving the last few years as steward of the king's eldest daughter, and was endowed with his own funerary temple, an unprecedented honor for a private citizen of his day.

Amenmose, scribe of Overseer of the Treasury Sebek-hotep, called Panehesy.

Amenmose, a palace steward of Amenhotep III.

Anen, brother of Queen Tiy, recorded as Second Prophet of Amun at Karnak in Year 20 on Nebnufer's statuette. Also a skilled astronomer and best known for his magnificent star-bedecked statue in Turin. Owner of Theban tomb 120. Predeceased Amenhotep III and was succeeded by Simut, son of Ramose.

Ankhesenamen, sister, wife, and widow of Tutankhamen, who tried to rescue her dying dynasty by writing to the Hittites for a suitable husband. One was sent but never arrived, and the throne passed into other hands.

Aper-el (Aperia; *see also* **Amanappa),** last northern vizier in reign of Amenhotep III, held over to reign of Amenhotep IV–Akhenaten, possibly envoy ambassador Amanappa of the Amarna letters. Tomb at Sakkara discovered by Alain Zivie in 1987 (*see also* Huy).

Ay, second to last king of Dynasty 18, possible brother of Queen Tiy, therefore uncle of Akhenaten and great-uncle of Tutankhamen. King's Valley 23 is his tomb.

Aziru (*see* Abdi-Ashirta).

Bak, son of Men, Chief of Sculptors in the Very Great Monuments of the King at Aswan. Bak served Amenhotep IV–Akhenaten, claiming to have been trained by the king himself. Bak moved to Amarna with his patron, where a brown quartzite stela of himself and his wife, both shown frontally like the figures on Ptahmose's group stela, was found.

Bengai, steward of the household of an important foreign woman, probably reign of Thutmose IV or Amenhotep III.

Burna-buriash, king of Babylon, corresponded with Amenhotep IV–Akhenaten (Amarna letters EA 6–12, 14).

Cleopatra (VII), ruled Egypt 51–30 B.C., and commanded Egypt's most lavishly decorated barge (as described by Plutarch) other than Amenhotep III's.

Diodorus Siculus, Sicilian (Greek) historian and traveler active during the mid-first century B.C.

Djoser, second king of Dynasty 3, builder of Sakkara's Step Pyramid and its surrounding complex, with its iconic jubilee scene.

Gilukhepa, daughter of Shuttarna, king of Mittani, and sister of his successor, Tushratta, who corresponded with Amenhotep III, Tiy, and Amenhotep IV in the Amarna letters. She arrived in Egypt in Year 10 as the first of Amenhotep III's recorded foreign brides, celebrated with a series of commemorative scarabs.

Haaramassi (var.) (*see* Ramose).

Hammurabi, king of Babylon, 1795–1750 B.C.

Hatshepsut, daughter of Thutmose I, sister and wife of Thutmose II, ruled as coregent with her stepson and nephew Thutmose III.

Hekareshu, name suggesting Nubian heritage, the elder of two schoolmasters at Karnak's Mut Temple school, where Thutmose IV and Amenhotep III both matriculated. His son was Hekarneheh.

Hekarneheh, formerly a palace cadet and cavalry officer. Hekarneheh taught with his father, Hekareshu, at Mut Temple and is shown with him in Theban tomb 64.

Henut–taneb, second daughter of Amenhotep III and Tiy.

Herodotus, Greek historian and traveler of the fifth century B.C.

Homer, epic poet thought to have flourished near the end of the eighth century B.C., attributed author of the *Iliad*, the story of the Trojan War, and the *Odyssey*, a sequel to the *Iliad*, describing the homeward journey of the Greek hero Odysseus (Ulysses) after the war.

Hor (*see* Suty and Hor).

Horemheb, army scribe, reign of Amenhotep III, owner of Theban tomb 78.

Horemheb, army general of Tutankhamen, rising to become last king of Dynasty 18, owner of a tomb at Sakkara, started when he was a general and revised when king, discovered by Geoffrey Martin in 1975. Also tomb KV 57 (*see also* Pa-Ramessu, vizier).

Huy, a charioteer mentioned in Amarna letters from the very end of Amenhotep III's reign and the beginning of Amenhotep IV's, who traveled with Amanappa, who may have been Aper-el (*see* his entry above). Aper-el had a son, a charioteer, named "Huy".

Huya, queen Tiy's steward at Amarna.

Iaret, a queen and sister (?) of Thutmose IV.

Ikheny, "the braggart," villain of Amenhotep III's Year 5 Nubian military campaign.

Imhotep, Djoser's architect and physician in Dynasty 3, centuries later venerated as a saint with Amenhotep son of Hapu.

Inena, son of Chief Craftsman Hamesh, member of Amenhotep III's nursery school, who became "Chief Craftsman of the Shipwrights of the Boats of All the Gods of Upper and Lower Egypt."

Ipy, son and successor of Memphite steward Amenhotep, nephew of Ramose. He closed Ptah Temple at Memphis before moving to Amarna to become steward to Akhenaten.

Isis, perhaps the youngest of Amenhotep III's daughters, who married him at the end of his reign, the second of his daughters to do so.

Joseph, biblical hero, thought by many to have coincided with the Second Intermediate Period.

Kadashman Enlil I, Kassite king of Babylon, the most contentious of Amenhotep III's Amarna letter correspondents (EA 1–3, 5). He was the brother of an anonymous, perhaps deceased, princess sent by his father, Kurigalzu, to Amenhotep III. Traded horses and an unnamed daughter (for gold, etc.) to Amenhotep III late in the reign. According to Amenhotep IV, the girl "died in a plague."

Kamose, last king of Dynasty 17, who turned back both Hyksos and Nubian invaders of the Second Intermediate Period, making way for Dynasty 18.

Keliya, royal messenger of Mitanni king Tushratta to Amenhotep III, mentioned in Amarna letters 17, 19, 20, 23, 24, 26, 27, 29 (*see* Ker, Kel).

Ker, Kel (*see also* Keliya), owner of a masterpiece *shawabti* in Leiden, probably Mitanni's royal messenger.

Keshy (Kashi?), huntsman portrayed on a wall in Ramose's tomb, possibly the Egyptian messenger Kashi of Amarna correspondence with Kadashman Enlil dating some years later.

Kha and Meryt, the venerable artist of Deir el Medina and his wife, buried in Theban tomb 8 with objects of exceptional quality, including artifacts inscribed with cartouches of Amenhotep II and Amenhotep III.

Khaefra (Chephren), fourth king of Dynasty 4, commissioned the middle of the three largest Giza pyramids and the Great Sphinx, where Thutmose IV, as prince, had his dream of becoming king.

Khaemhet, royal scribe and (later) granary overseer mentioned on Nebnufer's Year 20 statuette, owner of Theban tomb 57.

Khaemwaset, governor of northern foreign territories, that is, cities in Canaan, Palestine, and so on ("Overseer of the Hill Countries"). Depicted in fine statuettes with each of two wives, Khebunes and Manana.

Kheruef, best known steward of Queen Tiy, owner of Theban tomb 192 with its jubilee scenes, lived into the reign of Amenhotep IV.

Khufu (Cheops), second king of Dynasty 4, builder of the Great Pyramid at Giza.

Kikkuli, master horse trainer, whose minutely detailed manual of horsemanship and chariotry training, written in Hittite, is the earliest known, dating to about 1400 B.C., predating Greek horsemaster Xenophon's essay "On Horsemanship" by 1,000 years. It is preserved on large clay tablets found in Anatolia and now housed in the Vorderasiatisches Museum, Berlin.

Kiya (*see also* **Tadu-Hepa**), secondary wife of Akhenaten.

Kurigalzu, king of Babylon, father of Kadashman Enlil I. Sent Amenhotep III a daughter of unknown name with a suspicious outcome.

Mane (*see also* **Meniu**), royal messenger of Amenhotep III to Mitanni king Tushratta mentioned in Amarna letters 19–21 and 27–29.

Manetho, a priest of Heliopolis believed to have flourished in the third century B.C., credited with writing a history of Egypt recording a chronology of its kings, universally referenced by scholars, despite being given little weight for accuracy.

May, royal messenger represented in Ramose's tomb, scribe leaving graffito at Sneferu's pyramid in Year 30.

Memnon, Ethiopian king of Greek mythology, son of Eos, the Greek goddess of dawn, a Trojan ally killed by the Greek hero Achilles in the war. His name was applied by Greeks to Amenhotep III's colossi in front of his memorial temple because, as temperatures rose at dawn, the cracked stones of one emitted a sound, like a creature crying out for its mother.

Men (*see* Bak).

Menes, legendary unifier of Upper and Lower Egypt and founder of Egypt's Early Dynastic Period, circa 2920 B.C.

Meniu (see Mane), the name inscribed on a painted limestone portrait in the Louvre thought to represent Mane of the Amarna letters.

Menkaura (Mycerinus), fifth king of Dynasty 4, builder of the smallest of three large pyramids at Giza.

Menkheper, a Memphite mayor at some point in Amenhotep III's reign.

Menkheperra-seneb, First Prophet of Amun, reign of Thutmose III, owner of Theban tomb 86 (also of TT 112), with scenes of workshops in Karnak Temple.

Mentiu, a tribe thought to live northeast of Egypt in Sinai or Canaan.

Mentuhotep, Dynasty 12 vizier, statues found at Karnak Temple beside those of Amenhotep son of Hapu.

Mentuhotep II, native of Thebes, founder of Dynasty 11 after the First Intermediate Period.

Merneptah, son of Ramesses II, fourth king of Dynasty 19, built funerary temple at northwest corner of Amenhotep III's, probably covering and certainly usurping the earlier king's monuments and statuary.

Merymose, Viceroy of Nubia during Year 26 campaign, possible son of Mutemwia and brother of Amenhotep III, owner of Theban tomb 383.

Meryptah, First Prophet of Amun (Karnak). Possibly a (half-) brother of Amenhotep III (by mother Tawy – see later), and possibly the same as next Meryptah.

Meryptah, *sem* priest (chief) and steward of Amenhotep III's memorial temple at Kom el Hettan, possibly the same man as the preceding Meryptah since the memorial temple was in large part dedicated to Amun and likely received funds diverted from Karnak.

Meryra, supervisor of Prince Amenhotep when he was a small child, later Amenhotep III's treasurer and guardian of Prince Si-Atum. Sakkara tomb discovered in nineteenth century, lost, and rediscovered by Alain Zivie.

Meryt, daughter of the mayor of Shedet (Faiyum), wife of Sebek-hotep (see below), nurse of Thutmose IV's daughter Tiaa.

Merytptah, Royal Ornament, wife of Ramose.

Milkilu, headman of Gezer, received requests from the Egyptian court for beautiful cup bearers.

Mimmureya, Nimmureya, and so on, variations of the name of Amenhotep III (Nebmaatra) in the Middle Babylonian Akkadian of the Amarna letters.

Min, mayor of Thinis, father of Sebekmose, and archery tutor of Amenhotep II.

Minemheb, Army Scribe and Chief of Works in the Jubilee Temple, owner of an important granodiorite statue showing him holding a shrine topped by a baboon figure.

Mursilis II (ca. 1321–1295 B.C.), Hittite king whose texts mention plagues.

Mutemwia, a minor wife of Thutmose IV domiciled in the Faiyum, raised to Great Royal Wife at coronation of son Amenhotep III; possibly mother of Merymose.

Nebamun, police captain, owner of Theban tomb 90.

Nebetah, daughter of Amenhotep III.

Nebetia, daughter of Prince Si-Atum, granddaughter of Amenhotep III, effects found in mass burial of royal women.

Nebet-kebny, nurse to Sitamen.

Nebmerutef, master of ceremonies at Amenhotep III's First Jubilee, a role possibly requiring royal blood (*see* Sitamen).

Nebnufer, the granary scribe whose modest statue in Brussels, dated Year 20, breaks Amenhotep III's silence of eight years and records the names of several officials.

Neferhabef (aka Neby, Heby), Mayor of Memphis, companion on the Year 5 Nubian campaign, father of Steward Amenhotep Huy and of southern vizier Ramose by two different wives.

Neferirkara, third king of Dynasty 5, built a pyramid at Abusir, whose temple may have inspired the design of the Amun temple at Malkata (*see also* Sahura).

Nefer-neferu-aten, possibly the name of Smenkh-kara's wife and (half (?))-sister.

Neferronpet, butler, "clean of hands," of Amenhotep III.

Nefertiry, a queen of Thutmose IV.

Nefertiti, sister and chief queen of Akhenaten, mother of Tutankhamen.

Osorkon (II), fifth of 11 kings of Libyan lineage forming Dynasty 22, which lasted a mere 21 years. Osorkon built a jubilee hall at Bubastis, probably taking inspiration from Amenhotep III's monuments, and usurped the statue of an Amenhotep III queen (probably Tiy) for his own wife.

Pa-Ramessu, as vizier of King Horemheb, usurped Ramose's statues and at Horemheb's death became Ramesses I, first king of Dynasty 19.

Pa-Ramessu, a son of Ramesses II.

Panehesy (Sebek-hotep), succeeded father Sebek-mose as overseer of the treasury, led Year 36 campaign to Sinai in search of turquoise.

Paser, son of Faiyum mayor, treasurer, and royal mentor Sebek-hotep and (presumably) Meryt, who succeeded his father to the Faiyum mayoralty, his name recorded among the Year 30 jar labels at Malkata.

Penhet, governor of the northern territories, that is, Canaan, Palestine, and so on (Overseer of the Hill Countries).

Pepy I, third king of Dynasty 6, built a pyramid at Sakkara.

Plutarch (ca. A.D. 46–120), Roman citizen of Greek birth, prolific author. Biographer of Roman emperors and notables as well as Alexander III of Macedon and Cleopatra VII, and author of books on Egyptian religion.

Ptahmose, High Priest of Ptah at Memphis, owner of an important statue in Florence.

Ptahmose, a southern vizier and mayor of Thebes before Ramose; High Priest of Amun.

Ramesses II, third king of Dynasty 19, one of Egypt's longest-lived and most successful pharaohs, master usurper and/or upstager of monuments and statuary of Amenhotep III.

Ramesses III, second king of Dynasty 20, builder of a temple at Medinet Habu adjacent to Amenhotep son of Hapu's temple and between Amenhotep III's temple and his palace at Malkata.

Ramose, son of Mayor of Memphis Neferhabef (*see* above), half brother of Memphite steward Amenhotep (above), mayor of Thebes and southern vizier during later Amenhotep III to early Amenhotep IV–Akhenaten, likely the "magnate" Haaramassi (var.) of the Amarna letters who negotiated for foreign brides most notably with Tushratta. Owner of Theban tomb 55.

Re'a, royal herald of Thutmose IV, known from an inscription with Prince Amenhotep, owner of Theban tomb 201.

Rib-Hadda, mayor of Byblos, vassal of Egypt, most prolific author of Amarna letters 68–71, 73–79, 81–96, with few exceptions 119–138, 142, 362, detailing the political chaos and hardship in Canaan and along the Levantine coast at the end of the reign of Amenhotep III and the beginning of the next reign.

Roma, the gatekeeper of the "Polio" stela, donor to the king's jubilee in Year 30.

Sahura, second king of Dynasty 5, built a pyramid at Abusir whose temple may have inspired the design of Malkata's Amun temple (*see also* Neferirkara).

Sebek-hotep, mentor of Amenhotep III as a child, inherited mayoralty of Shedet (Faiyum) from the father of wife, Meryt (nurse of princess Tiaa), promoted to Royal Treasurer. Owner of Theban tomb 63.

Sebek-hotep, Sebek-mose's son (*see* Panehesy).

Sebek-mose, Overseer of the Treasury, father of Panehesy, supervisor of work at Luxor Temple, owner of important tomb at Er Rizeiqat.

Sebek-nakht, a royal steward.

Senenmut, chief architect and contractor for Hatshepsut's monuments at Thebes, in particular her memorial temple at Deir el Bahri, also chief steward for her and her (their?) daughter.

Senu, scribe of recruits late in Amenhotep III's reign, with monuments originally at Tuna el Gebel in Middle Egypt.

Senwosret I, son, coregent, and successor of Dynasty 12's first king, Amenemhet I (*see* Sinuhe).

Septimius Severus (A.D. 193–211), Roman emperor who patched the Memnon colossi.

Setau, Second Priest of (goddess) Neith, brother of Amenemhet Surer.

Shuttarna, king of Mitanni, contemporary of Thutmose IV and early Amenhotep III, father of Gilukhepa and Tushratta.

Si-Atum, son of Amenhotep III, nursling of Treasurer Meryra, father of a daughter, Nebetia, whose artifacts were found in a group burial of royal women at Thebes.

Simut, Fourth Prophet of Amun in Year 20 and Second Prophet of Amun at the end of the reign after Anen's death. Now identified as a son of Ramose, he is shown performing funeral rites in Ramose's tomb (there as fourth priest).

Sinuhe, legendary courtier of Amenemhet I, first king of Dynasty 12, who fled Egypt for western Asia on hearing of his liege's death, eventually returning to forgiveness and a warm welcome at the court of Amenmhet I's son, coregent, and successor, Senwosret I. The *Tale of Sinuhe* is a classic of Middle Kingdom Egyptian literature.

Sitamen, eldest daughter of Amenhotep III and Tiy, wedded her father in Year 30, possibly producing a son. If so, this may have been Nebmerutef.

Smenkh-kara, mysterious and controversial, short-lived coregent of Akhenaten or interim king between Akhenaten and Tutankhaten.

Sneferu, first king of Dynasty 4, builder of the Bent and Red pyramids at Dahshur, which were visited at the time of Amenhotep III's First Jubilee, according to an inscription left there by scribe May.

Suty and Hor, twins who worked late in the reign at Karnak Temple, supervising construction, their stela in the British Museum containing many references to the Aten sun god.

Tadu-Hepa, daughter of Tushratta, king of Mittani, and niece of Gilukhepa, Amenhotep III's first recorded foreign wife. Tadu-Hepa arrived as a new bride for Amenhotep in the mid-30s of his reign. After his death, she apparently became Amenhotep IV's secondary wife, likely changing her name to "Kiya".

Taitai, a priest at Hebenu in Middle Egypt, known from an exquisite statuette in Berlin.

Tarhundaradu, king of Arzawa, likely along the southern Lycian coast, who briefly and not entirely satisfactorily corresponded with Amenhotep III, his letter (EA 31) and Pharaoh's response (?) (EA 32) being found in the Amarna trove.

Tawy, "Lady of the House," mother of memorial temple steward Meryptah on the stela mentioned earlier for High Priest of Ptah Ptahmose.

Tentamen, a daughter of Thutmose IV who predeceased him, her canopics placed in his tomb (*see also* Amenemhet).

Thucydides (ca. 460–395 B.C.), Greek historian, author of the *History of the Peloponnesian War* (between Athens and Sparta), with its account of a devastating plague.

Thutmose I, third king of Dynasty 18. Kings' Valley tomb 38.

Thutmose II, fourth king of Dynasty 18. Kings' Valley tomb 42.

Thutmose III, fifth or sixth king of Dynasty 18, crowned as a toddler (coregent Hatshepsut), later the warrior king of Dynasty 18, often called the "Napoleon of Egypt." Outlived Hatshepsut to be sole ruler. Great-grandfather of Amenhotep III. Kings' Valley tomb 34.

Thutmose IV, eighth king of Dynasty 18, son of Amenhotep II, father of Amenhotep III. Kings' Valley tomb 43.

Thutmose, tomb painter, son of Director of Painters Amenemwia.

Thutmose, sculptor with extensive workshop found at Amarna, possible artist of at least part of Ramose's tomb.

Thutmose, son of Amenhotep III and Tiy, pictured as a young prince in the Apis cemetery with his father, became High Priest of Ptah, commissioned a huge limestone coffin for his pet cat Ta-mit. He predeceased his parents, leaving the succession to a younger brother.

Thuya, mother of Queen Tiy, wife of Yuya, buried with him in Kings' Valley 46. Mother-in-law of Amenhotep III, mother of Anen.

Tiaa, wife of Amenhotep II, mother of Thutmose IV, who promoted her to queen after his coronation. Grandmother of Amenhotep III.

Tiaa, daughter of Thutmose IV, (half-) sister of Amenhotep III, nursling of Treasurer Sebek-hotep's wife, Meryt. Recorded in a group burial of royal women.

Tiy, Great Royal Wife and Chief Queen of Amenhotep III; mother of Prince Thutmose, Amenhotep IV–Akhenaten (and his wife, Nefertiti), Prince Si-Atum (?), Princesses Sitamen, Henut-taneb, Nebetah, and Isis. Grandmother of Tutankhamen and Ankhesenamen.

Tjanuna, Royal Steward of Thutmose IV, guardian and mentor to Prince "Temy."

Tjenuro, a mayor of Memphis, and his wife, Ipay, a royal nurse, are represented by two large, limestone, *shawabti*-shaped (*sab*) funerary figures, both dated by style to the reign of Amenhotep III, now in Leiden.

Tushratta, king of Mitanni, brother of Gilukhepa, Amenhotep III's first recorded foreign bride. Author of Amarna letters 17, 19–29.

Tutankhamen, of the golden tomb (Kings' Valley 62), discovered by Howard Carter in 1922, son of Nefertiti and Akhenaten, grandson of Amenhotep III and Tiy.

Unas, last king of Dynasty 5, built pyramid at Sakkara.

Userhet, harem steward, likely at Malkata since his Year 30 jar label was found there. Owner of Theban tomb 47.

Yuya, father of Queen Tiy, master horseman, husband of Thuya, the pair buried in King's Valley tomb 46.

BIBLIOGRAPHY

ABBREVIATIONS

In addition to those abbreviations listed in Bergman, D. and Bergman, D. 2009, Abbreviations in Egyptology, BES 18: 1–82, use the following:

ACE — Australian Centre for Egyptology.

AEMT — *Ancient Egyptian Materials and Technology*, ed. P. T. Nicholson and I. Shaw. Cambridge: Cambridge UP, 2000.

Amarna Diplomacy — *Amarna Diplomacy: The Beginnings of International Relations*, ed. R. Cohen and R. Westbrook. Baltimore: Johns Hopkins UP, 2000.

AmSc — *American Scientist*.

AIIIP — *Amenhotep III: Perspectives on His Reign*, ed. D. O'Connor and E. Cline. Ann Arbor: University of Michigan Press, 1998.

Archaeology of Africa — *The Archaeology of Africa: Food, Metals, and Towns*, ed. T. Shaw, P. Sinclair, B. Andah, and A. Okpoko. London: Routledge, 1993.

Beyond Babylon — *Beyond Babylon: Art, Trade, and Diplomacy in the Second Millennium B.C.*, ed. J. Aruz, K. Benzel, and J. Evans. New York: MMA, 2008.

Civilizations — *Civilizations of the Ancient Near East*, ed. J. Sasson. 4 vols. Peabody, MA: Hendrickson, 1995.

Delange — *Aménophis III: L'Égypte à son Apogée*, ed. É. Delange. DossArch no. 180 (March 1993).

EA — Amarna letter, except when in inventory number of British Museum.

EDS — Kozloff, A. P., and Bryan, B. M., with Berman, L. M., and Delange, É. *Egypt's Dazzling Sun: Amenhotep III and His World*. Cleveland: Cleveland Museum of Art, 1992.

Fs.	Festschrift (see following list for abbreviated titles).
GI	Griffith Institute.
Halkedis	*The Collector's Eye: Masterpieces of Egyptian Art from the Thalassic Collection, Ltd.*, Courtesy Theodore and Aristea Halkedis, ed. P. Lacovara and B. Trope, with S. D'Auria. Atlanta: Michael C. Carlos Museum, Emory University, 2001.
Hatshepsut	*Hatshepsut: From Queen to Pharaoh*, ed. C. Roehrig. New Haven and London: Yale UP, 2005.
HUAM	Harvard University Art Museums.
Kingship	*Ancient Egyptian Kingship*, ed. D. O'Connor and D. P. Silverman. Leiden: Brill, PÄ 9, 1995.
LCL	Loeb Classical Library.
MMAP	Metropolitan Museum of Art Papers.
NINO	Nederlands Instituut voor het Nabije Oosten
OHAE	*The Oxford History of Ancient Egypt*, ed. I. Shaw. Oxford: Oxford UP, 2000.
OEAE	*Oxford Encyclopedia of Ancient Egypt*, 3 vols., ed. D. B. Redford. Oxford: Oxford UP, 2001.
OI	Oriental Institute of the University of Chicago
Pharaohs/Sun	*Pharaohs of the Sun: Akhenaten-Nefertiti-Tutankhamen*, ed. R. Freed, Y. Markowitz, and S. D'Auria. Boston: Museum of Fine Arts/Boston with Bulfinch Press/Little Brown, 1999.
Race	*Race and Identity in the Nile Valley: Ancient and Modern Perspectives*, ed. C. Fluehr-Lobban and K. Rhodes. Trenton, NJ: Red Sea Press, 2004.
Reines	*Reines d'Égypte d'Hétephérès à Cléopâtre*, ed. C. Ziegler, exh. cat. Monaco: Grimaldi Forum, 2008.
RMN	Réunion des musées nationaux (France).
Royal Women	*The Royal Women of Amarna: Images of Beauty from Ancient Egypt*, ed. Do. Arnold. New York: MMA, 1996.
Temples	*Temples of Ancient Egypt*, ed. B. E. Shafer. Ithaca: Cornell UP, 1997.
Temple in AE	*The Temple in Ancient Egypt: New Discoveries and Recent Research*, ed. S. Quirke. London: BM, 1997.
UP	University Press.

Festschriften and Memorial Volumes, Abbreviated Titles

Fs. Aldred *Chief of Seers: Egyptian Studies in Memory of Cyril Aldred*, eds. E. Goring, N. Reeves, and J. Ruffle. London: Kegan Paul, 1997.

Fs. Baer *For His Ka: Essays Offered in Memory of Klaus Baer*, ed. D. P. Silverman. SAOC 55, 1994.

Fs. Bell *Ancient Egypt, The Aegean, and the Near East: Studies in Honour of Martha Rhoads Bell*, ed. Jacke Phillips. San Antonio: Van Siclen Books, 1997.

Fs. Fazzini *Servant of Mut: Studies in Honor of Richard A. Fazzini*, ed. S. D. Auria. PÄ 28. Leiden: Brill, 2008.

Fs. Fecht *Form und Mass: Beiträge zur Literatur, Sprache und Kunst des alten Ägyptens: Festschrift für Gerhard Fecht zum 65. Geburtstag am 6. Februar 1987*, ed. J. Ösing and G. Dreyer. ÄUAT 12. Wiesbaden: Harrassowitz, 1987.

Fs. Geus *Mélanges offerts à Francis Geus*, ed. B. Gratien. CRIPEL 26. Lille: Éditions Universitaires, 2007.

Fs. Goedicke *Essays in Egyptology in Honor of Hans Goedicke*, ed. B. Bryan and D. Lorton. San Antonio: Van Siclen Books, 1994.

Fs. Griffiths *Studies in Pharaonic Religion and Society in Honour of J. Gwyn Griffiths*, ed. A. B. Lloyd. London: EES, 1992.

Fs. Hansen *Leaving No Stones Unturned: Essays on the Ancient Near East and Egypt in Honor of Donald P. Hansen*, ed. E. Ehrenberg. Winona Lake, IN: Eisenbrauns, 2002.

Fs. Leclant *Hommages à Jean Leclant*, ed. C. Berger, G. Clerc, and N. Grimal. Varia, BdÉ 106. 4 vols. Cairo: IFAO, 1993.

Fs. Murnane *Causing His Name to Live: Studies in Epigraphy and History in Memory of William J. Murnane*, ed. P. Brand and L. Cooper. Leiden: Brill, 2009.

Fs. Redford *Egypt, Israel, and the Ancient Mediterranean World: Studies in Honor of Donald B. Redford*, ed. G. N. Knoppers and A. Hirsch. PÄ 20. Leiden: Brill, 2004.

Fs. Sauneron *Hommages à la Mémoire de Serge Sauneron 1927–1976. I. Égypte Pharaonique*, ed. J. Vercoutter. BdÉ 81. Cairo: IFAO, 1979.

Fs. Säve-Söderbergh *Sundries in Honour of Torgny Säve-Söderbergh*. Boreas 13. Uppsala Press: University of Uppsala Press, 1984.

Fs. Silverman *Millions of Jubilees: Studies in Honor of David P. Silverman*, ed. Z. Hawass and J. H. Wegner. Publications du Conseil Suprême des Antiquités de l'Égypte, Cahier 39, 2010.

Fs. Simpson *Studies in Honor of William Kelly Simpson*, ed. P. Der Manuelian. Boston: MFA, 1996.

Fs. Smith *Studies on Ancient Egypt in Honour of H. S. Smith*, ed. A. Leahy and J. Tait. London: EES, 1999.

Fs. Stricker *Hermes Aegyptiacus: Egyptological Studies for BH Stricker*, ed. T. DuQuesne. Oxford: DE Publications, 1995.

Fs. te Velde *Essays on Ancient Egypt in Honor of Herman te Velde*, ed. J. van Dijk. Groningen, Netherlands: Brill/Styx, 1997.

Fs. Vermeule *The Ages of Homer: A Tribute to Emily Townsend Vermeule*, ed. J. Carter and S. Morris. Austin: University of Texas, 1997.

Fs. Wente *Gold of Praise: Studies on Ancient Egypt in Honor of Edward F. Wente*, ed. E. Teeter and J. Larsen. SAOC 58, 1999.

Fs. Wilson *Studies in Honor of the Seventieth Birthday of John A. Wilson*, ed. E. B. Hauser. SAOC 35, 1969.

Abd el-Maksoud, M. 1998 *Tell Hebuoa (1981–1991)*. Paris: Éditions Recherche sur les Civilisations.

————. 1998a Tjarou, Porte de l'Orient. In *Le Sinai durant l'antiquité et le Moyen Âge*, ed. C. Bonnet and D. Valbelle, 61–65. Paris: Éditions Errance.

Adams, W. Y., and Nordström, H. 1963 The Archaeological Survey on the West Bank of the Nile: Third Season, 1961–62. *Kush* 11: 10–46.

Alberge, D. 2003 Tomb Reveals Ancient Egypt's Humiliating Secret. *The Times* (London), July 28.

Aldred, C. 1988 *Akhenaten: King of Egypt*. London: Thames/Hudson.

Aling, C. F. 1977 *A Prosopographical Study of the Reigns of Thutmosis IV and Amenhotep III*. Ann Arbor: Xerox University Microfilms.

Allam, S. 1981 Quelques aspects du mariage dans l'Égypte ancienne. *JEA* 67: 116–135.

Allen, J. P. 1996 The Religion of Amarna. In *Royal Women*, 3–5.

————. 2001 *Middle Egyptian: An Introduction to the Language and Culture of Hieroglyphs*. Cambridge. Cambridge UP.

————. 2009 The Amarna Succession. In *Fs. Murnane*, 9–20.

Alliott, M. 1932 Fouilles de Deir el-Médineh 1930–1931. Un puits funéraire à Qournet-Mora'i, 21 février – 7 mars 1931. *BIFAO* 32: 70–71, 74–79, plates 1–2.

Ambraseys, N., Melville, C., and Adams, R. 1994 *The Seismicity of Egypt, Arabia, and the Red Sea*. Cambridge: Cambridge UP.

Anderson, R., and Fawzy, I., eds. 1987 *Egypt Revealed: Scenes from Napoleon's Description de l'Égypte*. Cairo: AUC.

Andreadaki-Vlazaki, M., et al. 2008 *From the Land of the Labyrinth: Minoan Crete, 3000–1100 BC*, exh. cat. New York: Onassis Foundation.

Andreu, G. 2002 *Les artistes de pharaon: Deir el-Médineh et la Vallée des Rois*. Paris: Louvre.

Anthes, R. 1976 Die höhen Beamten namens Ptahmose in der 18. Dynastie. *ZÄS* 72: 60–67.

Anus, P., and Sa'ad, R. 1971 Habitations de prêtres dans le temple d'Amon de Karnak. *Kêmi* 21: 217–238.

AOL News 2010 Huge Sculpture of Pharaoh's Head Unearthed in Egypt. http://www.aolnews.com/2010/02/28/huge-scupture-of-pharaohs-head-unearthed-in egypt/.

Arnold, D. 1977 Gurob. *LÄ* 2: 922–923.

————. 1997 Royal Cult Complexes. In *Temples*, 31–85.

————. 2003 *The Encyclopaedia of Ancient Egyptian Architecture*, trans. S. H. Gardiner and H. Strudwick, ed. N. Strudwick and H. Strudwick. Princeton: Princeton UP.

Arnold, Do. 1996 An Artistic Revolution: The Early Years of Amenhotep IV/Akhenaten. In *Royal Women*, 17–39.

————. 2005 Mirror. In *Hatshepsut*, 220.

Arnold-Biucchi, C. 2006 *Alexander's Coins and Alexander's Image*. Cambridge, MA: HUAM.

Assmann, J. 1983 *Sonnenhymnen in Thebanischen Gräbern. Theben I*. Mainz: Von Zabern.

———. 1989 State and Religion in the New Kingdom. In *Religion and Philosophy in Ancient Egypt*, ed. W. K. Simpson, 55–88. YES 3. New Haven: Yale UP.

———. 1995 *Egyptian Solar Religion in the New Kingdom: Re, Amun, and the Crisis of Polytheism*. New York: Kegan Paul.

Aston, B., Harrell, J., and Shaw, I. 2000 Stone. In AEMT, 5–77.

Aston, D. A. 1997 Cemetery W at Gurob. In Fs. Bell I: 43–66.

Aufrère, S., Golvin, J.-C., and Goyon, J.-C. 1997 *L'Égypte Restituée, I: Sites et temples de Haute Égypte*. Paris: Éditions Errance.

———. 1997a *L'Égypte Restituée, 2: Sites et temples des déserts*. Paris: Éditions Errance.

Azzaroli, A. 1985 *An Early History of Horsemanship*. Leiden: E. J. Brill/Dr. W. Backhuys.

Babled, T. 1993/1994 Les grands projets d'Aménophis III sur la rive occidentale de Thèbes: du contexte originel à la situation contemporaine. *Memnonia* 4–5: 131–146.

Baedeker, K. 1902 *Egypt: Handbook for Travellers*. Leipzig: Karl Baedeker.

———. 1929 *Egypt and the Sudan: A Handbook for Travellers*. Leipzig: K. Baedeker.

Bailey, D. M., Davies, W. V., and Spencer, A. J. 1982 *British Museum Expedition to Middle Egypt: Ashmunein 1980*. London: BM.

Bailey, E. 1996 Circumcision in Ancient Egypt. *BACE* 7: 15–28.

Baines, J. 1985 Egyptian Twins. *Orientalia* 54/4: 461–482.

———. 1991 Religious Experience and Piety: New Kingdom Developments. In *Religion in Ancient Egypt: Gods, Myths, and Personal Practice*, ed. B. E. Shafer, 123–200. Ithaca: Cornell UP.

———. 1998 The Dawn of the Amarna Age. In AIIIP, 271–312.

Baines, J., and Málek, J. 1984 *Atlas of Ancient Egypt*. New York: Facts on File. (Revised edition: *Cultural Atlas of Ancient Egypt*. New York: Checkmark Books, 2000)

Baker, S. W. n.d. *The Nile Tributaries of Abyssinia*, chapter 2. Worldwide School library. http://www.archive.org/details/niletributarieso00bakerich.

Bakry, H. S. 1971 The Discovery of a Temple of Sobk in Upper Egypt. *MDAIK* 27: 131–146.

Barber, E. J. W. 1991 *Prehistoric Textiles: The Development of Cloth in the Neolithic and Bronze Ages*. Princeton: Princeton UP.

———. 1994 *Women's Work: The First 20,000 Years: Women, Cloth, and Society in Early Times*. New York: W.W. Norton.

Barbotin, C. 1997 Le buste du scribe royal Meniou, une sculpture du règne d'Aménophis III (v. 1391–1353 av. J.-C.). RduL: *Études* 5–6: 51–56.

Beckman, G. 2008 Horse Training Manual. In Beyond Babylon, 158.

Bell, L. 1985 Luxor Temple and the Cult of the Royal Ka. *JNES* 44: 251–294.
———. 1997 The New Kingdom "Divine Temple": The Example of Luxor. In Temples, 127–184.
Bell, M. 1990 An Armchair Investigation of KV 55. *JARCE* 27: 97–137.
Bennett, J. 1939 The Restoration Inscription of Tut'ankhamun. *JEA* 25: 8–15.
Berg, D. 1987 The Vienna Stela of Meryre. *JEA* 73: 213–216.
Bergman, D., and Bergman, D. 2009 Abbreviations in Egyptology, ed. J. P. Allen. *BES* 18: 1–82.
Berlandini-Keller, J. 1993 Aménophis III, pharaon à Memphis. In Delange, 16–27.
———. 1993a Amenhotep III et le concept de Heh. *BSEG* 17: 11–28.
———. 1994 La statue thébaine de Kherouef et son invocation à Nout. In Fs. Leclant, 389–406.
Berman, L. M. 1992a Amenhotep III and His Times. In EDS, 33–66.
———. 1992b Commemorative Scarabs. In EDS, 67–72.
———. 1992c Funerary Equipment. In EDS, 305–330.
———. 1992d Amenhotep Son of Hapu as a Scribe. In EDS, 251–252.
———. 1997 Merymose at Vassar. In Fs. Aldred, 29–33.
———. 1999 *Catalogue of Egyptian Art: The Cleveland Museum of Art*. Cleveland: Cleveland Museum of Art.
Berman, L. M., and Bryan, B.M. 1992 Three Carved Gems. In EDS, 442–444.
Bianchi, R. S. 1994 *Daily Life of the Nubians*. Brookfield, CN: Millbrook Press.
Bickel, S. 2002 Aspects et fonctions de la déification d'Amenhotep III. *BIFAO* 102: 63–90.
———. 2006 Amenhotep III à Karnak, L'étude des blocs épars. BSFÉ 167 (October): 12–32.
Bidoli, D. 1970 Zur Lage des Grabes des Amenophis Sohn des Hapu. *MDAIK* 26: 11–14.
Bierbrier, M. 1984 *Tomb Builders of the Pharaohs*. New York: Scribner's.
Bietak, M., Marinatos, N., and Palivou, C. 2007 *Taureador Scenes in Tell el-Dab'a (Avaris) and Knossos*. DÖAW 43. Vienna: ÖAW.
Bietak, M. 2009 Perunefer: The Principal New Kingdom Naval Base. *EA* 34 (spring): 15–17.
Bigler, R. R., and Geiger, B. 1994 Eine Schenkungsstele Thutmosis' IV. *ZÄS* 121: 11–17.
Binder, S. 2008 *The Gold of Honour in New Kingdom Egypt*. ACE/S 8. Oxford: Aris and Phillips.
Birkstam, B. 1984 Reflections on the Association between the Sun-god and Divine Kingship in the 18th Dynasty. In Fs. Säve-Soderbergh, 34–42.
Bisset, N. G., Bruhn J. H., Curto, S., Holmestedt, B., Nyman, U., and Zenk, M. 1996 An Examination of Materials from the Tomb of the Chief Royal Architect Kha. *E&L* 6: 199–201.

Bisset, N. G., Bruhn, J. H., and Zenk, M. 1996a The Presence of Opium in a 3,500 Year-Old Cypriote Base-Ring Juglet. *E&L* 6: 203–204.

Bissing, Fr. W. von 1904 Ausradierungen im Tempel Amenophis III zu el Kab. *ZÄS* 41: 126.

Blankenberg-van Delden, C. 1969 *The Large Commemorative Scarabs of Amenhotep III*. Leiden: E. J. Brill.

Bleiberg, E. 1985–1986 Historical Texts as Political Propaganda during the New Kingdom. *BES* 7: 5–13.

Blyth, E. 2006 *Karnak: Evolution of a Temple*. London: Routledge.

Bonnet, C., and Valbelle, D. 2004 Kerma, Dokki Gel. In *Sudan: Ancient Treasures*, ed. D. A. Welsby and J. R. Anderson, 109–113. London: BM.

Booth, C. 2009 *Horemheb: The Forgotten Pharaoh*. Gloucestershire: Amberley.

Borchardt, L. 1911 *Der Porträtkopf der Königin Teje im Besitz von Dr. James Simon in Berlin*. Leipzig: J. C. Hinrichs.

———. 1911–1936 *Statuen und Statuetten von Königin und Privatleuten*. CG, nos. 1–1294. 5 vols. Berlin/Cairo. The Egyptian Museum.

———. 1914 Ausgrabungen in Tell el Amarna. *MDOG* 55: 30–34.

———. 1936 Jahre und Tage der Krönungs-Jubiläen. *ZÄS* 72: 52–59.

———. 1938 *Ägyptische Tempel mit Umgang mit Zeichnungen von Herbert Ricke*. BÄBA 2. Cairo: private.

Bosse-Griffiths, K. 1955 The Memphite Stela of Meryptah and Ptahmose. *JEA* 41: 56–63.

Bothmer, B. V. 1969–1970 A New Fragment of an Old Palette. *JARCE* 8: 5–8.

Bovot, J.-L. 2003 *Chaouabtis: Des travailleurs pharaoniques pour l'éternité*. Dossier du Musée du Louvre 63. Paris: RMN.

Bowman, H., Stross, F. H., Asaro, F., Hay, R. L., Heizer, R. F., and Michel, H. V. 1984 The Northern Colossus of Memnon: New Slants. *Archaeometry* 28, no. 2: 218–229.

Breasted, J. H. 2001 *Ancient Records of Egypt*, intro. and bibl. by P. Piccione. Urbana: University of Illinois Press.

Brinkman, J. 2008 Babylone entre deux empires: La dynastie kassite (vers 1595–1155), sources historiques (and) Les lettres d'Amarna. In *Babylone*, ed. Beatrice André-Salvini, exh. cat., 105–109. Paris: Hazan, Louvre.

British Museum, Keeper and Department of Ancient Egypt and the Sudan. 2007 *The British Museum Book of Ancient Egypt*. London: BM.

Brunner, H. 1986 Trunkenheit. *LÄ* 6: 773–777.

Brunton, G. 1943 The Inner Sarcophagus of Prince Ramessu from Medinet Habu. *ASAE* 43: 133–148, plates VII–XI.

Brunton, G., and Engelbach, R. 1927 *Gurob*. London: BSAE.

Bryan, B. M. 1982 The Etymology of Hnr "Group of Musical Performers." *BES* 4: 35–54.

———. 1985 Evidence for Female Literacy from Theban Tombs of the New Kingdom. *BES* 6: 17–32.

————. 1989 The Tombowner and His Family. In E. Dziobek and M. Abdel Raziq, *Das Grab des Sobekhotep, Theben Nr. 63*, 81–91. AV 71. Mainz: Von Zabern.

————. 1991 *The Reign of Thutmose IV*. Baltimore: Johns Hopkins UP.

————. 1992a Small-Scale Royal Representations. In EDS, 193–214.

————. 1992b Designing the Cosmos: Temples and Temple Decoration. In EDS, 73–120.

————. 1992c Private Statuary. In EDS, 237–260.

————. 1992d Royal and Divine Statuary. In EDS, 125–184.

————. 1992e Tomb Relief of Chancellor Meryra and Lady Baketamen. In EDS, 292–293.

————. 1992f Royal and Divine Images in Animal Form. In EDS, 215–222.

————. 1992g Shawabty of Lady Sati. In EDS, 328–329.

————. 1992h Entries on Three Shawabtis of Amenhotep III. In EDS, 325–327.

————. 1997 The Statuary Program for the Mortuary Temple of Amenhotep III. In Temple in AE, 57–81, plates 5–29.

————. 2000 The 18th Dynasty before the Amarna Period (1550–1352 B.C.). In OHAE, 218–271.

————. 2000a The Egyptian Perspective on Mitanni. In Amarna Diplomacy, 71–84.

————. 2008 A Newly Discovered Statue of a Queen from the Reign of Amenhotep III. In Fs. Fazzini, 32–43.

Bryce, T. R. 1990 The Death of Niphururiya and Its Aftermath. *JEA* 76: 97–105.

Buhl, M.-L. 1947 The Goddesses of the Egyptian Tree Cult. *JNES* 6: 80–97.

Buikstra, J., Baker, B., and Cook, D. 1993 What Diseases Plagued Ancient Egyptians? A Century of Controversy Considered. In *Biological Anthropology and the Study of Ancient Egypt*, eds. W. V. Davies and R. Wallem, 24–53. London: BM.

Bunbury, J. M., Graham, A., and Hunter, M. A. 2008 Stratigraphic Landscape Analysis: Charting the Holocene Movements of the Nile at Karnak through Egyptian Time. *Geoarchaeology: An International Journal* 23, no. 3: 351–373.

Cabrol, A. 1995 La Tombe de Khâbekhenet et les Dromos de Karnak-Sud. *Karnak* 10: 33–57, plates 1–6.

————. 1995a Les Criosphinx de Karnak: Un nouveau dromos d'Amenhotep III. *Karnak* 10: 1–28, plates 1–4.

————. 2000 *Amenhotep III: Le Magnifique*. Paris: Éditions Rocher.

————. 2001 *Les voies processionelles de Thèbes*. OLA 97. Louvain: Peeters.

Callaghan, G. 1992 The Education of Egyptian Scribes. *BACE* 3: 7–10.

Caminos, R., and James, T. G. H. 1963 *Gebel el-Silsilah. I. The Shrines*. ASE 31. London: EES.

Caminos, R. 1974 *The New Kingdom Temples of Buhen*. I = ASE 33. II = ASE 34. London: EES.

_____. 1987 Amenhotep III's Vizier Amenhotep at Silsilah East. *JEA* 73: 207–210.

Campbell, E. F., Jr. 1964 *The Chronology of the Amarna Letters with Special Reference to the Hypothetical Coregency of Amenophis III and Akhenaten.* Baltimore: Johns Hopkins UP.

Capart, J. 1935 Nouvelles: Bruxelles. *CdÉ* 10: 322–324.

_____. 1938 Une statue de Sebekhotep, précepteur royal. *BMRAH* 4: 83–86, figures 8 and 9.

Capart, J., and Spiegelberg, W. 1902 Une statuette du Temple de Wazmose à Thèbes. *ASAB* 16: 160–169.

Carlotti, J.-F. 2003 Essai de datation de l'agrandissement à cinq barres de portage du pavois de la barque d'Amon-Rê. *Karnak* 11, no. 1: 235–248, plates 1–6.

Carter, H., and Newberry, P. 1904 *The Tomb of Thoutmôsis IV.* CG 46001–46529. Westminster: Archibald Constable. (Reprinted. London: Duckworth 2000)

Castiglioni, A., and Castiglioni, A. 2004 Gold in the Eastern Desert. In *Sudan: Ancient Treasures,* ed. D. A. Welsby and J. R. Anderson, 122–131. London: BM.

Cenival, de, J.-L. 1991 Les deux frères (une statue de Souty frère de Hor). *CRIPÉL* 13: 47–52.

Chassinat, E. 1901 Une tombe inviolée de la XVIIIe dynastie découverte aux environs de Médinet el-Gorab dans le Fayoúm. *BIFAO* 1: 225–234, plates 1–3.

_____. 1910 Une statuette d'Aménôthès III. *BIFAO* 7: 169–172, plates 1–3.

Cheal, C. 2004 The Meaning of Skin Color in Eighteenth Dynasty Egypt. In *Race,* 89–122.

Chevrier, H. 1950 Rapport sur les travaux de Karnak 1949–1950. *ASAE* 50: 429–442, plates 1–13.

_____. 1956 Chronologie des constructions de la salle Hypostyle. *ASAE* 54: 35–38.

_____. 1971 La construction dans l'ancienne Égypte. *RdÉ* 23: 67–111.

Chittick, H. N. 1955 An Exploratory Journey in the Bayuda Region. *Kush* 3: 86–92.

Christie's 2003 *Collection de Monsieur Georges Halphen.* Paris, November 20, 2003.

_____. 2008 Antiquities. London, October 13, 2008.

Churchill, W. S. 1899 *The River War: An Account of the Reconquest of the Sudan.* New York: Carroll and Graf, 2000. (Repr. with shortened preface)

Clarke, S. 1916 Ancient Egyptian Frontier Fortresses. *JEA* 3: 154–179.

_____. 1922 El Kâb and its Temples. *JEA* 8: 16–40.

Clayton, P., and Price, M. 1988 *The Seven Wonders of the Ancient World.* London: Routledge.

Clère, J. J. 1968 Nouveaux fragments de scènes du jubilé d'Aménophis IV. *RdÉ* 20: 51–54.

Cline, E. 1990 An Unpublished Amenhotep III Faience Plaque from Mycenae. *JAOS* 110, no. 2: 200–212.

———. 1998 Amenhotep III, the Aegean, and Anatolia. In AIIIP, 236–250.

———. 2001 Mycenae. In OEAE 2: 457–459.

Collins, P. 2008 *From Egypt to Babylon: The International Age 1550–500 BC.* Cambridge, MA: Harvard UP.

Collins, R. O. 2002 *The Nile.* New Haven: Yale UP.

Cooney, K. M. 2007 *The Cost of Death: The Social and Economic Value of Ancient Egyptian Funerary Art in the Ramesside Period.* Leiden: NINO.

Corteggiani, J.-P. 1994 Une dyade privée d'un type particulier. In Fs. Leclant IV: 45–63.

Cotterell, A. 2005 *Chariot: From Chariot to Tank, the Astounding Rise and Fall of the World's First War Machine.* Woodstock: Overlook Press.

Crawford, O. G. S. 1953 Field Archaeology of the Middle Nile Kingdom. *Kush* 1: 2–29.

Croutier, A. L. 1989 *Harem: The World behind the Veil.* New York: Abbeville.

Crum, W. E. 1893 Stelae from Wadi Halfa. *PSBA* 16: 16–19.

Cruz-Uribe, E. 1992 The Lake of Moeris: A Reprise. In *Life in a Multi-cultural Society: Egypt from Cambyses to Constantine and Beyond,* ed. J. Johnson, 63–65. SAOC 51. Chicago: OI.

Curto, S. 1961 *L'Egitto antico nelle collezioni dell'Italia settentrionale,* exh. cat. Bologna: Museo Civico.

D'Auria, S. 1999 Preparing for Eternity. In Pharaohs/Sun, 162–175.

Darnell, J., and Manassa, C. 2007 *Tutankhamun's Armies: Battle and Conquest during Ancient Egypt's Late 18th Dynasty.* Hoboken: John Wiley.

David, A. R. 1982 *The Ancient Egyptians: Religious Beliefs and Practices.* London: Routledge, Kegan Paul.

———. 2002 *Religion and Magic in Ancient Egypt.* London: Penguin.

Davies, B. G. 1992 *Egyptian Historical Records of the Later Eighteenth Dynasty.* Fasc. 4. Warminster: Aris and Phillips.

———. 1994 *Egyptian Historical Records of the Later Eighteenth Dynasty.* Fasc. 5. Warminster: Aris and Phillips.

———. 1995 *Egyptian Historical Records of the Later Eighteenth Dynasty.* Fasc. 6. Warminster: Aris and Phillips.

Davies, N. de G. 1923 Akhenaten at Thebes. *JEA* 9: 132–152.

———. 1925 The Place of Audience in the Palace. *ZÄS* 60: 50–56.

———. 1941 *The Tomb of the Vizier Ramose.* Mond Excavations at Thebes 1. London: EES.

Davies, W. V. 2001 Kurgus 2000: The Ancient Egyptian Inscriptions. *Sudan and Nubia, the Sudan Archaeological Research Society Bulletin* 5: 46–58.

———. 2003 La frontière méridionale de l'empire: Les Égyptiens à Kurgus. *BSFÉ* 157: 23–37.

———. 2003a Kouch en Égypte: Une nouvelle inscription historique à El-Kab. *BSFÉ* 157: 38–44.

Davies, W. V., and Friedman, R. 1998 *Egypt*. London: BM.

Davis, T. M. 1908 *The Tomb of Siphtah: With the Tomb of Queen Tiyi*. London: Constable. (Repr. London: Duckworth, 2000)

Davis, T. M., et al. 1907 *The Tomb of Iouiya and Touiyou: With the Funeral Papyrus of Iouiya*. London: Constable. (Repr. London: Duckworth, 2000)

———. 1910 *The Tomb of Queen Tiyi*. London: Constable.

Delvaux, L. 1992 Amenhotep, Horemheb et Paramessou: les grandes statues de scribes à la fin de la 18e dynastie. In *L'atelier de l'orfèvre: Mélanges offerts à Ph. Derchain*, ed. M. Broze and P. Talon, 47–53. Leuven, Netherlands: Peeters.

Der Manuelian, P. 1987 *Studies in the Reign of Amenhotep II*. HÄB 26. Hildesheim: Gerstenberg.

Desroches, C. 1938 Une modèle de maison citadine du nouvel empire. *RdÉ* 3: 17–25, plate II.

Desroches-Noblecourt, C. 1986 *La femme au temps des pharaons*. Paris: Éditions Stock.

———. 1999 *Secrets des temples de la Nubie*. Paris: Éditions Stock.

Dewachter, M. 1984 Les premiers fils royaux d'Amon. *RdÉ* 35: 83–94, plate 8.

Diodorus Siculus. *See Oldfather*.

Dobbs, D. 2010 The Risks and Rewards of Royal Incest. *NatGeo*, September 2010, 60–61.

Dodson, A. 1990 Crown Prince Djhutmose and the Royal Sons of the Eighteenth Dynasty. *JEA* 76: 87–96.

———. 1999 The Canopic Equipment from the Serapeum at Memphis. In Fs. Smith, 59–75.

———. 2000–2001 Thutmose IV, an Usurper. *KMT* 11, no. 4: 4.

———. 2008–2009 Alexander Henry Rhind at Sheikh Abd el Gurna. *KMT* 19, no. 4: 38–52.

Dodson, A., and Hilton, D. 2010 *The Complete Royal Families of Ancient Egypt*. London: Thames/Hudson.

Dodson, A., and Janssen, J. 1989 A Theban Tomb and Its Tenants. *JEA* 75: 125–138.

Donadoni, S. 1994 Una statua reimpiegata da Ramesse II ad Antinoe. In Fs. Leclant I, 449–453.

Dorman, P. F. 1993 A Note on the Royal Repast at the Jubilee of Amenhotep III. In Fs. Leclant I, 455–470.

———. 2009 The Long Coregency Revisited: Architectural and Iconographic Conundra in the Tomb of Kheruef. In Fs. Murnane, 65–82.

Dreyfus, R. 2005 Decorative Arts: Metalwork. In Hatshepsut, 245–253.

Duhoux, Y. 2003 *Des Minoens en Égypte?: "Keftiou" et "les îles au milieu du Grand Vert."* PIOL 52. Louvain: Peeters.

DuQuesne, T. 2001 Concealing and Revealing: The Problem of Masking in Ancient Egypt. *DE* 51: 5–31.

Dziobek, E., and Abdel Raziq, M. 1989 *Das Grab des Sobekhotep, Theben Nr. 63*. AV 71. Mainz: Von Zabern.

Eaton-Krauss, M. 1988 Tutankhamun at Karnak. *MDAIK* 44: 1–11, plates 16–17.

———. 1993 Toutankhamon et les monuments d'Aménophis III. In Delange, 48–55.

Edel, E., and Görg, M. 2005 *Die Ortsnamenlisten im nördlichen Säulenhof des Totentempels Amenophis' III.* ÄUAT 50. Wiesbaden: Harrassowitz.

Edwards, D. 2004 *The Nubian Past: An Archaeology of the Sudan.* London: Routledge.

Edwards, D. and Osman, A. 2001 New Kingdom and Kushite Sites in the Third Cataract Region, Sudanese Nubia. *GM* 182: 17–30.

Eigner, D. 1983 Das Thebanische Grab des Amenhotep, Wesir von Unterägypten: Die Architektur. *MDAIK* 39: 39–50.

El Menshawy, S. 2003 The Protocol of the Ancient Egyptian Royal Palace. In *Egyptology at the Dawn of the 21st Century*, ed. Z. Hawass. 8th ICE 2, 400–406. Cairo: AUP.

El Sabban, S. 2000 The Cat's Coffin of *DHwty-ms* in the Cairo Museum. *DE* 46: 65–78.

El Saghir, M. 1991 *The Discovery of the Statuary Cachette of Luxor Temple.* SDAIK 26. Mainz: Von Zabern.

El Shahawy, A., and Atiya, F. 2007 *Luxor Museum: The Glory of Ancient Thebes.* Cairo: Farid Atiya Press.

Engelbach, R. 1943 Statues of the "Soul of Nekhen" and the "Soul of Pe" of the Reign of Amenophis III. *ASAE* 42: 71–73.

Epigraphic Survey. 1980 *The Tomb of Kheruef: Theban Tomb 192.* OIP 102. Chicago: OI.

———. 1994 *The Festival Procession of Opet in the Colonnade Hall. Reliefs and Inscriptions at Luxor Temple*, 1. OIP 114. Chicago: OI.

———. 1998 *The Facade, Portals, Upper Register Scenes, Columns, Marginalia, and Statuary in the Colonnade Hall. Reliefs and Inscriptions at Luxor Temple*, 2. OIP 116. Chicago: OI.

Erman, A. 1890 Neues aus den Tafeln von el Amarna. *ZÄS* 28: 112.

Ertman, E., Wilson, R., and Schaden, O. 2006 Unraveling the Mysteries of KV63. *KMT* 17, no. 3: 18–27.

Eyre, C. J. 1998 The Market Women of Pharaonic Egypt. In *Le commerce en Égypte ancienne*, ed. N. Grimal and P. Menu. BdÉ 121, 173–189. Cairo: IFAO.

Fabre, D. 2005 *Seafaring in Ancient Egypt.* London: Periplus.

Fagles, R., trans. 1990 *Homer: The Iliad.* London: Penguin.

Faulkner, R. O. 1941 Egyptian Seagoing Ships. *JEA* 26: 3–9.

———. 1953 Egyptian Military Organization. *JEA* 39: 32–47.

———. 1955 The Installation of the Vizier. *JEA* 41: 18–29.

———. 1962 *A Concise Dictionary of Middle Egyptian.* Oxford: GI.

Fay, B. 1985 *Egyptian Museum Berlin.* Berlin: Ägyptisches Museum.

Fazzini, R. 2002 Some Aspects of the Precinct of the Goddess Mut in the New Kingdom. In Fs. Hansen, 63–76.

———. 2005 The Precinct of the Goddess Mut at South Karnak, 1996–2001. *ASAE* 79: 85–94.

Feldman, M. 2006 *Diplomacy by Design: Luxury Arts and an "International Style" in the Ancient Near East, 1400–1200 BCE.* Chicago: University of Chicago.

Fenner, F. 1989 *Smallpox and Its Eradication.* History of Public Health 6. Geneva: World Health Organization.

Filer, J. 1995 *Disease.* Austin: University of Texas Press.

Finkel, I. 2008 Cuneiform Tablet with Manual for Glass Manufacture. In Beyond Babylon, 421–422.

Firth, C. M. 1915 *The Archaeological Survey of Nubia: Report for 1909–1910.* Cairo: Government Press.

Fischer-Elfert, H.-W. 2003 Representations of the Past in New Kingdom Literature. In *'Never Had the Like Occurred': Egypt's View of Its Past,* ed. J. Tait, 119–137. UCL Press.

Flaubert, G. *See* Steegmuller.

Fletcher, J. A. 2000 *Chronicle of a Pharaoh: The Intimate Life of Amenhotep III.* New York: Oxford UP.

Foster, J. L. 1995 *Hymns, Prayers, and Songs: An Anthology of Ancient Egyptian Lyric Poetry* (trans.), ed. S. T. Hollis. Atlanta: Scholars Press.

———. 1999 The New Religion. In Pharaohs/Sun, 97–109.

Frankfort, H. S. 1948 *Kingship and the Gods.* Chicago: University of Chicago Press.

Freed, R. E. 1999 Observations on Some Amenhotep IV Colossi from Karnak. *Memnonia* 10: 195–200, plates LV–LVIII.

———. 1999a Akhenaten's Artistic Legacy. In Pharaohs/Sun, 187–197.

———. 1999b Art in the Service of Religion and the State. In Pharaohs/Sun, 110–129.

Freed, R. E., Berman, L.M., and Doxey, D. 2003 *MFA Highlights: Arts of Ancient Egypt.* Boston: MFA.

Gaballa, G. 1970 Nefer, Third Prophet of Amun. *MDAIK* 26: 50–54.

Gaballa, G. A., and Kitchen, K. A. 1969 The Festival of Sokar. *Orientalia,* N.S. 38: 1–76.

Gabolde, L., and Rondot, V. 1996 Le temple de Montou n'était pas un temple à Montou. *BSFÉ* 136: 27–41.

Gabolde, M. 1993 La posterité d'Aménophis III. *Égyptes* 1: 29–34.

———. 2002 La parenté de Toutânkhamon. *BSFÉ* 155: 32–48.

———. 2004 Tenttepihou, une dame d'Atfih, épouse morganatique du futur Thoutmosis IV. *BIFAO* 104, no. 1: 229–243.

Galán, J. M. 2000 The Ancient Egyptian Sed-Festival and the Exemption from Corvée. *JNES* 59, no. 4: 255–264.

————. 2002 Amenhotep Son of Hapu as Intermediary between the People and God. In *Egyptology at the Dawn of the 21st Century*, ed. Z. Hawass and L. Brock, 221–229. 8th ICE 2. Cairo: AUC.

Gale, R., Gasson, P., Hepper, N., and Killen, G. 2000 Wood: Common Box. In AEMT, 337–338.

Gardiner, A. H. 1906 A Statuette of the High Priest of Memphis, Ptahmose. *ZÄS* 43: 55–58.

————. 1913 The Inscription of Amenhotep. In *Tarkhan I and Memphis V*, ed. W. M. F. Petrie, 33–36. BSAE 23. London: BSAE.

————. 1916 An Ancient List of the Fortresses of Nubia. *JEA* 3: 184–192.

————. 1917 A Stela in the MacGregor Collection. *JEA* 4: 188–189, plate 37.

————. 1937 *Late Egyptian Miscellanies*. Brussels: E. J. Brill.

————. 1948 *The Wilbour Papyrus II: Commentary*. London: Brooklyn Museum/ Oxford UP.

————. 1953a The Harem at Miwer. *JNES* 12: 145–149.

————. 1953b The Coronation of King Haremhab. *JEA* 39: 13–31.

————. 1961 *Egypt of the Pharaohs*. Oxford: Oxford UP.

————. 1969 *Egyptian Grammar: Being an Introduction to the Study of Hieroglyphs*. 3rd ed., rev. London: Oxford UP.

Gardiner, A. H., and Bell, H. I. 1943 The Name of Lake Moeris. *JEA* 29: 37–50.

Gardiner, A. H., and Peet, T. E. 1955 *The Inscriptions of Sinai*, ed. J. Černý. Part II: Translations and Commentary. London: EES.

Gee, J. 2001 Notes on Egyptian Marriage: P. BM10416 Reconsidered. *BES* 15: 17–25.

Germond, P. 1981 *Sekhmet et la protection du monde*. ÄH 9. Geneva: Belles-Lettres.

Geus, F. 1994 L'île de Saï à travers l'histoire du Soudan. *DossArch* 196 (September): 22–25.

Giddy, L. L. 1980 Some Exports from the Oases of the Libyan Desert in the Nile Valley: Tomb 131 at Thebes. In *Livre du Centenaire, 1880–1990*, ed. J. Vercoutter, 119–125. Cairo: IFAO.

Glanville, S. R. K. 1932 Records of a Royal Dockyard of the Time of Tuthmosis III. *ZÄS* 68: 39–41, plate 2.

————. 1932a Scribes' Palettes in the British Museum. *JEA* 18: 53–61, plates 4–9.

Gnirs, A. 2009 In the King's House: Audiences and Receptions at Court. In *Egyptian Royal Residences: 4th Symposium on Egyptian Royal Ideology*, ed. R. Gundlach and J. Taylor, 13–43. Königtum, Staat und Gesellschaft Früher Hochkulturen 4.1. Wiesbaden: Harrasowitz.

Goebs, K. 2001 Crowns. OEAE I: 321–326.

Goedicke, H. 1984 The Canaanite Illness. *SAK* 11: 91–105.

————. 1992 *Problems Concerning Amenophis III*. Baltimore: Halgo.

Goetze, A. 1955 Plague Prayers of Mursilis. In ANET, 394–396.

————. 1955a Suppiluliumas and the Egyptian Queen. In ANET, 319.

————. 1955b Hittite Treaties. In ANET, 201–206.

Gomaà, F. 1977 Hebenu. *LÄ* 2: 1075–1076.

Gordon, A. 1983 The Tomb of the Vizier Amenhotep at Thebes. *MDAIK* 39: 71–80.

————. 1989 Who Was the Southern Vizier during the Last Part of the Reign of Amenhotep III? *JNES* 48, no. 1: 15–23.

Gore, R. 2001 Pharaohs of the Sun. *NGM* 199, no. 4: 43–57.

Graham, A., and Bunbury, J. 2005 The Ancient Landscapes and Waterscapes of Karnak. *EA* 27: 17–19.

————. 2008 Paleogeography of the Delta (unpublished).

Green, L. 1996 The Royal Women of Amarna: Who Was Who. In Royal Women, 7–15.

Griffith, A. S. 1910 *Catalogue of Egyptian Antiquities of the XII and XVIII Dynasties from Kahun, Illahun, Gurob.* Manchester: Sherratt and Hughes.

Griffith, F. L. 1943 Ethiopia. *Encyclopaedia Britannica* 8: 778–779. Chicago: University of Chicago Press.

Gundlach, R. 1982 Mutemwia. *LÄ* 4: 251–252.

————. 1986 Taduhepa. *LÄ* 6: 144–145.

————. 1987 Die Felsstelen Amenophis' III. am 1. Katarakt. In Fs. Fecht, 180–217.

Habachi, L. 1957 The Graffiti and Work of the Viceroys of Kush in the Region of Aswan. *Kush* 5: 13–36.

————. 1957a Tell Basta. *SASAÉ* 22: 1–140.

————. 1960 Five Stelae from the Temple of Amenophis III at Es-Sebua' now in the Aswan Museum. *Kush* 8: 45–52.

————. 1971 The Jubilees of Ramesses II and Amenophis III with Reference to Certain Aspects of Their Celebration. *ZÄS* 97: 68–69.

————. 1972 *The Second Stela of Kamose and His Struggle against the Hyksos Ruler and His Capital.* ADAIK 8. Glückstadt: J. J. Augustin.

————. 1974 Aménophis III et Amenhotep, fils de Hapou à Athribis. *RdÉ* 26: 21–33.

————. 1980 Königssohn von Kush. *LÄ* 3: 630–638.

Haeny, G. 1981 *Untersuchungen im Totentempel Amenophis' III.* BÄBA 11. Wiesbaden: Franz Steiner.

————. 1982 La fonction religieuse des chateaux de millions d'années. In *L'Égyptologie en 1979: axes prioritaires de recherches,* vol. 1, 111–116. Paris: CNRS.

————. 1997 New Kingdom "Mortuary temples." In Temples, 86–126.

Häggman, S. 2002 *Directing Deir el-Medina, The External Administration of the Necropolis,* USE 4. Uppsala: Uppsala University.

Hall, H. R. 1925 *Hieroglyphic Texts in the British Museum,* part 7. London: Harrison and Sons.

————. 1931 Objects Belonging to the Memphite High-Priest Ptahmose. *JEA* 17: 48–49, plate 7.

Hall, R. M. 1986 *Egyptian Textiles*. Aylesbury: Shire.

Handoussa, T. 1979 Á propos de l'offrande *Sbt*. *SAK* 7: 65–74.

Hankey, V. 1999 The Whirligig of Time: The Aegean and Egypt in the Second Millennium BC. In Fs. Smith, 115–119.

Hankey, V., and Aston, D. 1995 Mycenean Pottery at Saqqara: Finds from Excavations by the EES of London and the RMO of Leiden, 1975–1990. In Fs. Vermeule, 67–92.

Hansen, N. B. 2005 The Ancient Egyptian Wedding Ceremony Rediscovered. Paper presented at ARCE, April 22–24, Boston.

Hardwick, T. 2003 The Iconography of the Blue Crown in the New Kingdom. *JEA* 89: 117–141.

_____. 2006 Festivals and Expeditions: Sculptures at the End of the Reign of Amenhotep III. Paper presented at ARCE April 7–9, Jersey City.

Haring, B. J. J. 1997 *Divine Households: Administrative and Economic Aspects of the New Kingdom Royal Memorial Temples in Western Thebes*. EU 12. Leiden: NINO.

Harrell, J. A. 1999 The Tumbos Quarry at the Third Nile Cataract, Northern Sudan. In *Recent Research in Kushite History and Archaeology, Proceedings of the 8th International Conference for Meroitic Studies*, ed. D. A. Welsby. BMOP 131: 239–250.

_____. 2002 Pharaonic Stone Quarries in the Egyptian Deserts. In *Egypt and Nubia: Gifts of the Desert*, ed. R. Friedman, 232–243. London: BM.

Harris, J. E. 1999 The Mummy of Amenhotep III. In Fs. Wente, 163–174.

Harris, J. E., and Weeks, K. R. 1973 *X-Raying the Pharaohs*. New York: Scribner's.

Hartwig, M. 2008 A Vignette Concerning the Deification of Thutmose IV. In Fs. Fazzini, 120–125.

Haslauer, E. 2001 Harem. OEAE 2: 76–80.

Hassan, F. 1993 Town and Village in Ancient Egypt: Ecology, Society, and Urbanization. In Archaeology of Africa, 551–569.

Hassan, S. 1949 *The Sphinx: Its History in the Light of Recent Excavations*. Cairo: Government Press.

Hawass, Z. 2004 *Hidden Treasures of Ancient Egypt: Unearthing the Masterpieces of Egyptian History*. Washington, DC: NatGeo.

_____. 2010 King Tut's Family Secrets. NatGeo, September 2010, 34–58.

_____. 2011 New discoveries on Luxor's west bank. http://english.ahram.org .eg/NewsContent/9/40/13339/Heritage/Ancient-Egypt/New-discoveries-on-Luxors-west-bank.aspx:

Hawass, Z., et al. 2010 Ancestry and Pathology in King Tutankhamun's Family. *Journal of the American Medical Association* 303, no. 7: 638–647.

Hayes, W. C. 1935 *Royal Sarcophagi of the XVIIIth Dynasty*. Princeton Monographs in Art and Archaeology, Quarto Series, 19. Princeton: Princeton UP.

————. 1938 A Writing-Palette of the Chief Steward Amenhotpe and Some Notes on Its Owner. *JEA* 24: 9–24.

————. 1939 *The Burial Chamber of the Treasurer Sobk-mose from er-Rizeikat.* MMAP 9. New York: MMA.

————. 1949 La 36e et la 37e année de règne d'Aménophis III. *CdÉ* 24: 96.

————. 1951 Inscriptions from the Palace of Amenhotep III. *JNES* 10: 35–40, figures 1–16; 82–104, figures 17–23; 156–183, figures 24–33; 231–242, figures 34–38.

————. 1959 *The Scepter of Egypt: A Background for the Study of the Egyptian Antiquities in the Metropolitan Museum of Art, vol.* 2, *The Hyksos and the New Kingdom* (1675–1080). New York: MMA.

Healy, M. 1992 *Armies of the Pharaohs.* Oxford: Osprey.

Heizer, R. F. 1973 The Colossi of Memnon Revisited. *Science*, December 21, 1973, 1219–1225.

Helck, W. 1955–1958 *Urkunden der* 18.*Dynastie*, Heft 17–22. Berlin: Akademie.

Herodotus. *See* Waterfield.

Herrera, C. 2008 De la KV 46 aux nécropoles d'Akhmim: À la recherche de l'élite "Akhmimy" du nouvel empire. *Égypte: Afrique et Orient* 50: 37–46.

Hill, M. 2007 Shifting Ground: The New Kingdom from the Reign of Thutmose III (ca.1479–1070 B.C.). In *Gifts for the Gods: Images from Egyptian Temples*, ed. M. Hill, 23–37. New York: MMA.

Hoch, J. E. 1994 *Semitic Words in Egyptian Texts of the New Kingdom and Third Intermediate Period.* Princeton: Princeton UP.

Hoffmeier, J. 2002 Tell el-Borg in North Sinai. *EA* 20:18–20.

————. 2004 Tell el-Borg on Egypt's Eastern Frontier: A Preliminary Report on the 2002 and 2004 Seasons. *JARCE* 41: 85–111.

Hoffmeier, J., and Abd el-Maksoud, M. 2003 A New Military Site on the 'Ways of Horus'–Tell el-Borg 1999–2001: A Prelimary Report. *JEA* 89: 169–197.

Homer. *See* Fagles 1990.

Hope, C. 1977 *Excavations at Malkata and Birket Habu 1971–1974: Jar Sealings and Amphorae.* Warminster: Aris and Phillips.

Hornung, E. 1992 *Idea into Image*, trans. E. Bredeck. New York: Timken.

————. 1995 Thomas Mann, Akhnaten, and the Egyptologists. In Fs. Stricker, 101–113.

————. 1999 *Akhenaten and the Religion of Light.* Ithaca Cornell UP.

————. 1999a *The Ancient Egyptian Books of the Afterlife*, trans. D. Lorton. Ithaca: Cornell UP.

Hornung, E., and Staehelin, E. 1974 *Studien zum Sedfest.* AH 1. Geneva: Belles-Lettres.

————. 2006 *Neue Studien zum Sedfest.* AH 20. Basel: Schwabe.

Hough, L., and Paget, W. 1895 *For Fortune and Glory: A Story of the Soudan War.* London: Cassell.

Hyland, A. 2003 *The Horse in the Ancient World.* Gloucestershire: Sutton.

Ikram, S. 1995 *Choice Cuts: Meat Production in Ancient Egypt*. OLA 69. Leuven: Peeters.

Izre'el, S. 1997 *The Amarna Scholarly Tablets*. Cuneiform Monographs 9. Groningen: Styx.

Jacquet, J. 1971 Trois Campagnes de Fouilles à Karnak-Nord 1968–1969–1970. *BIFAO* 69: 267–281, plates 33–48.

Jacquet-Gordon, H. 1999 Excavations at Tabo, Northern Province, Sudan. In *Recent Research in Kushite History and Archaeology: Proceedings of the 8th International Conference for Meroitic Studies*, ed. D. A. Welsby. *BMOP* 131: 257–263.

James, A. 2000 Egypt and Her Vassals. In Amarna Diplomacy, 112–124.

James, T. G. H. 1996 The Earliest History of Wine and Its Importance in Ancient Egypt. In *The Origins and Ancient History of Wine*, ed. P. McGovern, S. Fleming, and S. Katz. Food and Nutrition in History and Anthropology Series 11: 197–213. Amsterdam: Gordon and Breach.

Janssen, J. J. 1973 Prolegomena to the Study of Egypt's Economic History During the New Kingdom. *SAK* 3: 127–185.

———. 2008 *Daily Dress at Deir el-Medina: Words for Clothing*. Egyptology 8. London: GHP.

Janssen, R. M. and Janssen, J. J. 1990 *Growing Up in Ancient Egypt*. London: Rubicon.

———. 1992 The 'Ceremonial Garments' of Tuthmosis IV. *SAK* 19: 217–224.

———. 1995 Costume in New Kingdom Egypt. In *Civilizations of the Ancient Near East*, ed. J. Sasson. vol. 1, 383–394. Peabody, MA: Hendrickson.

Johnson, G. B., and Forbes, D. 2007 Given Life Forever: The Funerary Monuments of Amenhotep III. *KMT* 18, no. 3: 36–52.

Johnson, J. 1994 "Annuity Contracts" and Marriage. In Fs. Baer, 113–132.

Johnson, W. R. 1990 Images of Amenhotep III in Thebes: Styles and Intentions. In *The Art of Amenhotep III: Art Historical Analysis*, ed. L. Berman, 26–46. Cleveland: Cleveland Museum of Art.

———. 1994 Honorific Figures of Amenhotep III in the Luxor Temple Colonnade Hall. In Fs. Baer, 133–144.

———. 1996 The Revolutionary Role of the Sun in the Reliefs and Statuary of Amenhotep III. OI News and Notes 151, Fall 1996, http://oi.uchicago.edu/research/pubs/nn/fal96 epi.html.

———. 2001 Ptah-Sokar-Osiris with the Features of Amenhotep III. In Halkedis, frontispiece, 20–22 (no. 11).

———. 2006 Portrait of Nebetah. In *Objects for Eternity from the W. Arnold Meijer Collection*, ed. C. Andrews and J. Van Dijk, 135–137. Mainz: Von Zabern.

Jones, D. 1988 *A Glossary of Egyptian Nautical Titles and Terms*. London: Kegan Paul.

Jørgensen, M. 2007 The Ny Carlsberg Glyptotek's Egyptian Collection. In *Ancient Art to Post-Impressionism: Masterpieces from the Ny Carlsberg Glyptotek, Copenhagen*, ed. F. Johansen, 28–47. London: Royal Academy.

Karig, J. 1975 Achmim. *LÄ* 1: 54–55.

_____. 1976 Fackelhalter. In *Nofretete.Echnaton*, exh. cat., ed. H. W. Müller and J. Settgast no. 61, unpag. Berlin: Ägyptisches Museum.

Karlshausen, C. 1995 L'évolution de la barque processionnelle d'Amon à la 18e dynastie. *RdÉ* 46: 119–137.

Kemp, B. J. 1976 Review of Reiser. *JEA* 62: 191–192.

_____. 1977 A Building of Amenophis III at Kôm el-'Abd. *JEA* 63: 71–82.

_____. 1978 The Harim-Palace at Medinet el-Ghurab. *ZÄS* 105: 132–133.

_____. 2001 *The Ancient Textile Industry at Amarna*. London: EES.

Kemp, B. J., and Merrillees, R. S. 1980 *Minoan Pottery in 2nd Millennium Egypt*. Mainz: Von Zabern.

Kemp, B., and O'Connor, D. 1974 An Ancient Nile Harbour: University Museum Excavations at the 'Birket Habu.' *IJNA* 3, no. 1: 101–136.

Kemp, B. J., Samuel, D., and Luee, R. 1994 Food for an Egyptian City: Tell el-Amarna. In *Whither Environmental Archaeology*, ed. R. Luff and P. Rowley-Conwy, 133–170. Oxford: Oxford.

Kendall, T. Gebel Barkal and Ancient Napata. *Arkamani*.

_____. 2001 Napata. OEAE 2: 492–493.

Kessler, D. 2001 Bull Gods. OEAE 1: 209–213.

Kitchen, K. A. 1982 Punt. *LÄ* 4: 1198–1201.

_____. 1993 The Land of Punt. In Archaeology of Africa, 586–608.

_____. 1998a Amenhotep III and Babylon. In AIIIP, 253–256.

_____. 1998b Amenhotep III and Mitanni. In AIIIP, 256–261.

_____. 1998c Amenhotep III and Mesopotamia. In AIIIP, 250–256.

_____. 1999 Further Thoughts on Punt and Its Neighbours. In Fs. Smith, 173–178.

Klemm, D., Klemm, R., and Murr, A. 2002 Ancient Gold Mining in the Eastern Desert of Egypt and the Nubian Desert of Sudan. In *Egypt and Nubia: Gifts of the Desert*, ed. R. Friedman, 215–231. London: BM.

Klemm, R., and Klemm, D. D. 2008 *Stones and Quarries in Ancient Egypt*, trans. Translate Ltd., ed. N. Strudwick. London: BM.

Koltsida, A. 2007 A Dark Spot in Ancient Egyptian Architecture: The Temple at Malkata. *JARCE* 43: 43–57.

Kozloff, A. P. 1992a Tomb Decoration: Paintings and Relief Sculpture. In EDS, 261–296.

_____. 1992b Ritual Implements and Related Statuettes. In EDS, 331–359.

_____. 1992c Glass Vessels. In EDS, 373–392.

_____. 1992d Molded and Carved Vessels and Figurines. In EDS, 393–412.

_____. 1992e Jewelry. In EDS, 434–451.

_____. 1992f Enthroned Amenhotep III Re-cut by Ramesses II. In EDS, 172–175, no. 14.

_____. 1992g Amenhotep III as Sphinx. In EDS, 223–224.

_____. 1992h The Lioness Goddess Sekhmet. In EDS, 225–226.

_____. 1996 A Masterpiece with Three Lives. In Fs. Simpson, 477–485.

_____. 1997 The Malqata/El-Amarna Blues. In Fs. Aldred, 178–192.

_____. 1997a Statue of Queen Arsinoe. In Miho Museum: South Wing, ed. T. Umehara, 34–37. Kyoto: Miho Museum.

_____. 2002 A Revision of Amenhotep III's Age at Coronation. Paper presented at ARCE, April 27.

_____. 2004 Amenhotep, King's Son of Kush: Did He Become Amenhotep III? Paper presented ARCE.

_____. 2006a The Artistic Production of the Reign of Thutmose III. In Thutmose III: A New Biography, ed. E. Cline and D. O'Connor, 292–324. Ann Arbor: University of Michigan Press.

_____. 2006b Bubonic Plague during the Reign of Amenhotep III? KMT 17, no. 3: 36–84.

_____. 2007 Proof of the True Use of "Cosmetic" Spoons as Funerary Ritual Spoons. Paper presented at ARCE, April 20–22, 2007, Toledo.

_____. 2008 Visual Observations on the Process and Order of Theban Tombs from the Reign of Amenhotep III. Paper presented at ICE/Montepulciano.

_____. 2009 The Banks and Mounds of the Birket Habu as a Training Ground for Chariot Horses. ARCE April 24–26, Dallas.

_____. 2010 Chips off the Old Block: Amenhotep IV's Sandstone Colossi, Re-cut from Statues of Amenhotep III. In Fs. Silverman 1, 279–294.

Kozloff, A., and Meltzer, E. 2010 Have Ramose's Statuary and Sarcophagi Been Right under our Noses All This Time? Paper presented at ARCE April 23–25, Oakland, CA.

Laboury, D. 2010 Akhénaton. Paris: Pygmalion.

Labrousse, A. 1994 Sedeinga, métropole régionale au coeur de l'Empire méroïtique. In La Nubie, DossArch 196 (September 1994): 34–37.

_____. 1996 Temple de la Reine Tiy à Sedeinga. In Soudan: 5000 Ans d'Histoire, DossArch hors série 6: 66–67.

Lacau, P. 1913 Suppressions et modifications des signes dans les textes funéraires. ZÄS 51: 1–64.

Lacovara, P. 1997 Gurob and the New Kingdom 'Harim' Palace. In Fs. Bell 2, 297–306.

_____. 1997b The New Kingdom Royal City. London: Kegan Paul.

_____. 1999 The City of Amarna. In Pharaohs/Sun, 61–71.

_____. 2009 The Development of the New Kingdom Royal Palace. In Egyptian Royal Residences: 4th Symposium on Egyptian Royal Ideology, ed. R. Gundlach and J. Taylor, 83–110. Königtum, Staat und Gesellschaft Früher Hochkulturen 4.1. Wiesbaden: Harrassowitz.

Lane, M. E. 1985 Guide to the Antiquities of the Fayyum. Cairo: AUC.

Larché, F., and Letellier, B. 1979 La cour à peristyle de Thoutmosis IV à Karnak. In Fs. Sauneron 1, 51–71, plates 10–12.

Latjar, A. 2006 *Deir el-Bahari in the Hellenistic and Roman Periods: A Study of an Egyptian Temple Based on Greek Sources. Journal of Juristic Papyrology*, suppl. IV. Warsaw: Institute of Archaeology, Warsaw University and Fundacja im. Rafal Taubenschlaga.

Lauffray, J. et al. 1970 Rapport sur les travaux de Karnak: Tremblement de terre. *Kêmi* 20: 99.

Laurent, V. 1993 Un personnage hors du commun: Amenhotep, fils de Hapou. In Delange, 64–71.

Lawler, A. 2006 A Mystery Fit for a Pharaoh. *Smithsonian* 37, no. 4: 64–69.

————. 2010 Collapse? What Collapse? Societal Change Revisited. *Science* 330: 907–909.

Leahy, M. A. 1978 Excavations at Malkata and the Birket Habu 1971–1974: The Inscriptions. *Egyptology Today* 4, no. 2. Warminster: Aris and Phillips.

Leblanc, C. 1997 Quelques reflections sur le programme iconographique et la fonction des temples de "millions d'années." In Temple in AE, 49–56.

————. 2005 Research, Development and Management on the Left Bank of the Nile: Ramesseum and Its Environs. *Museum* 57: 80–81.

————. 2005a Un fragment de statue naophore au nom de Paiây et les Gouverneurs de Thèbes. *Memnonia* 16: 59–83, plates 9–10.

————. 2007a À propos de quelques lettres addressées de Babylonie et du Mitanni par Burra- Buraryaš et Tušratta II à Naphurereya-Amenhotep IV. *Memnonia* 18: 127–138.

————. 2007b Anubis criocéphale, Une manifestation du soleil nocturne. *Memnonia* 18: 139–143, plates 27–30.

Leclant, J. 1963 Le sarcophage de Oabset de la nécropole de Soleb. *Kush* 11: 141–158.

————. 1977 Soleb. *LÄ* 5: 1076–1080.

————. 1996 Le temple jubilaire d'Aménophis à Soleb. In *Soudan: 5000 Ans d'Histoire. DossArch, hors série no.* 6: 64–65.

Lefebvre, G. 1929 *Histoire des grands prêtres d'Amon de Karnak jusqu'à la XXIe Dynastie.* Paris: Paul Geuthner.

Legrain, G. 1903 Fragments de canopes. *ASAE* 4: 138–149.

————. 1904 Seconde note sur des fragments de canopes. *ASAE* 5: 139–141.

————. 1914 Les statues de Paramessou, Fils de Seti. *ASAE* 14: 29–38.

————. 1914a Pylone d'Harmhabi à Karnak (Xe Pylone). *ASAE* 14: 13–39.

Leitz, C. 1999 *Hieratic Papyri in the British Museum VII: Magical and Medical Papyri of the New Kingdom.* London: BM.

Lepsius, C. R. 1900 *Denkmäler aus Aegypten und Aethiopien.* Leipzig: J. C. Hinrichs.

Lesko, L. 1996 Egyptian Wine Production during the New Kingdom. In *The Origins and Ancient History of Wine*, ed. P. McGovern, S. Fleming, and S. Katz, 215–230. Food and Nutrition in History and Anthropology Series 11. Amsterdam: Gordon and Breach.

Lewis, N. 1983 *Life in Egypt under Roman Rule.* Oxford: Clarendon.

Lichtheim, M. 1975 *Ancient Egyptian Literature, vol. 1, The Old and Middle Kingdoms.* Berkeley. University of California Press.

———. 2006 *Ancient Egyptian Literature, vol. 2, The New Kingdom.* Berkeley: University of California Press.

Lilyquist, C. 1997 Descriptive Notes from the Valley. In Fs. Aldred, 201–206.

Littauer, M. A., and Crouwel, J. H. 1985 *Chariots and Related Equipment from the Tomb of Tut'ankhamun.* Tut'ankhamun's Tomb Series VIII. Oxford: GI.

Liverani, M. 2008 The Late Bronze Age: Materials and Mechanisms of Trade and Cultural Exchange. In Beyond Babylon, 161–168.

Loat, L. 1904 *Gurob. BSAE 10th memoir,* 2: 21–45.

Lobban, R. A., Jr. 2004 Afrocentric Perspectives on Race Relations in Dynastic Egypt. In Race, 57–88.

Lorton, D.1974 Review of Reiser 1972. *JARCE* 11: 98–101.

———. 1991 What Was the Pr-nsw and Who Managed It? *SAK* 18: 291–316.

Lurson, B. 2004 Les Sekhmets retrouvées au Ramesseum. *Memnonia* 15: 103–111, plates 15–20.

———. 2006 Note complémentaire sur la statuaire d'Amenhotep III retrouvée au Ramesseum. *Memnonia* 17: 91–93.

Lythgoe, A. 1919 Statues of the Goddess Sekhmet. *BMMA* 14: 3–22.

MacDowell, A. G. 1999 *Village Life in Ancient Egypt.* Oxford: Oxford UP.

Madsen, H. 1904 Zwei Inscriften in Kopenhagen. *ZÄS* 41: 114–115.

Mahfouz, E. S. 2005 Les directeurs des deserts aurifrères d'Amon. *RdÉ* 56: 55–78.

Mahoney, R. 2007 *Down the Nile in a Fisherman's Skiff.* New York: Little, Brown.

Málek, J. 1981 Two Problems Connected with New Kingdom Tombs in the Memphite Area. *JEA* 67: 156–165.

———. 2000 The Old Kingdom (c. 2686–2125 B.C.). In OHAE, 89–117.

Manetho. *See* Waddell.

Manniche, L. 1982 The Maru built by Amenophis III, Its Significance and Possible Location. In *L'Égyptologie en 1979* 2: 271–273. CICNRS 595. Paris: CNRS.

Mariette, A. 1857 *Le Sérapeum de Memphis découvert et décrit par Aug. Mariette.* Paris: Gide.

Markowitz, Y. 1999 Statuette of a woman, Statuette of Tiya, Chief of the Household. In Pharaohs/Sun, 206.

Martin, G. T. 2005 *Stelae from Egypt and Nubia in the Fitzwilliam Museum, Cambridge, c. 3000 BC–AD* 1150. Cambridge: Cambridge UP.

Martinez, P. 2004 Un monument préamarnien ignoré: Le Ramesseum. *Memnonia* 15: 123–150.

Maruéjol, F. 2007 *Thoutmosis III et la corégence avec Hatchepsout.* Paris: Pygmalion.

Masson, E. 1998 *L'art de soigner et d'entraîner les chevaux: Texte hittite du maitre écuyer Kikkuli.* Lausanne: Favre.

Matthiew, M. 1930 A Note on the Coronation Rites in Ancient Egypt. *JEA* 16: 31–32.

McClain, J. B. 2009 Preliminary Report on the Work of the Epigraphic Survey at the Temple of Khonsu at Karnak, 2008–2009. Paper presented at ARCE, April 24–26. Dallas.

McDermott, B. 2004 *Warfare in Ancient Egypt*. Gloucestershire: Sutton.

McRae, M. 2005 Mystery of the Black Pharaohs. *Discover* 26: 46–53.

Meiss, M. 1951 *Painting in Florence and Siena after the Black Death: The Arts, Religion and Society in the Mid-Fourteenth Century*. New York: Harper and Row.

Meltzer, E. S. 1974 A Funerary Cone of Merymose, Viceroy of Kush. *SSEA Newsletter* 5, no. 2: 9–11, plate 7.

————. 1989/1990 The Commemorative Scarab: A "Gem" of a Text. *BES* 10: 91–94.

————. 1996 Who Knows the Color of God? Review of T. DuQuesne, Black and Gold God. *JAC* (Changchun, Northeast Normal University) 11: 123–129.

————. 2000 Scots Verdict on Thutmose IV. *KMT* 11, no. 3: 15.

————. 2001 Children of the Kap – Upwardly Mobile, Talented Youth in Ancient Egypt. *Seshat* 5 (Winter): 20–26.

Meltzer, E., and Bianchi, R. 2009 An Unpublished Dated Stela of Thutmose IV. Paper presented at ARCE April 24–26, Dallas.

Meskell, L. 2002 *Private Life in New Kingdom Egypt*. Princeton: Princeton UP.

Meyer, C. 1984 Satamun II. *LÄ* 5: 485–487.

————. 1984a Zum Titel "Hmt Njswt" bei den Töchtern Amenophis' III. und IV. und Ramses' II. *SAK* 11: 253–263.

————. 1986 Tura. *LÄ* 6: 807–809.

Minault-Gout, A. 1994 Une nécropole du Nouvel Empire. In *La Nubie, DossArch* 196: 28–31.

————. 1996 Une tête de la reine Tiyi découverte dans l'île de Sai, au Soudan. *RdÉ* 47: 37–41, plates V–VIII.

Mond, R., and Myers, O. H. 1934 *The Bucheum* I, III. EESM 41. London: EES.

Montet, P. 1964 Le rituel de fondation des temples égyptiens. *Kêmi* 17: 74–100.

Moran, W. L. 1992 *The Amarna Letters*. Baltimore: Johns Hopkins UP.

Morenz, S. 1973 *Egyptian Religion*, trans. A. E. Keep. Ithaca: Cornell UP.

Moret, A. 1902 *Du caractère religieux de la royauté pharaonique*. Paris: E. Leroux.

Morgan, de, J. et al. 1894 *Catalogue des monuments et inscriptions de l'Égypte antique*. Vienna: Adolphe Holzhausen.

Morkot, R. G. 1987 Studies in New Kingdom Nubia, vol. 1, Politics, Economics, and Ideology: Egyptian Imperialism in Nubia. *Wepwawet* 3: 29–49.

————. 1990 NB-M3'T-R'–UNITED-WITH-PTAH. *JNES* 49, no. 4: 323–337.

————. 2000 *The Black Pharaohs: Egypt's Nubian Rulers*. London: Rubicon.

Morris, E. F. 2006 Bowing and Scraping in the Ancient Near East: An Investigation into Obsequiousness in the Amarna Letters. *JNES* 65, no. 3: 179–195.

————. 2010 Opportunism in Contested Lands, B.C. and A.D. In Fs. Silverman, 413–438.

Mueller, T. 2010 Valley of the Whales. *NatGeo* August 2010, 118–137.

Muhammad, M. A. 1966 Recent Finds: Karnak Third Pylon. *ASAE* 59: 143–155, plates 1–29.

Munro, I. 2010 The Evolution of the Book of the Dead. In Taylor, J. 2010 *Journey Through the Afterlife: Ancient Egyptian Book of the Dead*, 34–79. Cambridge, MA: Harvard UP.

Murnane, W. J. 1977 *Ancient Egyptian Coregencies*. SAOC 40. Chicago: OI.

————. 1979 The Bark of Amun on the Third Pylon at Karnak. *JARCE* 16: 11–27, plates 3–7.

————. 1990 *The Road to Kadesh*, 2nd ed., rev. SAOC 42. Chicago: OI.

————. 1991 Servant, Seer, Saint, Son of Hapu Amenhotep, Called Huy. *KMT* 2, no. 1: 9–13, 56–59.

————. 1992 Too Many High Priests? Once Again the Ptahmoses of Ancient Memphis. In Fs. Baer, 187–196.

————. 1993 Dans le domaine d'Amon, L'oeuvre d'Aménophis III à Karnak et à Louxor. In Delange, 28–39.

————. 1995 *Texts from the Amarna Period in Egypt*, ed. E. S. Meltzer. Atlanta: Scholars Press.

————. 1997 "Overseer of the Northern Foreign Countries": Reflections on the Upper Administration of Egypt's Empire in Western Asia. In Fs. te Velde, 251–258.

————. 1998 The Organization of Government under Amenhotep III. In AIIIP, 173–221.

————. 1999 Observations on Pre-Amarna Theology during the Earliest Reign of Amenhotep IV. In Fs. Wente, 303–316.

————. 1999a Return to Orthodoxy. In Pharaohs/Sun, 177–186.

Musée Borély 1973 *Le Nil et la société égyptienne: Hommage à Champollion*, exh cat. Marseille: Musée Borély.

Na'aman, N. 2000 The Egyptian Canaanite Correspondence. In *Amarna Diplomacy: The Beginnings of International Relations*, ed. R. Cohen and R. Westbrook, 125–138. Baltimore: Johns Hopkins UP.

————. 2005 *Canaan in the Second Millennium B.C.E.: Collected Essays*, 2. Winona Lake, IN: Eisenbrauns.

Naville, E. 1878 Les quatre stèles orientées du Musée de Marseille. In *Congrès provincial des orientalistes, Lyon, 1878. Compte rendu* 1: 275–293, plates 12–15.

————. 1891 *Bubastis (1887–1889)*. Egypt Exploration Fund, Memoir 8. London: Kegan Paul, Trench, Trübner.

————. 1908 *Funerary Papyrus of Iouiya*. London: A. Constable.

Newberry, P. E. 1928 The Sons of Tuthmosis IV. *JEA* 14: 82–85.

Nims, C. F. 1965 *Thebes of the Pharaohs: Pattern for Every City*. London: Elek.

————. 1973 The Transition from the Traditional to the New Style of Wall Relief under Amenhotep IV. *JNES* 32: 181–187.

Nord, D. 1975 Review of Reiser 1972. *JNES* 34: 142–145.

Nunn, J. F. 1996 *Ancient Egyptian Medicine.* Norman, OK: University of Oklahoma Press.

O'Connor, D. 1980 Malqata. *LÄ* 3: 1173–1177.

————. 1989 City and Palace in New Kingdom Egypt. *Sociétés urbaines en Egypte et au Soudan.* CRIPEL 11: 73–87.

————. 1993 Urbanism in Bronze Age Egypt and Northeast Africa. In Archaeology of Africa, 570–586.

————. 1995 Beloved of Maat, the Horizon of Re: The Royal Palace in New Kingdom Egypt. In Kingship, 263–299.

————. 1995a The Social and Economic Organization of Ancient Egyptian Temples. In Civilizations 1, 319–329.

————. 1998 Amenhotep III and Nubia. In AIIIP, 261–270.

————. 1998b The City and the World: Worldview and Built Forms in the Reign of Amenhotep III. AIIIP, 125–172.

————. 2003 Egypt's Views of 'Others.' In *"Never Had the Like Occurred": Egypt's View of Its Past,* ed. J. Tait, 155–185. London: University College London.

————. 2010 The King's Palace at Malkata and the Purpose of the Royal Harem. In Fs. Silverman, 55–80.

Ogdon, J. 1985–1986 Some Notes on the Iconography of the God Min. *BES* 7: 29–41.

Oldfather, C. H. 1933 *Diodorus of Sicily: The Library of History,* Books 1–2.34. Cambridge, MA: Harvard UP, LCL.

Oren, E. 1987 The 'Ways of Horus' in North Sinai. In *Egypt, Israel, Sinai, Archaeological and Historical Relationships in the Biblical Period,* ed. A. F. Rainey, 69–119. Tel Aviv: Tel Aviv University.

Ortiz, G. 1994 *In Pursuit of the Absolute: Art of the Ancient World from the George Ortiz Collection,* exh. cat. London: Royal Academy.

Ossian, C. 1999 The Most Beautiful of Flowers: Water Lilies and Lotuses in Ancient Egypt. *KMT,* 10, no. 1: 49–59.

Pamminger, P. 1993 Zur Gottlichkeit Amenophis' III. *BSÉG* 17: 83–92.

Panagiotokopulu, E. 2004 Pharaonic Egypt and the Origins of Plague. *Journal of Biogeography* 31, no. 2: 269–275.

Parkinson, R. B. 1997 *The Tale of Sinuhe and Other Ancient Egyptian Poems 1940–1640 BC.* Oxford: Oxford UP.

————. 2008 *The Painted Tomb-Chapel of Nebamun.* London: BM.

Partridge, R. B. 1994 *Faces of Pharaohs: Royal Mummies and Coffins from Ancient Thebes.* London: Rubicon.

————. 2002 *Fighting Pharaohs: Weapons and Warfare in Ancient Egypt.* Manchester: Peartree.

————. 2009 The Mortuary Temple of Merenptah. *Ancient Egypt* 10, no. 2: 31–35.

Patch, D. C. 2005 Mirror with Two Falcons. In Hatshepsut, 221.

Pendlebury, J. D. S. 1933 Report of the Excavations at Tell el-Amarneh. *JEA* 19: 113–118, plates 12–19.

Pernigotti, S. 1980 *La Statuaria Egiziana nel Museo Civico Archeologico di Bologna*. Bologna: Istituto per la Storia di Bologna.

Petrie, W. M. F. 1890 *Kahun, Gurob, Hawara*. London: K. Paul, Trench, Trübner.

————. 1891 *Illahun, Kahun, Gurob*. London: David Nutt.

————. 1897 *Six Temples at Thebes: 1896*. London: Bernard Quaritch.

Phillips, J. P. 2002 *The Columns of Egypt*. Manchester: Peartree.

Piankoff, A. 1955 *The Shrines of Tut-Ankh-Amon*. Bollingen 40.2. New York: Pantheon.

Pillet, M. 1925 Rapport sur les travaux de Karnak 1924–1925, 4. La Fouille du Pylône d'Amenhotep III. *ASAE* 25: 9–24.

Pinch, G. 1993 *Votive Offerings to Hathor*. Oxford: GI.

Pinch-Brock, L. 2006 Harvesting a Pharaoh. *Ancient Egypt* 7, no. 1: 20–24.

Pino, C. 2005 The Market Scene in the Tomb of Khaemhat (TT 57). *JEA* 91: 95–105.

Pischikova, E. 2001 Head of a Block Statue. In Halkedis, 23.

Plutarch. *See* Scott-Kilvert.

Podany, A. 2010 *Brotherhood of Kings: How International Relations Shaped the Ancient Near East*. Oxford: Oxford UP.

Podgórski, T. 1991 The Horus Dress as Represented in the Temple of Amenhotep III in Luxor. *Studies in Ancient Art and Civilizations* 4: 27–31.

Posener, G. 1985 *Le Papyrus Vandier*. BiGén 7. Cairo: IFAO.

Prisse d'Avennes, E. 2000 *Atlas of Egyptian Art* (repr.), with introduction by M. Raven. Cairo: Zeitouna.

Pulak, C. 1998 The Ulu Burun Shipwreck: An Overview. *IJNA* 27, no. 3: 188–224.

————. 2008 The Uluburun Shipwreck and Late Bronze Age Trade. In Beyond Babylon, 289–310.

————. 2008a Glass Ingots. In Beyond Babylon, 311–335.

Quaegebeur, J. 1986 Aménophis, nom royal et nom divin. *RdÉ* 37: 97–106.

Quibell, J. E. 1908 *Tomb of Yuaa and Thuiu*. CG 51001–51191.

Quirke, S. 1992 *Ancient Egyptian Religion*. London: BM.

Quirke, S., and Spencer, A. J. 2007 *The British Museum Book of Ancient Egypt*. London: BM.

Randall-MacIver, D., and Woolley, C. L. 1911 *Buhen*. Philadelphia: University of Pennsylvania Press.

Raoult, D., et al. 2000 Molecular identification by 'suicide PCR' of *Yersinia pestis* as the agent of Medieval Black Death. *Proceedings of the National Academy of Science*, 97, no. 23: 12,800–12,803.

Redford, D. B. 1967 *History and Chronology of the Eighteenth Dynasty of Egypt: Seven Studies*. Toronto: University of Toronto Press.

———. 1984 *Akhenaten, the Heretic King*. Princeton: Princeton UP.

———. 1986 *Pharaonic King-Lists, Annals and Day-Books*. Mississauga: Benben.

———. 1990 *Egypt and Canaan in the New Kingdom*. Beer-Sheva 4. Beer-Sheva: Ben-Gurion University of the Negev Press.

———. 1992 *Egypt, Canaan, and Israel in Ancient Times*. Princeton: Princeton UP.

———. 1995 The Concept of Kingship during the Eighteenth Dynasty. In Kingship, 157–184.

Redford, S. 2002 *The Harem Conspiracy: The Murder of Ramesses III*. DeKalb: Northern Illinois University Press.

Redford, S., and Redford, D. 1994 *The Tomb of Re'a (TT 201)*. (Aegypti texta propositaque 3 =) Akhenaten Temple Project 4. Toronto: SSEA.

Reeves, N. 1999 The Royal Family. In Pharaohs/Sun, 81–95.

———. 2001 *Akhenaten: Egypt's False Prophet*. London: Thames/Hudson.

Reeves, N., and Wilkinson, R. 1996 *The Complete Valley of the Kings: Tombs and Treasures of Egypt's Greatest Pharaohs*. London: Thames/Hudson.

Reiser, E. 1972 *Der königliche Harim im alten Ägypten und seine Verwaltung*. Vienna: Notring.

Reisner, G. A. 1918 The Barkal Temples in 1916. *JEA* 5: 99–103.

———. 1920 The Viceroys of Ethiopia. *JEA* 6: 28–34, 78–83.

Rhind, H. 1862 *Thebes: Its Tombs and Their Tenants*. London: Longman, Green, Longman, and Roberts.

Riefstahl, E. 1964 *Thebes in the Time of Amunhotep III*. Norman: University of Oklahoma Press.

Robichon, C., and Varille, A. 1936 *Le temple du Scribe royal Amenhotep, fils de Hapou*. FIFAO 11.

Robins, G. 1993 *Women in Ancient Egypt*. Cambridge, MA: Harvard UP.

———. 1995 *Reflections of Women in the New Kingdom: Ancient Egyptian Art from the British Museum*. San Antonio: Van Siclen Books.

Roehrig, C. H. 1996 Woman's Work: Some Occupations of Nonroyal Women as Depicted in Ancient Egyptian Art. In *Mistress of the House, Mistress of Heaven: Women in Ancient Egypt*, ed. A. E. Capel and G. E. Markoe, 13–24. New York: Hudson Hills Press, in association with the Cincinnati Art Museum.

———. 1997 Cult Figure of a Falcon-Headed Deity. In *Miho Museum: South Wing*, ed. T. Umehara, 18–21. Kyoto: Miho Museum.

———. 2010 New Thoughts on the Cleared Strip in the Western Desert of Thebes. Paper presented at ARCE, April 2010, Oakland, CA.

Romano, J. F. 2000 Jewelry and Personal Arts in Ancient Egypt. In *Civilizations of the Ancient Near East, III, 7. Technology and Artistic Production*, ed. J. M. Sasson, 1605–1621. Peabody, MA: Hendrickson.

Romano, J., et al. 1979 *The Luxor Museum of Ancient Egyptian Art: Catalogue*. Cairo: ARCE.

Rommelaere, C. 1991 *Les chevaux du nouvel empire égyptien: origines, races, harnachement.* Brussels: Connaissance de l'Égypte ancienne, no. 3.

Rössler-Köhler, U. 1982 Per-haa. *LÄ* 4: 930–931.

Rowe, A. 1931 The Eckley B. Coxe, Jr., Expedition Excavations at Meydum, 1929–30. *University Museum Bulletin* 22, no. 1: 190–194.

Sa'ad, R. 1970 Les travaux d'Aménophis IV au IIIe Pylône du Temple d'Amon Re' à Karnak. *Kêmi* 20: 187–193.

Sadek, A. I. 1988 *Popular Religion in Egypt during the New Kingdom.* Hildesheim: Gerstenberg.

Saleh, M. 1993 La tombe de Youya et de Touyou. In Delange, 56–63.

————. 1998 Varia from the Egyptian Museum in Cairo. In *Stationen: Beiträge zur Kulturgeschichte Ägyptens*, eds. H. Guksch and D. Polz, 353–361. Mainz: Von Zabern.

Saleh, M., and Sourouzian, H. 1987 *The Official Catalogue of The Egyptian Museum Cairo.* Mainz: Von Zabern.

Sauneron, S. 1968 Quelques monuments de Soumenou au Musée de Brooklyn. *Kêmi* 18: 57–78.

————. 2000 *The Priests of Ancient Egypt*, trans. David Lorton Ithaca: Cornell UP.

Sauneron, S., and Vérité, J. 1969 Fouilles dans la zone axiale du IIIe pylône à Karnak. *Kêmi* 19: 249–276.

Säve-Söderbergh, T. 1946 *The Navy of the Eighteenth Egyptian Dynasty.* Uppsala: Lundequistska bokhandeln.

————. 1957 *Four Eighteenth Dynasty Tombs: Private Tombs at Thebes I.* Oxford: GI.

————. 1964 Preliminary Report of the Scandinavian Join Expedition 1962–63. *Kush* 12: 19–39.

Sayce, A. H. 1908 *The Archaeology of the Cuneiform Inscriptions.* 2nd ed., rev. London: Society for Promoting Christian Knowledge.

————. 1922 The Geographical Position of Arzawa. *JEA* 8: 233–234.

Scamuzzi, E. 1965 *Egyptian Art in the Egyptian Museum of Turin.* New York: Abrams.

Schaden, O. 1987 Tutankhamun-Ay Shrine at Karnak and Western Valley of the Kings Project: Report on the 1985–1986 Season. *NARCE* 138: 10–15.

Schiaparelli, E. 1927 *Relazione sui lavori della Missione Archeologica Italiana in Egitto* (anni *1903–1920*). 2. *La tomba intatta dell'architetto Cha nella necropoli di Tebe.* Turin: Giovanni Chiantore.

Schiff Giorgini, M. 1961 Soleb. Campagna 1959–60. *Kush* 9: 182–197.

————. 1962 Soleb. Campagna 1960–61. *Kush* 10: 152–169.

————. 1965 *Soleb I, 1813–1963* (in collaboration with C. Robichon and J. Leclant). Florence: Sansoni.

————. 1965a The First Season of Excavations at Sedeinga. *Kush* 13: 112–130, plates 30–32.

————. 1971 *Soleb II, Les nécropoles* (in collaboration with C. Robichon and J. Leclant). Florence: Sansoni.

————. 2002 *Soleb.* Ed. N. Beaux. 5 vols. Cairo: IFAO.

Schmidt, H. 1993 Foreign Affairs under Egypt's "Dazzling Sun." *RdÉ* 44: 153–160.

Schmitz, B. 1984 Schatzmeister. *LÄ* 5: 539–543.

Schneider, H. D. 1977 *Shabtis: An Introduction to the History of Ancient Egyptian Funerary Statuettes with A Catalogue of the Collection of Shabtis in the National Museum of Antiquities at Leiden*. Parts 1 and 2. Leiden: Rijksmuseum von Oudheden.

_____. 1999 *Life and Death Under the Pharaohs. Egyptian Art from The National Museum of Antiquities in Leiden, The Netherlands*. Perth: Western Australia Museum.

Schoske, S. 2008 Au centre du pouvoir: Tiy, Âahotep, Hatchepsout. In Reines, 188–190.

Schoske, S., and Wildung, D., et al. 1995 *Staatliche Sammlung Ägyptischer Kunst München*. Mainz: Von Zabern.

Schulman, A. R. 1964 *Military Rank, Title, and Organization in the Egyptian New Kingdom*. Berlin: B. Hessling.

_____. 1978 Ankhesenamun, Nofretity and the Amka Affair. *JARCE* 15: 43–48.

_____. 1979 Diplomatic Marriage in the Egyptian New Kingdom. *JNES* 38: 177–193.

_____. 1980 Chariots, Chariotry, and the Hyksos. *JSSEA* 10, no. 2: 105–153.

Schulz, R. 2008 Small but Beautiful – The Block Statue of Khaemwaset. In Fs. Fazzini, 216–222.

Scott-Kilvert, I. 1965 *Plutarch: Makers of Rome*. London: Penguin.

Seipel, W. 1977 Harim, Harimsdame, Harimsverschwörung, Harimszögling. *LÄ* 2: 982–992.

_____. 1992 *Gott, Mensch, Pharao. Viertausend Jahre Menschenbild in der Skulptur des Alten Ägypten*, exh. cat. Vienna: Kunsthistorisches Museum.

Seki, K. 2008 A Note on the "Hb-Sd" and *Sed*-Pavilion in Ancient Egyptian Architecture. Report of the Study at OCEES. Mansfield College, Oxford, April–August 2008. http://home.kanto-gakuin.ac.jp/~kg064302/txt/a%20note%20on%20the%20hbsd_0826fr2.pdf.

Sesana, A., and Nelson, M. 1998 Exercices d'élèves-artisans découverts au sud-ouest du temple de "millions d'années" d' Aménophis II. *Memnonia* 9: 192–199.

Shaltout, M., Fekri, M., and Belmonte, J. 2006 The Ancient Egyptian Monuments and Their Relationship to the Position of the Sun, Stars, and Planets. *CASAE* 35: 93–112.

Shaw, G. J. 2008 *Royal Authority in Egypt's Eighteenth Dynasty. BAR* 1822.

Shaw, I. 2008 Une ville-harem du Nouvel empire: Nouvelle Étude archéologique du site de Gourob. In Reines, 104–115.

Shelley, P. B. *See* Wellesley.

Shipman, P. 2004 *To the Heart of the Nile: Lady Florence Baker and the Exploration of Central Africa*. New York: William Morrow/HarperCollins.

Shore, A. F. 1992 Human and Divine Mummification. In Fs. Griffiths, 226–235.

Siliotti, A. 1999 *Egypt Lost and Found: Explorers and Travelers on the Nile*. New York: Stewart, Tabori, and Chang.

Silverman, D. P. 1995 The Nature of Egyptian Kingship. In Kingship, 49–92.

Simpson, W. K. 2003 *The Literature of Ancient Egypt*. 3rd ed. New Haven: Yale UP.

Smith, G. E. 1912 *The Royal Mummies*. CG 61051–61100.

Smith, S. T. 1995 *Askut in Nubia: The Economics and Ideology of Egyptian Imperialism in the 2nd millennium* BC. London: Kegan Paul.

————. 2003 *Wretched Kush: Ethnic Identities and Boundaries in Egypt's Nubian Empire*. London: Routledge.

Smith, W. S. 1981 *The Art and Architecture of Ancient Egypt*, rev. and with additions by William Kelly Simpson. New York: Pelican.

Sotheby's 1990 *Antiquities*. London, July 10.

Sourouzian, H. 1993 La statuaire royale sous Aménophis III dans les grands sites d'Égypte. In Delange, 4–15.

————. 1994 Inventaire iconographique des statues en manteau jubilaire de l'époque thinite jusqu'à leur disparition sous Amenhotep III. In Fs. Leclant 1, 499–530.

————. 2002 New Colossal Statues at Kom el-Hettân. *EgArch* 21: 36–37.

————. 2006–2007 The Theban Funerary Temple of Amenhotep III. *EgArch* 29: 21–24.

Sourouzian, H., and Lawler, A. 2007 Unearthing Egypt's Greatest Temple. *Smithsonian Magazine* 38, no. 8: 46–54.

Sourouzian, H., and Stadelmann, R. 2003 The Temple of Amenhotep III at Thebes: Excavation and Conservation at Kom el- Hettân. *MDAIK* 59: 425–446.

————. 2008 Charme und Anmut im Grossformat. *AntWelt* 6: 73–76.

Sourouzian, H., et al. 2004 The Temple of Amenhotep III at Thebes: Excavation and Conservation at Kom el- Hettân. *MDAIK* 60: 171–236.

————. 2006 Three Seasons of Work at the Temple of Amenhotep III at Kom el Hettân. Part 2: Investigations at the Second Pylon and Work on the Royal Colossi. *ASAE* 80: 367–399.

————. 2006b Three Seasons of Work at the Temple of Amenhotep III at Kom el Hettân. Part 3: Works in the Dewatered Area of the Peristyle Court and the Hypostyle Hall. *ASAE* 80: 401–487.

Spalinger, A. 2001 Festivals. In OEAE, 521–525.

————. 2005 *War in Ancient Egypt: The New Kingdom*. Malden, MA: Blackwell.

Spar, I. 2008 The Amarna Letters. In Beyond Babylon, 168–169.

Spence, K. 2004 The Three-Dimensional Form of the Amarna House. *JEA* 90: 128–152.

Spence, K., and Rose, P. 2009 New Fieldwork at Sesebi. *EA* 35 (Fall): 21–24.

Spencer, A. J. 1982 *Death in Ancient Egypt*. Harmondsworth: Penguin.

————. 1989 *Excavations at El-Ashmunein II: The Temple Area*. London: BM.

Stadelmann, R. 1967 *Syrisch-Palästinensische Gottheiten in Ägypten.* PÄ 5.

———. 1978 Tempel und Tempelnamen in Theben-Ost un-West. *MDAIK* 34: 171–180.

———. 1979 Totentempel und Millionenjahrhaus. *MDAIK* 35: 303–321.

———. 1994 Royal Palaces of Late New Kingdom in Thebes. In Fs. Goedicke, 309–314.

———. 2000 Kom el-Hettân: The Mortuary Temple of Amenhotep III. *EgArch,* 16: 14–15.

———. 2001 Sphinx. *OEAE* 3: 307–310.

Steegmuller, F., trans. and ed. 1972 *Flaubert in Egypt: A Sensibility on Tour.* New York: Penguin.

Steindorff, G. 1900 Eine ägyptischen Liste syrischen Sklaven. *ZÄS* 38: 15–18, esp. 17–18.

Stewart, H. M. 1976 *Egyptian Stelae, Reliefs, and Paintings from the Petrie Collection. Part 1: The New Kingdom.* Warminster: Aris and Phillips.

Strassler, R. B., ed. 1996 *The Landmark Thucydides: A Comprehensive Guide to the Peloponnesian War.* New York: Free Press.

Stross, F. H., Hay, R. L., Asaro, F., Bowman, R., and Michel, H. V. 1988 Sources of the quartzite of some ancient Egyptian sculpture. *Archaeometry* 30, no. 1: 109–119.

Strudwick, N. 1996 *The Tombs of Amenmose, Khnummose, and Amenmose at Thebes.* Oxford: GI/Ashmolean.

Suys, E. 1934 Un vénetien en Égypte et en Nubie au XVIe siècle. *CdÉ* 9: 51–63.

Sweeney, D. 2004 Forever Young? The Representation of Older and Ageing Women in Ancient Egyptian Art. *JARCE* 41: 67–84.

Tait, J. 2003 Introduction – '. . . since the time of the Gods.' In *'Never Had the Like Occurred': Eqypt's View of Its Part,* ed. J. Tait, 1–13. UCL Press.

Taylor, J. 2010 *Journey through the Afterlife: Ancient Egyptian Book of the Dead.* Cambridge, MA: Harvard UP.

Teeter, E. 1997 *The Presentation of Maat: Ritual and Legitimacy in Ancient Egypt.* SAOC 57.

te Velde, H. 1982 Mut. *LÄ* 4: 246–248.

Thomas, A. 1981 *Gurob.* 2 vols. Warminster: Aris and Phillips.

Thucydides. *See* Strassler.

Tietze, C. 2003a Tell Basta: Vorläufiger Bericht der XIV. Kampagne. *ARCUS* 5: 21–28.

———. 2003b Reconstruction und Restaurierung in Tell Basta. *ARCUS* 6: 101–112.

Tietze, C., and Abd el-Maksoud, M. 2004 *Tell Basta: Ein Führer über das Grabungsgelände.* Potsdam: Universitätsverlag.

Topozada, Z. 1988 Les deux campagnes d'Amenhotep III en Nubie. *BIFAO* 88: 153–165.

Török, L. 2009 *Between Two Worlds: The Frontier Region between Ancient Nubia and Egypt, 3700 BC–AD 500*. PÄ 29. Leiden: Brill.

Trad, M., and Mahmoud, A. 1993 Aménophis III au Musée Égyptien du Caire. In Delange, 40–47.

Trapani, M. 2001 Shawabty Belonging to Ptahmes. In *The Illustrated Guide to the Egyptian Museum in Cairo*, ed. A. Bongioanni and M. Sole Croce, 489. Cairo: AUC.

Trigger, B. 1965 *History and Settlement in Lower Nubia*. New Haven: Yale UP.

———. 1976 *Nubia under the Pharaohs*. London: Thames/Hudson.

Troy, L. 1986 *Patterns of Queenship in Ancient Egyptian Myth and History*. Boreas Uppsala Studies in Ancient Mediterranean and Near Eastern Civilization 14. Uppsala: Alqvist and Wiksell International.

———. 1997 Mut Enthroned. In Fs. te Velde, 301–315.

Tylor, J. J., Clarke, S., and Griffith, F. L. 1895–1900 *Wall Drawings and Monuments of El Kab. 3 The Temple of Amenhetep III*. London: B. Quaritch.

Tytus, R. 1903 *A Preliminary Report on the Re-excavation of the Palace of Amenhotep III*. New York: MMA.

Ullmann, M. D. 2009 The Temple of Amenhotep III at Wadi es-Sebua. Paper presented at ARCE, April 24–26, Dallas.

Uphill, E. 1965 The Egyptian Sed-Festival Rites. *JNES* 24, no. 4: 365–383.

Valbelle, D. 2004 Egyptians on the Middle Nile. In *Sudan: Ancient Treasures*, ed. D. A. Welsby and J. R. Anderson, 92–99. London: BM.

Valloggia, M. 1976 *Recherche sur les "messagers" (wpwtyw) dans les sources égyptiennes profanes*. Hautes Études Orientales 6. Geneva: CRHPR 2.

Van Den Boorn, G. P. F. 1988 *The Duties of the Vizier: Civil Administration in the Early New Kingdom*. London: Kegan Paul.

Van Der Vliet, J. 1985 Raising the Djed. *BSAK Beihefte* 1–5, vol. 3: 405–411.

Van Dijk, J. 1997 The Noble Lady of Mitanni and Other Royal Favorites of the Eighteenth Dynasty. In Fs. te Velde, 33–46.

Van Siclen, C., III. 1973 The Accession Date of Amenhotep III and the Jubilee. *JNES* 32: 290–300.

Van Walsem, R. 1997 The Struggle against Chaos as a 'Strange Attractor' in Ancient Egyptian Culture: A Descriptive Model for the 'Chaotic' Development of Cultural Systems. In Fs. te Velde, 317–342.

Varille, A. 1936 Un colosse d'Aménophis III dans les carrières d'Assouân. *RdÉ* 2: 173–176.

———. 1968 *Inscriptions concernant l'architecte Aménophis, fils de Hapou*, ed. J. Vercoutter. BdÉ 46. Cairo: IFAO.

———. 1985 Mut, the Eye of Re. *BSÄK Beihefte* 1–5, no. 3: 395–403.

———. 1997 Mut and Other Ancient Egyptian Goddesses. In Fs. Bell 2, 455–462.

Vercoutter, J. 1956 New Egyptian Texts from the Sudan. *Kush* 4: 66–82, plates 7–9.

———. 1959 The Gold of Kush. *Kush* 7: 124–153.

———. 1973 La XVIIIe Dynastie à Sai et en Haute-Nubie. *CRIPEL* 1: 9–38, plates 1–10.

———. 1974 État des Recherches à Sai. *BSFÉ* 70–71: 28–36.

———. 1980 Le pays Irem et la pénétration égyptienne en Afrique (Stèle de Saï S. 579). In *Livre du Centenaire IFAO*, 157–178. Cairo: IFAO.

Vivian, C. 2008 *The Western Desert of Egypt*. Cairo: AUC.

Waddell, W. G. 1964 *Manetho*. Cambridge, MA: Harvard UP/LCL.

Walle, B. van de 1963 Précisions nouvelles sur Sobek-hotep fils de Min. *RdÉ* 15: 77–85.

———. 1971 La statue bloc de Hor. *ZÄS* 97: 130–140.

Ward, W. A. 1983 Reflections on Some Egyptian Terms Presumed to Mean 'Harem, Harem-Woman, Concubine.' *Berytus Archaeological Studies* 31: 67–74.

Warner, C. D. 1876 *My Winter on the Nile*. Boston: Houghton Mifflin.

Waterfield, R., trans. 1998 *Herodotus: The Histories*, with introduction and notes by C. Wald. Oxford: Oxford UP.

Weeks, K. R. 2005 *The Treasures of Luxor and the Valley of the Kings*. Vercelli: White Star.

Weigall, A. E. P. 1907 A Report on Some Objects Recently Found in Sebakh and Other Diggings. *ASAE* 8: 39–50.

Weinstein, J. 1998 Egypt and the Levant in the Reign of Amenhotep III. In *AIIIP*, 223–236.

Wellesley, D. *Shelley*. London: Britain in Pictures.

Welsby, D. 1996 The Northern Dongola Reach Survey: The 1995/6 Season. *Sudan Archaeological Research Society Newsletter* 10.

———. 2004 Egyptian Invasions of Nubia: The Last 5000 Years. In *Fifty Years in the Archaeology of Africa: Themes in Archaeological Theory and Practice. Papers in Honour of John Alexander*, ed. L. Smith, P. Rose, G. Wahida, and S. Wahida. *Azania* 39: 283–304.

Welsby, D., and Sjöström, I. 2007 The Dongola Reach and the Fourth Cataract: Continuity and Change during the 2nd and 1st Millennia B.C. In Fs. Geus, 379–398.

Wente, E. F. 1969 Hathor at the Jubilee. In Fs. Wilson, 83–91.

———. 1990 *Letters from Ancient Egypt*, ed. E. S. Meltzer. SBLWAW 1.

Whale, S. 1989 *The Family in the Eighteenth Dynasty of Egypt*. Warminster: Aris and Phillips.

White, K., and Mattingly, D. J. 2006 Ancient Lakes of the Sahara. *AmSc* 94: 58–65.

Wiese, A., and Brodbeck, A. 2004 *Tutankhamun: The Golden Beyond: Tomb Treasures from the Valley of the Kings*. Basel: Antikenmuseum Basel und Sammlung Ludwig.

Wild, H. 1979 Une stèle memphite du regne d'Aménophis III à Lausanne. In Fs. Sauneron 1, 305–318, plate 48.

Wildung, D. 1977 *Imhotep und Amenhotep*. MÄS 36. Munich: Ägyptisches Museum.

_____. 1998 Le frère aîné d'Ekhnaton: réflexions sur un décès prématuré. *BSFÉ* 143: 10–18.

_____. 1999 Relief of Prince Thutmose ("Thutmose V"). In Pharaohs/Sun, 205.

Wilfong, T. 2001 Marriage and Divorce. In OEAE, 340–344.

Wilkinson, R. H. 1991 Ancient Near Eastern Raised-Arm Figures and the Iconography of the Egyptian God Min. *BES* 12: 109–118.

_____. 2000 *The Complete Temples of Ancient Egypt*. New York: Thames/Hudson.

_____. 2003 *The Complete Gods and Goddesses of Ancient Egypt*. London: Thames/Hudson.

Wilson, H. 1988 A Recipe for Offering Loaves. *JEA* 74: 214–217.

Wilson, R. S. 2010 *KV 63: The Untold Story of the New Tomb in Egypt's Valley of the Kings*. Jedburgh, Scotland: Ferniehirst.

Wolf, W. 1924 Miszellen. *ZÄS* 59: 157–158.

_____. 1924a Amenhotep Vizekönig von Nubien. *ZÄS* 59: 157–158.

_____. 1931 *Das schöne Fest von Opet*. Leipzig: J. C. Hinrichs.

Yeivin, S. 1965 Who Were the Mentyw? *JEA* 51: 204–206.

Yoshimura, S. 1985 Some Remarks on the Relic at South Malkata "Kom el Samak" in Comparison with the Relic at "Kom el Abd," Luxor, Egypt. *Orient* 21: 132–149.

Yoshimura, S., Capriotti, G., Kawai, N., and Nishisaka, A. 2004 A Preliminary Report on the Conservation Project of the Wall Paintings in the Royal Tomb of Amenophis III (KV 22) in the Western Valley of the Kings: 2001–2004 Seasons. *Memnonia* 15: 203–212.

Yoshimura, S., and Kondo, J. 2004 The Tomb of Amenophis III. *ASAE* 78: 205–207.

Young, G. D., ed. 1981 *Ugarit in Retrospect*. Winona Lake, IN: Eisenbrauns.

Yoyotte, J. 1959 Le Bassin de Djaroukha. *Kêmi* 15: 23–33.

_____. 1980 Une monumentale litanie en granite: Les Sekhmets d'Aménophis III et la conjuration permanente de la déesse dangereuse. *BSFE* 87–88: 46–75.

_____. 1993 La réligion d'Aménophis III. *Égyptes: Histoire et culture* 1: 22–28.

Yoyotte, M. 2008 Gouvernante avec un prince et trois princesses sur les genoux. In Reines, 293, cat. 110.

_____. 2008a Le "harem" dans l'Égypte ancienne. In Reines, 76–93.

Žába, Z. 1950 Un nouveau fragment de sarcophage de Merymose. *ASAE* 50: 513.

Zibelius, K. 1972 *Afrikanische Orts-und Völkernamen in hieroglyphischen Texten*. TAVO 1. Wiesbaden: Ludwig Reichert.

Zibelius-Chen, K. 1988 *Die Ägyptische Expansion nach Nubien*. TAVO 78. Wiesbaden: Ludwig Reichert.

Ziegler, C. 1994 Notes sur la Reine Tiy. In Fs. Leclant 1, 531–548.

Zivie, A.-P. 1985 Tombes rupestres de la falaise du Bubasteion à Saqqarah – IIe et IIIe campagnes (1982–1983). *ASAE* 70: 225–232.

———. 1989 Le Trésor Funéraire du Vizir 'Aper-el. *BSFE* 116 (October): 31–44.

———. 1990 *Découverte à Saqqarah: Le vizir oublié.* Paris: Seuil.

———. 2004 Hatiay, scribe du temple d'Aton à Memphis. In Fs. Redford, 223–231.

———. 2005 Le point sur les travaux de la mission archéologique française du Bubasteion à Saqqara. *BSFE* 162 (March): 28–45.

Zivie, C. M. 1976 Giza au Deuxième Millénaire. *BdÉ* 70.

———. 1983 Une curieuse statue de la reine Ti'aa à Giza. *BSFE* 98: 40–56.

Zivie, C. M. 1986 Tiaa. *LÄ* 6: 551–555.

Zivie-Coche, C. 2002 *Sphinx: History of a Monument,* trans. D. Lorton. Ithaca: Cornell UP.

Zyhlarz, E. 1958 The Countries of the Ethiopian Empire of Kash (Kush) and Egyptian Old Ethiopia in the New Kingdom. *Kush* 6: 7–38.

INDEX